Beyond Reconstruction in Afghanistan

Lessons from Development Experience

Edited by
John D. Montgomery and
Dennis A. Rondinelli

BEYOND RECONSTRUCTION IN AFGHANISTAN
© John D. Montgomery and Dennis A. Rondinelli, 2004

First published 2004 by
PALGRAVE MACMILLAN™
175 Fifth Avenue, New York, N.Y. 10010 and
Houndmills, Basingstoke, Hampshire, England RG21 6XS
Companies and representatives throughout the world

PALGRAVE MACMILLAN is the global academic imprint of the Palgrave Macmillan division of St. Martin's Press, LLC and of Palgrave Macmillan Ltd. Macmillan® is a registered trademark in the United States, United Kingdom and other countries. Palgrave is a registered trademark in the European Union and other countries.

ISBN 1–4039–6511–0 hardback
Library of Congress Cataloging-in-Publication Data
    Beyond reconstruction in Afghanistan : lessons from development experience / edited by John D. Montgomery and Dennis A. Rondinelli.
        p. cm.
    Includes bibliographical references and index.
    ISBN 1–4039–6511–0 hardback
    1. Afghanistan-Economic policy. 2. Afghanistan-Politics and government.
I. Montgomery, John Dickey, 1920– II. Rondinelli, Dennis A.

HC417.B49 2004
338.9581—dc22   2003062261

A catalogue record for this book is available from the British Library.

Design by Newgen Imaging Systems (P) Ltd., Chennai, India.

First edition: April 2004
10 9 8 7 6 5 4 3 2 1

Printed in the United States of America.

Contents

Acknowledgments

The research leading to the production of these chapters emerged after a series of conferences among the authors. They first convened in Cambridge, Massachusetts in January 2002, supported by the Pacific Basin Research Center of Soka University of America and by the Boston Research Center for the Twentieth Century. A second meeting occurred at Magdelen College, Oxford University in March 2002, with support from the Toda Institute for Global Peace and Policy Research and its project, "Globalization, Regionalism, and Democracy." A third meeting in Cyprus in March 2002 gathered additional participation, and was provided for by the Centre for World Dialogue and the Toda Institute. A final session occurred at Harvard University, in Cambridge, Massachusetts in November 2002, with support from the Pacific Basin Research Center. The completion of the writing phase, including aid for the distribution of our findings, was made possible by a grant from the Smith Richardson Foundation. For the generous support of each donor, the editors and authors are very grateful. This manuscript also benefited from suggestions and criticisms proffered by Michael Loo, Virginia Kosmo, and Kristen Eichensehr.

About the Authors

KAMOLUDIN N. ABDULLAEV, Independent Scholar, Tajikistan, has specialized in modern Central Asian history and analysis for conflict transformation. He participated in the Fulbright Program (1994, the George Washington University, USA). In 2001–2003, Abdullaev taught contemporary history of Central Asia at Yale and at Ohio State University. His latest books include *What Peace Five Years After the Signing of the Tajik Peace Agreement?: Strategic Conflict Assessment and Peace Building Framework, Tajikistan* (coauthored with Sabine Frasier); *Politics of Compromise: The Tajikistan Peace Process* (with coeditor Catherine Barnes); and *Historical Dictionary of Tajikistan* (coauthored with Shahram Azbarzadeh).

YURI V. BOSSIN, Associate Professor of History and Central Asian Studies at Moscow State University, is a member of the Institute of Oriental Studies, Russian Academy of Sciences, Moscow. His most recent monograph is *Afghanistan: Multi-Ethnic Society and State Power in Historical Context.*

MILTON J. ESMAN is John S. Knight Professor of International Studies and Professor of Government, Emeritus, at Cornell University. His recent books are *Carrots, Sticks, and Ethnic Conflict: Rethinking Development Assistance* (coedited with Ronald J. Herring) and *Why Americans Need the Feds.*

RICHARD N. FRYE began his years of residence in the Middle East with WWII service in Afghanistan with the OSS. He is Aga Khan Professor of Iranian Emeritus at Harvard University. His most recent book on the region is *The Heritage of Central Asia.*

PAULA GUTLOVE, DMD, is director of the International Conflict Management Program at the Institute for Resource and Security Studies (IRSS) and founder of Health Bridges for Peace.

JOHN M. HEFFRON, Professor of History at Soka University of America, has lectured and published extensively on reconstruction policies in post–Civil War United States and on problems of post-War reconstruction in Europe, Central Asia, and the Far East.

JOHN D. MONTGOMERY is Ford Foundation Professor of International Studies, Emeritus, Harvard University. He is the author or editor of numerous books, including *Forced to be Free, The Artificial Revolution in Germany and Japan, The Politics of Foreign Aid, American Experience in Southeast Asia,* and *Aftermath: Tarnished Outcomes of American Foreign Policy.*

ROBERT J. MUSCAT has served as economic advisor to the development authorities in Thailand and Malaysia; Chief Economist of the Agency for International

Development; planning director of UNDP; and as consultant to UN agencies and the World Bank. He has been a visiting scholar at Columbia University's East Asian Institute and at George Mason University's Institute for Conflict Analysis and Resolution. His most recent book is *Investing in Peace: How Development Aid Can Prevent or Promote Conflict.*

EDEN NABY began her teaching and research as a cultural historian with service in the Peace Corps in Afghanistan. She has published extensively on regional ethnic issues from Tajikistan to Iraq and is co-author of *Afghanistan: Mullah, Marx, and Mujahid.*

CHARLES H. NORCHI is an international lawyer, Professor at Sarah Lawrence College, Fellow at Yale University, and consultant to the World Bank. He has worked in Afghanistan as a human rights advocate, educator, and journalist writing about the country for the *Cleveland Plain Dealer*, the *New York Times*, and the *Los Angeles Times*. He is a coeditor of *Afghanistan: The Essential Field Guide.*

DENNIS A. RONDINELLI, Glaxo Distinguished International Professor of Management, Kenan-Flagler Business School, University of North Carolina at Chapel Hill, has done research for 30 years on international development assistance and foreign aid policy and on economic transformation in emerging market countries in Asia, Central and Eastern Europe, Latin America, and Africa. In 2002, he was appointed by the U.N. Secretary General as a member of the Expert Committee on Public Administration of the United Nations Economic and Social Council. He is the author of *Development Projects as Policy Experiments: An Adaptive Approach to Development Administration*, as well as many other books and articles.

JACOB HALE RUSSELL is a research assistant in public health studies.

GORDON THOMPSON, executive director of IRSS, has more than 25 years' experience in technical and policy analysis on security issues.

CHAPTER ONE

INTRODUCTION

John D. Montgomery and Dennis A. Rondinelli

This book assesses plans and prospects for the reconstruction and development of Afghanistan drawing on 50 years of previous experience with international development. Although many international planners were conscious that "lessons of experience" could be drawn from similar post-conflict situations, they devoted little attention to applying them in Afghanistan. But they could have. For although in many ways Afghanistan is unique, it is one of a long list of countries that have undergone postwar reconstruction and development; neither international donors who have pledged billions of dollars to Afghanistan's recovery nor the national planners who will implement development programs and projects would be wise to ignore that experience. They do so at serious peril to their ultimate objectives and further risk to the future of the Afghan people.

Plans for this book began very soon after Osama Bin-Laden mounted the infamous attack that is now known and mourned as 9/11/01. By the time it had become known that he and the closest of his terrorist followers had been tracked to an unknown lair in Afghanistan, it was clear that they had not found a permanent sanctuary. A few quick military strikes by the United States and its allies ended their moment of safety. A much-battered Afghanistan came once more under foreign control. What was to follow?

The period immediately after the fall of the Taliban regime was one of euphoric planning in the international community. This time Afghanistan was not to be left to patch itself together when the war was over, as it had been after several previous encounters with foreign invaders. Late in 2001 the governments of the United States, European and Asian countries, and several Middle Eastern nations, along with international organizations and regional development banks sent representatives to Bonn and Tokyo to formulate plans to lift Afghanistan out of decades of devastation caused successively by colonization, war, and military occupation. They pledged billions of dollars in aid and technical help to rebuild Afghanistan's economy, society, and political system.

The plans were ambitious, but they could draw on a half-century of experience with the aftermath of war destruction and rehabilitation—the military occupations of Japan and Germany, the Marshall Plan for the reconstruction of Europe, and postcolonial nation-building efforts in Asia, Africa, Central America, and the Balkans. Foreign aid of that kind was one of the unique features of the second half of the twentieth century; each effort was undertaken afresh, but experience accumulated.

Not all of the previous reconstruction efforts were successful, of course; some were abandoned because donor nations had lost interest, or their attention had been diverted to new conflicts in other parts of the world. Some of the plans were inappropriate and doomed to failure. Old questions took on new meaning: Would the history of reconstruction and development in Afghanistan be recorded as a triumph like that of the Marshall Plan in Europe, or was it simply another disaster in the wake of good intentions easily forgotten? Was the refrain in the Afghanistan chorus to be "Seduced and Abandoned," "Love's Labours' Lost," or "Born Again"?

It had quickly become clear that the people of Afghanistan had long-term development needs far beyond physical reconstruction or the kind of building that they could satisfy with their own resources even if they were supplemented by routine foreign assistance. The ambitions of political leaders, military logisticians, foreign aid specialists, and nongovernmental organizations (NGOs) far transcended physical reconstruction. Could so many donors, working independently, bring together their collective half-century of experience with development, scattered as it was over different times and places?

These donors, from east and west and north and south, had interests as diverse as their technologies and customs. Even if the language of their early plans was coherent and complementary, implementation would have to be turned over to detached and independent agencies, whose strategies and interests could conflict as they mixed revenge and the desire for reparations with their deeper motives for world peace. In any case, restoring the previous order would not produce needed new economic and political institutions. To add to these troubles, it was not long before the donors had to pause in their speculations about new and unfamiliar reconstruction programs in Afghanistan to begin wondering about similar plans for Iraq, Palestine, and perhaps other Islamic states.

A Tale of Two Countries

Although international organizations such as the United Nations (UN) and the World Bank have been involved in post-conflict reconstruction since the 1950s, some reconstruction experience was fresh and even contemporary. The transition from plans to programs in East Europe revealed two approaches and outcomes, each of which was seemingly successful in its own context (Bosnia and Kosovo). The first approach, which encouraged self-reliant governance, was a necessity in the absence of a strongly coordinated international presence. The second was administered largely by external agents, where the priority was to ameliorate the damages of war and engage in many tasks of physical rebuilding, with fewer consequences for institutional development. While local capacity that existed in both countries was unlike that of Afghanistan's, the two approaches each implied ways of accomplishing relevant objectives.

Bosnia had received substantial early investments in social and political infrastructure. A coalition of donors worked under a High Representative who had little authority except to coordinate activities not unlike those contemplated for Afghanistan. Much of the actual implementation was left to interim governing regimes, pending elections that would be strongly contested. The "software" investments for the American program from 1998 to 2002 reached one billion dollars for reconstruction, plus one billion dollars in humanitarian aid following the Dayton Accords of 1995, and included $25 million annually for economic institutions, assistance to accounting and banking reforms, projects on management of the national treasury, and local public sector improvements. In order to cope with the return of increasing numbers of refugees, an enlarged Community Reintegration and Stabilization Program helped resettle more than 100,000 minority refugees after 2002. A $265 million rehabilitation program for Municipal Infrastructure and Services rebuilt water, rail, and other physical facilities. Assistance to free and independent media, a business development program, several small-scale projects supporting the rule of law, and grants to NGOs for improving the status of women and children, all aimed at enhancing public participation and local institutional capacities. The strengthening of internal administration contributed to various forms of political participation, culminating in a democratic election that produced a leadership that was quite unexpected by the international community.

In Kosovo, on the other hand, although foreign donors supported objectives similar to those for Afghanistan, they had to concern themselves primarily with providing urgently needed services. The legal circumstances required establishing international tribunals, a task that was pursued more urgently than that of improving the indigenous judiciary. As a result, international organizations under UN Resolution 1244 actually managed most legal problems and donors concentrated on immediate post-conflict problems of reconstruction and left the development of indigenous institutions for the future.

The subsequent outcomes still reflect the original constraints on Kosovo's ultimate sovereignty and legal status, unresolved after years of occupation. Kosovo postponed its desired separation from Serbia, although by December 29, 2002, the *New York Times* reported the emergence of an independence movement. Several years were to pass before the UN was ready to assign major responsibilities to self-governing authority, and even then it was necessary to retain important powers under international authority, including security, the treatment of minorities, external relations, and organized crime.

The Bosnia ethnic model seemed to offer more hope for Afghanistan, where the primary objective is to strengthen the central state without relying on combative local warlords as intermediaries. International aid has permitted central governance to develop very slowly, with international bodies, including NGOs, providing essential services, with little decentralization except of sporadic rule by warlords.

Parsing Reconstruction Experience

Two groups of specialists can claim expertise for Afghanistan: scholars and practitioners of international development who are familiar with reconstruction and development in war-torn and poverty-stricken countries, and experts on Afghanistan, the Middle East, and Islamic societies who have observed conditions of change and continuity in recent history. The issues they can contemplate seriously range from postcolonial rehabilitation to post-Communist reconstruction, and the resistance or amenability of Afghanistan's culture to the creation of a stable polity, a growing economy, and a peaceful society.

By the time the authors of this book met initially in January 2002, they were already worried that after the fighting was over the U.S. government might abandon Afghanistan in spite of the optimistic scenarios it had ceremoniously presented to the newly installed Afghan authorities. There was no guarantee that "nation-building" would continue to be on the government's agenda, especially after it had been unwilling to acknowledge it as a legitimate function of foreign policy. Although the cost of abandonment is one of the primary lessons of development experience, soldiers are especially vulnerable to the temptation of retreating from the field when the appetite for military adventure had been satisfied. Even Douglas MacArthur, the prototype of a caring proconsul in Japan, had labeled his quarterly Occupation reports, "Nonmilitary Activities," thus conveying a foreboding preview of what was to be a decaying commitment even before the Cold War had ushered in the "reverse revolution" of 1948.

Planners of Afghanistan's reconstruction took preventive measures. Thoughtful resolutions and detailed planning documents began to emerge from the World Bank, the U.S. Agency for International Development, the UN, and a host of NGOs that were contemplating rescue missions for Afghanistan. Their plans entered the funding phase even after the United States had begun to turn its attention away from Afghanistan (the host for terrorists) toward Iraq (the presumed harbor of weapons of mass destruction and the will to use them). The aid administrators persisted even after the importance of the task in Afghanistan seemed diminished by these events. As a reminder of the urgency of acting, Afghanistan was threatening to return to pre-Taliban insecurity to capture the wandering international attention.

Moreover, issues of reconstruction would continue to rise in still more diverse settings than that of Afghanistan. Certainly it would be no frivolous exercise to consult previous experiences in international assistance that might illuminate the outcomes of similar ventures elsewhere. Wherever applied, there could be much to learn from programs that assisted indigenous efforts at political stability, as well as from some that did not; from some that encouraged democracy and from others that attempted political neutrality; from some that contributed to economic viability and some that led to plunder. In the details there lurked relevant lessons for reconstruction and development in Afghanistan and for other countries seeking a better postwar future.

The Search for a Model

The most obvious risk in translating lessons from history to the present is that no two sets of experiences are interchangeable parts of a static paradigm. The only way to minimize false analogies is to focus on the antecedents and consequences of similar actions. In short, though history was not created to solve current problems, most current policies cannot be quarantined from earlier ones.

Supreme Commander MacArthur's Japan is often cited as the model for democratic nation-building because its outcome is considered a hopeful omen for a future success in similar circumstances. But it is not a template: many of its best features were unique. A few officers in the Occupation's Government Section had drafted Japan's new constitution in record time; other members had produced a translation of the New York State civil service regulations to satisfy the needs of Japanese bureaucracies that had survived almost intact; a universal education system already existed that could be "reformed" by adopting the American junior high approach in middle schools that were already functioning well. But the parallel to Afghanistan is mythical. No one wants to install a foreign proconsul in Kabul; American laws and regulations are rarely considered models in the Islamic world; a new constitution would have to be drafted by qualified Afghans, not by foreign advisors; and above all, there was no internal security in the country to guarantee continuity, no revered emperor to provide stability, and no resident occupation troops to discourage rebellion. Even in Iraq, where a complex civil society survived and economic institutions were readily at hand, there was no inclination to emplace, or accept, a supreme commander and a quasi-governing staff.

But in the donors' aspirations for Afghanistan was an implied model of hope derived from past experience. The model was less prescriptive than historical; it concentrated on ends rather than means; and its nation-building functions were to be discharged by Afghans themselves with international donors performing only supporting roles. Whatever the donors might carry in their minds as a model of nation-building, their prime expectations were to serve mutually desired ends in the light of experience.

Rondinelli, in chapter two, traces these expectations in the plans of the World Bank, the United States and other national donors, the Asian Development Bank, the United Nations Development Programme, and a variety of NGOs. All of them were intended to respond to national needs in Afghanistan, but they were developed in light of previous reconstruction programs from other parts of the world. Reference to these experiences made it possible for the donors to make their decisions speedily, without sacrificing complexity and comprehensiveness.

In chapter three, Montgomery considers theoretical and historical elements that underlay these plans, which constituted the outlines of the donors' preferred model for Afghanistan. The model was never stated as such, of course, but it may be inferred from relevant experiences, including previous postwar reconstructions as well as other recent events such as emerged from military defeat, from colonial rule, from the collapse of communism, and from the aftermath of dictatorship. It was a wealth of such historical data that encouraged donors to affirm the need for the rule of law; the use of competitive markets to promote economic efficiency; the practice of free speech; the protection of human rights; and participatory and balanced governmental institutions, all of which they presumed to be relevant to Afghanistan, thus constituting the "donors' model" explored in chapter three.

Lessons can also be drawn from more remote times and circumstances, as Heffron shows in his description of reconstruction and restoration following the American Civil War and the two World Wars (chapter four). Most of the post–Civil War assistance, like that following World Wars I and II, was of a humanitarian nature, aimed at recovery and the maintenance of minimal living standards. But the origins and vicissitudes of political and economic circumstances in Afghanistan indicate the need for reconstruction as well as restoration. Heffron explores the divergent and sometimes conflicting needs of these two convergent goals.

Most of the donor experiences described in this book deal with other countries, but in chapter five, Bossin provides a parallel description of previous assistance programs in Afghanistan itself (which date from the Britain's imperial ambitions about 150 years ago and continued during the Cold War's competitive giving). Competitive giving also accompanied support to the five-year and seven-year plans of the 1950s and beyond. The major surviving asset from those years is the Helmand Valley project, an irrigation and resettlement scheme that was plagued with inefficiencies but is still serving as a source of irrigation and stream control in the region.

Chapter six, by Muscat, draws extensively on program evaluations from Thailand, Taiwan, Botswana, Turkey, South Korea, Vietnam, Mozambique, and Uganda, to the encouragement provided by the European Marshall Plan, and to less successful experiences in The Democratic Republic of Congo (formerly Zaire), Sri Lanka, Rwanda, and the East–West Pakistan division. Although these country situations had little in common, they all faced problems endemic to underdevelopment or resulting from severe combat destruction like that in Afghanistan.

Norchi discusses in chapter seven the prospects for a rule of law, setting forth the pre-constitutional history and conditions in Afghanistan, as well as analyzing the implications of initiated in the constitutional debates of 2003.

During the past half-century donor governments and international assistance agencies have consciously chosen to deal more with economic than political issues, resting their hopes more on comprehensive national planning of macro policies than on constitutions. In chapter eight, Rondinelli shows how deeply Afghanistan's economic needs had impressed the donors as they considered how they could contribute to the task of reconstructing public works and the industrial infrastructure, while also creating conditions that would enable the country to initiate and sustain further development in the private sector. Their plans had to supplement those of the Interim Government, which was carrying out its own needs assessment analysis.

Recognition of Afghanistan's plight is further deepened by consideration of its most long-standing characteristic, its domination by centrifugal ethnic forces, which are described in chapter nine by Esman and chapter ten by Abdullaev. Both chapters emphasize the need for political centralization and the dangers of warlordism.

Esman describes the ethnic, linguistic, and religious structure of the tribes that occupy most of the country's regions and presents their relationship with outsiders as a special problem for donors who are concerned with national development. His approach suggests the need for establishing appropriate structures to carry out national functions as part of the strategy for national reconstruction, drawing on positive as well as negative examples from South Asia, Bosnia, Kosovo, Cambodia, Mozambique, East Timor, and, especially, South Korea and Taiwan.

Abdullaev builds on this approach by examining several unique features of Afghanistan's "warlordism" that make it necessary to find ways of co-opting armed regional rulers. He finds their roots in civil society and thus possible sources of social capital. In chapter ten he contrasts them with "state-based" warlords like Slobodan Milosevic, Franjo Tudjman, and Radovan Karadzic in the former Yugoslavia, Saddam Hussein in Iraq, and Pol Pot and Hun Sen in Cambodia, and considers how the special circumstances of Afghanistan's warlords permit their integration into a viable state.

Introducing the major social programs that Afghanistan will require in the near future could well take the form of organized interventions into the diverse local lifestyles, but experience warns against using remote instruments for that purpose. Community-directed programs can provide needed services and at the same time become an instrument of social and political development. Examples range from small-scale credit programs managed by village women to public health programs delivered by their intended beneficiaries. In chapter eleven, Gutlove, Thompson, and Russell review how health programs centered around human security can become essential components of social reconstruction, especially at local levels.

The regional possibilities for linking traditional ethnic groups across the artificial boundaries of Central and South Asia suggest other ways of providing international support to development, a topic that Eden Naby and Richard Frye consider in chapter twelve that may be relevant to other parts of the Islamic world as well.

All the chapters in this book unfold lessons of experience on which donors can draw in implementing plans for reconstruction and development in Afghanistan. Some reveal successful policies that can be modified and adapted to Afghanistan's conditions and needs, and others are derived from less successful programs and mistakes that donors can avoid. None of the successful programs of the past can be extended to Afghanistan without considering the conditions of success, and some may not be replicable at all. It is certain, however, that policies that are informed by knowledge and understanding of the past offer better prospects of success than can those that merely respond to immediate needs, however urgent.

PART 1
HOPES BEYOND RECONSTRUCTION

CHAPTER TWO

INTERNATIONAL GOALS AND STRATEGIES FOR AFGHANISTAN'S DEVELOPMENT: RECONSTRUCTION AND BEYOND

Dennis A. Rondinelli

Not since the modern era of international assistance began with the Marshall Plan in Europe in the late 1940s have donor countries dealt with such a complex and seemingly intransigent morass as they encounter in attempting to help Afghanistan recover from the past 25 years of external military intervention and internal conflict. Although wealthy nations attending the 2002 International Conference on Reconstruction Assistance for Afghanistan in Tokyo pledged more than $4.5 billion toward the nearly $15 billion that international organizations estimate it will cost to develop the economy of Afghanistan over the next decade, the prospects for success are uncertain.

The difficulties of making international assistance successful in Afghanistan cannot be attributed to lack of experience. As the Afghanistan Interim Administration recognized in its national development framework, foreign aid has been a major instrument of international policy for more than 50 years. Over the past 60 years the United States and other countries intervened frequently to help war-torn nations recover from devastating conflicts and to rebuild their governments and economies.[1] Prior to and immediately after the end of World War II, the United States provided emergency relief through the United Nations Relief and Rehabilitation Administration (UNRRA) and the International Bank for Reconstruction and Development (the World Bank) to the Philippines, European countries, Greece, and Turkey. The Marshall Plan, a concerted U.S. effort launched in 1947 to provide loans and technical assistance to European countries to rebuild their war-devastated infrastructure and economies and to alleviate poverty, hunger, and joblessness, served for years after as the model for postwar reconstruction assistance and the talisman for many kinds of international actions.

Through its Economic Cooperation Administration, the U.S. government assisted 16 European countries to develop long-range plans for restoring production and trade to prewar levels. The United States played a direct and extensive role in the reconstruction and development of Japan and Germany under military occupation after their surrender in World War II.[2]

The United States and its military and political allies provided substantial aid for economic development to South Korea in the wake of its invasion by North Korea and China, to the Kuomintang government in Taiwan during and after its conflicts with the Communist regime in China in the 1950s, and to governments recovering from insurgency and civil war in Southeast Asia during the 1960s.[3] The World Bank Group and regional development banks in Asia, Africa, and Latin America all channeled assistance to countries recovering from military incursions or insurgencies. Throughout the 1970s and 1980s, the United States, Japan, and Western European countries, the United Nations (UN), and international lending organizations came to the aid of countries in Africa, Asia, Central and South America, and other regions of the world where war tore apart societies and destroyed economies. In the 1990s, they formed the European Bank for Reconstruction and Development to help Central and Eastern European and Western Asian countries rebuild their economies and governance systems after the collapse of the Soviet Union and the end of the Cold War. The World Bank, the UN, and national governments provided reconstruction assistance in El Salvador, Nicaragua, Cambodia, the West Bank and Gaza, Lebanon, East Timor, Mozambique, Bosnia-Herzegovina, Kosovo, and other countries recovering from conflicts.

The Context of International Assistance to Afghanistan

The extensive experience of Western nations and international assistance organizations in providing aid for postwar reconstruction and development, however, is no guarantee of success in Afghanistan. The uncertainty arises from at least three sources. First, many of the decisions about how to promote the development of Afghanistan are likely to be made rapidly, reactively, and in response to uncertain and ever-changing political forces. Careful deliberation is likely to be in short supply in the face of rapidly changing political trends and complex social and cultural conditions in Afghanistan. Second, the political resolve of donor countries and organizations to see through to completion the difficult and complex long-term tasks of development in Afghanistan over the next two or three decades remains suspect, both by the diverse political factions in the country and by governments in neighboring nations that have seen the Great Powers abandon their posts after immediate threats to donor interests pass.[4] Third, unlike many other countries to which wealthy nations and international organizations have provided assistance for postwar reconstruction and development, Afghanistan has political, social, and economic characteristics that make implementing external assistance plans as complex as any previous case.

Unlike many other countries that have received international assistance for redevelopment, Afghanistan is a nation in name only. Powerful ethnic leaders forged territories controlled by diverse clans and tribes into what is now the country of Afghanistan by forcible consolidation during the seventeenth and eighteenth centuries and through wars with Great Britain and Russia, both of which sought control of warm-water ports and outposts in Central Asia in the nineteenth and twentieth centuries.[5] In response to Russian expansion in the late 1800s, the British supported the "Iron Amir" Abdur Rahman Khan's suppression of ethnic tribes and displacement of Pashtun enemies to create the present-day nation as a political convenience for maintaining ethnic and colonial interests in the region.[6] Between external invasions, much of the conflict in Afghanistan has been among ethnic, religious, and regional groups led by heavily armed warlords. Except for a brief period of relative liberalization under King Mohammad Zahir Shah from 1933 to 1973, Afghanistan has been under the control of one ethnic warlord or another. The Marxist revolt in 1978, accompanied by Soviet military occupation, led to abolition of the monarchy and to a long and destructive guerilla war supported by the United States until the Soviet defeat in 1992. The *mujahidin* victory, however, simply created conditions for continuing internecine warfare among ethnic clan and religious groups.[7]

The suppression of ethnic and religious groups by powerful warlord allies of the British and Russians forced diverse factions into political confederations that have never really accepted a strong central regime or pledged loyalty to a unified national government. The ethnic Pashtun, Tajik, Hazara, Aimaq, Turkmen, Baluch, and Uzbek groups that control various districts and regions of Afghanistan form temporary alliances of convenience but jealously guard their territory and identity. The majority Sunni Muslim groups are often in conflict with the minority Shi'a Muslims. Warlords forge alliances with ethnic and religious counterparts in politically diverse neighboring states of Pakistan, Iran, China, Tajikistan, Turkmenistan, and Uzbekistan.

The Taliban, which overthrew the ruling Afghan government in 1996, was the only faction that had been able to assert some degree of control over a large part of the country. Its extreme political and religious authoritarianism, however, incited opposition among groups that formed the Northern Alliance. After Islamic terrorist groups, coordinated by the Arab religious extremists of the al-Qaeda, based themselves in Afghanistan, the factional conflicts accelerated. The al-Qaeda-inspired attack on the New York World Trade Center and the Pentagon on September 11, 2001 brought American and British military forces into Afghanistan to support the Northern Alliances' defeat of the Taliban in late 2001.

An Interim Authority established by contending factions at an international conference organized by the UN in Bonn, Germany, brought some degree of temporary stability and governance—at least in the districts immediately surrounding the capital, Kabul—in 2001.[8] The Bonn Agreement called for an emergency meeting of the Loya Jirga—a traditional convening of elders to settle disputes—in June 2002 to form a transitional government and a parliament that would develop a new constitution. The temporary head of government, Hamid Karzai, was elected president, but the Loya Jirga could not agree on a cabinet, and Karzai appointed members on his own. The Grand Council disbanded before agreeing on guidelines for electing a parliament. Continuing disagreement among warlords and ethnic factions rendered uncertain the fate of compromises reached by the Loya Jirga.

Initial Conditions of Reconstruction and Development

Given Afghanistan's long history of internal conflict, one of the most difficult challenges facing donors is how to channel large amounts of foreign aid into the country in the absence of a central government with national authority and to prevent the dissipation of aid through corruption, favoritism, or incompetence.

Donor countries attempting to reconstruct and develop Afghanistan face multiple and complex problems. Although many of the countries receiving external assistance in the past have been poor, most had functioning economic and social institutions in the prewar period that provided at least a subsistence livelihood in agriculture and small business. Afghanistan never had much of an economy to reconstruct. Even before the conflicts with Russia and the Taliban, Afghanistan was one of the poorest places on earth.[9] The estimated population of 25 million in this land-locked country of rugged mountains and dry plains—smaller in size than the state of Texas—subsisted traditionally on seasonal agriculture and goat- and sheep-raising. Only about 12 to 15 percent of the terrain is arable and only about half of that was actually cultivated. Agricultural land in Afghanistan yields few permanent crops. Prior to and after Taliban rule, many farmers turned to poppy cultivation; Afghanistan became the world's largest supplier of illicit opium, which international donors are now seeking to eliminate.

The country is subject to frequent droughts, floods, and earthquakes. From 1999 to 2002, Afghanistan was devastated by both war and widespread drought. Educational levels were low, basic social services did not exist in most of the country, infrastructure had been destroyed, and health conditions were poor. About 70 percent of the Afghan population was estimated to be malnourished in 2000. More than 64 percent—nearly two-thirds of Afghan adults—were illiterate.[10] Only about 35 percent of people living in urban areas and 19 percent living in rural areas had access to safe drinking water, mostly from public wells.[11] The Asian Development Bank (ADB) estimated the per capita Gross Domestic Product (GDP) at only about $200.[12] Only 13 percent of roads were paved in 1991, and most of those fell into disrepair during the following ten years of warfare. Less than 30 percent of boys were enrolled in elementary school, and under Taliban rule girls were forbidden to be educated and women were not allowed to be trained, obtain access to health services, or work outside of their homes. The United Nations Development Programme (UNDP) estimated that more than one million Afghans were displaced persons, with an additional 3.5 million Afghan refugees in Pakistan and Iran, in 2002.[13] Much of the country was plagued with land mines and unexploded ordnance from previous wars. Although Afghanistan possesses unknown quantities of natural resources, including natural gas, petroleum, coal, copper, and minerals, few had been exploited for commercial purposes. Nearly half the population of Afghanistan was estimated to be below 14 years or over 65 years of age, although life expectancy in the country barely reached 44 years for men and 45 years for women. One in four children died of preventable diseases before their fifth birthday.[14]

Before the most recent military conflicts, more than 70 percent of the estimated 10 million people in the labor force worked in subsistence agriculture and another 15 percent in small-scale trading and services. A 25-year period of war not only destroyed much of the physical and social infrastructure and disrupted whatever social services were available, but also disabled small-scale business and trade.

International Assistance Programs for Afghanistan

During the period of Taliban domination in Afghanistan external foreign assistance was limited to occasional emergency aid by nongovernmental organizations (NGOs), but the Taliban obstructed even their missions if they sought to help women or girls or funded activities that the ruling *mullahs* considered suspect. Prior to the Taliban takeover, Afghanistan received relatively small amounts of the billions of dollars dispersed annually in official development assistance. From 1980 to 1986 official development assistance to Afghanistan never exceeded $20 million a year. Between 1988 and 1998, Official Development Assistance (ODA) averaged a little more than $200 million a year, and during the years of Taliban rule, external aid fell to a little more than $130 million a year.[15] From 1992 to 2001, the United Nations provided only a total of about $160 million in aid.[16]

During the *mujahidin* guerilla war against the Soviet armies, the United States provided substantial amounts of military equipment and supplies to the Northern Alliance, but largely ignored Afghanistan after the Russians were driven out. As Afghanistan became an increasingly dangerous base for extremist terrorism under the Taliban, the United States and Western European countries took greater interest in preparing reconstruction and development assistance plans, in addition to providing military aid to the Northern Alliance and other forces fighting the Taliban and its allies. Only in late 2001, after the Taliban had been removed from power, did international organizations and governments in Western countries begin thinking seriously about reconstruction and development efforts.

The plans for international assistance were driven both by the immediate conditions and needs in Afghanistan and, inevitably although more implicitly, by conceptual models of development and modern society that have generally been embedded in Western foreign aid strategies for more than two decades. All the components of this implicit virtual model, discussed in more detail elsewhere in this volume, are reflected in both the immediate reconstruction and longer-term development plans that were initially formulated by international aid agencies and the Interim Administration in Afghanistan. A broad consensus emerged on the priorities for international assistance in part because of the pressing requirements emerging from 25 years of war and destitution and in part from a comprehensive needs assessment compiled by three international assistance organizations in the absence of alternative sources of information.

The World Bank "Approach Paper"

The World Bank developed an "approach paper" in 1999 that anticipated formulating a reconstruction strategy and plan for Afghanistan and establishing a trust fund through which its own and other donor funds could be channeled.[17] Based on limited information about conditions in Afghanistan, the World Bank identified priorities for international assistance in the short and medium terms.

In the short term, the World Bank suggested that external assistance be focused on: (1) agricultural recovery and food security; (2) providing basic services and small-scale development programs in communities; (3) generating livelihoods for returning refugees and displaced people; (4) rehabilitation of the main road networks; (5) public works programs for generating short-run employment; (6) restarting and expanding education and health programs, especially for girls and women; (7) building human capacity in areas of social service delivery, infrastructure development and public administration; and (8) expanding the program to remove land mines.

The World Bank report noted that reconstruction assistance was not enough in Afghanistan and that "merely restoring the pre-1978 economic situation would still leave the country one of the poorest in the world in terms of both incomes and social indicators."[18] After addressing immediate needs, international donors would have to help Afghanistan with long-term economic and social development. Among the most important development priorities were: (1) establishing sound economic management institutions such as a Central Bank and ministries of finance and treasury as well as a reliable statistic system; (2) developing educational and health systems that serve a large majority of the population; (3) creating lean, honest, effective, and publicly accountable civil service institutions and urban management capability; (4) establishing an "enabling environment" for private sector development; (5) developing exports of agricultural, livestock, and mineral products; (6) managing effectively natural (especially forestry) and environmental resources; and (7) managing and developing energy resources.

The Preliminary Needs Assessment

Following the al-Qaeda terrorist attacks in New York and Washington in September 2001, the United States intervened militarily in Afghanistan to capture al-Qaeda leaders and drive the Taliban from power. Western nations began preparing for postwar reconstruction in late 2001. UN Resolution 1378 called for a framework for recovery and reconstruction efforts in preparation for a senior officials' meeting cochaired by Japan and the United States in Washington in November 2001 and a donor's meeting in Tokyo in January 2002 cosponsored by Japan, the United States, the European Union, and the Kingdom of Saudi Arabia. At the meeting in Washington, senior officials agreed that a coordinated assistance plan should be implemented among all parties providing financial aid and technical support.[19]

At the request of the senior officials attending the Washington meeting, UNDP, the World Bank, and the ADB jointly conducted a needs assessment in Afghanistan to estimate the required types and costs of external assistance.[20] This preliminary needs assessment became the most comprehensive and authoritative plan for international aid to Afghanistan, providing the basis not only for reconstruction and development assistance by international organizations, but a reference point for national governments' aid efforts. For all practical purposes, it became the only reliable guide for understanding international donor's objectives and strategies for reconstruction and development in Afghanistan.

The needs assessment suggested that internationally assisted reconstruction and development programs in Afghanistan should focus on poverty reduction and creation of economic opportunities. The intended outcomes included establishing political stability and security, providing widespread access to basic services, creating an adequate standard of living for the Afghan people, and generating economic growth and—in the long term—independence from foreign aid.[21]

The immediate priorities for international assistance included establishing a national security force and mobilizing the support of local institutions and civil society leaders. Creating sound and trusted basic governance structures at the central and local levels was seen as a precondition for development, along with investment in labor-intensive public works programs to rehabilitate infrastructure and provide jobs.

At the same time, the needs assessment placed high priority on the expansion of health and education services, especially for women and girls. The report noted the critical importance of having Afghans implement reconstruction and development programs and engaging the support and participation of local communities in the process.

Among the most important immediate international assistance programs, the needs assessment identified the following:

- *Establishing effective institutions for security, justice, and protection of human rights*—including establishing professional police forces, reestablishing a judicial system at the central government and municipal, district, and provincial levels, redeveloping the legal profession, implementing human rights education programs and creating an independent human rights commission.
- *Reintegrating war combatants*—including demobilizing militias and armed groups and reintegrating war combatants into the economy through public works and other job-creation programs, and developing training programs to prepare combatants for alternative livelihoods.
- *Controlling drugs*—including enacting a poppy cultivation ban, creating viable law enforcement to monitor and eliminate poppy cultivation and drug trafficking, formulating alternative livelihood strategies to poppy cultivation and establishing countrywide drug rehabilitation and prevention programs.
- *Eliminating mines*—including resuming regular mine and unexploded ordnance clearance operations and creating mine awareness and risk reduction education programs.

Although these immediate priorities were paramount in the needs assessment, the report emphasized that reconstruction and development could not take place without good governance and economic management. Among the most important needs in the short and medium terms were creating a sound civil service administration, staffing government agencies, implementing a reliable and appropriate salary system to pay government employees a living wage, and fighting corruption.

In the long run the needs assessment noted the requirement that external aid to Afghanistan be focused on helping build "a limited, but effective state that takes full advantage of existing capacity at the community level," based on a balance of centralized and decentralized functions, simple and transparent procedures to minimize corruption and discrimination, and effective aid management within a lean government bureaucracy.[22] The report emphasized the importance of "using the full variety of institutional actors to help in the reconstruction effort, including the civil service, private sector, community and non-government organizations (NGOs)" and that the recovery and development activities be carried out as much as possible by Afghans themselves.

The wide-ranging program of potential immediate and long-term development activities identified in the needs assessment is summarized in Table 2.1. The needs assessment also calculated potential costs of these programs, and by implication, the ranges of international assistance that would be needed to carry them out over a 10-year period. The estimates, based on total costs of aid in other postwar countries and recalculated into per capita expenditures for application in a country of Afghanistan's population size, are summarized in Table 2.2. Over a 10-year period,

Table 2.1 Afghanistan reconstruction and development needs assessment

Sector	Immediate actions ("reconstruction")	Longer-term actions ("development")
Security	—Establish professional police force of 30,000 people	—Expand police and law enforcement forces and a national plan for counterterrorism and drug interdiction —Create capacity to investigate threats to national security and customs, tax, and financial crimes
Drug control	—Establish drug control commission in Kabul and control units in key provinces —Monitor illicit opium poppy cultivation —Provide assistance to landholders and sharecroppers —Establish sanctions for poppy cultivation	—Build sustainable livelihoods in poppy growing areas —Reduce opium cultivation and drug trafficking —Provide effective enforcement of drug ban
Mine action	—Support Department of Mine Clearance —Create Mine Action Program for training and equipment —Clear mines and unexploded ordnance from roads	—Develop programs to significantly clear and mark mined areas —Provide mine awareness/risk education —Destroy stockpiles of mines —Integrate mine action into overall national development plans
Social protection	—Provide disabled with limbs, cash benefits, and special needs education —Create rural and urban public works employment programs —Establish micro-finance schemes to encourage business start-ups —Develop affirmative action programs to employ women in civil administration, health, and education sectors	—Gradually phase out public works programs as economy grows —Scale up micro-finance services in rural and urban areas —Develop and implement a national policy and safety net program for disabled and other social groups, including orphans and widows
Gender	—Support a Ministry of Women's Affairs	—Ensure participation of women in political process —Promote social recovery, provision of education, professional training, economic opportunities, access to health care, social security, and other services designed specifically for vulnerable groups of women
Governance	—Establish rules and procedures for the civil service —Establish pay scales and pensions —Fund NGO programs supporting community development —Create intergovernmental institutional framework to define roles and responsibilities of different levels of government	—Establish sound and trusted basic governance arrangements —Support the interim and transitional governments in building legitimacy and accountability —Assist in holding of elections for a more permanent administration —Build government's capacity to take responsibility for coordination and

Table 2.1 continued

Sector	Immediate actions ("reconstruction")	Longer-term actions ("development")
	—Design and implement demand-driven funding mechanisms	management of overall recovery and reconstruction efforts
Judicial system	—Review compatibility of Afghanistan laws with international legal obligations —Provide financial support for salaries and supplies of judicial system —Recruit judges and prosecutors —Provide technical assistance for a Human Rights Commission	—Formulate and implement program of legal literacy and communication —Extend professional development in legal profession —Establish a Judicial Commission to rebuild the domestic justice system in accordance with Islamic principles, rule of law, and Afghan legal traditions —Support organization of legal aid services —Create legal affairs offices to assist central government institutions with legal reform, court administration, and professional development
Economic management	—Establish Central Bank, payments system and banking supervision framework —Prepare interim budget —Establish treasury single account to receive funds and make payments —Create economic forecasting capacity —Support Aid Coordination Unit in Ministry of Finance	—Create investment climate conducive to attracting foreign direct investment —Create legislative framework for protecting investors' rights —Formulate policy framework for developing oil, gas, and mineral resources —Develop secure, efficient, and corruption-free financial institutions and services
Health	—Carry out national child immunization programs —Expand supplementary and therapeutic feeding program —Provide basic health services package —Conduct refresher training for health sector personnel	—Control communicable diseases, including TB, malaria, sexually transmitted diseases, and HIV/AIDS —Promote child health, including management of pneumonia and diarrhea —Develop reproductive health programs including maternal and newborn health and birth spacing and family planning services —Create nutrition supplementation and micronutrient programs —Expand district and community public health facilities
Education	—Undertake "back to school" programs to expand primary school enrollment and provide teaching materials —Rebuild and equip school buildings —Repair and reopen Kabul University and regional colleges	—Increase gross enrollment rate to 85% and the net enrollment rate to 75% combined for boys and girls —Raise proportion of qualified teachers to 80% —Lower teacher–pupil ratio to 1 : 40 —Improve transition rate between primary and secondary schooling to about 40%

Table 2.1 continued

Sector	Immediate actions ("reconstruction")	Longer-term actions ("development")
Cultural heritage	—Protect cultural sites, survey monuments, protect buildings from further damage	—Continue protection of cultural sites
Roads and civil aviation	—Establish policy and institutions for national, provincial, and local roads —Rehabilitate core highway network —Remove bottlenecks from main road networks —Establish institutions for airport rehabilitation and operation	—Continue to expand and extend roads and civil aviation facilities
Water, sanitation and energy	—Establish institutional frameworks and policy for water, sanitation, and energy development —Repair urban piped water systems —Expand access to water in priority rural areas —Provide technical assistance to develop energy strategy and supply emergency fuels —Restore minimum power supply in major cities	—Continue to expand and extend water, sanitation, and energy facilities and services
Communications	—Establish radio broadcast services —Create telecommunications policy to expand investment and services —Provide legal services to support the government in regulating contracts of incumbent operators —Support telecommunications sector reform	—Continue to expand communications facilities and improve quality of telecommunications services
Urban infrastructure	—Establish mechanisms to resolve property ownership disputes —Develop municipal management framework to plan urban reconstruction —Provide shelter and basic services to urban residents and returnees —Initiate urban planning that leads to rapid establishment of services for housing	—Continue to reconstruct and expand urban road network, piped water and sewerage networks, sanitary facilities, and urban housing
Agriculture and Natural resources	—Distribute essential agricultural inputs (seeds, tools, fertilizer, etc.) —Design irrigation rehabilitation programs —Implement environmental assessments and pilot projects for forestry and watershed management	—Implement policy framework to support competitive markets and private sector provision of agricultural support, marketing and agro-processing services —Develop the hydrological monitoring network —Promote improved technologies in irrigated and rain-fed crops, livestock, horticulture, forestry, and irrigation sectors

Table 2.1   continued

Sector	Immediate actions ("reconstruction")	Longer-term actions ("development")
		—Foster development and outreach of sustainable rural and micro-finance system —Expand watershed management and forestry and agro-forestry programs in priority areas —Rebuild and strengthen public institutional capacity to develop environmental policy and regulation

Source: Compiled from United Nations Development Programme, World Bank, Asian Development Bank, "Afghanistan: Preliminary Needs Assessment for Recovery and Reconstruction" (New York: UNDP, 2002).

Table 2.2   Base Case—cumulative estimates of funding requirements on commitment basis (US$ millions)

	2.5 years	5 years	10 years
Range of Estimates			
Base Case	4,900	10,200	14,600
Low Case	4,200	8,300	11,400
High Case	6,500	12,200	18,100
Sector			
Security			
Security Force and Police	320	320	320
Mine Action	150	450	660
Drug Control	110	290	380
Subtotal	570	1,060	1,360
Governance & Economic Management			
Governance and Public Administration	330	500	520
Local Governance & Community Development	300	600	800
Private Sector Development	110	200	200
Gender	10	20	40
Environment	20	30	30
Cultural Heritage	20	30	30
Subtotal	780	1,370	1,620
Social Protection, Health & Education			
Education	210	650	1,240
Health	210	380	640
Social Protection	350	400	490
Subtotal	760	1,430	2,380
Infrastructure			
Transport	180	1,030	2,390
Civil Aviation	30	60	70
Water and Sanitation	100	230	580
Energy	240	760	1,330

Table 2.2 continued

	2.5 years	5 years	10 years
Telecommunications	40	80	120
Urban Management, Services, Housing	130	250	320
Subtotal	720	2,400	4,810
Agricultural & Natural Resource Management	280	850	1,360
Total Capital Expenditures	3,110	7,110	11,530
Of which Technical Aid & Inst. Devel.	330	550	830
Base Case Total Recurrent Costs	1,800	3,100	3,100

Source: United Nations Development Programme, World Bank, Asian Development Bank, "Afghanistan: Preliminary Needs Assessment for Recovery and Reconstruction" (New York: UNDP, 2002).

the estimates ranged from $11.4 billion for a low case-scenario to $18.1 billion for a high case scenario, with the base case costing about $14.6 billion.

Afghanistan's Draft National Development Framework

In April 2002, the Interim Administration in Afghanistan formulated a draft *National Development Framework* in consultation with international assistance organizations and donor governments that reflected many of the same priorities and projects described in the preliminary needs assessment. The framework pointed out five lessons from experience that should guide Afghanistan and international donors in using aid to promote reconstruction and development.[23] First, it noted that the "developmental agenda must be owned domestically, and the recipient country must be in the driver's seat." Second, it declared that the "market and the private sector is a more effective instrument of delivering sustained growth than the state." Third, it held that "without a state committed to investing in human capital, the rule of law, the creation of systems of accountability and transparency, and providing the enabling environment for the operation of the private sector, aid cannot be an effective instrument of development." Fourth, it proclaimed that the people in general, and particularly the poor, "are not passive recipients of development but active engines of change." Thus, Afghanistan needed a governance system that allows people to take part in decision making "on issues that affect them and their immediate surroundings." And fifth, structural adjustment programs funded by donors would not be sustainable or result in reform unless they are translated into feasible projects and the projects "are anchored in coherent programs of government."

The national development strategy was based on three pillars. First, because Afghanistan had undergone a humanitarian crisis following the defeat of the Taliban, the development strategy gave highest priority to programs focused on strengthening human and social capital—resettling refugees and returnees, developing secure livelihoods, reestablishing the educational system, establishing vocational training, investing in health and nutrition programs, and preserving the national heritage. Second, the development strategy would be based on projects of physical reconstruction and natural resource management—using public works programs to offer employment opportunities to rebuild roads, water and sanitation, and energy facilities. Physical infrastructure programs would invest heavily in cities to create hubs of economic activity and link those activities to rural areas. The third pillar of Afghanistan's proposed development strategy was to stimulate the private sector and begin creating a competitive export-oriented economy. Building a market-based economy would require developing policy and legal frameworks for attracting foreign direct investment and meeting international standards on health, organic agriculture, child labor, certificates of origin, and other technical requirements so that Afghan products would be accepted in world markets.

Donor Assistance Programs for Afghanistan's Reconstruction and Development

International organizations, governments of rich nations around world, and foundations pledged more than $4.5 billion in assistance for reconstruction and development of Afghanistan at the Tokyo conference in January 2002.

International Organizations. Three international organizations—the UNDP, the World Bank Group, and the ADB—took the lead in coordinating assistance to Afghanistan. The UNDP focused its immediate recovery assistance on seven programs: (1) governance; (2) community empowerment and participation; (3) the return and reintegration of refugees and internally displaced populations; (4) stronger capacity of women' s organizations to participate in political and social activities; (5) drug control; (6) peace building and conflict prevention; and (7) human rights. The UNDP assumed a coordinating role in bringing UN assistance to nearly all the activities identified in the preliminary needs assessment. Creating an effective governance capacity was seen as a fundamental condition for carrying out other assistance programs in Afghanistan. The UNDP noted that "effective governance is built on sound economic policy, transparent and accountable public institutions, a free media, robust and independent legal frameworks and judicial mechanisms which, *inter alia*, protect and promote the rights of all citizens."[24] The UN's role would be to assist the Interim Authority and the transitional government through programs focusing on justice and security, drug control, public administration and support for the civil service, development planning and aid coordination and management, and local governance and community-led development. The United Nations also saw a role for itself in helping Afghanistan create employment opportunities and provide alternative livelihoods to prevent the spread of poppy cultivation.

Sector strategies and activities included food assistance to meet emergency conditions and to improve self-sufficiency through rapid expansion of food production and nutritional programs to treat the severely malnourished children and pregnant and lactating women. Health programs would focus on reducing the high levels of morbidity, mortality, and disability in Afghanistan and to extend water and sanitation facilities. UN assistance programs also sought to improve the protection of at-risk civilians from continued armed conflicts and to protect and promote human rights in Afghanistan. Gender-oriented assistance would target programs for ensuring the inclusion of women in governance and peace-building efforts, ensure women's economic and social security, promote an end of violence against women, and support women's involvement in UN-supported recovery and development efforts. The United Nations also took an active role in supporting mine- and ordnance-clearing activities.

The UN assistance programs would also attempt to increase access to primary and secondary education and help develop the educational system. The UN High Commission for Refugees sought to promote the repatriation and return of refugees and help reintegrate them in Afghanistan.

The World Bank Group's assistance also covered most of the activities identified in the needs assessment. The International Monetary Fund (IMF) took the lead in helping Afghanistan establish a functional financial and payment system, assist in the reactivation of governmental economic institutions, including creation of a regulatory environment to support a productive private sector and improvement of the government's capacity to prepare and implement macroeconomic policies to dampen the inflationary pressures from reconstruction and development assistance.[25] The IMF's assistance for longer-term development will focus on strengthening the government's economic management and restoring economic and financial institutions, creating a predictable, transparent and liberal trade regime, and restoring the Ministry of Finance's full capacity to carry out treasury functions.

The World Bank announced its first operation in Afghanistan in April 2002—a $10-million grant to assist the Afghanistan Interim Administration to begin to develop key public administration functions so that public resources and donor funding could be used effectively to rebuild and redevelop the country.[26] The support for medium-term development focused on the specific goals of "(1) rebuilding or strengthening essential governance institutions and capacity; (2) kickstarting high-priority, high-impact reconstruction programs to help restore livelihoods, generate economic activity, create employment, facilitate the development of the private sector, and restore essential infrastructure, communications, and social services; (3) facilitating effective coordination of assistance efforts by the international community under the leadership of the Afghan government; and (4) building a knowledge base and analytical underpinning for the work of the international community and future Bank assistance." The World Bank followed up with a $42-million program to fund labor-intensive public works and housing and infrastructure community grants for rural villages, $33 million for emergency infrastructure reconstruction projects in Kabul and other provincial cities, and $15 million to support education rehabilitation and development. The World Bank Group's International Development Association also pledged grants for high-impact assistance projects focusing on community-driven investments in infrastructure and for education.

The ADB's assistance program gave highest priority to basic education, reconstruction of transport infrastructure, and rehabilitation of irrigation systems and agriculture.[27] The ADB would also provide supplementary assistance for health, energy, finance and trade, environment, and community development programs, following the recommendations outlined in the preliminary needs assessment and Afghanistan's draft national development framework.

Government and NGO Assistance Programs. At the donors' conference in Tokyo in January 2002, many Western countries pledged contributions of nearly $4.5 billion to assist Afghanistan in reconstruction, initially over a two-and-a-half year period, and for longer-term development.[28] Most donor countries referenced the preliminary needs assessment report as the basis for focusing their assistance either through a temporary UNDP trust fund or through specialized international assistance organizations.

Most national governments focused their assistance grants on specific programs or interventions identified in the preliminary needs assessment. Japan's aid, for example, focused on resettlement of refugees, improving education and health care, the empowerment of women, and the removal of land mines. The United States announced that its assistance had to give highest priority to projects that quickly create jobs, generate income, stimulate the economy, rebuild infrastructure, and resettle refugees and displaced persons. The United States would also focus on creating agricultural alternatives to poppy cultivation and rebuilding infrastructure and education and health systems.[29] The European Union (EU) pledged aid in promoting the Bonn Agreement and its implementation for creating a permanent national government in Afghanistan, providing technical support for civil, social, and military structures and services, providing aid for refugees and displaced persons, and promoting democracy and the inclusion of women.[30] Much of the EU's aid would be channeled through United Nations Specialized Agencies and NGOs.

Germany committed assistance for basic education, health care, development of the private sector and micro-finance institutions, water and sanitation, the development of state structures, support for women' s programs, and establishing police structures. Germany took the lead in training a new Afghanistan police force.[31] Canada's assistance was targeted to mine removal programs, for World Health Organization tuberculosis control projects, for the UNICEF national vaccination campaign, to the UN High Commissioner for Refugees projects, and to the International Committee for the Red Cross to protect citizens in conflict-affected areas and provide health care, water, relief supplies, and sanitation facilities. Canada also distributed its contribution to NGOs including CARE Canada and the Red Crescent Society, and to other United Nations Specialized Agencies to carry out reconstruction and development activities in Afghanistan.[32]

In addition, private organizations, such as the Aga Khan Foundation pledged support for development activities. The Aga Khan Development Network committed $75 million to create a "safety belt" through project investments in areas in the region around Afghanistan plagued by poverty, isolation, or lack of opportunity, to resettle refugees and integrate former combatants, to help establish "accountable institutions," and strengthen democracy.[33] Oxfam expanded its programs in Afghanistan for food distribution, education, health, snow clearance on mountain passes, and de-mining activities.[34] CARE International extended its emergency assistance programs for displaced families and returning refugees, for food assistance and food-for-work, and security of livelihoods. Moreover, it further developed its water and sanitation projects in the poorest areas of Kabul, its community organization for primary education program, and its widows feeding program.[35] By mid-2002, more than 100 NGOs ranging from CARE, Oxfam, Médécins Sans Frontières, and the

International Catholic Migration Commission to Handicap International, the Islamic Relief Agency, and the Organization for Humanitarian Assistance were working in Afghanistan.[36]

Managing International Assistance to Afghanistan

A critical question initially surrounding international assistance to Afghanistan was how to channel significant resources from national governments and international organizations into a country with no permanent democratically chosen government, where national government ministries and agencies had to be reestablished, where the civil service had been decimated and those remaining at their posts had not been paid, and where the Interim Administration hardly exercised authority outside Kabul. In a country divided into areas controlled by armed militias, and with a reputation for high levels of corruption, how could donors be sure that their assistance would not be wasted, dissipated on ineffective projects, or simply diverted into the pockets of government officials or regional warlords? Following the Tokyo conference in early 2002, the major donors established a steering group for Afghanistan's reconstruction and an implementation group chaired by the Government of Afghanistan and supported by the ADB, the Islamic Development Bank, the UNDP, the World Bank, and the chair of the Afghan Support Group. Initial assistance to provide short-term emergency funding for civil servant salaries was channeled through a temporary UNDP Trust Fund.

The World Bank distributed a proposal at donor meetings early in 2002 to create a multi-donor Afghanistan Reconstruction Trust Fund (ARTF) that would manage donor assistance contributions and coordinate aid activities in Afghanistan at least until 2006.[37] The ARTF would help promote transparency and accountability of reconstruction assistance, reduce the burden on government capacity, and build its ability to take on increasing responsibility over time. The Trust Fund would also help reinforce the national budget as the means for aligning the reconstruction and development program and national objectives and to fund essential recurrent budget expenditures. The ARTF would manage three categories of expenditure. First, it would cover running costs—salaries and nonproject technical assistance, operations and maintenance, and other recurrent expenditures of the government budget. Second, it would manage the investment and program component—investment activities and quick-impact postwar recovery projects. Third, it would cover costs of reconstruction efforts by expatriate Afghan experts as well as training programs in Afghanistan.

The World Bank would serve as the Administrator of the ARTF, supervised by a Management Committee composed of representatives of the World Bank, the UNDP, the Islamic Development Bank, and the ADB, with participation by contributing donors. The Government of Afghanistan would not be a member of the governance structure but would play a strong role in reviewing proposals for ARTF funding and submitting proposals to the Management Committee. The ARTF would accept only grant contributions from donors that were not earmarked for a specific component, activity, or program.

World Bank procedures would generally apply to procurement, disbursement, financial management, environmental and social impacts, corruption monitoring and evaluation, and conflict of interest. The World Bank would also appoint a Monitoring Agent to oversee financial transactions and report on the developmental impacts of expenditures. The World Bank, with approval of participating donors, launched the ARTF in May 2002, accepting the first installment of a five million pound contribution from the United Kingdom.

Learning from International Experience

The implementation of international assistance programs in Afghanistan faces complex challenges. Donors and the recipient recognized that external aid could not be delivered and used wisely unless guided by sensitivity to local needs and conditions and informed by experience with economic and technical assistance in other countries. As the Afghanistan Interim Administration's draft *National Development Framework* recognized, "we must internalize the lessons of 50 years of experience of international assistance. Afghanistan offers a unique opportunity to prove to the skeptics that the aid system is relevant in postconflict context and that difficult challenges can be met with determination, partnership and vision."[38]

However, the underlying goals and strategies of international donors are shaped almost unconsciously by a "virtual model" (as described by Montgomery in chapter three that) reflects their long-term aspirations for a developed society. It remains to be seen, however, whether that model fits the conditions and needs in Afghanistan. Because of its history of involvement in Afghanistan and the surrounding region, Russia's position on military, political, and economic issues may again strongly influence how quickly and in what direction reconstruction and development take in the future and how conflicts in its surrounding region limit or expand the potential for Afghanistan's economic growth and political stability. The geopolitical context of foreign aid to Afghanistan, and how Afghans maneuver among donor governments, will also influence the pace and direction of development. Equally important will be the influence of neighboring countries with which different ethnic and religious groups have made alliances. Pakistan, Iran, and China all have strong interests in Afghanistan's political and economic future, but those interests may not be compatible or able to be reconciled.

Complicating the process of reconstruction and development in Afghanistan is the need to implement external assistance programs in a fragmented political system in which internal ethnic and religious differences will remain a source of tension for years to come. The conflicts between warlord-dominated areas and the central government, between the Shi'a and Sunni communities, and between Shi'a and Hazara political components of the Northern Alliance-dominated Transitional Authority raise complex questions about how closely diverse political factions in Afghanistan will work together for recovery and development. Moreover, implementation of reconstruction and development programs will be carried out in part by a central government so weak that it is generally referred to as a "failed state." How resources will be distributed and how powers will be shared among warlord leaders and with the central government remain open questions. Without a recognized central government that can impose the rule of law, provide security, mediate continuing conflicts, protect human rights, reconstruct infrastructure, extend basic health and educational services, and earn the loyalty of people throughout the country, development will remain a slow and uncertain process. Although the lessons of experience with international assistance to post-conflict countries can provide strong guidelines for effective assistance to Afghanistan, it must be noted that in none of these countries has the process of international assistance gone perfectly smooth. In an assessment of external assistance to Cambodia, Mozambique, El Salvador, the Palestinian Territories, South Africa, and Bosnia-Herzegovina, Patrick found that similar problems plagued assistance efforts in all these countries during the post-conflict recovery period.[39]

Although in most of these countries donors formulated a strategic framework similar to the needs assessment developed for Afghanistan, donors and assistance organizations did not always follow the strategy or coordinate their activities. Nor did assistance organizations have the mechanisms to mobilize resources quickly to address unanticipated problems or unique transitional situations. In some of these countries, donor pledges did not correspond to realistic needs or recipient priorities. Many of the donors placed conditions on their grants that either conflicted with each other or that undermined the capacity of other assistance organizations or the government to carry out development programs effectively. Monitoring, assessment, and evaluation of aid impacts were often fragmented, uncoordinated, and incomplete. Procedures for tracking aid flows usually were not standardized or coordinated among assistance organizations.

A mid-2002 assessment of initial assistance efforts by the Afghan Assistance Coordination Authority (AACA) indicated that many of the same problems were beginning to appear in Afghanistan. The UN-sponsored organization found that "assistance agencies (both international and Afghan) are most often 'doing their own thing,' with very little advance consultation with local authorities or even with each other."[40] Local authorities, largely isolated from the government in Kabul, did not have the tools or qualified personnel to implement donor projects. External assistance efforts were carried out in areas in which there were "uneven relations between regional and provincial centers on the one hand and districts or local communities on the other." The trust and confidence among various stakeholders of international assistance organizations were extremely weak. Moreover, although most of the donors had honored their pledges of assistance during the first year, nearly all of the funds went to United Nations agencies or NGOs for programs in Afghanistan rather than to the Transitional Authority or Afghan ministries or agencies.

In order to improve the process of reconstruction and development assistance, the AACA called for the acceleration of capacity-building initiatives and for international organizations to provide material assistance to local authorities, establish provincial coordination bodies and program-area working groups, and find ways of identifying and agreeing upon local assistance priorities. The AACA noted the importance of extending the outreach of government agencies and international organizations from Kabul to other parts of Afghanistan and of sensitizing aid workers to local conditions.

The chapters that follow attempt to assess political, economic, and social issues that can affect the design and implementation of international assistance programs and projects in Afghanistan and to identify and describe critical issues surrounding the use of international assistance for postwar reconstruction and development based on 50 years of experience with international aid. They cull from past experience the factors that contributed to the success and failure of international economic and technical assistance to poor or war-torn countries and analyze the relevance of that experience to the potential for successfully implementing development policies, programs, and projects in Afghanistan.

Whether or not external aid will be effective in achieving reconstruction and development will depend on complex political, economic, and social factors that were only partially known as the international assistance programs were designed and will be difficult to forecast as the government of Afghanistan and international organizations attempt to implement them during the next decade.

Notes

1. Dennis A. Rondinelli, *Development Administration and U.S. Foreign Aid Policy* (Boulder, CO: Lynne Rienner Publishers, 1987).
2. John D. Montgomery, *Forced to be Free: The Artificial Revolution in Germany and Japan* (Chicago, IL: University of Chicago Press, 1957).
3. John D. Montgomery and Dennis A. Rondinelli, eds., *Great Policies: Strategic Innovations in Asia and the Pacific Basin* (Westport, CT: Praeger Publishers, 1995).
4. Peter Baker and Susan B. Glasser, "What's Next for Afghanistan? Reconstruction Plan Should be in Place Before we Run Off to Another Crisis," *Washington Post National Weekly Review*, Vol. 19, No. 34 (June 17–23, 2002): p. 21.
5. Peter R. Blood, ed., *Afghanistan: A Country Study* (Washington, DC: U.S. Library of Congress, 1997).
6. U.S. Department of State, "Background Notes: Afghanistan" (Washington, DC: U.S. Department of State, 1994).
7. Barnett R. Rubin, *The Search for Peace in Afghanistan: From Buffer State to Failed State* (New Haven, CT: Yale University Press,1995).
8. United Nations, "Agreement on Provisional Arrangements in Afghanistan Pending the Reestablishment of Permanent Government Institutions" (New York: United Nations, 2001).
9. U.S. Central Intelligence Agency, *The World Factbook* (Washington, DC: CIA, 2002).
10. United Nations, "Afghanistan: Facts and Figures at a Glance" (New York: United Nations, 2002).
11. United Nations, "Immediate and Transitional Assistance Programme for the Afghan People, 2002" (New York: United Nations, 2002).
12. Asian Development Bank, *Asian Development Outlook 2002* (Manila: ADB, 2002).
13. United Nations Development Programme, "Afghanistan Crisis: UNDP Strategy" (New York: UNDP, 2002).
14. United Nations, "Afghanistan and the United Nations" (New York: United Nations, 2002).
15. Development Assistance Committee, "Destination of Official Development Assistance and Official Aid" (Paris: Organization of Economic and Community Development, 2001).
16. United Nations, "A Transition Strategy for Afghanistan and the Immediate Region" (New York: United Nations, 2002).

17. World Bank, "Afghanistan: World Bank Approach Paper" (Washington, DC: World Bank, 1999).
18. Ibid., p. 2.
19. Government of Japan, "Senior Officials Meeting on Reconstruction Assistance to Afghanistan" (Tokyo: Ministry of Foreign Affairs, 2001).
20. United Nations Development Programme, World Bank and Asian Development Bank, *Afghanistan: Preliminary Needs Assessment for Recovery and Reconstruction* (New York: UNDP, 2002).
21. Ibid., p. 3.
22. Ibid., p. iv.
23. Afghanistan Interim Administration, *National Development Framework*, Draft for Consultation (Kabul: AIA, 2002), quote at pp. 5–6.
24. United Nations Development Programme, "Immediate and Transitional Assistance Programme for the Afghan People 2002" (New York: United Nations, 2002), quote at p. 12.
25. Zubair Iqbal, "Preparing for Afghanistan's Reconstruction," remarks delivered at UNDP, World Bank, Asian Development Bank Conference on Preparing for Afghanistan's Reconstruction, Islamabad, Pakistan (November 2001).
26. World Bank, "Afghanistan: World Bank Approves $10 Million in Grants to Afghanistan for Public Administration," News Release No. 2002/269/SAR (April 4) (Washington, DC: World Bank, 2002).
27. Asian Development Bank, "ADB Approves Strategy for Afghanistan," News Release No. 094/02 (Manila: ADB, 2002).
28. UNDP, press release (January 22, 2002). The pledges of international assistance included:

   - Japan—$500 million over 30 months
   - United States—$296 million over 1 year
   - European Union—$500 million over 1 year (including $180 million from the European Commission
   - Saudi Arabia—$220 million over a 3-year period
   - World Bank—$500 million over 30 months
   - Iran—$560 million over 5 years
   - India—$100 million
   - United Arab Emirates—$36 million
   - Turkey—$5 million over a 5-year period
   - Norway—$40 million for 1 year
   - Switzerland—$18.1 million over 2 years
   - Australia—$17 million for an unspecified time
   - Pakistan —$100 million over 5 years

29. United States Department of State, "Powell Announces U.S. Giving $296 Million for Afghan Aid," Press release (Washington, DC: U.S. Department of State, January 21, 2002).
30. European Commission, "The EU's Relations with Afghanistan" (Brussels, Belgium: European Commission, 2002).
31. Federal Republic of Germany, "Germany's Contribution to Reconstruction and Development in Afghanistan" (Bonn, Germany: FRG, 2002).
32. Government of Canada, "Minister Susan Whelan Announces Details of Assistance for Afghanistan," Press release (Ottawa, Canada: Ministry of International Cooperation, March 25, 2002).
33. Aga Khan Development Network, "Aga Khan Announces US$75 Million for Afghanistan," Press release (Geneva, Switzerland: AKDN, January 21, 2002).
34. Oxfam International, "Humanitarian Assistance to Afghanistan" (Ottawa, Canada: Oxfam Canada, 2002).

35. CARE International, "CARE International in Afghanistan" (London: CARE International, 2001).
36. Afghanistan Information Management Service, "AIMS Directory of Organizations Working in Afghanistan" (Islamabad, Pakistan: Humanitarian Information Service, 2002).
37. World Bank, "Afghanistan Reconstruction Trust Fund" (Washington, DC: The World Bank, 2002).
38. Afghanistan Interim Administration, *National Development Framework*, Draft for Consultation (Kabul: AIA, 2002), quote at p. 5.
39. Stewart Patrick, "The Donor Community and the Challenge of Post Conflict Recovery," in Shepard Forman and Stewart Patrick, eds., *Good Intensions: Pledges of Aid for Post-Conflict Recovery* (Boulder, CO: Lynne Reinner Publishers, 2000), pp. 35–65.
40. Afghan Assistance Coordination Authority, "Local Coordination and Capacity Building: Conclusions from Five AACA-UNAMA-Donor Joint Missions" (Kabul, Afghanistan: AACA, 2002), quote at p. 3.

CHAPTER THREE

SUPPORTING POSTWAR ASPIRATIONS IN ISLAMIC SOCIETIES

John D. Montgomery

When international planners first began to consider how to deal with the aftermath of war in Afghanistan, they recognized, reluctantly, that eventually they might have to embark on a little-known journey that would extend their role beyond addressing the need for physical reconstruction.[1] Their reluctance was understandable, even prudent, given the mixed results of past international assistance in the aftermath of war. The observant donors could see all too clearly the chance element in foreign aid, the ultimate outcome of which they could not decisively control. They viewed the notion of nation-building as a politically hazardous enterprise, even though they did not hesitate to profess lofty purposes like "democratization," "sovereignty," "decentralization," and "marketization," while actually planning much humbler, more discrete programs.

Their loftier hopes were not entirely unreasonable, however. Previous experience in postwar reconstruction included several noteworthy cases where international efforts had helped a reviving population move toward a peaceful, productive, and promising society; where a government finally emerged that provided education for children of both sexes; where national policies did improve public health and facilitate access to justice and economic opportunity; where foreign aid was able to help stabilize power relations among divergent ethnic groups; where new support emerged for entrepreneurial, competitive commerce and industry; and where some of the political leaders who came to power were willing to accept most of the obligations of responsible government.[2] Such consequences would be far from inevitable in Afghanistan, of course, much less in Iraq or Palestine, where current conditions and trends would do little to encourage such optimistic hopes. But in their preliminary negotiations in Bonn, Tokyo, and a dozen capital cities and organizational headquarters, professionals among the donors—their political leaders had different views in many cases, to be sure—dared to hope that their work, beginning in Afghanistan, would contribute to results that resembled their rhetoric.

The projections of all international donors are not so optimistic, however. Forces in the government of India, for example, hoped to "neuter" Afghanistan, leaving it a helpless toy in a regional tug-of-war. Less ambitious counselors, especially in neighboring countries, preferred to set aside thoughts of promoting a modern democratic state in such infertile soil; others instead offered aid directly to villages and nongovernmental organizations (NGOs) so as to bypass warlords and local power centers, and to use international servants for the purpose rather than risking a strengthened central government.[3] Meanwhile, off in the anterooms of the future, most donors continued daring to hope for the best, or at least the better.

This chapter will address the prospects for their most ambitious outcomes by examining experiences in other transitional countries, none of which replicated conditions in Afghanistan or other Islamic countries, but all of which shared some aspirations or anticipated some trajectories leading to a better future. What would such a future look like? Can there be a desired "model" of development that donors might justifiably seek for these countries, and if so, what are its principal elements? Have they appeared in other countries that have made similar transitions? How can such elements be observed and compared to give them the greatest relevance to current planners for Afghanistan and perhaps other Islamic countries? Do the features donors prefer contribute to long-term outcomes like better productivity, equity, stability, and perhaps even "democracy"? These questions cannot be answered as decisively as one might hope, but history provides valuable suggestions for thinking about them.

A Possible Donors' Model

Their positive hopes reflect a generalized set of value preferences derived from experience and observation, which donors can interpret as desirable outcomes of international aid. This template of aspirations corresponds to selective realities in "modern" or "developed" societies, and it thus serves as a model that gives coherence and continuity to their hopes for the best.[4] Some current national leaders in Afghanistan and other Muslim countries accept them as well.

This acceptance can be self-deluding when it leads to an uncritical, mechanical pursuit of the template. Practice has demonstrated both the benefits and the risks of relying too heavily on such generally desirable innovations as popular elections, active political parties, a prosperous press, and unregulated, spirited markets. Present prospects in Afghanistan counsel less nuanced aims at first, starting with a central government that is strong enough to protect the nation's diverse people against each other and their neighbors, and restrained enough not to collapse into a renewal of the familiar machinery of oppression. It is a guide to the future that gives us perspective on how to consult history and experience, so that the country can aspire toward a better future that is informed by past realities there and elsewhere.

There is no such thing as a standard made-to-order democracy, and the donors' model should not yield to the alluring fantasy of fixed and interchangeable institutions that can serve everywhere as reliable mechanisms of change. History provides countless examples of elections that have led to internal conflict as well as to democratic transition. As long ago as Napoleon's popular rise to power or Kaiser Wilhelm's modernizing government, or even Adolf Hitler's electoral triumphs, and the recent ethnic agreements in Yugoslavia, Azerbaijan, Russia, and most of Africa, elections have not automatically produced democratic and virtuous outcomes.[5] Political parties have been seized and used by Nazis, neo-Nazis, and nationalistic strutting generals; free markets have been captured by gangsters and local Communist warlords. Unguarded marketization has permitted ethnic oligarchs to take advantage of democratic freedoms to exploit an unwary majority.[6] Modern history offers bountiful warnings against relying on political magic, in spite of encouraging signs marking the rise of instant democratization in Sri Lanka, India, South Africa, Lebanon, Israel, Palestine, and Romania.

There are grounds for supporting the implied model for post-conflict Afghanistan nevertheless, even though the model itself may be ephemeral. If it is virtual rather than actual, and hinted as much as acknowledged, it can be inferred from program designs and other official documents, and it is possible to consider it as carefully as if it were a generally accepted, integrated set of policy prescriptions. Indeed, it gains plausibility as a logical construct when its elements are consciously identified and traced to informed studies of social and political development.[7] It is part of the reality of a post-conflict transition.

Our understanding of this model is largely derived from the foreign aid programs of the past 50 years in which the United States and other industrial countries have observed and assisted national transitions of many kinds, including those of countries that have escaped from authoritarianism, militarism, colonialism, and communism,[8] and some that moved from preindustrial traditions toward a more "modern," "progressive," and "productive" state. Donors have constantly relived and reexamined lessons from these cumulative experiences and can use them as a source of normative standards even as they adapt and amend them. Their common elements provide reassuring validation for a modest effort at model-building, since international donors have used them as a source of principles to be consulted in designing acts of foreign occupation, military government, and development assistance. These principles include changing perceptions as well as fixed constants, but they are recurrent themes of foreign policy.

There is also a vast comparative literature about democratization and modernization, and even though it has not produced precise universal formulae, it has gained in plausibility because it is so often drawn upon for operational guidance. Democratization does not necessarily improve the prospects for peace,[9] in spite of hopeful rhetoric to the contrary: but most Western scholars, at least, regard it as a good in itself. In relying on such models of development, policymakers have to overlook their intuitive, fragmentary, and impressionistic hopes as they record their "successes" in the annals of America and the United Nations. For the "failures" to introduce democracy in the wake of conflict and postwar aid can be taken as admonitions against ignoring the important institutional requirements that are the subject of this chapter. The list of failures is longer than the reports of success: Haiti (1994), Cambodia (1970–1973), Vietnam (1965–1973), the Dominican Republic (1965–1966), and, much earlier, Cuba (1917–1922), Haiti (1915–1919), Honduras (1924–1925), Nicaragua (1909–1927), Mexico (1914), and Cuba (1906–1909).[10]

It is no wonder that nations that are supposed to benefit from such international interventions tend to view the record with skepticism and suspicion, although it shines only a little shakily, as a hopeful beacon in foreign policy planning, having survived many challenges and disappointments over the past 50 years. Many of the elements of "success" reappear in plans for Afghanistan and in the aspirations underlying other programs for Central Asia (see chapter two, this volume).

Elements of the Donor Model

The elements of the model, even when not stated as formal objectives, therefore have some claim to universality. It probably is more influential than its critics acknowledge, lurking as it does in the background of international assistance and consulted both inside and outside Europe and America. Although it does not prescribe a universal solution for "underdevelopment," it does identify universal requirements of "development," and because these elements are found in so many countries, they cannot be dismissed as merely an expression of Western values. Suspicion of its provenance deserves respect, but not dismissal.

Five elements of the model recur frequently in the literature describing the development of modern democratic states, and they can be treated as "status variables" to be used to compare the standing of posttransition states and to observe country needs in defining program rationales. Clearly, they are not equally represented in all countries, nor are they in balance in any one country; but because they appear in various combinations and relationships, they can become useful diagnostic tools. When they are simply enumerated, there is no obvious priority among them, and they are not closely linked to a desired outcome; but in tandem they are often used to calibrate such outcomes as "democracy," "economic freedom," and "transparency." The list includes

(1) the "rule of law,"[11] which refers to universality of access to courts,[12] compatibility with widespread cultural aspirations,[13] stable and independent institutions for interpretation and application,[14] a professional class of lawyers or accredited advocates, openness to change,[15] and the capacity to enforce observance;[16]

(2) a productive economy based on different types of viable enterprises,[17] including "private," industrial, or commercial organizations[18] that incorporate policies in support of competition,[19] prevailing psychological and social proclivities toward entrepreneurship and innovation,[20] widespread access to credit,[21] regulatory functions to protect consumers and other public stakeholders,[22] restraints on excessive consumption in the public sector,[23] and fluid social networks that give investment and employment opportunities to people with appropriate talents;[24]

(3) a regime of "free speech," which implies pluralistic politics,[25] open and competing media,[26] and multiple outlets for self-expression, including vehicles for dissent and the protection of offenders;[27]

(4) protections for the "universal human rights,"[28] including procedures for assuring access by women and minorities,[29] social supports for disadvantaged groups,[30] educational opportunities and minimum levels of science and technology,[31] and widespread access to schooling;[32]

(5) good governance at the national level, incorporating both legislative and administrative units, and including separate systems for lawmaking, interpretation, and execution,[33] the decentralized capacity to deal with local problems,[34] a "professional" bureaucracy with open careers for civil servants,[35] civilian control of the military,[36] transparency and self-correcting mechanisms in both the public and private sectors,[37] arrangements for the devolution or decentralization of authority with protection against capture by local elites,[38] and accountability, including rotation of leaders through removal and retirement procedures.[39]

Each one of these elements, *in extremis*, can become a vice as well as a virtue: (1) the rule of law can degenerate into the rule of lawyers—litigious, costly, and dilatory; (2) economic efficiency can turn into profligacy—piratical and predatory; (3) free speech can reward superficiality and extremism; (4) the demand for unfulfilled rights can invite invidious reverse discrimination; (5) checked-and-balanced governmental institutions can yield policy stasis. Examples can be cited from recent history: the rule of law has justified the abuses of a Taliban theocracy; productive marketization and competition have produced plutocratic authoritarianism in East Europe; the shrill-voiced media arising out of free speech regimes have exhorted populations to ethnic violence in South Asia; affirmative action derived from human rights aspirations has produced inhumane reverse discrimination in America; the separation of powers associated with good governance has yielded gridlock in Western Europe.

Experience also implies the possibility of arranging a corrective balance among these elements: well-conceived *laws* can restrain predatory economic practices, equilibrate the domination of excessive views, control unjustified terms or conditions of social relations, and even provide escape from political gridlock; competitive *economies* can neutralize repressive laws, highlight suppressed views, protect exploited groups, and lubricate the immobilized machinery of government; transparency, a product of *free speech*, can expose unjust legalisms, exploitive plutocracies, the abuse of privileges, and governmental repression; a regime of *rights* can restrain judicial abuses, compensate for economic injustice, assert suppressed opinions, and negate political and bureaucratic neglect; and in the end, regulation by responsive *government* can establish rules and standards against the abuse of any of these elements.

The present status of these five conditions in Afghanistan is not in any kind of balance, but each can enrich others: for example, the rule of law under the Shari'a, in its more extreme form, lacks judicial elements that constitute the usual institutions of the law. Like the other elements, however, it calls for the kinds of programs that can restrain arbitrary exploitation. Where the rule of law has left behind the sequelae of tyranny, it can accept institutional devices that can provide a balance; where economic efficiency has developed most conspicuously in illegal narcotic enterprises, donors can help develop substitutes for an opium and smuggling industry; where free speech is limited, external forces can extend it beyond its present confinement to Kabul; where progress in human rights, especially of women, is receiving most of its encouragement from international sources, new forces can open sealed-off pockets of warlords' resistance and ethnic abuses; and what checks there are on a potentially onerous, burdensome government can become the basis for seeking a balance among counters to an effective central power.

While there is no sensible way of standardizing these dimensions on behalf of the perfect society, there are multiple ways of applying them. That process requires exploring how they have emerged elsewhere and assessing priorities among them.

Using Indicators to Define the Model

Exploring these relationships and priorities begins with observing and evaluating data that have been gathered by international agencies for planning purposes. Standard indicators of their presence and intensity in different nations can make it possible to compare and measure these features of the donors' model. Though they are still incomplete and fragmentary, they can serve as status variables in order to appraise their potential contributions to desired developmental outcomes (the appendix to this chapter lists these variables for 30 Asian countries).

International agencies have been using global indicators of such status variables for several decades in order to compare and interpret economic, social, and political conditions in countries receiving aid. Planners recognize, of course, that the raw indicators displayed in their monumental tables are less than perfect representations of the conditions they purport to measure; but planners accept them nevertheless, because they provide a modest cover of objectivity for making external judgments about country needs. Experience helps explain implausible findings and untoward comparisons (Saudi Arabia, with its oil-based economy, will show a much higher output per worker than Sri Lanka or China, for example; and similarly, reverence for the Shari'a or Islamic legal tradition makes a country appear not only stable but also as adherent to the rule of law). Since these indicators are often misleading when interpreted in Western terms, international organizations are careful not to denigrate a member country that ranks low in certain desirable variables even though they must consult such data as evidence of internal constraints on social development.

In appraising the evidence available for studying the elements of the donors' model, this chapter will summarize indicators that seemed close to these five conditions in the 30 North African and Asian countries.[40] Existing tables for this purpose are abundant and readily available.[41]

"Ideal Countries" as Planning Models

International observers occasionally view certain countries as "living models" for others on the basis of their presumed religious character or because of certain economic or cultural achievements or historical associations. For various reasons, Korea, Malaysia, Philippines, Turkey, and Morocco are often held up as examples to other countries, even though their status variables show how different they are. On the overall indicators in our sample, Korea ranked best among these countries, Turkey worst; and Malaysia, Morocco, and the Philippines occupied the middle grounds (figure 3.1). These divergent indicators offer more guidance than the totality that would seem to make them "model" countries. The use of Morocco and Turkey as exemplars for planners may satisfy some cultural expectations, but their critical characteristics are significantly different.

The use of country models such as these risks overlooking needs that require special attention. Among these five countries, for example, freedom of speech was the weakest variable, human rights was the strongest, followed by economic competitiveness. To view any of these countries as an ideal model would mask such differences.

Experience has shown as well that familiar presumptions about transferability of country models distort the perception of other countries' prospects and needs.[42] Figure 3.1 suggests the relative position of these countries by showing the frequency distribution of the five variables among them, as they are listed in the appendix. From this matrix, we can readily observe the variance among the countries in terms

	Rule of law	Competitive economic systems	Protection of free speech	Protection of human rights	Government competence	Total
Korea	3	3	3	2	5	16
Malaysia	4	4	9	5	3	25
Morocco	5	(6)	11	4	6	32
Philippines	13	7	4	3	7	34
Turkey	11	(10)	19	5	15	50
Total	44	30	52	22	45	

Figure 3.1   Selected country models

Note: Countries are ranked from highest to lowest in the indicated categories. Some of the rankings were identical, i.e., a tie. Numbers in parentheses are the average of all status indicators for any country for which the economic system was not ranked.

of their relative ranking on the desired variables. Countries that are sometimes presented as "ideal" poster children of development do not necessarily rank well in all respects.

Dominant Variables as Country Models

Another possible use of a country model would be to select those that rank best on a single variable rather than on the basis of more conventional features such as religion or economic status. Since the variables are relatively independent of each other, it would be possible to cluster all 30 countries we examined most closely according to their outstanding elements, recognizing that a high ranking under one variable would not necessarily imply similar standing on others. This approach is demonstrated in figure 3.2. The five countries that ranked at the top for one or two of the variables did not score uniformly well on the others. In three of the five clusters, indeed, country rankings for the other variables were widely scattered.

Two of the variables were fairly predictive. The most competent governments among them according to the database were Malaysia, Tunisia, Morocco, the Philippines, and China. They also had the best cumulative rankings and were near the top ranking in competitiveness as well (note that China ranked low in both rule of law and free speech categories). This clustering did not occur for the other variables. The top five human rights countries (Thailand, Morocco, Malaysia, Iran, and Saudi Arabia) were significantly deficient in three other categories (rule of law, free speech, and government competence). A similarly uneven profile was found in the free-speech countries (Philippines, Indonesia, Thailand, Bangladesh, and Malaysia), where Bangladesh was disappointing in both rule of law and government competence. The countries that were rated best for their human rights record seemed to enjoy the least spillover of all to the other desirable elements in the model. Political theorists in the J.S. Mill tradition might be disappointed at the fact that top rating in freedom of speech did not seem to "drive" the other variables in the sense of improving society.

For donors to concentrate an assistance program on any one of these three variables, however desirable it might be in itself, would require a degree of confidence in probable spillover benefits that intercountry comparisons do not support. Nepal has a lower rating for its observance of the rule of law than it has for free speech and human rights, but donors can hardly be expected to begin to require exquisite legal procedures in an era when the government, already weak, is being assailed by terrorists. And if the Philippines, after years of American occupation, still finds adherence to the rule of law the weakest of its five status variables, aid donors would do well to consider the reasons for failure in that regard before making large investments in its legal system.

	Rule of law	Competitive economic systems	Protection of free speech	Protection of human rights	Government competence
1. *Rule of law countries*					
Malaysia	X	4	9	5	3
Morocco	X	(6)	11	4	6
Tunisia	X	(7)	16	5	4
Saudi Arabia	X	(12)	23	7	14
Thailand	X	5	6	3	9
2. *Competitive economies*					
Malaysia	4	X	9	5	3
Thailand	8	X	6	3	9
China	12	X	25	6	8
Philippines	13	X	4	3	7
Egypt	10	X	17	5	10
3. *Free speech countries*					
Philippines	13	7	X	3	7
India	9	10	X	3	11
Thailand	8	5	X	3	9
Bangladesh	26	14	X	4	18
Malaysia	4	4	X	5	3
4. *Human rights countries*					
Thailand	8	5	6	X	9
Morocco	5	(6)	11	X	6
Malaysia	4	4	9	X	3
Iran	17	(12)	15	X	13
Saudi Arabia	8	(12)	23	X	14
5. *Competent governments*					
Malaysia	4	4	9	5	X
Tunisia	6	(7)	16	5	X
Morocco	5	(6)	11	4	X
Philippines	13	7	4	3	X
China	12	6	25	6	X

Figure 3.2 (a) Status variables in the five clusters by rank

Note: Countries are ranked from highest to lowest in the indicated categories. Some rankings resulted in ties. Numbers in parentheses are the average of all status indicators for that country as data are missing.

	Rule of law	Competitive economic systems	Protection of free speech	Protection of human rights	Government competence
1. *Rule of law countries*					
Malaysia	1	4	9	5	3
Morocco	2	(6)	11	4	6
Tunisia	3	(7)	16	5	4
Saudi Arabia	4	(12)	23	7	14
Thailand	5	5	6	3	9
2. *Competitive economies*					
Malaysia	4	1	9	5	3
Thailand	8	2	6	3	9
China	12	3	25	6	8
Philippines	13	4	4	3	7
Egypt	10	5	17	5	10
3. *Free speech countries*					
Philippines	13	7	1	3	7
India	9	10	2	3	11
Thailand	8	5	3	3	9
Bangladesh	26	14	4	4	18
Malaysia	4	4	5	5	3
4. *Human rights countries*					
Thailand	8	5	6	1	9
Morocco	5	(6)	11	2	6
Malaysia	4	4	9	3	3
Iran	17	(12)	15	4	13
Saudi Arabia	8	(12)	23	5	14
5. *Competent Governments*					
Malaysia	4	4	9	5	1
Tunisia	6	(7)	16	5	2
Morocco	5	(6)	11	4	3
Philippines	13	7	4	3	4
China	12	6	25	6	5

Figure 3.2 (b) Status variables in the five clusters by rank, suggested emendation

Note: Countries are ranked from highest to lowest in the indicated categories. Some rankings resulted in ties. Numbers in parentheses are the average of all status indicators for that country as data are missing.

A more promising approach is to follow the implication of the finding that the countries that ranked highest for their economic competition and government competence variables had the most satisfactory general rankings for the other elements. The use of such "dominant-variable" country models in aid programming would predictably have the greatest effect if the two institutional criteria (i.e., political and economic status) were to receive priority assistance, with the expectation that the results would most likely contribute to other positive features. High rank in economic competitiveness and government competence seemed to yield the best prospects for achieving success in the other arenas. (Three of the 30 baseline countries, Australia, Japan, and Korea, were not used in identifying these clusters because they ranked high on all the variables.)

Clusters of Variables

It would be convenient for planners if all of the variables were systematically related to each other, so that donors could design assistance programs in such a way as to obtain the maximum reinforcement effect. But the evidence does not support that expectation strongly enough to provide much more guidance than is already suggested.

The Implication of Sequential Regularity

A more useful finding is that there is enough regularity in the rise of some status variables to suggest a likely sequence in their development, notably in the case of successful political and economic institutions. There are no historical data to prove that these two characteristics developed first, or to identify a uniform sequence in their rise, but the tables showed a suggestive frequency in their appearance jointly with other variables at the top of the list. Using the frequency count of high rankings is not a substitute for historical data, but it provides a rough explanation for some processes of development. It is probably significant that competitiveness of economic enterprises appears as a high-ranked variable more coherently clustered with others than do freedom of speech, human rights, or rule of law. This ranking offers modest support to the priority that donors commonly assign to the development of a competitive market economy.[43] The other status variables appear to rise independently, suggesting that they should be addressed one by one without expecting that any of them will bring improvement throughout the social system.

This approach does not discredit the notion of using a balanced development model as a diagnostic tool or template for noting deficiencies, or for avoiding the imposition of intuitive judgments about priority areas for improvement. A balanced approach can coexist with the probability that in many, if not most, cases, economic competitiveness and good governance variables dominate other desirable qualities sought during the course of development.[44]

That does not mean, of course, that donors should skimp on assistance to the other features of the model, especially when extremely low performance on any of them degrades a country's prospects for participating in the international order. In such cases, donors can help compensate for deficiencies without attempting to improve everything at once. A donor might conclude on the basis of their rankings on different variables that Morocco and Tunisia would especially benefit from aid to free speech (e.g., to the media) even if other elements of assistance were neglected, while Nepal and the Philippines would probably attract private investors seeking stable contract obligations if assistance were offered primarily for establishing the rule of law, which is as likely to serve economic purposes as it does political and social goals.[45] In countries like Egypt, with many needs to fill, donors might speculate on the possibility that they could best concentrate on the two leading institutional variables and postpone action on the others. In very few cases should donors expect that helping to bring a single feature up to par would necessarily improve standing in the others and thus contribute to a balanced society. The fact that all the variables are subject to improvement by internal domestic policies reaffirms the wisdom of placing a high priority on programs that contribute the most to good political and economic governance. That would appear to be the case in Afghanistan.

Encouraging economic competition as the top priority in the case of Afghanistan would ignore the need for assigning at least equal priority to central governmental competence. Both variables are related even in countries at the bottom of the list (failure for either is likely to be associated with failure of both), and it seems reasonable to conclude that neither should be pursued in the absence of progress in the other. To rely on government competence as a prelude to economic competitiveness might be welcomed by "strong-state" economists who believe that aiding the public sector might somehow encourage private competition, especially at the low end of the scale of economic development; but experience teaches that strong states may not be ready to step aside even when independent economic forces are available to dominate the agenda of productivity. In many of the mid-range countries, the rank in economic competitiveness is higher than that for governmental competence. The relation between political and economic development is not constant, however.[46]

Donor Applications of the Model

Fads in foreign aid tactics have changed conspicuously over the past half-century, but the five elements of the preferred model have remained relatively fixed. Donors' economic goals have fluctuated with advances in theory, with changing global preferences, or with short-term domestic needs, but their long-term consequences have accompanied the commitment to democratic outcomes. Mood swings have accompanied aid programming, but they have been designed to improve its appeal to the public more than to indicate changes in basic purposes.

Some of the changes in operational doctrines have had significant effects on outcomes in the host country. The switch from grants to loans, and back to grants again, from technical to capital assistance, and from institution-building to nation-building and then from government-to-government aid efforts to bolster private and "third-sector" organizations: all have had consequences for timing and survivability, though not necessarily for their final effect. Some of the changes in aid doctrine have had long-term consequences (e.g., technical progress comes more promptly than does institutional development, and the time schedule needs to reflect that fact); some tactics have succeeded in extending the donor's influence modestly for a time (management of loans takes longer than accepting grants); and some have an immediate and sometimes significant impact on the local economy (grants, procurement, and "local ownership" conditionalities). These fluctuations in implementation strategies, with unchanged objectives under the donors' virtual model, have become important parts of the mythology of aid.

These strategies have also influenced the relationships between donor and host country, even though they were not chosen for that reason. For example, the change from Truman's Point Four-style technical assistance to programs of capital "investments" altered the links between donors and public and private institutions because they extended the relationship beyond individual tours of duty. Early nation-building activities went out of style because they preferentially strengthened some government units; and foreign aid to governments had to give way to expanded encouragement of private initiatives and to elements in the civil society. Rule-of-law programs have come to penetrate society more deeply than do more limited civil service reforms; and technical improvements in economic development planning have enlarged influence on the host society more conspicuously than the old-style public administration, agricultural, and other technical expertise did. The prestige of the relevant experts in these fields declined as the influence of lawyers and economists made their presence more conspicuous in the international donor community. These shifts do not always reveal points of change in a learning curve, but even if sometimes they have been capricious, their variety makes aid history a valuable source of experimental knowledge.[47]

The most important recurrent theme in the rhetoric of international assistance has been its hopeful references to developments favoring global democracy. Even when the "donors' model" has not been consciously incorporated in development plans, there have been increasingly frequent acknowledgments of the contributions that democratic achievements make to other goals. As already suggested, experience with democratization, especially of reliance on stereotypical organizational features, warns against treating any one democratic feature as a surrogate for all of them, however. In the case of Afghanistan, the relation between democratic elections and ethnic violence calls attention to a disturbing feature of this popular nostrum in other contexts.[48] On the global scale, the number of countries that have held elections since 1980 has doubled to 140, but only 82 had a free press or independent judiciary.[49] The texture of democracy requires more than elections.

The amount of aid money specifically devoted to democracy and improved structures of governance has gradually risen over the decades and it has expanded in its reach.[50] In the U.S. program, about $700 million is devoted annually to political aid, and 85 percent of its country and regional programs include aid to one aspect or another of democracy. Germany ranks next in such political efforts; at the other extreme, Japan has none of its own, but even it supports some such assistance through the United Nations and the Asia Development Bank (ADB). The U.S. Agency for International Development set up an Office of Transitional Initiatives in its Bureau for Democracy, Conflict and Humanitarian Assistance; it also has an Office of Democracy and Governance; America's freestanding National Endowment for Democracy entered the field in 1983; the State Department now administers a Democracy and Human Rights Fund through its embassies, each of which is authorized to spend up to $100,000 per year for those purposes; and both major American political parties have sponsored international programs. These developments follow earlier efforts, most notably those of Title IX of the 1967 assistance act, which had enjoined the agency to pay special attention to democratic development (less conspicuous forerunners, in fact, were found as early as 1961). Perhaps these programs have survived more on the basis of faith than of evidence; but many hopes for foreign assistance rest upon this trend toward democratization.

Europe, too, has established agencies to express their interest in political outcomes, including an Initiative for Democracy and Human Rights and similar program elements of the Organization for Security and Cooperation (OSCE). The European Bank for Reconstruction and Development has extended loans to post-communist countries in Central and Eastern Europe for the purpose of promoting market economies and private business in the context of "multi-party democracy, pluralism, and market economics."[51] Germany's effort is the largest and oldest among them, now boasting resident political specialists in 100 countries and making extensive use of foundations that specialize in race relations and other topics.[52] Britain's Department for International Development also concerns itself with removing obstacles to party competition. These concerns are also visible in the United Nations' support of free elections and the United Nations Development Program' (UNDP's) contributions to better governance through support to organizations in civil society.

Even some development banks, although not created to assist political development, have decided nevertheless to promote transparency and accountability, both to encourage democratic links and to promote the efficient use of resources. The World Bank, which began its work with NGOs in the 1980s, has promoted NGOs that facilitate debate on public policies. In 1999, it started the Global Development Network to enhance public participation research, and it has supported national think tanks and workshops for parliamentarians and their staff. Even the more technically oriented Inter-American Development Bank now lists "democratic governability" as a criterion for assistance.

Prospects

These activities overlap and even contradict each other at times, but such is the price of democratization, especially if its elements are to incorporate diverse aspects of the donors' virtual model. Moreover, democratization does not necessarily produce improved outcomes in other areas such as productivity, stability, and equity. The evidence is against the assumption that any one of the status variables will necessarily improve these ultimate outcomes, which are often contradictory and in any case often the consequence of other factors. Indeed, the first finding from the fragmentary data consulted for this chapter confirms that improvements in the status variables do not necessarily associate positively with each other, and they do not necessarily produce the other features contemplated in the donors' model.

No one should be surprised any longer to learn that even these desired outcomes are not always mutually compatible. It is an old and commonplace, though still debatable, observation that equity, as measured by the Gini index and similar indicators, is negatively related to productivity at some points in the development process. Concentrating on productivity to relieve poverty is quite different from promoting equity in distribution. At early stages of industrialization as well as in advanced cases, there are often widening gaps between the rich and poor. Nor does better equity always accompany progress in political rights and civil liberties (reassurance comes to activists who support policies that benefit the poor in such measures as spending on education, since, according to the indicators, they are modestly related to political rights and civil liberties). Since donors cannot always hope to achieve such goals as productivity, stability, or equity by contributing to the rule of law, a market economy, good governance, free speech, or human rights, it is surely enough if these latter are pursued for their own merits. Most international observers must be satisfied if their efforts bring about improvements in any of them.

Moreover, aid to democracy in the Arab world, including hundreds of projects directed to legislative, judicial, and civic institutions, has encountered resistance even among groups that were its intended beneficiaries.[53] Governments have objected to aid from NGOs as "violations" of their sovereignty, and to political reform that "threatened" their stability; women's groups there have been annoyed by glib Western assumptions about their conditions and aspirations; donor NGOs have attracted criticism as "foreign agents" or Central Intelligence Agency (CIA) cutouts; and some beneficiaries have even been prosecuted for having access to foreign funds. Even though donors have promised to walk softly in Afghanistan and the Middle East, leaving only "light footprints," it has not helped much that they have concentrated their efforts in Kabul and in international conventions; and when they relied on indigenous people and institutions to minimize interference, they have been challenged as the causes of distortion in the local labor market, contributors to the brain drain of critical specialists, and as hypocritical do-gooders engaged in some kind of internal colonization.[54] Delays, bureaucratic procedures, and shortfalls in funding have only sharpened the inherent ambiguity of foreign assistance.

The programs planned for Afghanistan aim at the component elements of the model rather than at the abstractions of democracy and globalization. As Rondinelli's chapter suggests, current plans are designed to promote the rule of law for all (including components such as legislative advice, suggestions for judicial reform, and improvements in public access to courts); more competitive economies (through protection of foreign direct investment and promotion of trade liberalism); free speech (including assistance to the media, promotion of civil society through support to advocacy groups and professional associations, and support to a democratic political culture); human rights (more and more support to NGOs); and improved governance (which may still start with civil service reform and decentralization schemes, later moving toward citizen participation programs and conditionalities favoring transparency).

The prospects for these aspirations can be estimated on the basis of experience.[55] Success in achieving results at the sectoral or micro level is easier than large-scale institutional change,[56] and support to local government and participation does not necessarily contribute to improvements at the national level.[57] In spite of some disappointments, however, support to elections in post-conflict situations has often improved the political prospect for harmonious development.[58] Each element of the donors' model has surfaced in the experience of transitional countries in diverse ways: the *rule of law* has advanced significantly in Latin America and East Europe where local institutions have received financial and technical assistance from abroad;[59] a *productive economy* is the most conspicuous product of foreign aid, especially when competitive[60] and outward-based, though there are risks of new forms of colonization;[61] *free speech* and media diversity have risen with foreign presence even when there are setbacks to daring critics;[62] *human rights* are at least as much protected by foreign intervention as by domestic politics;[63] and for all its impreciseness, the congeries of qualities involved in *good governance* have included special elements immediately associated with productivity, such as emergent agricultural technology,[64] as well as advances in accountability,[65] transparency, efficiency, absence of corruption, and support to competitive markets, which are the hallmarks of government most preferred by the international banks. There is often a spillover effect in well-designed aid projects that serve purposes of equity and opportunity, while reinforcing institutional aims and enriching a public sense of national identity and purpose.[66]

Other chapters in this book will examine in greater detail how experience with previous transitions suggests lessons that can apply to Afghanistan and its Islamic neighbors, near and far. It is encouraging that recent history presents many examples of aid that has helped countries progress beyond authoritarian and semi-authoritarian governments. These results have led already to modification of older nostrums of foreign aid: standard reforms in civil service and economic planning have improved with the participation of strongly independent local challengers; technical assistance addresses the needs of civil society as well as those of government agencies; NGOs have had to confront their own uneven development and the ambiguity of their relations with central government organizations; support to free speech includes encouragement of diversity in media; off-the-shelf programs of assistance to party organizations have adapted to regional and ethnic conditions that are divisive and hostile; and election and post-election monitoring is improved by contemplations of mixed successes and failures in Cambodia, Armenia, and Zimbabwe.[67]

History joins comparative analysis in advising donors against trying to promote all good things at once. Studies of the rise of democratic states have emphasized the importance of attaining institutional strength at the center first, before local autocrats or other rival groups can interrupt a transition to responsible government. Programs to promote the rule of law, support media diversity, and train a corps of professional civil servants should usually precede pressures for competitive elections and partisan activism.[68] Although the data reviewed here show that applications of the virtual model have not always produced the results that donors had anticipated, there is no reason to doubt that these relationships would apply to the Islamic world: they are not merely an expression of Western donors' preferences. The path to development there, as elsewhere, will be shaped more by indigenous factors and events in the field than by donors' underlying values; whatever may be the role of political culture,[69] most scholars agree that nothing in the Islamic world makes democratic aspirations impossible.[70] What the donors may expect in the light of history is that although their own aspirations may not have changed much over the past 50 years, there will continue to be surprising and even wondrous developments abroad as the host countries take control over their own destiny.

As Mark Twain is often quoted as saying, history may not repeat itself so much as it rhymes. Aspiring donors would do well to consider the poetry not as that of a sonnet, but that of a limerick, full of surprises. Moreover, not all of them are humorous. Some are deadly serious.

Appendix

Table I   Status variables of 30 baseline Asian countries

Country	Rule of law	Competitiveness of economic enterprises	Free speech regime	Human rights status	Government competence
Algeria	−1.103		−1.310	5	−1.087
Australia	1.596	5	1.628	1	1.459
Azerbaijan	−0.563		−0.919	5	−0.833
Bangladesh	−0.929	71	−0.015	4	−0.565
Cambodia	−0.235		−0.909	6	
China	−0.040	39	−1.296	6	0.016
Egypt	0.128	51	−0.674	5	−0.138
Georgia	−0.494		−0.291	4	−0.512
India	0.160	57	0.498	3	−0.264
Indonesia	−0.918	64	−1.165	4	−0.528
Iran	−0.364		−0.559	6	−0.339
Japan	1.422	21	1.163	2	0.839
Kazakhstan	−0.590		−0.712	5	−0.824
Korea (South)	0.943	23	1.002	2	0.409
Laos	−1.204		−1.050	6	
Malaysia	0.834	30	−0.144	5	0.714
Morocco	0.678		−0.240	4	0.267
Nepal	−0.558		0.047	4	
Pakistan	−0.760		−0.441	5	−0.744
Philippines	−0.078	48	0.614	3	0.126
Saudi Arabia	0.494		−1.103	7	−0.349
Sri Lanka	−0.361	61	−0.157	4	−0.612
Syria	−0.291		−1.358	7	−1.181
Tajikistan	−1.335		−1.565	6	−1.423
Thailand	0.413	33	0.215	3	0.010
Tunisia	0.648		−0.589	5	0.633
Turkey	−0.010	54	−0.859	5	−0.412
Uzbekistan	−0.870		−1.343	6	−1.305
Vietnam	−0.437	60	−1.416	6	−0.300
Yemen	−1.008		−0.415	6	−0.621

See Key for Abbreviations, Data Definitions, and Data Sources for Table I.

Key   Abbreviations, Data Definitions, and Data Sources

Indicator	Definition	Source
Rule of law	Index of aggregate measures of perceptions of the rule of law, effectiveness of the judiciary, and incidence of crime. The Maximum/Minimum Score Range is from 2.5 (indicating the least instability and violence) to −2.5 (indicating the most instability).	Kaufmann, Daniel, Aart Kraay, and Pablo Zoido-Lobaton (1999a). "Aggregating Governance Indicators." World Bank Policy Research Department Working Paper No. 2195, and Kaufmann, Daniel, Aart Kraay, and Pablo Zoido-Lobaton (1999b), "Governance Matters." World Bank Policy Research Department Working Paper No. 2196. http://www.worldbank.org/wbi/governance/datasets.htm#dataset

Table I continued

Indicator	Definition	Source
Competitiveness of economic enterprises	Growth Competitiveness Index Ranking (out of a total of 75 countries) that measures sustained economic growth in the medium term based on an index of technology, public institutions, and macroeconomic environment.	John W. McArthur and Jeffrey D. Sachs, "chapter 1.1: The Growth Competitiveness Index: Measuring Technological Advancement and the Competitiveness of Stages of Development," Global Competitiveness Report 2000–2001, Center for International Development, Harvard University, Oxford University Press, http://www.cid.harvard.edu/cr/pdf/2001Growth_Competitiveness.pdf
Free speech regime	Voice and Accountability Index: Index of aggregate measures of perceptions of political process, civil rights, political rights, media independence, and the extent to which citizens can participate in the selection of governments. The Maximum/Minimum Score Range is from 2.5 (indicating the highest level of voice and accountability) to −2.5 (indicating the lowest level of voice and accountability).	Kaufmann, Daniel, Aart Kraay, and Pablo Zoido-Lobaton (1999a). "Aggregating Governance Indicators." World Bank Policy Research Department Working Paper No. 2195, and Kaufmann, Daniel, Aart Kraay, and Pablo Zoido-Lobaton (1999b), "Governance Matters." World Bank Policy Research Department Working Paper No. 2196. http://www.worldbank.org/wbi/governance/datasets.htm#dataset
Human rights status	Civil Liberties: Measured on a one-to-seven scale, with one representing the highest degree of freedom in 2000–2001. Countries whose combined averages for political rights and for civil liberties fall between 1.0 and 2.5 are designated "free"; between 3.0 and "not free." Civil liberties 5.5, "partly free"; and between 5.5 include freedom of expression, assembly, association, and religion generally equitable system of rule of law.	Freedom House, "Freedom in the World: the Annual Survey of Political and Civil Liberties 2000–2001," Annual Freedom in the World Country Scores 1972–1973 to 2000–2001, http://www.freedomhouse.org/ratings/
Government effectiveness	Index of aggregate measures of perceptions of such indicators as the quality of public service provision, bureaucracy, civil service independence from political process. The Maximum/Minimum Score Range is from 2.5 (indicating the most effective) to −2.5 (indicating the least effective).	Kaufmann, Daniel, Aart Kraay, and Pablo Zoido-Lobaton (1999a). "Aggregating Governance Indicators." World Bank Policy Research Department Working Paper No. 2195, and Kaufmann, Daniel, Aart Kraay, and Pablo Zoido-Lobaton (1999b), "Governance Matters." World Bank Policy Research Department Working Paper No. 2196.http://www.worldbank.org/wbi/governance/datasets.htm#dataset

Notes

The author gratefully acknowledges suggestions from Kristen Eichensehr, Milton J. Esman, Virginia A. Kosmo, Robert J. Muscat, Pippa Norris, Anne Piehl, Joseph Stern, Dennis A. Rondinelli, and James Seward, who prepared the appended table.

1. Naomi Weinberger, "Civil-Military Coordination in Peacebuilding: The Challenge in Afghanistan," *Journal of International Affairs*, Vol. 55, No. 2 (Spring 2002); Barnett R. Rubin, Ashraf Ghani, William Maley, Ahmed Rashid, and Oliver Roy, *Afghanistan: Reconstruction and Peacebuilding in a Regional Framework*, KOFF Peacebuilding Report 1/2001, Center for Peacebuilding (KOFF) and Swiss Peace Foundation (June 2001), at <http://www.swisspeace.ch/html/navigation/fr_publications.html>.

2. Anne O. Krueger, Constantine Michalopoulos, and Vernon W. Ruttan, *Aid and Development* (Baltimore, MD: Johns Hopkins University Press, 1989), pp. 1–10; John D. Montgomery and Dennis A. Rondinelli, eds., *Great Policies: Strategic Innovations in Asia and the Pacific Region* (Westport, CT: Praeger Publishers, 1995).

3. Marina Ottaway and Anatol Lieven, "Rebuilding Afghanistan: Fantasy versus Reality," New York, Carnegie Institute for International Peace, Policy Brief No. 12, January 17, 2002.

4. John D. Montgomery, ed., *Values in Education, Social Capital Formation in Asia and the Pacific* (Hollis, NY: Hollis Publishing, 1997).

5. Jack Snyder, *From Voting to Violence, Democratization and Nationalist Conflict* (New York: W.W. Norton, 2000), pp. 28, 267, 287, 295–296.

6. Amy Chua, *World on Fire* (New York: Doubleday, 2002).

7. Vernon W. Ruttan, "What Happened to Political Development?" *Economic Development and Cultural Change*, Vol. 39, No. 2 (1991): pp. 265–292.

8. Michael McFaul, "The Fourth Wave of Democracy and Dictatorship, Noncooperative Transitions in the Postcommunist World," *World Politics*, Vol. 54, No. 3 (January 2002): pp. 212–244.

9. Edward D. Mansfield and Jack Snyder, "Democratic Transitions, Institutional Strength, and War," *International Organization*, Vol. 56, No. 2 (Spring, 2002): pp. 297–337; "Democratization and the Danger of War," *International Security*, Vol. 20, No. 4 (1995): pp. 5–38.

10. Minxin Pei and Sara Kasper, "Reconsider the US Success Rate before Forcing Democracy Again," *Christian Science Monitor*, January 15, 2003, p. 9.

11. David A. Grigorian and Albert Martinez, "Industrial Growth and Quality of Institutions: What Do (Transition) Economies Have to Gain from the Rule of Law?" Private and Sector Development Unit, Europe and Central Asia Region, World Bank.

12. Friedrich Hayak, *Law, Legislation, and Liberty, Vol. I, Rules and Order* (Chicago, IL: University of Chicago Press, 1973); and *Vol. III, The Political Order of a Free People* (Chicago, IL: University of Chicago Press, 1979); Zheng Yong, "Access to Justice: Legal Aid in the People's Republic of China," in John D. Montgomery, ed., *Human Rights: Positive Policies in Asia and the Pacific Rim* (Hollis, NY: Hollis Publishing, 1998), pp. 131–149.

13. J.P. Platteap, *Order, Rule of Law, and Moral Norms* (Geneva: UN Conference on Trade and Development, 2000); Lucian W. Pye and Sidney Verba, eds., *Political Culture and Political Development* (Princeton, NJ: Princeton University Press, 1965); Gabriel A. Almond and Sidney Verba, *The Civic Culture: Political Attitudes and Democracy in Five Nation* (Princeton, NJ: Princeton University Press, 1963).

14. Peter H. Russell, "Toward a General Theory of Judicial Independence," in Peter H. Russell and David M. O'Brien, *Judicial Independence in the Age of Democracy: Critical Perspectives from around the World* (Charlottesville and London: University Press of Virginia, 2002). See also Christopher Clague, Philip Keefer, Stephen Knack, and Mancur Olson, "Institutions and Economic Performance: Property Rights and Contract Enforcement," in C. Clague, ed., *Institutions and Economic Growth and Governance in Less-Developed and Post-Socialist Countries* (Baltimore, MD: Johns Hopkins University Press, 1997), pp. 67–90.

15. Michael T. Hayes, *The Limits of Policy Change: Incrementalism, Worldview, and the Rule of Law* (Washington: Georgetown University Press, 2001).

16. Joel S. Migdal, *Strong Societies and Weak States, State-Society Relations and State Capabilities in the Third World* (Princeton, NJ: Princeton University Press, 1988).

17. Adam Przeworski, Michael E. Alvarez, Jose Antonio Cheibub, and Fernando Limongi, *Democracy and Development* (Cambridge: Cambridge University Press, 2000).

18. Fernando H. Cardoso, "Entrepreneurs and the Transition Process: The Brazilian Case," in Guillermo O'Donnell, Philippe C. Schmitter, and Laurence Whitehead, eds., *Transitions from Authoritarian Rule: Comparative Perspectives* (Baltimore, MD: Johns Hopkins University Press, 1986), pp. 137–153.

19. P.T. Bauer, *Equality, the Third World, and Economic Delusion* (Cambridge, MA: Harvard University Press, 1981); Michael E. Porter, *The Competitive Advantage of Nations* (New York: The Free Press, 1998); Richard P. Appelbaum and Jeffrey Henderson, eds., *States and Development in the Asian Pacific Rim* (Newbury Park, CA: Sage, 1992); and Mancur Olson, *The Rise and Decline of Nations* (New Haven, CT: Yale University Press, 1982).

20. B.W. Hodder, *Economic Development in the Tropics* (London: Methuen, 1980).

21. Bruce F. Johnston and William C. Clark, *Redesigning Rural Development: A Strategic Perspective* (Baltimore, MD: Johns Hopkins University Press, 1982); Ronald J. Herring, *Land to the Tiller: The Political Economy of Agrarian Reform in South Asia* (New Haven, CT: Yale University Press, 1983); and Dale W. Adams, Douglas H. Graham, and J.D. von Pischke, eds., *Undermining Rural Development with Cheap Credit* (Boulder, CO: Westview Press, 1984).

22. James E. Anderson and Leslie Young, *Trade Implies Law: The Power of the Weak*, Cambridge: National Bureau of Economic Research, Working Paper No. 7702 (2000).

23. R.J. Barro, *Determinants of Economic Growth: A Cross-Country Empirical Study* (Cambridge, MA: MIT Press, 1997).

24. Milton J. Esman and Norman T. Uphoff, *Local Organizations: Intermediaries in Rural Development* (Ithaca, NY: Cornell University Press, 1984).

25. Samuel P. Huntington, *Political Order in Changing Societies* (New Haven, CT: Yale University Press, 1968), pp. 397–461.

26. Pippa Norris, *Politics and the Press: The News Media and Their Influences* (Boulder, CO: Lynne Rienner, 1997); and *Digital Divide: Civic Engagement. Information Poverty, and the Internet Worldwide* (New York: Cambridge University Press, 2001).

27. A.J.M. Milne, *The Right to Dissent: Issues in Political Philosophy* (Amersham, UK: Avebury, 1983).

28. Roger C. Kormendi and Philip G. Meguire, "Macroeconomic Determinants of Growth: Cross-Country Evidence," *Journal of Monetary Economics,* Vol. 16 (1985): pp. 141–163; and Gerald W. Scully, "The Institutional Framework and Economic Development," *Journal of Political Economy*, No. 3 (1988): pp. 652–662.

29. Amartya Sen, *Poverty and Famines: An Essay on Entitlement and Deprivation* (Oxford: Clarendon Press, 1981); William Ascher, *Scheming for the Poor* (Cambridge, MA: Harvard University Press, 1984).

30. Partha Dasgupta, *An Inquiry into Well-being and Destitution* (Oxford: Clarendon Press, 1993).

31. Vernon W. Ruttan, *Technology, Growth, and Development, an Induced Innovation Perspective* (New York: Oxford University Press, 2001); David S. Landes, *The Wealth and Poverty of Nations: Why Some are So Rich and Some So Poor* (New York: W.W. Norton, 1998); Paul Bairoch, *The Economic Development of the Third World Since 1900* (Berkeley, CA: University of California Press, 1977), trans Cynthia Postan.

32. James S. Coleman, ed., *Education and Political Development* (Princeton, NJ: Princeton University Press, 1965).

33. Arend Lijphart, *Patterns of Democracy: Government Forms and Performance in 36 Countries* (New Haven, CT: Yale University Press, 1999).
34. David Morawetz, *Twenty-five Years of Economic Development, 1950 to 1975* (Baltimore, MD: Johns Hopkins University Press for the World Bank, 1977).
35. Joseph LaPalombara, ed., *Bureaucracy and Political Development* (Princeton, NJ: Princeton University Press, 1963).
36. Larry Diamond and Marc F. Plattner, eds., *Civil-Military Relations and Democracy* (Baltimore, MD: Johns Hopkins University Press, 1996); Peter D. Feaver and Richard H. Kahn, eds., *Soldiers and Civilians: The Civil-Military Gap and American National Security* (Cambridge, MA: MIT Press, 2001); and Michael W. Doyle and Nicholas Sambanis, "International Peacebuilding: A Theoretical and Quantitative Analysis," *American Political Science Review*, Vol. 94, No. 8 (December 2000): pp. 779–801.
37. William Easterly, *The Elusive Quest for Growth: Economists' Adventures and Misadventures in the Tropics* (Cambridge, MA: MIT Press, 2001).
38. Youssev Cohen, Brian R. Brown, and A.F.K. Organski, "The Paradoxical Nature of State-Making: The Violent Creation of Order," *American Political Science Review*, Vol. 75, No. 4 (1981).
39. Adam Przeworski, *Democracy and the Market* (Cambridge: Cambridge University Press, 1991).
40. The countries were Algeria, Australia, Azerbaijan, Bangladesh, Cambodia, China, Egypt, Georgia, India, Indonesia, Iran, Japan, Kazakhstan, Korea (South), Laos, Malaysia, Morocco, Nepal, Pakistan, Philippines, Saudi Arabia, Sri Lanka, Syria, Tajikistan, Thailand, Tunisia, Turkey, Uzbekistan, Vietnam, and Yemen.
41. The World Bank's World Development Indicators 2001, the UN Human Development Report 2001, the World Bank's Global Development Network, the World Bank's Worldwide Governance Research Indicators Dataset 1998, and the UN University World Institute for Development Economics Research, 2000.
42. I once called this error the "beanbag effect." John D. Montgomery, "Crossing the Culture Bars: An Approach to the Training of American Technicians for Overseas Assignments," *World Politics*, Vol. XIII, No. 4 (July 1961).
43. Fraser Institute, *Annual Economic Freedom of the World Report*, June 2003, at <www.FreeTheWorld.com>.
44. This finding was confirmed by the Fraser Institute report.
45. Ruttan, "What Happened to Political Development?" *Economic Development and Cultural Change* (1991): p. 269.
46. Vernon W. Ruttan, "What Happened to Political Development," op. cit., Irma Adelman and Cynthia Taft Morris, *Society, Politics and Economic Development: A Quantitative Approach* (Baltimore, MD: Johns Hopkins University Press, 1967) and *Economic Growth and Social Equity in Developing Countries* (Stanford, CA: Stanford University Press, 1973); and Cynthia Taft Morris and Irma Adelman, *Comparative Patterns of Economic Development, 1850–1914* (Baltimore, MD: Johns Hopkins University Press, 1988).
47. Thomas Carothers, *Aiding Democracy Abroad: The Learning Curve*, Washington, DC: Carnegie Endowment for International Peace, 1999, esp. chapters 2 and 3.
48. Snyder, *From voting to violence, Democratization and Nationalist Conflict.*
49. United Nations Development Program, *Human Development Report 2002* (New York: Oxford University Press, 2002).
50. Peter Burnell, ed., *Democracy Assistance: International Cooperation for Democratization* (London, UK: Frank Cass, 2000), p. 26.
51. *Economist*, October 5, 2002, p. 39.
52. Burnell, op. cit., p. 36.
53. Sheila Carapico, "Foreign Aid for Promoting Democracy in the Arab World," *Middle East Journal*, Vol. 56, No. 3 (Summer 2002): pp. 379–305.

54. Simon Chesterman, "Walking Softly in Afghanistan: The Future of UN State-Building," *Survival*, Vol. 44, No. 3 (Autumn 2002): pp. 37–46.
55. David Morawetz, *Twenty-Five Years of Economic Development* (Baltimore, MD: Johns Hopkins University Press, 1977); Robert Cassen et al., *Does Aid Work? Report to an Intergovernmental Task Force* (Oxford: Oxford University Press, 1986); and Krueger, Michalopoulos, and Ruttan, op. cit.
56. Robert J. Muscat, *Investing in Peace, How Development Aid can Prevent or Promote Conflict* (Armonk, NY: M.E. Sharpe, 2002), p. 38.
57. Muscat, op. cit., pp. 179–180.
58. Carothers, op. cit., pp. 123–140.
59. Carothers, op. cit., pp. 163–177.
60. Robert Cassen and Associates, *Does Aid Work? Report to an Intergovernmental Task Force* (Oxford: Clarendon Press, 1987), pp. 321–333.
61. Krueger et al., p. 306.
62. Carothers, op. cit., pp. 235–244.
63. John D. Montgomery, ed., *Human Rights: Positive Policies in Asia and the Pacific Rim.* (Hollis, NH: Hollis Publishing, 1998).
64. Cassen, op. cit., pp. 60, 117–131.
65. Cassen, op. cit., pp. 97–100.
66. Muscat, op cit., pp. 74–99, Ruttan, "What Happened to Political Development?" op. cit., p. 276.
67. Boutros Boutros-Ghali, *Agenda for Peace*, New York: United Nations (1992); David M. Malone, "UN Peacekeeping: Lessons Learned," *Global Governance*, Vol. 7, No. 1 (January–March 2001), pp. 11–18.
68. Mansfield and Snyder, "Democratic Transitions, Institutional Strength, and War."
69. Lawrence E. Harrison and Samuel P. Huntington, *Culture Matters: How Values Shape Human Progress* (New York: Basic Books, 2000).
70. Mitchell A. Seligson, "The Renaissance of Political Culture or the Renaissance of the Ecological Fallacy," *Comparative Politics*, Vol. 34, No. 3 (April 2002): pp. 273–292. Mark Tessler, "Islam and Democracy in the Middle East, The Impact of Religious Orientations and Attitudes Toward Democracy in Four Arab Countries," *Comparative Politics*, Vol. 34, No. 3 (April 2002): pp. 337–354.

CHAPTER FOUR

BETWEEN RECONSTRUCTION AND RESTORATION: THREE HISTORICAL CASE STUDIES

John M. Heffron

What are the most salient features of Afghanistan's latest bid for social, economic, and political reconstruction? How has the presence of a weak central government, made weaker by a long devastating war, affected foreign aid to the country, now and in the recent past? Are language, culture, and a common historical heritage sufficient to unite a nation? Are they sufficient to heal it in the aftermath of the long war?

This chapter examines these issues and a broader historical question that applies as much to the current recovery programs in Afghanistan as it did to the redevelopment efforts after the American Civil War and World Wars I and II. That question is the subtle but important one of the relationship between *reconstruction* and *restoration*. To be sure, there are physical structures—roads and other transportation facilities, public buildings, private homes, farm and industrial equipment—that, once destroyed, plainly need reconstruction and rebuilding. Humanitarian agencies often dominate the postwar battlefield, but their work is neither of reconstruction nor, strictly speaking, of restoration. It is largely maintenance work, an uphill battle to maintain minimal living standards in the face of institutional collapse and human destitution. Political and economic relations and the fabric of lives are not as easily rebuilt or replaced as new roads. At some point, policymakers have to ask themselves the difficult political question whether it is preferable to restore and preserve a nation's postwar institutions or to reconstruct them on a new basis. Even if a return to "normalcy" is an illusion, it is sometimes a necessary one.

This issue occupied the leading minds of three generations separated by three wars: the American Civil War, World War I, and World War II. In the wake of the current war in Afghanistan, it dominates official thinking in the Afghan Interim Government (AIG) and among its international allies, including both governments and nongovernmental organizations (NGOs). As the Afghan experience since 2000 testifies, resolving this issue can be a painful experience, especially in the absence of political will and public support for the difficult work of postwar reorganization. The pain is always worse and the dislocations deeper when the military victory is also a moral one, carrying with it humanitarian and political promises that the winners are not always able or willing to fulfill. What can follow in the wake of such engagements—at least in the four analyzed here—is a syndrome of "noble purpose leading to excessive ambition and, finally, discouragement and withdrawal."[1]

This was certainly the pattern leading up to the withdrawal of federal troops from the American South in 1877 and the collapse of the carpetbagger governments they were sent there to protect—a *denouement* of the moral exhaustion of radical reconstruction. It was also the case after World War I, when American idealists, faced with the loss of their prerogatives, abandoned collectivist hopes as exemplified by the League of Nations and reverted to notions of "Open Door" and the ascendancy of the private sector. Not long after the end of World War II, the syndrome made its appearance again in Japan, resulting in the "reverse course" of American foreign policy from liberal reconstruction to conservative restoration. Moreover, it looms in Afghanistan today as American national self-interest threatens to trump any long-standing commitment to the region.[2]

Afghanistan: The Historical Context of Current Recovery

Two competing trends, the one toward modern state formation, the other toward tribal and ethnic particularism, are persistent elements in the recent history of Afghanistan, and they continue to define and complicate the process of recovery. The Islamicization of the Afghan state, although it may be said to have reached a certain high point in the Taliban regime, has also been a point of contention. Periods of religious reformation alternated with movements of counterreformation and reactionary change, with tribal and religious loyalties often set against each other in decisive ways.[3] Thus, the westernizing reforms of Shah Amanullah (1919–1929) provoked a counterreformation in the Constitution of 1931, which made the Hanafi Shari'a law of Sunni Islam the basis of Afghanistan's social and legal system. This system, following a series of political struggles fought in the shadow of the "Big Game," yielded the liberal Constitution of 1964 and ultimately to the Peoples' Democratic Party of Afghanistan, the first non-Islamic political party in Afghanistan and a precursor of communist rule. With the emergence of the Taliban in 1994, the pendulum swung decisively to the right again. A new constitution, one that will presumably try to incorporate liberal democratic reforms within a balanced local and transnational Islamic framework, was pursued in post-Taliban Afghanistan. To these two salient features of Afghanistan's recent past—a troubled history of state-building and the country's imperfect Islamicization—may be added a third: the failure of reconstruction in the wake of the Afghan–Soviet War (1979–1989) and the civil war that followed it.[4]

For an understanding of the rapid rise of the Taliban, its sudden collapse in November 2001, and the current debate over Afghanistan's subsequent development, two events in the recent history of the country are particularly relevant. The first of those events—British withdrawal from the region in 1947 and the creation of the newly independent Islamic state of Pakistan—brought to a climax internecine struggles among Muslims of both Central and South Asia. These struggles, principally fought over competing Pan-Islamic, tribal, and nationalist ideals, continue to play themselves out in Afghanistan to this day. Forty-five years after the collapse of the British Empire, the fall of the Soviet-backed Najibullah government and the occupation of Kabul by a *Mujahidin* (resistance) government introduced into the Afghan state-building process the same unstable set of forces, creating new opportunity costs for the chief benefactor of those changes, the dominant Pushtun populations of both Afghanistan and Pakistan.[5]

Pakistan, it should be remembered, was the reluctant stepchild of an Indian independence movement rent asunder by age-old political hatreds between India's Muslim and Hindu populations. More relevant for Afghanistan, the struggle for statehood also gave rise to a bitter rivalry between the two leading Muslim organizations in British-held India, the All-India Muslim League (AIML) and the all-Pushtun Khudai Khidmatgar (Servants of God) movement in the North-West Frontier Province (NWFP). For Indian nationalists like Gandhi and Nehru, the prospect of a united India included the NWFP and, with it the hope of a *rapprochement* between Hindus and Muslims in the region. The election of Pushtun representatives to the Indian National Congress, where Pushtun Muslims advocated not territorial sovereignty or statehood but independent status within one India, gave some basis for this hope. British maneuvering and the creation of Pakistan dealt a crippling blow to Pushtun dreams of independence within a single successor state, dividing the group's loyalties between four opposing alternatives: (1) the Islamicism preached by Pakistani extremists; (2) the status quo embodied in liberal Afghan statehood; (3) a new Pushtunistan that would unite all Pushto-speaking peoples of Afghanistan and the former NWFP (now Pakistan) into an independent Pushtun state; and (4) the traditional prerogatives of local, khanate rule. This last alternative, in which the Pushtun submitted to a tribal code of Pushtunwali and only indirectly to Islamic Shari'a Law, was, if nothing else, the solution most compatible historically with the fierce independence of the Pushtun people.[6]

Pushtun independence, as pronounced as it was in Pakistan, was not confined to the tribes living within the corridor separating the former British-held India from the fledgling state of Afghanistan, the so-called Durand Line imposed by the British in 1893. Representing its most militantly nonaligned and recidivist expression, Pushtuns were and continue to be the dominant ethnic group in the south and southwest areas of the country. Their resistance not only to external invasion and conquest but to the "internal imperialism" of Afghanistan's own empire-builders helped to preserve a nomadic, pastoral way of life that has rendered this large ethnic majority politically redundant in the postcolonial Afghan state. The formation of Pakistan accelerated this process, launching a civil war in Afghanistan between pan-Islamic forces in the region led by Pakistan and pronationalist modernizers in Kabul supported by the Soviet Union. Except as mercenaries for a lost cause, this and subsequent civil wars left the majority Pushtun, until the Taliban regime, more or less out of the equation. The combination of non-Pushtun Islamic fundamentalism and an Afghan nationalism driven by hopes of postcolonial tribal reunification has divided Afghanistan against itself and turned inherently unstable Afghan–Pakistani border relations into a political football for disparate tribal and religious organizations seeking their own advantage.[7]

In 1947, the real conflict was over Muslim identities and territorial prerogatives, not over Hindu nationalism or the right of Pakistan to exist as a state. In 1992, at the end of the Soviet occupation of Afghanistan and the overthrow of the Najibullah government, the outbreak of civil war between rival groups within the *Mujahidin* took place along similar fault lines. Separated by half a century, these two events—the formation of Pakistan and the Soviet occupation and ensuing civil war—are part and parcel of a larger crisis of state-building that has haunted the country from the beginning. As early as 1973, Afghanistan was still "just barely a state, and separate ethnic and tribal communities," writes Selig Harrison, "paid obeisance to Kabul only as long as it accorded them substantial autonomy."[8] The divisions are ethnoreligious, but they depend for their survival on contending sources of foreign support that have reintroduced new Great Game rivalries between an expanded list of players: Pakistan, Iran, Russia (and its two breakaway republics, Uzbekistan and Tajikistan), the United States, and Saudi Arabia.

The marriage of religion and politics is unique in Afghanistan, where rather than producing a unified Muslim state it has tended to have instead a splintering effect. Muslim Sunni (80%) and Shi'a populations (20%) in the country divide principally along class and ethnic lines, relegating religious to political solutions that are otherwise inimical to Islam. The Taliban represented a short-lived effort to reverse this trend by implementing an Islamic regime that was intolerant of political views incompatible with its own narrow reading of Qur'anic law. Nation-building for the Taliban had to begin logically with tearing down what little was left of the post-Soviet state, even if that meant alienating Pakistan, its one friend in the region, isolating and ultimately driving into resistance the vast northern, non-Pushtun tribal areas of Afghanistan, and paradoxically forcing still greater divisions among the Islamic parties, some seven in all, that comprised the former *Mujahidin*.

Not that the *Mujahidin* were particularly unified themselves, either politically or around Islamicist ideals. The latter were confined to an urban elite, a "thin upper crust" of the opposition to Communism and to the Soviet occupation in the 1980s, before they were later subsumed by a relatively young and rootless Taliban rank and file. According to one source, the Islamicist parties at the time of the Soviet withdrawal represented only about 15,000 of a *Mujahidin*-led army numbering in the hundreds of thousands. Many *Mujahidin* commanders had little or no political affiliations beyond the four walls of the jirga or village unit or within the limits of their own province. "By the late 1980s," writes Antonio Giustozzi, "there were at least 6,000 *Mujahidin* commanders in Afghanistan, about a third without affiliation to any political party and most of the others with only loose affiliations. They controlled areas ranging from a single village to a whole province or more." What the Afghan–Soviet War had begun the Taliban were able to complete in a little less than six years—the effective dismantling not only of Afghanistan's rich Kandaharan cultural heritage but also of the consensual politics that had once held together, however loosely, its traditional federated state system.[9]

In a further erosion of Afghanistan's independent development, political and religious discord has made it easy for Pakistan to view its neighbor as a client state made to serve its own economic and religions ambitions in the region. Zia ul-Haq's Islamicization program from 1977 until his death in 1988 extended from political to economic to cultural and legal institutions in a thoroughgoing religious revolution aimed at displacing irredentist nationalist movements within both Pakistan and Afghanistan and in drawing the latter more firmly within the orbit of a Pan-Islamic

Central Asian *zollverein*. The Soviet invasion of Afghanistan precipitated this trend by making Pakistan home to an Islamicist liberation movement (the multiparty *Mujahidin*) over which Pakistan, through its Directorate of Inter-Services Intelligence (ISI), assumed direct military control.[10]

Between 1980 and 1989, vast amounts of money and arms flowed from U.S., Chinese, Saudi, and other Arab sources into Pakistani coffers. Besides simply making life hard for the Soviets, foreign aid had the effect of militarizing and ultimately fueling the physical destruction of an entire society.

Pakistan endeavored not only to control the political and material conditions of the Afghan–Soviet War but also to manipulate the restructuring process that followed it, installing, for example, one of its own Wahhabi cronies as prime minister of the hastily organized Pakistan-based "Interim Islamic Government of Afghanistan." As we know today, these hopes never fully materialized, foundering on the nationalist sentiment of the former *Mujahidin* commanders as well as on the growing ethnopolitical divide between Pushtun and non-Pushtun tribal families.[11] The declining influence of the Pushtuns had a curious effect. Deracination revived still vivid memories of the Pushtunistan movement of 1947 and its resistance, born of India's dismemberment, to absorption into either Afghanistan or the new Pakistan. Since then Pushtun nationalism has found expression in demands ranging from complete independence to "relatively moderate demands for regional auton-omy," always with an underlying awareness of "the same one blood, One God, one prophet, one language and land."[12]

The source for much of the warlordism that today threatens to undermine Afghanistan's fragile ethnic peace and undo Karzai's neoliberal economic reforms, the Pushtun are nevertheless heirs to a potent, long-running tradition of anticolonialism in the region. To the extent that Afghanistan's reconstruction is managed from above by what, in Pushtun eyes, appears to be only another foreign invader, a neocolonial international cartel of external governments and assistance agencies armed now with butter if not with guns, Pushtun irredentism will continue to pose problems of legit-imacy for the Afghan state. Not unlike the unification of the powerful nineteenth-century Prussian state, beginning from a weak confederation of 36 independent Germanic states, Pushtun dreams of Afghan sovereignty having had to await the fragmentation of its domestic competitors and the weakness of its neighbors, India and Pakistan (it was France, one will remember, in the case of the Prussians). The Pushtun are still waiting and watching. The recent war in Afghanistan brought an end to Taliban rule but not to the ambitions of its Pushtun majority, repatriated but still largely disenfranchised within a power-sharing arrangement not of its own making.

If one meaning of restoration, as opposed to reconstruction, implies the reconcil-iation of historic claims of Afghan statehood, ethnic identity, and independence, then it stands to reason that before any real reconstruction can begin, Afghanistan's political leaders and their allies in the international financial community must confront the Pushtun problem and its special challenges. If either history or current events are any indication, the prospects for such a *rapprochement* are dim. This remains true in spite of the fact that Pushtun occupy several key government posts, including the office of the president. Most are returning exiles from the West imbued with an ethos that has put them out of touch with the nonmaterial needs of the Afghan people. A preference for regional solutions to national problems and for private sector growth and investment, as opposed to greater public spending, not the idiosyncrasies of cultural history, dominates the thinking of the men and women leading Afghanistan's reconstruction effort.[13]

The recent tripartite trade and investment agreement among Afghanistan, Pakistan, and Iran is a good case in point. Representing Afghanistan, Hedayat Amin-Arsala (Pushtun), a former World Bank official and the country's new Finance Minister, commented that Kabul sees the private sector as "the force behind reconstruction." Another delegate to the conference, the United Nations Development Programme (UNDP) Administrator, Mark Malloch Brown, noting that Afghanistan had entered a "new era of peace," declared, "commerce can resume." "A vibrant, dynamic private sector for the speedy recovery of the Afghan economy is needed," opined Nigel Fisher, deputy special representative of the secretary-general in Afghanistan. Afghan "self-reliance, entrepreneurship and productivity" were the keys, not a national preoccupation with the wages of history. The pronouncements of American economic officials are a piece with this point of view. Undersecretary of Treasury for International Affairs and cochair of the Afghanistan Reconstruction Steering Group John Taylor, in remarks to the Council of Foreign Relations in October 2002, made it clear that only "the creation of higher productivity jobs by the private sector" (a euphemism for the introduction of new labor-saving technologies that would actually reduce the number of available jobs) would generate enough economic growth to keep the country out of poverty. The hustle and bustle of a revived private sector witnessed by Taylor on a recent trip to Kabul—"storefront after storefront selling uncut logs, bricks, mortar, trowels, handsaws, shovels; people streaming of out of the shops carrying building material to rebuild their homes and businesses"—was quaint and heartwarming but hopelessly inefficient. "I could only imagine," he told his audience, "the huge improvements in productivity and the better life that precut lumber and cheap saws could bring; perhaps foreign investment by firms like Home Depot could some day be the agents of such change." The image of grizzled Pushtun warlords, their heavily armed sons and veiled daughters, *mullahs*, and Sufi masters all lining up for precut lumber, Big Macs, and other mass-produced American products may be a comforting one but it completely ignores the reality of Afghanistan's cultural circumstances and background, however antediluvian those may seem to Western eyes.[14]

Three Cases of Post–Conflict Recovery Assistance

For purposes of historical comparison, this chapter looks closely at reconstruction policies in the postbellum American South, in Europe after World War I, and in Japan after World War II. That the United States should figure so prominently in the latter two cases is a reminder of its formidable role, both in the fighting and in the peace that followed. Its subsequent responsibilities within a new international order were not, necessarily, of its own making. As Stanley Hoffman has recently written, "A hegemon concerned with prolonging its rule should be especially interested in using internationalist methods and institutions, for the gain in influence far exceeds the loss of freedom of action."[15] The United States has understood this for some time, nevertheless choosing its bedfellows carefully and only as its own national interests dictate. The enormity of the terrorist events of September 11, 2001 and the seriousness of the terrorist challenge in general has brought it, reluctantly perhaps, to a greater appreciation of the need for an international division of the tasks of war, peace, and reconstruction. The chapter concludes by extrapolating from the three case studies specific historical parallels and, in some cases, lessons for Afghanistan's current problems and the wide range of responses, internal and external, available to donor governments, NGOs, and other international assistance agencies.[16]

The Case of the American Postbellum South
Compared to Afghanistan's war of 23 years, the American Civil War was of relatively short duration, four years from the first shots at Fort Sumter to Lee's surrender at Appomattox in April 1865. And yet the constellation of forces leading up to it, the legacy of economic and social problems that followed it, and the sheer magnitude of its human and physical destructiveness present striking parallels to the Afghan experience. Not unlike the Pushtun, Southerners identified themselves historically with the country's oldest and most cherished traditions—state and territorial rights, yeoman individualism, God and family, even slavery, which white Southerners viewed positively as an eleemosynary institution for the moral and practical uplift of their inferiors. Paeans to "southernness" stressed the ascendancy but also the compatibility of Southern values and culture with all that was fundamentally American.[17] The construction of regional identities in both the United States and Afghanistan, sometimes but not always along ethnic lines, has served to reinforce the same common norms of personal and group honor, integrity, and autonomy that nonetheless have made political union in these countries so difficult.

In the civil war's brief years, about 618,000 Union and Confederate soldiers and sailors died, a figure that exceeds by more than 50 percent the number of U.S. casualties at the end of World War II. Besides the great loss of life and limb, the War had an equally crippling effect on the financial and physical infrastructure of the Confederate South.[18] This scorched-earth policy, culminating in Sherman's famous "March to the Sea" and a "devastation more or less relentless" from Atlanta to Raleigh, North Carolina, had ruinous long-term social and economic consequences for the South.[19] Not only, as many historians now believe, did postwar policymakers fail to address these costs adequately; they permitted the much deeper wounds to Southerner pride and honor to grow and fester, leading only to more aberrant forms of regional self-consciousness—the religion of the Lost Cause, the Ku Klux Klan, America's preeminent terrorist organization, and the Redeemer's New South. Still reeling from defeat and disgrace, it is not surprising that Southerners should have clung to the sense of regional self-importance that marked Dixie during the antebellum period.[20]

The road from war to reconstruction to the restoration of 1876, when Congress returned home rule to the South, follows the familiar pattern of high purpose, withdrawal, disillusionment, and neglect that we are beginning to see in Afghanistan, notwithstanding the success of its neoliberal market reforms or growing prospects for the country's democratic transformation. The image of a foreign-occupied South ruled over by military governments and by a Bureau of Refugees, Freedman, and Abandoned Lands—the famous Freedman's Bureau run and funded by the War Department—ultimately failed to capture the imagination of the American people, the majority of whom were anxious to return to prewar, peacetime federal spending levels. More immediately, it also failed to keep up with the reality of troop movements on the ground. By fall of 1867, the Northern Union army had been so rapidly demobilized (from over a million active soldiers in May 1865 to 152,000 by the end of the year and to 38,000 by the end of 1867) that most peacekeeping operations in the South were doomed to ineffectiveness. Add to this the refusal of the federal government to subsidize the South's economic recovery, and it is not difficult to see how great the obstacles must have been to any serious effort at reconstructing the former slave South.[21]

In the South, reconstruction implied at least three things that would have been anathema to Andrew Johnson, Lincoln's successor and the government's most prominent proponent of restoration. It implied the complete overhaul, from above, of the South's antebellum social and economic system. It implied federal enforcement of a "free soil, free labor, free men" ideology at odds with the needs of the postwar plantation economy. And it would cause a weakening of local self-determination, the key, in Johnson's mind, to intersectional harmony.

"General, there is no such thing as reconstruction," he told John A. "Blackjack" Logan, the Illinois pro-southernist, Union army general, and later Republican Senator. "These states have not gone out of the Union, therefore reconstruction is unnecessary." It was the responsibility of the Executive, representing "the will of the people" and not of a partisan Congress, to carry out the "rehabilitation of these rebellious states" and to bring them back to "their former condition as quickly as possible."[22] In discussions with Grant in March of 1865, just weeks before Lee's surrender at Appomattox, Lincoln himself cautioned patience and forbearance toward the apostates: "Let them once surrender and reach their homes [and] they won't take up arms again . . . . Let them have their horses to plow with. . . . Give them the most liberal and honorable terms."[23] Conciliating Southern whites came down in practical terms to restoring social order, forgiving the Confederate debt, and putting the South, especially its black labor force, back to work. The Lincoln–Johnson policy of leniency and easy restoration met bitter resistance from a Republican Congress spoiling for retribution, protective of the fragile social and political rights of the freedman, and yet fearful of the premature return of the South as a powerful new political bloc, with or without black suffrage. Archaist restoration also had to face an initial upsurge of federal enthusiasm and support for government intervention at all levels.[24]

In 1867 and 1868, a series of Military Reconstruction Acts passed by Congress (over Johnson's veto) declared "illegal" southern state governments restored under presidential order, imposed new, stricter requirements for their readmission, and set up temporary military governments to enforce the 14th Amendment. Although impressive in scope, the real effect of these four laws was minimal and short lived. A combination of southern white intransigence, dwindling troop strength in the

South, and moderate Republican fears of growing federal power and a desire for speedier restoration succeeded in drawing many of the teeth out of the Radical Reconstruction program.[25]

The Freedmen's Bureau suffered a similar fate. During its brief life, this government within a government did much to guarantee ex-slaves greater access to religion, education, and a wide range of social services normally denied them in the former Confederacy. "Scarcely any subject that has to be legislated upon in civil society," averred its chief administrator, General Oliver O. Howard, "failed at one time or another, to demand the action of this singular Bureau." It made laws and established its own court system, the so-called freedman's courts, raised and collected taxes, built schools, churches, and hospitals in the hundreds, negotiated and enforced labor contracts, settled land disputes, and presided over marriages between former slaves. In humanitarian aid alone it distributed in 50 months of operation 21,000,000 free meals at a cost of over four million dollars. Underfunded and understaffed, the Bureau nevertheless fell a victim to federal neglect and New South boosterism, including a pervasive new philosophy of self-help that feared in the Bureau "a permanent welfare agency."[26]

The abandonment of the Freedman's Bureau went hand in hand with the abandonment of reconstruction in the South. Blacks and poor southern whites found themselves bound to the land as property-less agricultural workers within what was still essentially a one-crop cotton economy, while unrepentant, unreconstructed ex-Confederates filled the state courts and legislatures, dismantling Republican state governments and disenfranchising black voters.[27]

Nearly a century and a half later, the lessons for Afghanistan are striking. Like the nineteenth-century South, Afghanistan remains to this day a society of largely landless and illiterate agriculturalists, the vast majority of them sharecroppers or tenants employed in labor-intensive monocultivation of wheat or, in growing numbers today, poppy seed. The reintegration of Afghan refugees, some 1.3 million in only the last year, has placed enormous new burdens on this semi-feudal rural economy, one still struggling to overcome the effects, notes a recent Asia Development Bank (ADB) assessment, of "four years of drought, land loss through mines, degradation of irrigation systems and natural resources, population displacement and war."[28] These refugees, especially the many women and children among them, are perhaps the most vulnerable group. The extension of basic political and social rights, health and educational services, and new economic opportunities to this immiserated class poses challenges to the modern donor community not dissimilar to those faced by the Freedman's Bureau in the South. Humanitarian aid in the form of emergency rations and disaster relief—and there has been little dearth of either in Afghanistan in recent months (the World Food Programme (WFP), just one relief agency among hundreds, alone delivering over 400,000 tons of food to Afghanistan between October 2001 and June 2002) is no substitute, as the failure of reconstruction in the South demonstrates, for more equitable land and labor policies, desegregated political and educational institutions, and the protection of basic freedoms, backed by the credible threat of military force.[29]

The Case of Post–World War I Germany

Intervention relief seems to have certain overriding economic and political benefits to recommend it to foreign policymakers. "Food will win the war!" was the motto of Herbert Hoover, head of the United States Food Administration, responsible for regulating and directing food production in the United States during World War I. After the war ended in 1918, Hoover turned his Food Administration into a relief agency to send American surplus foodstuffs to the famine-stricken peoples of Eastern and Western Europe. Between December 1, 1918 and August 31, 1919, the United States provided food for some 300,000,000 people, shipping approximately 17.5 million tons of food to France, Italy, and the United Kingdom as well as to European neutrals at a cost of approximately $2.5 billion. Allied governments supplemented this amount with a distribution of another one billion dollars, a little over half of it to Germany, Poland, and Belgium, the three countries in greatest immediate need of relief. It is not too much to say that in the minds of leading policymakers in Europe and the United States food not only won the war; it won the peace.[30]

The rationale was that putting food in people's stomachs would not only stave off hunger; it also would stave off "Revolution, Unemployment, Suspicion, and Hate," Hoover's four "new recruits" to the Apocalyptic horsemen that were sweeping Europe. It would nurture "the frail plants of democracy in Europe against . . . anarchy or Communism," the "pit" into which the Horsemen of Famine and Pestilence were driving "frantic peoples." "The whole of American policies during the liquidation of the Armistice," Hoover stated in 1921, "was to contribute everything it could to prevent Europe from going Bolshevik or being overrun by their armies." For his friend and admirer, John Maynard Keynes, whose *Economic Consequences of the Peace* (1920) demonstrated so eloquently the futility of the League's reparations policy, hunger and starvation threatened the very foundations of European civilization. Mad with hunger and despair people "in their distress may overturn the remnants of organization, and submerge civilization itself in their attempts to satisfy desperately the overwhelming needs of the individual." The interdiction of famine and disease had to be made the basis of political and economic reconstruction. Against their danger "all our resources and courage and idealism," Keynes wrote, "must now co-operate."[31]

Hoover and Keynes also understood that without increasing productivity no amount of food or fuel would be sufficient to meet Europe's current or more serious future needs. To a return to full productivity Hoover nevertheless saw two great obstacles: the increased consumption of luxuries and the demoralizing affect of this on labor and the institution of price controls, including the artificial effect on prices of government-enforced blockades and trade embargoes and of continued military spending on large armies and navies. "Aid," he counseled Woodrow Wilson, "would not be forthcoming to any country that did not resolutely set in order its internal financial and political situations, that did not devote itself to the increase of productivity, that did not curtail consumption of luxuries and expenditures upon armament, and did not cease hostilities and did not treat other neighbors fairly."[32] Hoover was not entirely disinterested. Restoring Europe's financial stability and buying power, including German solvency, was essential to American industrial, agricultural, and capital interests, which required open, orderly, and growing markets to maintain the country's high levels of employment and productivity, the highest, in fact, in the world. Thus, aid to Europe was both carrot and stick—the carrot, Europe's share in the dividends of American prosperity; the stick, a goad against class warfare and incipient socialism.[33]

The exigencies of war required a level of central planning and government over-sight, including price and wage controls and the collectivization of key industries, that in peacetime was no longer acceptable to most Americans. The corporate state may have won the war, but individual initiative and private enterprise, Hoover and others insisted, would have to win the peace. Americans may have rejected Europe's League of Nations but they were not without their own global, collectivist ideals. In the League's place they offered their own covenant, one compounded of principles of democratic self-government, economic realism, and *noblesse oblige*. They were sure that only the United States, the world's largest creditor nation, possessed both the will and the resources to effect a recovery of Europe and by extension the world.[34]

At least one European diplomat agreed. Francesco Nitti, the former Italian Prime Minister, surveying a "Balkanized Europe" in 1923, doubted that the region could find within itself "the strength needed for its resurrection." America, Nitti argued, must "impose peace, as she imposed victory." Commanding the peace turned out to be in practice a difficult balancing act, for it required vetoing all inter-Allied economic action, moving American capital and raw resources quickly and efficiently, in other words, with as little government interference as possible, and exerting the country's moral leadership without, as Hoover stressed to Wilson and members of the American Peace Delegation in 1919, getting "dragged into detailed European entanglements over a period of years."[35]

Republican rejection of the punitive Treaty of Versailles was of a piece with these policies, expressed by Senator Henry Cabot Lodge that "the United States in acting with complete independence can be more helpful to the world than in any other way." American reconstruction policy in Europe in the period 1924–1930 was marked by an emphasis on a restoration of the prosperity and relative tranquility of pre-1914, a wistful desire shared by Europeans themselves. Hoover and other Republican leaders in the 1920s, following Wilson, elected for a postwar reconstruc-tion policy that would operate "through private rather than governmental channels" and that would tie such support to reinstatement of the gold standard, fiscal prudence, and marketplace control of economic development and capital movements (as opposed to government regulatory controls and more "economic planning").[36] Based on the slogan, "Business, not politics," Americans offered an economic plan, the Dawes Plan, for shoring up the mark and balancing the German budget, restor-ing German manufacturing output to its prewar levels (by demilitarizing and rein-dustrializing the Ruhrland), and subsidizing German war debt and reparations with a loan of 800 million gold marks—chiefly to secure political conditions that would incline investors of the world to look favorably again upon the German state.[37]

The Case of Postwar Japan

In each of the aftermaths we have reviewed up to this point two imperatives—economic development and security—combined to define an American policy that would begin in radical reconstruction, in a campaign of bold social experimentation, and end in moral retreat, in the conservation restoration of the status quo. The Radical Republican program to reconstruct the unreconstructed and install a pluralistic, egalitarian society ended ignominiously in the Compromise of 1876 and the return of self-rule to the traditional South. Visions of German democratization and one-worldism collapsed under the weight of American exceptionalism and a blind faith in the ameliorating effects of full production, "the doctrine of salvation by exports."[38] Afghanistan's fate too, it seems, swings between the two poles of economic development and security, notwithstanding a great deal of high rhetoric on the subject of democracy and human rights. But Afghanistan is not the American South, and it is not Germany. It is also not Japan, and yet among our three case studies, the lessons of America's seven-year occupation of Japan are perhaps the most poignant and for U.S. policymakers in Afghanistan today the most instructive.

Like the policy disputes that have split the development community over Afghanistan—questions ranging from how hard to push social and political reform in the country to the nature and extent of American military presence—those who had a hand in formulating America's occupation policy in Japan also served conflicting masters. There were those like Joseph C. Grew, a member of the Japan Crowd at the State Department in the early years of the war, who sued for a "soft peace" and counseled moderation in the terms of surrender, including possible retention of the Emperor. There was Harry F. Kern, *Newsweek*'s foreign editor, who in 1948–1949 with his friends in the American Council on Japan, the so-called Japan Lobby, took up cudgels against General MacArthur and his SCAP (Supreme Commander for the Allied Powers) organization, arguing for a cessation of reparations, business purges, land and labor reform, and an end to SCAP bureaucratization.[39] It was the aim of this group and its allies in Washington, including the influential George Kennan, to reduce SCAP power and influence drastically and in the process shore up Japan's own police establishment, restore to power the old ruling elites or Zaibatsu, and, wrote Kern, make Japan into " 'the workshop of the Far East' as part of the American policy of rebuilding the world and containing Communism."[40]

There were the civilian and military personnel at SCAP itself, including MacArthur, who offered a bewildering mix of New Deal reforming zeal, democratic messianism, and Bismarckian realism. They were not a homogeneous group, either ideologically or by disposition, but of one thing they were sure—the peace, like the defeat of Japan, belonged to the United States alone. A policy of noncooperation verging on willful intransigence guided its relations with the inter-allied Far Eastern Commission and the Allied Council for Japan.[41] SCAP's thinly concealed contempt for multilateral solutions to Japan's reconstruction not only underscored the agency's supreme power in the region, it revealed American hubris at its worst. In the harsh judgment of occupation historian John Dower there was nothing very generous, or for that matter very democratic, about SCAP's "democratic revolution from above." He points out, "their reformist agenda rested on the assumption that, virtually without exception, Western culture and its values were superior to those of 'the Orient.' At the same time, almost every interaction between victor and vanquished was infused with intimations of white supremacism."[42]

Although the United States has done much in recent decades to shed its image as the world's "Ugly American," the recent war on terrorism, albeit more cautious in its official stance toward Islam than the United States ever was toward Communism, has nevertheless reawakened in Washington some of the posturing and bombast of the past. More important, it has brought back into sharp relief the relationship between economic development and security that has governed foreign relations in the United States since the emergence of its archenemy Russia as an Asian power in the late nineteenth century.

As Afghan traditionalists, who far outweigh in number and influence the modernizers in the AIG, begin to reassert their cultural prerogatives in areas of self-governance, trade, and commerce, and with respect to the role of women in Afghan society; as peacekeeping efforts in the country devolve increasing to national police forces; and as Washington tires of promoting a social agenda that, for all its moral value, distracts from major U.S. policy goals in the region (namely, the disestablishment of al-Qaeda and the reintegration of Afghanistan into the world economy), the likelihood grows that America and her partners will embark, as they once did in Japan, on a "reverse course" in postwar reconstruction of Afghanistan. In Japan this policy reversal entailed a shift, although never a complete one, from the compulsory democratization of the enemy's institutions to a greater emphasis on local autonomy and economic stabilization. It entailed a shift from constitutionalism to cronyism and from deindustrialization to a variety of pump-priming measures—wage stabilization, price controls, Marshall Plan–like loans and subsidies, currency and tax reform, and the promotion of exports—designed to "force the economy to shake itself down," in the words of Japan's dean of occupation studies, Takemae Eiji, and thus to better enable Japan to convert its investments into real growth. In Afghanistan no less than in Japan in 1948, the creation of a postwar economic world order favorable to the American economy and open to American trade, not the formalities of democracy, threatens to dominate the development agenda as, ironically, local recidivist forces coalesce with apolitical, neoliberal economic ones to favor restoration over reconstruction.[43]

Toward a Policy of Tailored Commitment

In each of our three cases, fear and mistrust—a great deal of it justified, most of it unfounded and avoidable—have combined with a foreign policy of tailored commitment to produce a uniquely American approach to the management of post-war relations, first in its own backyard, then in Germany and Japan, and now in Afghanistan. The fears are usually opposing fears; the mistrust is as "valid" on one side of any given equation as on the other. Yet their functions have been the same—to complicate and divide the American response to peoples and countries in need of our help. In the aftermath of the American Civil War, fear and mistrust arose almost immediately over such vital issues to the country as black rights, economic recovery, and the restoration of normal relations between North and South. Northern commitments to the region vacillated between altruistic humanitarian impulses, aggressive schemes of social engineering, and the gathering *Weltanschauung* of *laissez-faire*. Northern and Southern "men of interest" feared alike the social revolution that reconstruction threatened to release in communities already dangerously attenuated by war and conflict. Reconstruction was bad business. Restoration, on the other hand, promised to restore to order not simply the South but the North, reeling from its own urban-industrial backlash. Restoration was good business. The result, at least for any kind of progressive reform, was moral and political paralysis ending in the nation's full acquiescence in 1876 to southern rehabilitation.

The fear of social revolution and mistrust of our former allies once again dominated American thinking in the wake of World War I. Two new revolutions, one from above, the other from below, now threatened the U.S. government's interests, as they are currently perceived. A revolution from above in the form of internationalism—the collective, multilateral agreements embodied in such postwar instruments as the League of Nations—compromised America's ability to act alone even while taking "Open Door" to its logical conclusion. Lenin's revolution from below gave Communism a territorial base from which to wage its war of world domination. No longer dismissible as the noxious political ideology of a deranged German intellectual, Communism had become with the Revolution of 1917 a major force in international affairs, one that it was in America's interest to actively curtail, contain, and if possible eradicate altogether. We have seen how the United States tailored its commitments to Europe to take these two new threats into account: in the case of the one, refusing membership in the League of Nations and privatizing commercial loans to its former allies and to Germany; in the case of the other, linking economic aid to European efforts to halt the spread of radicalism to its own working-class populations.

By 1945, Americans had emerged from much of their earlier provincialism, at the very least no longer finding "any incompatibility between devotion to our own country and joint action," as Secretary of the Treasury Henry Morgenthau put it at Bretton Woods in 1944. "Indeed," said Morgenthau, "we have found on the contrary that the only genuine safeguard for our national interests lies in international cooperation. We have to recognize that the wisest and most effective way to protect our national interests is through international cooperation—that is to say, through united effort for the attainment of common goals." The American occupation of Japan put Morgenthau's idealism ("the people of the earth are inseparably linked to one another by a deep, underlying community of purpose") to a severe test, too severe perhaps to survive it.[44] Here again, faced with a post-conflict situation in which they believed their vital interests to be at stake, Americans chose unilateral over multilateral policies and actions, clung to their own political and economic prerogatives, and generally followed their own instincts in peace as in war. America found itself in a Cold War with the Soviet Union that not only tailored its commitments to Japan but to the rest of the world as well. A chain of weak states stretching from Asia to Eastern Europe became "dominoes" of Communist expansionism. Propping up these weak links with American economic and military power, helping them to address the social and political inequities that bred instability and social revolution and that gave Communism a foothold in their countries, became from 1947 the major thrust of American foreign policy. Democratization remained as a means, and not always a very effective one; development and security, the ends.

A Revolution of Falling Expectations

The poor prospects for democracy in Afghanistan have little to do with ongoing ethnic conflict in the country or with the doctrines of Islam, neither of which pose insuperable obstacles to the successful implementation of democratic reforms. In the reigning Madisonian version of democracy, ethnic pluralism (and most notably the conflicts it tends to give rise to) has always been considered a safeguard against the worst abuses of democracy from elitism to tyranny of the majority. In Islam, a tradition of consensual decision-making, strong civic institutions, and an abundant supply of social capital suggest that democracy is not quite the alien transplant its detractors make it out to be.[45] The problem lies, rather, with changing conceptions in the West of what exactly democracy brings to or can be expected to accomplish in post-conflict states with little or no experience with democracy, countries such as Afghanistan, Japan, Germany, even regions of the United States. In Japan, occupation forces viewed democracy primarily as the most peaceful means available to an important short-term end—the pacification of the Japanese war economy and the suppression of militant nationalism. "The Allied goal was not so much to make the world safe *for* democracy," according to one firsthand account, "as to make it safe *through* democracy."[46] American policymakers in Afghanistan today no longer labor under the same illusion that democracy can accomplish as a means what it cannot accomplish as an end.[47] Democracy may still be the end game, but the priorities are demilitarization, humanitarian relief and economic revitalization, and the reestablishment of security. The strengthening of civil society, especially as a buffer against the influence of non-state actors, warlords, for example, is viewed as an important but nonessential good during this initial stage of development. Although it is important to involve them in all aspects of the recovery process, more effective than well-placed civic leaders is the policeman on the beat and an organized NGO presence to provide the necessary expertise and range of basic services.[48]

There is another, more critical consideration than either the pace of democratic reforms or their feasibility in theory. How the objects of democratic reconstruction respond to the reforms will largely determine their acceptance or rejection, success or failure. While a function of time and place, the latter also depends on what the individuals involved see themselves gaining or losing from the extension of democratic rights and responsibilities. Many initial SCAP reforms, especially those affecting the rights of women and minorities, labor and small independent farmers, and religious organizations, were greeted with approbation by the people they were intended to empower. A freer press, more independent unions, greater health and occupational opportunities for the underprivileged, a more open educational system, greater party competition, open entry to the civil service—these and other grassroots reforms appealed to millions of rank-and-file Japanese for whom MacArthur and the occupational forces were "liberators," releasing people from an oppressive past.[49]

Running hand-in-hand with the celebration of their new freedoms was a desire to "escape from freedom," a fear of what their new institutions would mean for Japanese traditions much older than democracy. Martha Mitchell's *Gone With the Wind*, her wistful vision of lost southern innocence contrasted against the angry defiance of her heroine ("I'm never going to be hungry again!"), made the bestseller lists in Japan for two years running (1949–1951). Mitchell's novel tapped into a powerful vein of nostalgia for a simpler, feudal past, a place where, many felt, personal honor and dignity still counted for something. "It did not take great imagination," writes John Dower, "to read Japan itself into this portrayal of the defeated Confederacy, where romantic evocation of a genteel civilization 'gone with the wind' were counterpoised against the vicissitudes of a war-torn landscape and a postbellum society plagued by Yankee interlopers and groping for a new identity."[50]

Nostalgia turned to bitterness and grief for the political, military, and industrial leaders of Japan's failed empire. Purged, defrocked, disenfranchised, and humiliated by the new freedoms, some former Japanese loyalists—from the decommissioned soldier in the street still loyal to the emperor to the top echelons of the Japanese command—committed suicide rather than submit to SCAP authority. The vindication of the dispossessed was slow in coming, but it was coming nonetheless. The conservative restoration of the Yoshida years, incipient as it was, reflected a truism of Japanese culture and politics: the readiness of most Japanese to accept uncritically the conqueror's terms, however unreasonable, revealed a tendency toward conformity, even slavishness that in the end would ill serve prospects for democracy in the country. No amount of democratization could ever completely eradicate old "habits of the heart." When the reverse course came in 1947–1948, after the first heady rush of freedom and democracy, it fit over the country like a comfortable old shoe.

The lesson is simple. In countries like Japan and Afghanistan, where the encounter with coercive democracy is separated by half a century, one ought to regard with suspicion facile expressions of acquiescence in changes that run fundamentally counter to local experience and that affect no two individuals or groups the same way. Democratic statesmen, for their own part, must not be so naïve as to accept at face value governmental reforms, especially market reforms and favorable trade agreements, that may or may not have anything to do with democracy at all.

Nation-Building in an Age of Divided Sovereignty

The Cold War ended for all intents and purposes with the dismemberment of the Soviet Union in 1990. The conflict between the superpowers had so shaped international events in the modern period that the fall of Communism felt like "the end of history" itself.[51] We know today that it was only the intermission in a drama that continues to play itself out with new actors and new dramatic materials and new and larger fears stalking the world stage. What are America's worst fears with regard to Afghanistan and how have those fears materialized in the reconstruction process there? How have they distorted the process, as all worst fears must? How have they defined and tailored American commitment to the region? Finally, what simple lessons can we draw from our three case studies of failed will and commitment?

The rise of a powerful, defensive new Central Asian empire, one geographically centered on Afghanistan, free of the historic influence of the United States, Great Britain, and Russia, and united around ancient Islamic ideals, while powered by modern neoliberal economic ones, presents a frightening scenario to Americans for several reasons. It suggests that state and nation-building, the focus of American postwar reconstruction policy for many years, may have to yield to regional trends over which Americans have less control. Besides the loss of competitive advantage, Americans fear that regional trade and political agreements, and the relaxation of borders that necessarily follows, will expand the breeding and staging ground for international terrorism, America's implacable foe after 9/11. What American dollars are doing to reconstruct roads and bridges, reopen schools, and legitimate central government will only, in our worst fears, serve a process of regional stabilization and Islamicization ultimately inimical to American interests. These fears have undercut the American commitment to Afghanistan, reducing its presence there to teams of military, political, and economic advisors and to a small international security force, with the bulk of American support going to the hunt for Osama Bin-Laden, al-Qaeda, and the remnants of the Taliban.[52]

In the postbellum American South fundamental changes cut across the traditionalists' grain. If changes just as elementary are opposed by conservative Islamicists in Afghanistan, this should demonstrate the difficulties of reconstruction compared to restoration. Donors, it seems, have as much of an interest in the latter as in the former. Officials in the U.S. Agency for International Development (USAID) talk not of restructuring but of "restoring" and "revitalizing," "improving" and "strengthening" the agricultural, health, and educational sectors of the economy. Although USAID is providing many critically needed goods and services to the region, many of these—cash-for-work and food-for-work programs, for example—are by its own admission temporary, stopgap measures designed less to force through major new changes in the country than to build or rebuild a capacity for self-sustaining development.[53]

Lack of federal subsidies and a weak army presence led in the American South to what Michael Ignatieff, writing recently about Afghanistan's reconstruction, has called "nation-building lite." In the South the most direct and direful consequence of "nation-building lite" was the disenfranchisement of four million free blacks and their reduction to a state of economic peonage. In Afghanistan, the consequences of neglect have included the rise of al-Qaeda, the revival of the opium trade, and most recently the recrudescence of warlordism. "The United States," Ignatieff observes, "wants a presence here, but not an occupation," when only the latter will buy the interim government the time it needs to build a coalition and to secure itself against it enemies.[54] Americans were reluctant in 1865 and are still reluctant today to support large armies of occupation. A new study by the Army's now defunct Center of Military History has estimated that it would take 300,000 armed peacekeepers to reconstruct Afghanistan on the scale that occurred in Germany and Japan after World War II.[55] All that Americans seem willing to support at this time, however, are the relatively modest peacekeeping efforts of the 30,000-member International Security Assistance Force (ISAF) headquartered in Kabul. Stability, not reconstruction, restoration, not nation-building, are the watchwords.

As in their efforts to help Europe recover after World War I, the United States and its allies in Afghanistan have sought to balance dynamic economic development with cultural and political stability to achieve sound public policy with private sector initiatives. When multilateral financial institutions such as the World Bank and the ADB have been unable or unwilling to fund Afghanistan's debt, which in some cases goes back 23 years, governments have stepped in to provide the necessary relief. Only very recently did the United Kingdom provide Afghanistan with a grant of $18 million to settle its accounts with the ADB, leading to approval of a new ADB $150 million post-conflict Multisector Program Loan for Afghanistan that will target governance and finance, transport, and energy.[56] Billions of dollars of subsidies flow from industrialized nation taxpayers through the channel of World Bank and IMF financing to provide loans to developing countries that not only target education, public health, and agricultural productivity but are predicated on creating "a sound investment climate" and "a sensible governance system," one that will allow private entrepreneurs to operate effectively and without unnecessary risk. According to the recent World Bank report, "Private Sector Development Strategy," firms and farms must be able to generate productive activity "without harassment, contracts and property rights to be respected and corruption to be reduced."[57]

Afghanistan finds itself in a position today vis-à-vis the major industrial powers paralleling that of the former colonies and territories that secured their independence at the end of World War I. Although nominally free, these countries remained in "practical effect" unfit and ill-prepared for self-government. Although the conditions for Afghanistan's reentry into the world of nations may not be as intrusive as those imposed by Europe on her former colonies, the principle remains the same: Territories inhabited by peoples unable to stand by themselves would have to be entrusted to advanced nations until such time as the local population could handle their own affairs.

A reasonable prescription perhaps for the ills of colonialism, but bad policy in a postcolonial world that, with Afghanistan as a perfect example, valorizes local culture and challenges traditional notions of sovereignty itself. Given the transnational nature of Islam—at once a religious philosophy, a code of ethics, and a system of governance—it is quite simply a mistake to view Afghanistan and other Islamic countries like it as weak or failed states and as such as havens for the settlement of nomadic terrorist groups. Yet this presumption or something like it has been a cornerstone of American foreign policy, whether the occupying force has been Union troops with plenipotentiary powers in the American South, interwar entrepreneurs plying dollar diplomacy, or bank officials and development workers in the case of modern Afghanistan.

Conclusion

The United States can still achieve its goals—development, security, and democratic state building—in Afghanistan and in the Central Asian region if its policymakers face and overcome traditional fears. I have touched here on those fears and their long history. They include a fear of isolation and encirclement, on the one hand, and of multilateral, collective decision-making processes, on the other; a fear of political and economic ideologies incompatible with our own; and strangest of all, a fear of democracy or at least of its "excesses"—grassroots populism, labor unions, ethnic pluralism, and multiculturalism. If Washington could recall its waffling of the "Negro question" at the end of the Civil War and its consequences down today for race relations in the United States, it might take a harder line on the rights of women and children in Afghanistan as well as a brighter view of Pushtun recidivism—a difficult balancing act to be sure, but an important one. If it could recall its stinginess at the end of World War I and the consequences that followed from an impoverished Germany, it might up the ante in Afghanistan, raising expenditures that today account for only a minuscule fraction of the American budget. If it could recall its relative largesse in Japan, it might also recall that no amount of money was in the end able to purchase the democratic reforms that alone could prevent a return to emperor worship, cronyism, and imperialism. Throwing more money at Afghanistan will not have the necessary saving effect without the effort to build the civil institutions and a civil society capable of absorbing such a large development package. These four lessons from the past—the priority of individual and customary rights over political solutions, the need for economic commitments commensurate with moral ones, the comparative advantage of bipartisan, multilateral agreements, and the limitations of pump-priming measures to bolster a weak economy—must guide the reconstruction process in Afghanistan. Only then will the friends of Afghanistan walk the necessary fine line between reconstruction and restoration.

Notes

1. John D. Montgomery, *Aftermath: Tarnished Outcomes of American Foreign Policy* (Dover, MA: Auburn House, 1986), p. x.
2. James Dobbins, "Afghanistan's Faltering Reconstruction," *New York Times*, September 12, 2002, pp. 27–29; Condoleeza Rice, "Promoting the National Interest," *Foreign Affairs*, Vol. 79, No. 1 (January/February 2000): pp. 45–62, which argues for the priority of America's "national interest" over either "humanitarian interests" or the interests of "the international community."
3. Larry P. Goodson, *Afghanistan's Endless War: State Failure, Regional Politics, and the Rise of the Taliban* (Seattle, WA: University of Washington Press, 2001), p. 18.
4. Peter R. Blood, ed., *Afghanistan: A Country Study* (Washington, DC: U.S. Library of Congress, 1997); Anthony Lake, ed., *After the Wars: Reconstruction in Afghanistan, Indochina, Central America, Southern Africa, and the Horn of Africa* (New Brunswick, NJ: Transaction, 1990).
5. Peter Marsden, *The Taliban: War and Religion in Afghanistan* (London: Zed Books, 2002).
6. Abdul Karim Khan, "The *Khudai Khidmatgar* (Servants of God)/Red Shirt Movement in the North-West Province of British India, 1927–1947," Ph.D. Diss., University of Hawaii, 1997; Ali Banuazizi and Myron Weiner, eds., *The State, Religion, and Ethnic Politics: Afghanistan, Iran, and Pakistan* (Syracuse, NY: Syracuse University Press, 1986); and Sayed Wiqar Ali Shah, *Ethnicity, Islam, and Nationalism: Muslim Politics in the North-West Frontier Province, 1937–47* (London: Oxford University Press, 1999).
7. Goodson, *Afghanistan's Endless War*, esp. pp. 3–53; Anwar ul-Haq Ahady, "The Decline of the Pushtuns in Afghanistan," *Asian Survey*, Vol. 35, No. 7 (July 1995): pp. 621–634.
8. Selig S. Harrison, "Afghanistan," in Lake, *After the Wars*, p. 48.
9. Antonio Guistozzi, *War, Peace, and Society in Afghanistan, 1978–1992* (Washington, DC: Georgetown University Press, 2000), p. 242.
10. Stephen P. Cohen, "State Building in Pakistan," in Banuazizi and Wiener, *The State, Religion, and Ethnic Politics*; John L. Esposito, "Islam: Ideology and Politics in Pakistan," ibid., esp. pp. 343–346; Barnett R. Rubin, *The Fragmentation of Afghanistan: State Formation and Collapse in the International System* (New Haven, CT: Yale University Press, p. 2002), pp. 250–255.

11. Barnett R. Rubin, *The Search for Peace in Afghanistan: From Buffer State to Failed State*, (New Haven, CT: Yale University Press, 1995), pp. 248–290.

12. Selig S. Harrison, "Ethnicity and the Political Stalemate in Pakistan," in Banuazizi and Wiener, op. cit., p. 288; Khan, op. cit., p. 564.

13. See, e.g., Martha Brill Olcott, "Preventing New Afghanistans: A Regional Strategy for Reconstruction," in Carnegie Endowment for International Peace, *Policy Brief*, No. 11 (January 2002) and International Trade Administration, "Afghanistan: The Commercial Landscape" (Washington, DC: Department of Commerce, September 13, 2002).

14. Amin-Arsala, Brown, and Fisher quoted in "IRAN: Tripartite Agreement on Trade and Investment," *IRIN News*, at <http://www.irinnews.org/report.asp?ReportID=27834> (May 20, 2002), p. 1; John B. Taylor, "Making Reconstruction Work in Afghanistan," Speech to Council on Foreign Relations in Washington, DC, October 9, 2002, p. 3 at <http://usinfo.state.gov/regional/nea/sasia/afghan/text/1009tayaf.htm>.

15. Stanley Hoffman, "Clash of Globalizations," *Foreign Affairs*, Vol. 81, No. 4 (July/August 2002): p. 115.

16. Within the nonprofit community alone, as of July 2002 there were 115 international NGOs working across 13 assistance sectors in Afghanistan. See Afghanistan Information Management Service, "Who's Doing What Where?" July 5, 2002, at <http://www. hic. org.pk/wdww/documents/wdww.html>. See the four most pertinent international policy documents: United Nations Development Programme (UNDP), World Bank (WB), and Asian Development Bank (ADB), *Afghanistan: Preliminary Needs Assessment for Recovery and Reconstruction* (New York: UNDP, 2002), leading to the establishment of the multinational Afghanistan Reconstruction Trust Fund; International Monetary Fund (IMF), *Islamic State of Afghanistan: Report on Recent Economic Developments and Prospects, and the Role of the Fund in the Reconstruction Process* (Washington, DC: IMF, 2002); Afghanistan Interim Administration (AIA), *National Development Framework*, Kabul: Republic of Afghanistan (2002), prepared in consultation with the Afghan Assistance Coordination, the Ministry of Planning, and the Ministry of Reconstruction; and United States Agency for International Development (USAID), *Rebuilding Afghanistan: Our Current Efforts in a War Torn Country* (Washington, DC: USAID, 2002).

17. See John M. Heffron, "Nation-Building for a Venerable South: Moral and Practical Uplift in the New Agricultural Education, 1900–1920," in Wayne J. Urban, ed., *Essays in Twentieth Century Southern Education: Exceptionalism and its Limits* (New York: Garland Publishing, 1999), pp. 43–51.

18. Maris A. Vinovskis, "Have Social Historians Lost the Civil War? Some Preliminary Demographic Speculations," *Journal of American History*, Vol. 76, No. 1 (June 1989): pp. 36–37; Claudia Golden, "Economic Cost of the American Civil War," *Journal of Economic History*, Vol. 35 (June 1975): pp. 299–326.

19. Sherman quoted in David Herbert Donald, Jean Harvey Baker, and Michael F. Holt, eds., *The Civil War and Reconstruction* (New York: W.W. Norton, 2001), p. 390.

20. See, e.g., Gaines Foster, *The Ghosts of the Confederacy: Defeat, The Lost Cause, and the Emergence of the New South, 1865–1913* (New York: Oxford University Press, 1987) and Charles Reagan Wilson, *Baptized in Blood: The Religion of the Lost Cause, 1865–1920* (Athens, GA: University of Georgia Press, 1980).

21. Donald et al., op. cit., pp. 481–482.

22. Johnson quoted in Brooks D. Simpson, *The Reconstruction Presidents* (Lawrence, KA: University Press of Kansas, 1998), p. 75.

23. Donald et al., op. cit., p. 469.

24. Kenneth M. Stampp, *The Era of Reconstruction, 1865–1877* (New York: Alfred A. Knopf, 1966). Stampp argues that to Lincoln, "restoring the old relationship between the southern states and the Union was the essence of reconstruction," p. 27.

25. Ibid., pp. 558–564.

26. Howard quoted in W.E.B. DuBois, "The Freedman's Bureau," at <http://eserver.org/history/freedmans-bureau.txt>, n.d., p. 7; Donald, ibid., p. 505; Randall M. Miller and Paul A. Cimbala, *The Freedman's Bureau and Reconstruction* (New York: Fordham University Press, 1999); and Donald G. Nieman, *Freedom, Racism and Reconstruction: Collected Writings of La Wanda Cox* (Athens, GA: University of Georgia Press, 1997), esp. pp. 149–171, provide positive reappraisals of the Bureau's effectiveness.
27. Gerald David Jaynes, *Branches Without Roots: Genesis of the Black Working Class in the American South, 1862–1882* (New York: Oxford University Press, 1986).
28. Asia Development Bank, *Afghanistan: Initial Country Strategy and Program, 2002–2004,* Appendixes, May 2002, p. 27, at <http://www.adb.org/Documents/CSPs/AFG/2002/>.
29. FAO Global Information and Early Warning System on Food and Agriculture and the World Food Programme, "Special Report: FAO/WFP and Food Supply Assessment Mission to Afghanistan" (August 16, 2002), p. 30.
30. Herbert Hoover, "Report to the President of the Supreme Council on Relief Operations Undertaken in Co-operation with the Allied Supreme Council, September 3, 1919," in Suda Lorena Bane and Ralph Haswell Lutz, eds., *Organization of American Relief in Europe, 1918–1919* (Stanford, CA: Stanford University Press, 1943), pp. 714–715; Herbert Hoover, *An American Epic*, Vol. III (Chicago, IL: Henry Reznery, 1961).
31. Herbert Hoover, "We'll Have to Feed the World Again," in Ibid., p. 7; Hoover quoted in Richard Hofstadter, *The American Political Tradition and the Men who Made it* (New York: Vintage Books, 1973), pp. 376–377; John Maynard Keynes, *The Economic Consequences of the Peace* (New York: Harcourt, Brace, and Howe, 1920), p. 228.
32. Herbert Hoover, "Memorandum on the Economic Situation of Europe, July 3, 1919," in Francis W. O'Brien, ed., *Two Peacemakers in Paris: The Hoover-Wilson Post-Armistice Letters 1918–1920* (College Station, TX: Texas A&M Press, 1978), pp. 202, 203.
33. Hofstadter, op. cit., pp. 368–409; Dan P. Silverman, *Reconstructing Europe after the Great War* (Cambridge, MA: Harvard University Press, 1982).
34. See Frank Charles Costigliola, "The Politics of Financial Stabilization: American Reconstruction Policy in Europe, 1924–30," Ph.D. Diss., Cornell University, 1973.
35. Francesco, Nitti, *The Decadence of Europe: The Path of Reconstruction* (London: T. Fisher Unwin, 1923), pp. 239, 261; Herbert Hoover, *America's First Crusade* (New York: Charles Scribner's Sons, 1942), p. 46.
36. Costigliola, op. cit., pp. 1, 4, 11.
37. William L. Langer, ed., and compiled, *An Encyclopedia of World History* (Boston, MA: Houghton Mifflin, 1948), p. 959; Louis Aubert, *The Reconstruction of Europe* (New Haven, CT: Yale University Press, 1925), esp. pp. 82–110; Carl Fink, Axel Frohn, and Jurgen Heideking, eds., *Genoa, Rapallo, and European Reconstruction in 1922* (Cambridge: Cambridge University Press, 1991).
38. Walter LaFeber, *America, Russia, and the Cold War 1945–1980* (New York: John Wiley, 1980), p. 63.
39. Howard B. Schonberger, *Aftermath of War: Americans and the Remaking of Japan, 1945–1952* (Kent, OH: Kent State University Press, 1989), pp. 11–39, 134–160.
40. Ibid., p. 150; Takemae Eiji, *Inside GHQ: The Allied Occupation of Japan and Its Legacy* (New York: Continuum, 2002), p. 338.
41. Schonberger, op. cit., pp. 47, 179; Eiji, ibid., pp. 96–103.
42. John Dower, *Embracing Defeat: Japan in the Wake of World War II* (New York: W.W. Norton, 1999), pp. 69–73, 211.
43. Ibid., p. 469. See also Walter LaFeber, *The Clash: A History of US–Japan Relations* (New York: Norton, 1997), pp. 271–274.
44. "Closing Address by Secretary of the Treasury Henry Morgenthau, July 22, 1944," in *Pillars of Peace*, Pamphlet No. 4, Bretton Woods Decisions (Carlisle Barracks, PA: Book Department, Army Information School, 1946), pp. 1–2, at <http://oll.temple.edu/his249/course/Documents/bretton_woods_decisions.htm>.

45. See, e.g., Mahmoud Mohamed Taha, *The Second Message of Islam* (Syracuse, NY: Syracuse University Press, 1987), pp. 62–84, who locates democratic traditions of individual freedom and community within Islam itself.

46. Montgomery, op. cit., p. 32.

47. Roy Licklider, "Obstacles to Peace Settlements," in Chester A. Crocker, Fen Osler Hampson, and Pamela Aall, eds., *Turbulent Peace: The Challenges of Managing International Conflict* (Washington, DC: United States Institute for Peace, 2001), pp. 707, 697–718; Krishna Kumar, "The Nature and Focus of International Assistance for Rebuilding War Torn Societies," in Krishna Kumar, ed., *Rebuilding Societies after Civil War: Critical Roles for International Assistance* (Boulder, CO: Lynne Rienner, 1997), pp. 1–38.

48. Karin von Hippel, "Democracy by Force: A Renewed Commitment to Nation Building," *Washington Quarterly*, Vol. 23, No. 1 (Winter 2000): pp. 95–112.

49. Montgomery, op. cit., pp. 31–40; Ray A. Moore, "Comment: Reflections on the Occupation of Japan," *Journal of Asian Studies*, Vol. 38, No. 4 (August 1779): pp. 721–734; Dower, op. cit., pp. 239–253.

50. Ibid., p. 528.

51. Francis Fukuyama, *The End of History and the Last Man* (New York: Free Press, 1992).

52. For a critique along something of the same lines, see "Penny Wise," *The New Republic*, Vol. 227, No. 14 (September 30, 2002): p. 7; and Spencer Ackerman, "Drop Zone, *The New Republic*, Vol. 227, No. 11/12 (September 9–16, 2002): pp. 10, 12.

53. USAID, op. cit., "Rebuilding Afghanistan."

54. Michael Ignatieff, "Nation-Building Lite," *New York Times*, July 28, 2002, p. 5 at <http://query.nytimes.co/search>.

55. Vernan Loeb, "Study: New Demands Could Take Military: Historical Precedent Suggests 100,000 Troops Would be Needed to Rebuild Iraq," *Washington Post*, September 23, 2002, p. 2 at <http://proquest.umi.com>.

56. "ADB Resumes Lending to Afghanistan after 23 Years," *Relief Web*, News Release No. 235/02, December 4, 2002, at <http://www.reliefweb.int/w/rwb.nsf/480fa8736b88bbc3c12564f6004c8ad5/624bb8d5dae35220c1256c850054cb93?OpenDocument>.

57. World Bank, "Private Sector Development Strategy—Direction for World Bank Group," April 9, 2002, p. ii, at <http://rru.worldbank.org/documents/PSDStrategy-April%209.pdfp>.

Chapter Five

The Afghan Experience with International Assistance

Yuri V. Bossin

Today, as never before, Afghanistan needs massive international assistance that extends beyond the current humanitarian effort in order to escape from its isolated and ostracized status. Afghanistan's long experience with foreign donors has failed to promote political and social stability. Optimistic plans for economic development from the 1950s to the 1970s did little to avert two decades of turmoil that drove the country to the brink of disintegration.

Afghanistan has undergone three periods of foreign assistance, beginning in the second half of the nineteenth century (when the British Empire offered regular subsidies to the Afghan Emirs, designed to entice cooperation from otherwise intractable local leaders), leading to the Cold War period (after the British Empire had waned and the new Great Powers—the United States and the Soviet Union—indulged in nearly 30 years of economic competition in Afghanistan), and continuing to a third period, which began during the civil war in Afghanistan in 1979 and extended through the fall of the Taliban regime in 2001. None of these activities overcame the defects of elite-directed development, domination by the public bureaucracy, and weak popular support. Political reform lagged dramatically behind economic modernization; democratic experiments in the 1960s failed to weaken autocratic rule and a rigid unitary state model, thereby precipitating the crisis of 1973 that broke the fragile political equilibrium and released formerly latent forces, splitting Afghanistan along ethnic, religious, and tribal lines. Thereafter, foreign assistance, particularly from the United States, dwindled and finally disappeared with the Marxist coup of 1978. The pervasive fighting that followed left no opportunity to maintain the development or the integrity of foreign assistance and produced a diverse stream of patron–client networks. Afghanistan entered the third millennium with a stigma of being one of the most ravaged countries of the world.

This chapter summarizes a century-and-a-half of international assistance given to Afghanistan, with the goal of helping donors avoid some of its pitfalls.

Defining Foreign Assistance to Afghanistan

Foreign assistance is not necessarily a product of philanthropy or even the expectation of an immediate payback or the reward of economic or political privileges.

For the most part, foreign aid to Afghanistan was offered with "strings attached." Sometimes foreign intervention was disguised as foreign aid, usually to establish a strategic foothold in the country. The assistance programs that contributed most to Afghanistan's economic and social progress came in the form of loans. During several decades following World War II, aid was a major source of economic growth and social reform, and Afghan regimes were able to maneuver successfully among donors and still maintain momentum for increasing economic productivity. There were many projects or programs, supported fully or partially by foreign donors, where the donors' motives were irrelevant to their contributions.

Early Stages of Foreign Assistance: British Subsidies

Afghanistan's sensitive geographic location made it party to the "Great Game" that began in the nineteenth century and continued through the end of the twentieth century. Though it was one of the poorest lands of the world, possessing scarce natural resources and low economic potential, Afghanistan was a magnet for attracting foreign powers, particularly Great Britain and Russia, who saw it as a strategically important buffer zone against each other. Although never formally colonized, Afghanistan experienced constant external pressures to prevent it from allying with either side. After the failure of the British military campaign of 1838–1842, foreign aid became the dominant instrument in the plan to win favor with Afghan Emirs.

In 1809, Shah Shuja al-Mulk was the first Afghan Emir to sign a treaty with the East India Company; almost immediately he was forced into a 20-year exile that ended only by British intervention in 1839.[1] He was soon toppled and assassinated, but all his successors on the Afghan throne accepted British patronage. "In the consideration of the efficient fulfillment of their entirety of the engagements stipulated by the treaties," the government of Great Britain "agreed to pay" annual subsidies, which, complemented by periodic donations of both financial funds and military supplies, almost constituted the only reliable source of Afghan revenues.[2] In 1885, for example, Abdur Rahman Khan was granted 120,000 rupees for the demarcation of the Russo-Afghan border along the Oxus (Amudarya) River.[3] In fact, during this 60-year period, annual subsidies rose from 600,000 Indian rupees in the 1850s to 2,050,000 rupees in the 1910s, by which time the subsidies covered approximately 10–20 percent of all Afghanistan's receipts. The emirs personally controlled these funds, disbursing them for army costs and for the needs of the royal court.

British subsidies, estimated at a total of 8–10 million pounds, had little developmental impact on the Afghan economy and social structure. Except for several ammunition workshops and the provision of "exotic" appliances to entertain the royal family, no Western technical advances came to the country. When the third Anglo-Afghan war erupted in 1919, the British government terminated the subsidies. Later, the British approached Emir Amanulla Khan with the offer of four million rupees per annum, but when he refused, the subsidies were never resumed.

Experience from past British interventions warns against using foreign assistance to maintain a desirable political balance in the country. Such a strategy would neither bring a new perspective to the Afghan people nor guarantee that Islamic radicalism will not be reborn in post-Taliban Afghanistan.

Foreign Assistance in the 1940s

World War II severely weakened the Afghan economy.[4] Foreign trade declined as did export earnings, which were the principal source of Afghan foreign exchange reserves. Galloping inflation and heavy expenditures depleted the state's finances. A subsistence agricultural economy prevailed over market-oriented production, making Afghan per capita income one of the lowest in the world. Educational facilities, public health, and social services were inaccessible to the overwhelming majority of the population.

The partition of the Indian subcontinent and the emergence of Pakistan posed another potential threat to Afghanistan. On the Northwest frontier, the defeat of the Pushtun movement, which sought to preserve its affiliation with India, animated the idea of Pushtunistan, a sovereign Pushtun enclave straddling the Durand Line.[5] This issue was the driving force behind the long-standing tension between Afghanistan and Pakistan at a time when Afghanistan's economy depended on the transit routes to seaports through Pakistani territory.

When 43-year-old Mohammad Daud, the king's cousin, headed the cabinet in 1953, Afghanistan had a medieval economy, weak government institutions, and a heterogeneous society in which many groups were openly hostile to the central power in Kabul. Despite the bitter experience with King Amanulla's reforms in the 1920s, the new prime minister was enthusiastic about giving modernization a fresh start.

In April 1954, Afghanistan passed its first law encouraging foreign investments to offset the lack of internal financial and technical resources for economic modernization. It was a highly bureaucratic and restrictive law, however, allowing foreigners only a 49 percent share in local businesses. It was also largely ineffective: Only two joint enterprises were established—a chinaware factory in Kunduz with the Japanese in 1955 and the Ariana Civil Aviation Company (Da Ariana Hawayi Sherkat) with the Americans in 1956.[6] International economic assistance was also disappointing, with most projects since the 1930s having been dropped at the embryonic stage: The construction of a highway to link northern Afghanistan with Kabul via the Salang Pass was negotiated with the Soviet Union in the late 1920s, but this project never materialized. In 1937 and 1938, Germans explored for mineral resources in Paktya province, to no practical consequence. In 1937, the American Inland Exploration Company of New York received an oil concession in northern Afghanistan but abandoned it two years later. In 1939, the Japanese began digging the Bogra Canal in Helmand Province, but gave it up after completing nine miles.[7]

The Helmand Valley Project

The first and most expensive foreign assistance project to be implemented in Afghanistan was the Helmand Valley development, originating from an official visit of the Afghan Minister of Finance and National Economy, Abdul Majid Zabuli, to the impressive irrigation network of the Tennessee Valley Authority in the United States.

The Helmand Valley project started commercially to strengthen Afghan–American relations, which had only been established in 1942.[8] After 1952, however, with advice from the U.S. International Cooperation Administration (ICA), the project began to receive American state assistance.[9] The final goals were highly ambitious—to settle 380,000 hectares of land with 2,000,000 people, mostly nomadic Pushtuns, and to transform the valley into the country's leading agricultural oasis. In 1946, the Afghan government signed a contract with the Boise, Idaho, firm Morrison-Knudsen Company to repair four dams, construct new irrigation canals, and develop a variety of infrastructure facilities including 450 km. of hard pavement roads. The $17 million contract was to be financed entirely by the Afghans and was equal to the Afghan exchange reserves in American banks that were accumulated from the karakul trade. Soon its initial budget exploded to an estimated total cost of $40 million. The Afghan government negotiated a $118 million loan with the U.S. Export–Import Bank, but received only $39.5 million in two installments— $21 million in 1949 and $18.5 million in 1954. The initial project cost eventually totaled $56.5 million.[10]

During and after the construction, Morrison-Knudsen was vigorously criticized. Critics blamed the company for faulty engineering that cost Afghanistan a tremendous amount but yielded little output. A subsequent criticism was that Morrison-Knudsen had overlooked the drainage facilities required to release excessive water and to maintain the correct salinity balance in the newly irrigated soils; the consequent waterlogging was said to have damaged vast expanses of land that yielded only a disappointing 1.18 tons of wheat, 0.85 tons of barley, 1.09 of corn, and 0.46 tons of cotton per hectare.[11]

In 1960, a team of Russian specialists surveyed the Morrison-Knudsen facilities. They discovered minor shortcomings resulting from high-speed blueprinting and lack of hydrological data (including annual river flow records). On the whole, however, the Russians concluded that the work had been done with high standard of quality and that the irrigation network was in perfect working condition.[12]

One reason that the project never justified its huge investments was because of mismanagement by the Afghan administration. The resettlement program moved slowly. By 1962, only 2,200 families had been settled on the new lands, and they were people of nomadic background, equipped with little knowledge of agricultural methods. Government support included a 20-year mortgage, cattle, seeds, and farming equipment that were primitive and outdated. No modern techniques were offered to match the magnitude of the project.[13]

Further improvements to rejuvenate the Helmand project extended for another two decades so that by the end of the 1970s, more than $200 million had been invested (mostly by Americans), exceeding the initial projected cost nearly fifteen-fold.

U.S.–Soviet Aid: Competition in the Mid-1950s

The Helmand project had generated hopes for swift economic progress, but its disappointing results tarnished the U.S. image in Afghanistan and challenged the validity of U.S. development strategy. This perception deepened when Americans demonstrated growing interest in Pakistan as its chief geopolitical ally in the Middle East and South Asia. Afghanistan painfully reacted to the U.S.– Pakistan rapprochement as it raised concerns on Pushtunistan, which had always been a highly charged and sensitive issue for the Afghans.

Essentially it was Afghanistan's reluctance to join regional security arrangements that accounted for the U.S. chill toward the country. The bipolar model of international relations had gathered momentum and ruled out toleration of Afghan neutrality. The Afghans resented the growing U.S. friendship with Pakistan and were deeply dissatisfied with the rejection of their requests for military assistance. U.S. President Dwight D. Eisenhower's approval of a multimillion dollar arms deal with Pakistan in 1954 reinforced the Afghan feeling of abandonment.

The logic of the Cold War prompted the Afghans to search for support in the East after failing to receive it from the West. Afghanistan critically needed heavy weapons to bolster its defenses against Pakistan and to control internal tribal and ethnic opposition, and the Soviet Union appeared to be a more constructive partner in fulfilling these needs.

The Soviet welcome persuaded the highly pragmatic Muhammad Daud to exploit competition between the Great Powers. His strategy was expressed in the motto: "Soviet matches, American cigarettes"; it survived for three decades.

In 1954, the first Soviet loan of $3.5 million was extended to Afghanistan to finance the construction of two grain towers, a bread bakery, and a flour mill. Six months later, the Soviets loaned $2.1 million to develop the Afghan asphalt industry. The enthusiasm surrounding the first steps in Afghan–Soviet cooperation reached its climax in 1955 when Nikita Kruschev and Nikolai Bulganin, returning from India, stopped in Kabul and approved an unparalleled $100 million line of credit to Afghanistan. The Americans were caught off-guard. Searching for effective means to deflect the Soviet advance, they decided to expand technical assistance to Afghanistan, which from 1951 to 1956 had totaled a modest $4.7 million, mostly channeled into educational projects and wheat grants. In comparison, during the same period, Pakistan received about $90 million in wheat grants and $37 million in technical assistance, which was four times higher per capita than what was delivered to Afghanistan.[14] The start of serious U.S.–Soviet economic rivalry in Afghanistan began in 1956. The U.S. ICA budget increased several times, and Americans became actively involved in promoting Afghan industrial development. By the end of the 1950s, Americans were bidding against the Soviets for projects.

Assistance to Five-Year Development Plans
After these diplomatic triumphs, Afghanistan began to receive assistance in unprecedented amounts. On the 1956 wave of euphoria, the Afghans even announced that they were no longer interested in loans, because grants and gifts covered all of the country's development needs. This optimism did not last long, however, as credit agreements multiplied rapidly. To channel the flow of new assistance, the Afghan government initiated a Five-Year Development Plan, which was designed with the help of a multinational board of advisors. Foreign sources were to finance 33.6 percent of the budget. After the plan was completed, they appeared to have financed 43.7 percent, which was then divided among the Soviet Union, the United States, West Germany, Czechoslovakia, the United Nations (UN), and several international charity organizations (see table 5.1).

Table 5.1 Foreign aid received by Afghanistan during 1956–1967 (in millions of U.S. dollars)

Aid-giving countries and organizations	1956–1961				1962–1967			
	Loans	Gifts*	Total	Percent	Loans	Gifts*	Total	Percent
Soviet Union	90.00	38.02	128.02	54	254.13	57.68	311.81	65.6
USA	10.43	67.16	77.60	32.7	12.80	80.60	93.40	20.0
West Germany		3.00	3.00	1.26	42.35	5.95	48.30	10.0
Czechoslovakia	4.38		4.38	1.84	3.20		3.20	0.7
France		0.11	0.11	0.04				
China					8.72		8.72	1.8
Japan		0.30	0.30	0.12				
United Nations		7.30	7.30	3.04		8.48	8.48	1.8
World Bank						0.35	0.35	0.1
U.S. Export–Import Bank**	15.20		15.20	6.4				
Asia Foundation		0.8	0.8	0.3				
MEDICO— Medical International Cooperative Organization		0.18	0.18	0.07				
CARE— Cooperative for American Relief Everywhere		0.56	0.56	0.23				
Total	120.01	117.43	237.44	100	321.20	153.06	474.26	100

* Including commodity grants.

** Export–Import Bank Loans prior to 1956 are not included.

Sources: Survey of Progress, 1961–1962, Ministry of Planning, Kabul, 1963, p. 34; Survey of Progress, 1967–1968, Ministry of Planning, Kabul, 1968, appendix S-2; Survey of Progress, 1968–1969, Ministry of Planning, Kabul, 1969, appendix S-2.

The primary economic goal of the First Five-Year Plan was to engage in "the most effective exploitation of natural resources in order to prepare the conditions for the further industrial development of the country."[15] The sectors that received the most foreign assistance were irrigation, surface and air transportation, food processing, and education. The Plan laid a long-term foundation for sustained economic modernization in Afghanistan. It also created a mechanism for managing international aid, which worked smoothly enough to accelerate the pace of development even after its main architect, Muhammad Daud, relinquished his post in 1963. Although the Second Five-Year Plan, launched in 1962, failed to raise the envisaged funds, it nevertheless attracted larger amounts of foreign assistance (see table 5.1 and chart 5.1). The economy grew steadily by 3–4 percent per year, and production in the state sector increased by 440 percent.[16]

Foreign assistance in the 1950s and early 1960s encouraged the Afghan elite to accelerate social modernization as well. In 1964, King Zahir Shah initiated challenging democratic reforms that he hoped would transform Afghan political

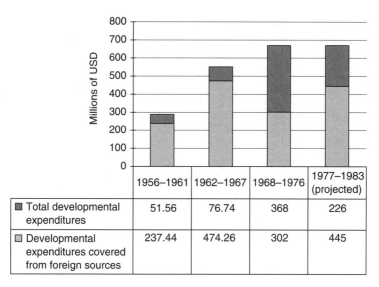

	1956–1961	1962–1967	1968–1976	1977–1983 (projected)
■ Total developmental expenditures	51.56	76.74	368	226
▢ Developmental expenditures covered from foreign sources	237.44	474.26	302	445

Chart 5.1 Foreign aid in Afghan development expenditures

institutions, but his first timid steps to establish parliamentary rule and political pluralism revealed serious tensions throughout society. The Third Five-Year Plan sought to reduce those tensions by raising "the standard of living of the depressed classes [in order to] rescue the oppressed . . . by increased agricultural and industrial production."[17] The amount of investment requested in the Third Plan was 32 percent higher than that of the Second Plan. The expected international aid was nearly equal to what had been received during the two previous five-year terms combined.[18]

Accelerating economic momentum required the Afghan government to increase domestic spending. To meet increasing financial obligations, the government tried raising taxes, but when this attempt was attacked by the upper classes, it retreated, thereby halting development. Foreign aid was directed to "carry over" ongoing projects. The GDP growth rate dropped to 2.5 percent per annum.

The Third Five-Year Plan brought a downturn in foreign assistance to Afghanistan, and its power as a driving force of economic progress began to wane. The heavy burden of social problems also undermined the development strategy. International assistance to Afghanistan never again reached its previous scale and productivity.

Assistance During the Republican Period

The bloodless coup in 1973 abolished the monarchy in favor of a republic. Muhammad Daud, the country's new leader, faced an urgent need to accelerate economic growth, which was slowing as foreign aid declined after the 1960s.

An experienced Cold War strategist, he reconfirmed Afghanistan's neutrality, hoping again to reap an economic harvest from the U.S.–Soviet geopolitical contest. His efforts, however, were largely in vain. To Americans, Daud did not represent the ideal leader after his overtures to the Soviets in the mid-1950s and his hard-line on the Pushtunistan issue in the early 1960s. In 1974, Washington, DC cut its assistance programs to Afghanistan and dropped the Helmand Valley project.

In contrast to the cool U.S. reaction, the Soviet Union seemed quite content to see the return of Muhammad Daud, who was associated with Afghanistan's pro-Soviet party. Daud reciprocated with a series of friendly gestures. On the day after the coup, the Afghan press reported that the Soviet Union was the first country to recognize the Afghan Republic (although officially this honor had belonged to India). Daud's first foreign trip was to Moscow, although Tehran or Islamabad would have been a more traditional choice. During his visit, he negotiated Soviet help for 25 projects, mostly under the Seven-Year Economic and Social Development Plan, three drafts of which were shaped by Soviet specialists in 1976.

In 1975, the United States resumed assistance to the Helmand Valley program. Because the Soviet Union could ill-afford to provide all the assistance that Afghanistan needed, Muhammad Daud embarked on a search for additional international donors. The Seven-Year Plan listed 126 carryover projects and 244 new projects affecting all Afghan economic and social spheres. The Soviet Union was to sponsor 62 projects; Iran 23; the UN 19; West Germany 16; the World Bank 12; Saudi Arabia 11; Czechoslovakia and the Asian Development Bank eight each; India and Bulgaria seven each; the United States five; Mainland China, Taiwan, UNICEF, and Kuwait, three each; the Industrial Development Bank and Iraq two each; and Sweden, Canada, Yugoslavia, Japan, Romania, Switzerland, and the International Civil Aviation Organization one each.[19] The Iranian pledge to expand assistance to Afghanistan was a U.S.-inspired move to keep American influence in the country through its closest ally in the region. This tactic had a positive effect. Daud still called the Soviet Union, "True Friend and Great Brother," but indicated his wish to rebalance Afghan policies. Although the United States indicated in 1977 that future assistance to Afghanistan would depend on how the Afghan government handled the problem of illegal drug trafficking, both sides seemed determined to rebuild bilateral relations. Daud planned to visit the United States in the autumn of 1978 to restore American aid, but he was assassinated that April.

Economic Assistance Projects: Successes and Failures
More than 150 economic projects in Afghanistan were constructed, equipped, or renovated with foreign assistance; almost all of Afghanistan's industrial, energy, and transportation facilities were built with foreign financial or technical support (see table 5.2).

Among the most significant technical and symbolic Soviet projects was the construction of the Salang highway across the Hindu Kush stronghold, which remains the only direct route connecting southern and northern Afghanistan. Some skeptics predicted that heavy snowfalls in winter would block the road six months a year, but the longest stoppage lasted for only two days. All of the foreign-assisted

Table 5.2 The largest economic projects constructed with the Soviet, American, and West German assistance in Afghanistan

Soviet Union	USA	West Germany
Kushka-Herat-Kandahar Hwy 680 km.	Kabul-Kandahar Hwy, 570 km.	Textile Factory in Puli-Khumri
Salang Hwy, 107 km.	Kandahar Spin-Baldak Hwy, 104 km.	Textile Factory in Jabal as-Seraj
Naglu Hydroelectric Station, 100,000 kw.h	Kabul-Turkham Hwy, 236 km.	Sarobi Hydroelectric Station, 22,000 kw.h
Irrigation Network in Jalalabad, 30,000 hectares	Herat-Islam-kala Hwy, 130 km.	Mahipar Hydroelectric Station, 15,000 kw.h
Darunta Hydroelectric Station, 11,000 kw.h	Irrigation Network in Helmand Valley, 300,000 hectares	Agricultural and Forestry Projects in Khost Province
Four Agricultural Farms in Jalalabad, 12,000 hectares	Kabul University Enlargement	Telephone and Telegraph Lines in Kabul
Gas Extracting Plant & Gas Pipelines, 365 km.	Auto Repair Workshops in Kabul and Kandahar	Transmitting Equipment for Kabul Radio Station
Fertilizer Factory, 105,000 metric tons of Carbamide per year	Kandahar International Airport	Textile Factory in Gulbahor
Kabul Polytechnic Institute	Ariana Airline	Wool Mill in Kabul
House Building Factory in Kabul	Kadjaki Hydroelectric Station, 33,000 kw.h	
Bread-Bakery Plant in Kabul		
Jangalak Auto Repair Workshop		

Sources: Survey of Progress, 1961–1962, Kabul: Ministry of Planning, 1963; Survey of Progress, 1967–1968, Kabul: Ministry of Planning, 1968; Survey of Progress, 1968–1969, Kabul: Ministry of Planning, 1969; The Third Five-Year Economic and Social Plan of Afghanistan 1966–1971, Kabul: Ministry of Planning, 1967; First Seven-Year Economic and Social Development Plan 1355–1361, vol. I–II, Kabul: Ministry of Planning, 1355 (1976); P. Franck, *Afghanistan Between East and West* (Washington, DC: National Planning Association, 1960), pp. 36–37; L. Dupree, *Afghanistan* (Princeton, NJ: Princeton University Press, 1980).

road construction yielded immediate and impressive benefits, as did Soviet, American, and German hydroelectric projects, relieving a power shortage that had produced severe voltage drops in Kabul in the evenings.

The other indisputable success was the U.S.-sponsored Afghan civil aviation program, which established the Afghan Ariana Airline and offered swift transportation of pilgrims to Mecca. Later it was purchased by Pan Am Airlines and continued to expand by offering reasonable prices for flights and attaining sustained profitability.

Among American failures, in addition to the notorious Helmand Valley project, the Kandahar airport appeared to be the most ill-conceived. Opened in 1962, the airport was designed as an international class facility to serve as a short-cut route for flights from Europe to Asia. Until the introduction of jet travel, the Afghans expected planes to refuel in Kandahar, but international flights began bypassing Kabul. Only one small shuttle plane from Kabul arrived in Kandahar once a week, and the project never justified its investments.

There were at least two disappointing Soviet projects as well—the Jangalak auto repair workshop in Kabul, and the Jalalabad irrigation network in Nangarhar Province. The Jangalak plant was designed to cover 30 percent of Kabul's auto repair needs, estimated at 1,373 vehicles per year. But Soviet engineers ignored the local mentality and tradition. The Afghans exploited commercial vehicles on a two-year basis. In the first year, the vehicle was paid for, and in the second year, it yielded a net profit. Then the vehicle was considered completely amortized, dismantled into parts, and recycled, generating extra income for the owner. The cost of repair at nearly 60 percent of the cost of a new car or truck, discouraged the Afghan owners, and the plant remained idle. An attempt to convert the plant into a hardware production factory generated products that were priced higher than Russian imports.

The Jalalabad irrigation network was designed after scrupulous analysis of the mistakes made by Morrison-Knudsen in the Helmand Valley. Soviet specialists stayed for three years beyond construction to supervise water-shedding and soil maintenance techniques. Although well engineered, the Jalalabad project was based on erroneous economic assumptions. Because the expected wheat crops would have taken 140 years to pay for the project, farmers were encouraged to grow more commercially relevant olive and citrus trees. But this alternative also encouraged sporadic growths of opium poppy plantations in the Jalalabad complex.[20]

The Soviet-built bakery in Kabul was also marginal, producing 64 tons of bread per day, which required wheat imports, mostly under American grants. Such volumes threatened about 220 small private bakeries located throughout the city. However, the Soviet-style loaves were not popular, since the Afghans preferred the oven-baked round *nan* bread; consequently the bakery began to produce army supplies and later introduced new lines of products, such as cakes, candies, and cookies, and became successful by the early 1990s.

Foreign Assistance Planning and Coordination

Most foreign assistance to Afghanistan was coordinated by Muhammad Daud's Ministry of Planning, which worked with the economic advisor at the Soviet embassy and the U.S. ICA Mission, later known as the Agency of International Development (USAID). Approximately 20 percent of the requests were rejected immediately for failing to meet certain economic or political criteria of the respective sponsors. Others led to preliminary agreements, but no final decision to begin a project was made until it was validated by a careful on-site survey. These agreements became so routine that the number with the Soviet Union alone increased from five in 1956 to 126 in 1977.[21] A few agreements remained controversial, however, including the Afghan demand in the early 1960s for a dam in Helmand to regulate the river flow into Iranian territory. This project became entangled in a century-long conflict over water resources and was ultimately denied. A proposed system of pumping stations on the Amudarya River to irrigate cotton crops in Northern Afghanistan was strongly resisted by Soviet Central Asian republics, which persuaded Moscow to freeze it. At the same time, the bargaining power of the Afghans was increased by competition among donors. For instance, the Germans rejected a cement plant project, as did the Americans, but the Czechs completed it.

Competition between the Great Powers made donors acquiesce, even when projects were unrelated to development, such as the Shindand military airfield near Herat. The Soviet Union was initially skeptical of supporting the airfield because a base already existed in Bagram, 20 km. north of Kabul. The Afghans convinced the Soviets, however, that the United States secretly intended to use it to establish roots near the southern Soviet border. To thwart the alleged American conspiracy, the USSR constructed the air base in Shindand quickly and at no cost to Afghanistan.

Attitudes of the Afghan Elite

Muhammad Daud's policy of accepting foreign assistance from any source encouraged subtle internal friction among the friends of the United States, the Soviet Union, and Germany. High-ranking officials, including the King's closest entourage, were traditionally oriented to the United States, with the expectation that after the British withdrawal from India, the United States could serve as a countervailing force to the Soviet Union. Lacking a history of colonization and possessing unrivaled technological and economic superiority, the United States was especially attractive, despite its pro-Pakistani leanings.

In contrast, the Afghans bore more ambiguous feelings toward the Soviet Union. The British-inspired fear of invasion made Afghanistan cautious about Soviet advances. Bilateral relations were initiated in 1919, and since then, the countries have remained formally on good terms, although Afghanistan openly supported the Basmach anti-Soviet movement in Central Asia in the 1920s and later became a home for thousands of Central Asian migrants. The Soviet Union also suspected the Afghans of pro-Nazi sympathies early in the 1940s; as for Afghanistan's part, even when Muhammad Daud opened the door to the Soviet Union in 1954, and although both King Zahir Shah and Prime Minister Daud proclaimed "the deepest deference and sincere gratitude to the great Soviet Union," they clearly underscored that the Soviet–Afghan relations were "a bright example of cooperation between the two countries with different social systems."[22]

The atheistic character of the Soviet Union made Afghans anxious about the possible ideological influence that might weaken the pillars of Islam. Although the Soviets offered many educational opportunities for young Afghans, the government usually declined them.[23] The only exception was for the middle-rank army personnel, many of whom trained in the Soviet military academies. In 1961, the first group of Afghan civil students was allowed to attend Soviet universities, but until the end of the 1970s, their number never exceeded the quota of 100 per annum. U.S. education, however, appeared more compatible, ideologically. American degrees were valued more greatly than others and usually offered better chances for promotion. Soviet technicians, though numerous, were welcomed for a single term, but never renewed; the Soviet Iron Curtain policy was strongly biased against any informal contacts extending beyond professional responsibilities. The most loyal supporters of the Soviet Union were Afghan businessmen that traded with the Soviets and a group of technocrats in the Ministry of Planning.

Finally, Germans had enjoyed a warm reception in Afghanistan since the beginning of the nineteenth century, and in the 1930s, the Nazi ideology was well received because of Pushtun intellectuals who admired German racial theories of Aryan ancestry.[24] After World War II, Germany quickly reestablished contacts with

Afghanistan and after the Second Five-Year Plan, became its third largest economic partner after the USSR and the United States of America.

Assistance Strategies

The U.S.–Soviet economic rivalry produced a competition amid philosophies of assistance and development. Among the Soviets, loans prevailed over grants, while U.S. aid emphasized gifts and donations. The Soviet ratio of credits to gifts was nearly 3.5 to one, including credits extended over 50 years. It was scarcely profit-oriented; the interest rate tended to be lower than that offered by the United States (the Americans were later forced to reduce it in order to compete against the Soviets). In part the Soviet Union preferred loan-based programs because they seemed more appropriate for long-payout projects; usually a single loan financed several independent projects. Except for the Helmand Valley irrigation network, which took 10 years to construct and two decades to complete, all U.S. investments generally assumed a short maturity period. Loans and grants were smaller and targeted at single, self-sufficient projects.

The Soviet and American aid models were derived from conflicting views of the assistance needs of poor countries. The Soviet Union emulated its own experience with industrialization in the 1930s, strongly believing that economic growth should take material form. Most of the Soviet-sponsored projects were aimed at creating production facilities and tangible assets. Investments in management and administration, the trade sector, or learning programs were subordinate in the Soviet view to "capital" investments. This concept resulted in longer payout schedules, larger credits, lower interest rates, and larger equipment expenditures per contract. Americans, on the other hand, while not denying the advantages of industrialization, assumed that applying advanced knowledge, methods, or general "know-how" was a more relevant strategy for Afghanistan.

Soviet and American assistance policies also differed in terms of economic rationality. The United States never sacrificed economic rationality for political reasons as readily as the Soviets did. U.S. loans outnumbered gifts, but Americans never agreed to repayment in commodities as the Soviets did. U.S. aid programs generally worked in a more pragmatic manner than the Soviet ones. The differences in policies especially affected the administration of wheat grants, which were a substantial part of both countries' aid to Afghanistan. The wheat grants, as well as some other commodity assistance, performed a double function, relieving the food reserve shortage while also providing an extra source of local currency to reinvest in development projects. The funds received from selling wheat in the Afghan market should have been deposited in special bank accounts from which all further transfers were to be donor-controlled. The Afghans resisted this practice implicitly when they asserted a right to control the wheat grants money. The Soviets preferred to ignore the abundant wheat grant embezzlements and financial losses in order to sustain the spirit of Soviet–Afghan cooperation. Americans, in a modest compromise, allowed the Afghans to calculate the wheat grants revenues at a higher Afghani-to-U.S. dollar conversion rate, but still required an American endorsement on all wheat-accounts transactions.

Foreign Assistance During the War

In April 1978, a revolt in Kabul toppled Muhammad Daud and established the Party Dictatorship.[25] Seeking support against rising internal opposition, the new Afghan leaders invited Soviet troops to stop the conflict. When these arrived, however, they were largely perceived as invaders, and Islamic forces started a guerrilla war. By the beginning of the 1980s, the Islamic forces took over the provinces while the Soviet-backed government controlled major urban centers and transportation routes. Western powers, as well as the majority of Muslim states, sided with the Mujahidin—regarding the Kabul regime as a Soviet "puppet."

In 1980, the Revolutionary Government revived Five-Year Planning. The two-volume draft, which covered the years from 1980 to 1985, provided an economic prognosis through 1990. Its contents essentially copied Daud's Seven-Year Plan with slight modifications in a Communist spirit. The Plan promised rapid development of heavy industry so that by 1985, it was to produce 36 percent of the Afghan GDP, as compared to 23 percent in 1980. Radical reform in the rural sector suggested ceilings for the ownership of land. The land in excess of the fixed limits (from 100 to 200 hectares depending on land quality) was to be repossessed and distributed to landless farmers. Average economic growth was expected at 7.8 to 9.3 percent per annum. Foreign assistance was estimated to contribute approximately 62 percent of the development budget and to total $1.32 billion (calculated at the rate of 50 Afs/USD).[26] Two-thirds of these funds were to come from the Soviet Union.

Most initiatives of the new Five-Year Plan never advanced beyond the outline stage. Fierce political antagonism split Afghanistan and provoked new rounds of violence and economic disarray. As a result, uninterrupted warfare paralyzed development. By 1980, military assistance to warring Afghan parties had crowded out the civil aid programs. The Soviet involvement in the Afghan crisis required extraordinary material and financial resources. For example, the 120,000 troops of the Fortieth Army that were deployed in Afghanistan (to help the Party regime foil Islamic resistance) cost the Soviet Union about one million per day, and another $300–400 million per year went to sustain the country economically.[27] In order to optimize the logistics for aid, the Soviet Union constructed the Khairaton Bridge over the Amudarya River, as well as the electric power line from Tajikistan to Northern Afghanistan, with the plan to extend it to Kabul. The two were the only notable projects accomplished in Afghanistan in the 1980s.

The largest portion of Soviet commodity assistance was delivered to Kabul, which raised its standard of living, while little aid reached the defiant provinces. Attracted by economic opportunities and relative security, numerous rural migrants moved to the capital city and doubled its population from 750,000 to 1,500,000. To make aid more accessible for the Afghan periphery, Moscow launched direct assistance programs from Soviet oblasts (administrative regions) to the Afghan provinces, bypassing the Kabul bureaucracy. The results were disappointing, however, because the oblasts lacked qualified staff to manage the assistance programs.

The U.S. strategy of assistance to Afghanistan was identical in that military assistance overshadowed humanitarian projects. From 1980 to 1984, the United States supplied $400 million worth of arms to Mujahidin through CIA covert channels.[28]

In 1985, Americans steadily and openly increased military aid from $250 million in 1985 to $1.2 billion in 1988, making the United States one of the chief financial sources for the Afghan rebellion.[29]

U.S. humanitarian assistance to Afghanistan was channeled through grants to UN agencies as well as nongovernmental organizations (NGOs) that focused on relief programs for Afghan migrants who had fled the country starting in 1980; there was a grant of $100 million administered by the UN High Commissioner for Refugees.[30] Other governments actively participating in humanitarian assistance to Afghanistan were Saudi Arabia, the Persian Gulf states, Western European countries, Japan, Canada, and Australia.[31] In 1980, they succeeded in raising combined funds of approximately one billion that were allocated for Afghan refugees' urgent humanitarian needs. Simultaneously, the United States initiated assistance programs for displaced persons inside Afghanistan, and after 1988, this program grew larger than the aid provided to refugees.[32] From 1980 to 1988, Americans contributed $750 million to humanitarian programs, which helped nearly four million Afghans who found asylum in the neighboring states to survive. After the 1989 Soviet withdrawal, the United States focused much of its humanitarian aid program on the return of refugees and disbursed $125 million over a three-year period.[33]

The 1992 fall of the Najibulla regime did little to stop the decline of the Afghan economy. The weakening of central power and the protracted political turmoil had devastating effects. Military actions forced massive displacement of population and destroyed material assets across the country. Islamic radicals, determined to annihilate everything bearing the hallmark of *Kafirs* (the unfaithful), later smashed the remaining projects. Of the 366 economic projects, including approximately 150 that were financed by foreign assistance, only six were still functioning in the mid-1990s.[34]

For 15 years, the Soviet Union and the United States gave Afghanistan roughly five to six billion in military outlays and a similar amount in humanitarian programs (with other donor countries). Tragically, the Afghan economy was ruined by the same Cold War dynamics that had earlier propelled its development.

The apparent stability in Afghanistan after the Taliban had established its authority did not result in any economic progress.[35] Despite the Taliban's anti-drug rhetoric, poppy cultivation expanded, and Afghanistan became one of the world's leading opium producers. Except for transitory pipeline proposals to link Turkmenistan oil reserves with Pakistani sea terminals via Afghan territory, no remarkable development initiatives emerged on the Taliban economic agenda. Islamic extremism made the Taliban regime an international outcast, eliminating its political and economic contacts with the rest of the world.[36]

Lessons and Recommendations for Donors

The history of foreign assistance to Afghanistan offers lessons of experience that current donors can ignore only at their own peril. Among the most important tasks they face are: creating a reliable statistical system in Afghanistan, setting priorities for aid, and addressing the problem of political stability.

Afghan Statistics

One of the challenges that donors inevitably will face in Afghanistan is a serious dearth of statistics. Two decades of hostilities and five years of Taliban rule shattered local statistical services. As a result, all that is known about the country today is based on unverified figures derived from prewar data. What makes these figures even more dubious is that statistical information has always been scarce and unreliable in Afghanistan. No censuses have ever been undertaken, except for partial polls in 1979 and 1983, because the Afghan government never had enough literate staff to conduct the survey. The population and ethnic and tribal group numbers have always been approximated. For instance, the estimated Baluch population in the late 1960s "fluctuated" in an enormously broad range from 40,000 to 200,000.[37] In addition, all information on ethnolinguistic groups has been highly precarious and politically colored to serve or to justify Pushtun domination in the ruling structures. Afghan authorities have not been interested in producing transparent vital statistics. Higher population figures automatically decreased per capita income estimates, which Afghanistan relied on to be eligible for international humanitarian programs.

Economic statistics have always been ambiguous in Afghanistan as well. For a long time, the Afghan Emirs did not distinguish between state and personal finances. Any records of government receipts and outlays were state secrets until 1919, when some fragmentary information was published in press. In 1920, a law introduced annual budgets; the first official budget appeared three years later in 1923–1924. However, the budget figures were often manipulated to hide a chronic deficit.

Keeping economic statistics vague was partly deliberate, but also reflected the volatile and chaotic structure of state finances, in which foreign trade was unrecorded. Economic planning in the 1950s required statistical data for the budget. A Department of Statistics and Research was established in the Ministry of Planning, but its annual reports were still far from the standards adopted in developed countries.

Kaleidoscopic exchange in the beginning of the 1960s included some 15 different official conversion rates (ranging from 20 to 40.50 Afs/USD), each designated for a specific foreign trade operation.[38] Some foreign commodity grants were calculated at irregular rates sometimes reaching 68.35 Afs/USD. The black market composed of numerous *Sarrafs* (private foreign exchange dealers, composed of mostly Hindus) established rates that were three to four Afs/USD higher than that offered by the National Bank.

The decade of Soviet presence (1979–1989) brought Communist ideological imperatives. Economic statistics were manipulated to show rapid progress under Marxist rule. Soviet aid reigned over Afghanistan but was mostly directed toward military needs, while the economy suffered from wartime disturbances. The largest part of the territory and population was beyond the control of the government and was barely included in the statistical reports.

Clearly, a workable and transparent statistics system is a prerequisite for building a modern Afghanistan.

Assistance and Priority Setting

When Afghanistan launched its First Five-Year Plan in 1956, the central question was where to start. The Afghans were obsessed with industrial development, but the shortage of surface transportation routes forced nearly two-thirds of the Five-Year budget to be assigned to constructing hard pavement roads, tunnels, and bridges. The power plants and related infrastructure indispensable for supplying energy to the growing industries became the second priority of modernization. The manufacturing facilities that were built later required qualified managers and operators in a country with 15 percent literacy—education was yet another high-priority item.

Today, designers of Afghan reconstruction must incorporate vital programs of food production, health care, housing construction, and repatriation of displaced people. Designers will survey more than 100 war-damaged projects from the 1950s, a few of which may now be reconstructed quickly.

Another important priority that should be considered is the allocation of assistance between the state and private sectors of the Afghan economy. In fact, the entire volume of foreign aid to Afghanistan since the 1950s has been rendered to the state sector. (The only exception was a seven million German loan to the privately owned Nassaji textile factory in Kunduz.) Afghan leaders assumed that the private sector was weak and unable to absorb large investments, especially ones with a long-term payout schedule. Also, many Afghans were biased against profiteering entrepreneurs, whom they blamed for graft and social injustice. Because donors did not consider the Afghan private sector to be worthwhile partner, the Afghan state sector enjoyed tremendous expansion during the period of foreign assistance. But state management, effectiveness, and profitability were weak. Foreign economic assistance played an important role in Afghanistan's industrial development, but failed to create a modern market economy that functioned through the business initiative of small- and medium-size private enterprises.

Today, the private sector may be the only possible instrument to foster self-sustained economic growth. Dynamic development of the private sector should become an integral part of reconstruction, thus providing abundant employment opportunities and establishing an attractive climate for foreign investments. Making the Afghan private sector robust requires more than financial support; it needs legal norms harmonized with a juridical tradition based on the mixture of religious laws (the *Shariat* code) and customary laws (the *'Adat* code). For the last two decades, Afghanistan had no rule of law. An effective legal system will be one of the chief prerequisites toward rehabilitating the Afghan private sector. Without it, the economy will be crippled.

The Problem of Political Stability

The structural requirements of political stability in Afghanistan are still uncertain. Some ardent voices urge a federation to follow the interim government; others challenge the possibility of an overnight democracy in a country with centuries of autocratic experience. In any case, a centralized power capable of curbing separatist forces must first be established. Even the confusion caused by foreign aid competition jeopardizes Afghan independence.

Foreign assistance to Afghanistan started as spontaneous maneuvers between the Great Powers during the Cold War, when the Afghans were unable to accommodate the projected volume of investment. The Afghans were expected to "pick and shovel" work equal to approximately 25–40 percent of a project budget.[39]

But the requirement that the Afghan government was to match every dollar of foreign aid with $0.25–$0.40 of its own placed a heavy burden on state finances. The country is still bankrupt and lacks banking and credit institutions, a stock market, and adequate purchasing power. The task of rebuilding its economy must be financed entirely by the donor community at greater costs than those of the 1950s–1970s.

Creating an attractive image of the donors in this xenophobic country requires highly professional knowledge and sensitivity about the local mentality and prejudices. No stereotypical approach will satisfy needs that extend far beyond economic goals in the Afghan reconstruction.

Notes

For his kind help in my research, I owe great thanks to Professor G. Ezhov whose incredible memory is a true history book of Afghanistan in the 1950s–1970s. The author appreciates the comments and suggestions from John D. Montgomery, Dennis A. Rondinelli, Robert J. Muscat, and Virginia Kosmo.

1. Mountstuart Elphinstone, *Account of the Kingdom of Cabul* (London: Munshiram Manoharial Publishers Private, Limited, 1998) is valuable for historical background.
2. C.U. Aitchinson, *Collection of The Treaties, Engagements and Sanads Relating to India and Neighboring Countries*, vol. XIII (Calcutta: Government of India Central Publication Brunch, 1933), p. 242.
3. Ricard Tapper, *Conflict of Tribe and State in Iran and Afghanistan* (New York: St. Martin's Press, 1983), pp. 235–237.
4. N.M. Gurevich, *The Economic Development of Afghanistan* (Moscow: Nauka, 1966), pp. 137–138 (in Russian).
5. The Durand line is the border between Afghanistan and British India (today Pakistan) established by Anglo-Afghan Treaty in 1893.
6. *Islah*, Kabul, July 31, 1956.
7. See Louis Dupree, *Afghanistan* (Princeton, NJ: Princeton University Press, 1980), p. 479.
8. Afghan–American official relations started in 1936, but the legations were established only in 1942.
9. The operation mission of American International Cooperation Administration (ICA) in Kabul was established in 1951.
10. For a detailed account of the Helmand Valley Project see P. Franck, *Afghanistan Between East and West* (Washington, DC: National Planning Association, 1960), pp. 36–37; Dupree, *Afghanistan*, pp. 499–500, and Donald N. Wilber, *Afghanistan* (New Haven, CT: Hraf Press, 1962), pp. 237–241.
11. The data covers the years 1959–1961, as compiled by G.P. Ezhov, *The Development of Afghan Economy 1956–1961*, No. 51 (Moscow: Institute of Peoples of Asia Special Bulletin, 1965), p. 141 (in Russian).
12. Interview with Georgiy P. Ezhov, former aide to the Soviet economic advisor in Kabul in 1958–1963 and in 1968–1973. Conducted on September 12, 2002.
13. I. Stevens and K. Tarzi, *Economics of Agricultural Production in the Helmand Valley, Afghanistan*, Denver, CO: U.S. Department of the Interior, Bureau of Reclamation, 1965.
14. Franck, op. cit., pp. 43–44.
15. Survey of Progress, 1961–1962 (Kabul: Ministry of Planning, 1963), p. 2.
16. *Afghanistan* (Moscow: Vostok, 2000), p. 80 (in Russian).
17. The Third Five-Year Economic and Social Plan of Afghanistan 1966–1971 (Kabul: Ministry of Planning, 1967), p. 25.
18. Ibid., pp. 41, 46–48.

19. First Seven-Year Economic and Social Development Plan 1355–1361, vol. II (Kabul: Ministry of Planning, 1976), pp. 39–143.
20. Interview with Georgiy P. Ezhov, former aide to the Soviet economic advisor in Kabul in 1958–1963 and in 1968–1973. Conducted on September 9, 2002.
21. Ibid., conducted on September 12, 2002.
22. For instance, *Anis*, January 16, 1960.
23. Franck, op. cit., p. 61.
24. Robert Byron, *The Road to Oxiana* (London: Lehman, 1950), p. 207.
25. People's Democratic Party of Afghanistan (PDPA) was founded in 1965 and was based on an eclectic mixture of democratic, nationalist, and Marxist ideology.
26. The Perspective of Economic and Social Development of Democratic Republic of Afghanistan Through the Year 1367, The Basic Documents of the First DRA Five-Year Economic and Social Development Plan for The Years 1358–1362 (1979/1980–1983/1984) and Prognosis Through the Year 1367 (1988/1989). (Russian translation from Dari), Kabul: Ministry of Planning of the Democratic Republic of Afghanistan, 1358 (1979/1980), vol. II, pp. 4, 8, tables 1, 14.
27. These are estimated figures. By the beginning of the 1990s, the Afghan debt to the Soviet Union reached $4.5 billion of the total $5.5 billion of external debt. *Afghanistan* (Moscow: Vostok, 2000), p. 154 (in Russian); see also *The CIA World Factbook 2002*, accessed on December 15, 2002 at http://www.cia.gov/cia/publications/factbook/geos/af.html.
28. Estimates vary. See *New York Times*, May 4, 1983; *US News and World Report*, #11, 1985, p. 51; *Wall Street Journal*, April 9, 1984; *Congressional Quarterly*, August 4, 1984, p. 103. See also Bob Woodward, *Veil: The Secret Wars of The CIA* (New York: Simon and Schuster, 1987).
29. 1985-$250 million—*Washington Post*, January 13, 1985.
    1986-$470 million—*New York Times*, June 17, 1985.
    1987-$660 million—*Washington Post*, January 3, 1988.
    1988-$1.2 billion—*Izvestia*, September 12, 1988.
    See also Tim Weiner, *Blank Check: The Pentagon Black Budget* (New York: Warner Books, 1991) and George P. Shultz, *Turmoil and Triumph* (New York: Charles Scribner's Sons, 1993).
30. Department of State Bulletin # 2048 (Washington, DC, 1981), p. 22.
31. Department of State Bulletin # 2095, "Afghanistan: Five Years of Occupation" (Washington, DC, 1985), p. 34.
32. Department of State Bulletin # 2144, "Afghanistan: Soviet Occupation and Withdrawal" (Washington, DC, 1989), p. 90.
33. "Recent Developments in U.S. Policy Towards Afghanistan," Hearing Before the Subcommittee on Asian and Pacific Affairs of the Committee on Foreign Affairs, House of Representatives. Congress 102nd, Session 1st, June 20, 1991 (Washington, DC: Government Printing Office, 1993).
34. *Afghanistan* (Moscow: Vostok, 2000), p. 124 (in Russian).
35. For a brief account of the Afghan economy in the 1990s see Barnett Rubin, "The Political Economy of War and Peace in Afghanistan," *World Development*, Vol. 28, No. 10 (2000): pp. 1789–1803.
36. On Taliban economy see Ahmed Rashid, *Taliban: Militant Islam, Oil and Fundamentalism in Central Asia* (New Haven: Yale University Press, 2000), especially chapter 9 (on pipeline plans) through chapter 13.
37. See Vartan, Gregorian, *The Emergence of Modern Afghanistan* (Stanford, CA: Stanford University Press, 1969).
38. Basic Statistics of Afghanistan (Kabul: Ministry of Planning, 1962), p. 5.
39. Franck, op. cit., p. 60.

CHAPTER SIX

LESSONS FROM POST-CONFLICT AID EXPERIENCE

Robert J. Muscat

Reconstruction and Its Defining Characteristics

The international assistance community has had vast experience with helping underdeveloped, often poverty-stricken countries reconstruct their economies after a period of violent conflict. Some development experience has been highly successful. In Thailand, Taiwan, Botswana, and Turkey, for example, foreign aid contributed significantly (although not without setbacks) to economic progress and modernization. The record of post-conflict assistance also includes some successful cases, such as South Korea, Vietnam, Mozambique, and Uganda, which were designed and implemented beyond the template of the European Marshall Plan.

Donor organizations have also experienced failures—where large-scale aid over long periods accomplished little or even contributed to corruption and institutional disintegration. The Democratic Republic of Congo (formerly Zaire) stands out as the worst case, being a corrupt and failed state that received large-scale, Cold War–driven aid for many years. In some countries, such as Sri Lanka, development assistance did little to prevent a slide into internal chaos; and in other situations, such as Rwanda and the East–West Pakistan conflict, aid programs ignored signs of impending conflict or inadvertently exacerbated the problems that led to violent confrontation.

Not surprisingly, given the varied circumstances of geography, culture, political history, and social structure in each society, experience with development assistance and post-conflict reconstruction has yielded much information. Years of systematic evaluation, including individual country case studies and cross-country comparative analyses by aid agencies, as well as independent scholarly research, provide rich literature on the commonalities, lessons, policy recommendations, and the problems that remain unresolved with post-conflict reconstruction.

To some extent, aid programs that address conditions and purposes in post-conflict situations are similar to those commonly faced in "normal," nonconflict circumstances: for example, high infant mortality due to malnutrition and lack of inoculation against infectious diseases; weak education systems and high levels of adult illiteracy; poorly developed and maintained physical infrastructure; deficiencies in government capacities for providing essential services; and a labor force lacking cadres of skilled workers and professionals sufficient for the requirements of modern economic development. Problems that arise from corruption erodes trust in government and discourages foreign investment; causes weaknesses in the legal and judicial framework; creates a substantial need for official development assistance to supplement low levels of domestic saving; and creates a paucity of resources available for public sector investment needs.

In addition to these generic problems, post-conflict aid programs also face a host of social and political difficulties that are the legacies of violent internal conflict in developing countries: decimation of human capital; physical capacity destruction; institutional destruction; distortion or extinction of economic activity; vast areas laced with land mines and unexploded ordnance; psychosocial disabilities and a legacy of distrust and hatred; and armies and militias that need to be disarmed, demobilized, and reabsorbed into the civilian economy. In some instances, the peace accords ending the conflict are designed by external powers and are imposed on reluctant antagonists, some of whom remain determined not to adhere to the provisions on governance and/or reluctant to embark on a course of reconciliation. All these legacies are found in contemporary Afghanistan.

In the face of such legacies, donor agencies have had to deepen their understanding of the consequences of their aid programs, and of prescribing policy advice. Politics and social relationships in post-conflict countries are commonly fragile. Countries that have recently emerged from disruption are at high risk of conflict resumption. The design of post-conflict assistance, as well as the content and management of its component programs and projects, should be tailored to avoid conflict resumption by accommodation of local circumstances and needs. Programs for supporting peace and stability may often be at odds with lessons that have been drawn from "normal" nonconflict development experience. As one World Bank study concluded, it may be folly to apply "conventional wisdoms of development practice" in situations of post-conflict devastation.[1]

It is not sufficient to conceive and implement aid programs within the traditional technical framework. It is not enough, for example, to be concerned that the beneficiaries of specific projects include the poor; that infrastructure projects meet tests of economic feasibility; or that economic policy recommendations are designed to meet macroeconomic requirements. Perhaps a more important consideration is that projects and policies contribute to interethnic toleration, if not reconciliation, or at least do not inadvertently aggravate the already poisoned relationships between former warring groups. A perception of fairness in the distribution of aid-generated benefits between ethnic groups (so-called horizontal equity) is likely to be more essential to sustain peace than is fairness in distribution among the population by income class ("vertical" equity). Where different ethnic groups are concentrated in different regions of a country, it may be necessary to allocate resources to relatively backward ethnogeographic areas where the inherently small returns to investment would otherwise suggest low prioritization. In this and other ways, economic development and sociopolitical stability criteria may need to be blended to produce allocation outcomes that depart from conventional development guidelines.

This chapter examines the objectives that have typically faced post-conflict assistance programs, and reviews lessons pertinent to Afghanistan that the development community has learned from its general post-conflict aid experience concerning program content and process.

Post-Conflict Objectives

In the first few years of all post-conflict aid programs, the overarching objective has been to help sustain peace. In recent years, aid agencies have bypassed their traditional reconstruction mandates to contribute to de-mining, demobilization, and other security-related tasks. Even under these expanded conceptions of what constitutes reconstruction, however, the assistance agencies alone cannot ensure continuing peace. Agencies may only have minimal impact if one or more of the parties to peacemaking are bent on undermining it, especially if such parties resist disarmament. Present circumstances in Afghanistan reiterate that reconstruction aid cannot effectively substitute for support for security, law and order, and political accommodation, or for pressures that must be exercised by international security, diplomatic, and other non-reconstruction actors. Aid may provide incentives to induce non-cooperating parties to move toward accommodation, but to be effective, such measures must be enacted with other kinds of pressures or interventions.

One of the most important post-conflict objectives of aid agencies has been the reconstruction of a ruptured polity. This often, as in Afghanistan today, amounts to creation of a polity based on international norms—rule of law, democracy, human rights, independent judiciary, free press—that are often new to the society in question. In practice, typical peace-cementing programs have comprised such efforts as helping to introduce open and participatory democratic processes; election and political party assistance; technical aid to new legislative bodies; legal drafting; education for judicials; training of journalists and support of independent media; "peace education" and reconciliation processes; and development of "peace curricula" for the school system. According to a recent comprehensive study of aid programs that promote democracy, Thomas Carothers concluded that practitioners were learning about democracy, but that efforts to transplant democratic institutions and democratic political culture into unpromising environments have not been very effective.[2] The introduction of democratic processes may serve to perpetuate the divisions within a conflicted society or may lead to greater disruption. Much depends on whether the party and electoral systems promote cross-ethnic or polarizing politics. From a different perspective, the initial burst of open politics can release and stimulate group antagonisms and fears that were repressed during years of authoritarian control.

In sum, post-conflict assistance programs have generally had five broad, inter-related purposes: sustaining the peace, establishing (or reestablishing) a polity, rebuilding physical capital, rebuilding human capital, and "jump-starting" economic activity and employment. The principal responsibility of post-conflict assistance programs rests with local authorities and political leaders. Donors may succeed relatively easily in rebuilding physical infrastructure. Rebuilding human capital takes more time. Jump-starting an economic recovery, even if sporadic, is almost an automatic result of aid expenditures pouring into a depressed economy.

Ironically, in Afghanistan, one of the major economic policies the new government has been obliged to reintroduce by donors—the suppression of poppy cultivation—may become an economic depressant. The 2002 crop increased over the previous year, providing the only significant income infusion other than aid flows. Aid projects to rehabilitate irrigation systems and to promote substitute crops that might be substitutes for poppies are unlikely to yield rapid results. If suppression of poppy cultivation achieves significant early results, there will be both general depressing economic effects and an increase in the numbers of rural families requiring emergency support. A second, more typical, jump-starting problem has also been recognized in Afghanistan from the beginning, that is, balancing the need for "quick-impact" projects with the need for careful redevelopment planning to avoid large mistakes.[3] Clearly, the needs must be undertaken together. Donors carrying out quick-impact projects must avoid eliminating options or launching irreversible major investments or processes that, if analyzed more carefully, shows the swift initiative to have been flawed.

Creating the basis for sustained economic growth in Afghanistan after stimulating aid flow begins to decline may be more difficult. In other countries, sustained recovery has depended on the outcome of peace and polity-building objectives. The principal responsibility for the latter rests squarely with the local political leaders and on the nature and functioning of their post-conflict governance. In retrospect, viewing the post-conflict effort as a whole, the record is mixed. Government authorities and the donors in the Afghanistan reconstruction effort have the opportunity to benefit from general and specific lessons from prior experiences.

External actors helping to sustain peace and rebuild a war-torn society typically face a wide range of problems and tasks. A list of such tasks, ordered approximately by priority, follows:[4]

1. *Immediate post-settlement tasks*: including providing civilian security; disarming military forces and creating new, apolitical security forces; ensuring survival with food, health care, shelter; addressing needs of the displaced and disaffected, including ex-combatants; jump-starting economic recovery, especially through creating employment; and promoting reconciliation and confidence-building.

2. *Tasks for longer-run peace-building*: including strengthening government capacity; reforming government institutions; strengthening civil society; developing institutions for dispute resolution and the rule of law—the judiciary, ombudsman, human rights, property adjudication; creating mechanisms that address with past abuses; rebuilding social and human capital; and exercising donor flexibility in planning, implementing, and financing, within a time frame as long as ten years.

The actors addressing these tasks are typically numerous, who more or less adopt the specialized roles of a humanitarian, economic, security, diplomatic, or good-offices character, and represent many international and bilateral organizations. Whereas all these organizations may not be present in every post-conflict situation, almost all are operating in Afghanistan. Some of the tasks require joint or coordinated action by organizations with different mandates and capabilities. Although practitioners and scholars have produced much literature on each task, this chapter focuses only on development assistance agencies. Since the reconstruction effort in Afghanistan is still in its initial stages, it is too soon to evaluate overall effectiveness. Instead, the next section will review relevant lessons taken from past post-conflict experiences elsewhere, and relate these connections to the situation in Afghanistan during the early phase of the reconstruction.

The donors clearly face daunting challenges. It may not be readily apparent how their reconstruction programs in health, education, transportation, agriculture, and other sector projects, or how their policy prescriptions for trade, taxation, or privatization, for example, relate to the sociopolitical dynamics of a society just emerging from conflict. The international development practitioners examining these subjects are likely to have little capacity to analyze the sociopolitical consequences of proposed projects and policies. Even when aid agencies attempt to apply lessons from past post-conflict experience to approach a new situation—as the World Bank, U.S. Agency for International Development (USAID), and other organizations in Afghanistan, have—it is essential to exercise caution and discrimination. A period of violent conflict usually represents a sharp discontinuity in a society's history. Lessons drawn from the past may no longer be apt. For example, the point is often made (correctly, e.g., in Bosnia) that the particular society being torn apart in contemporary ethnic conflict was not characterized historically by deep ethnic enmities; instead, the ethnic aspects of the conflict were manipulated by cynical "ethnic entrepreneur" leaders. The historical point is valid, but recent conflicts' legacies of ethnic hatred are the new reality and cannot be ignored by donors anxious to solidify the peace through reconstruction and development.

Afghanistan may represent precisely such a discontinuity. Not surprisingly, Afghans themselves have varying views about the present nature of their society. The issue of ethnic division, for example, sparked important discussion and revealed some fundamental disagreements. Some participants believed that ethnic division was an inherent part of Afghan history and society. Although elites may believe in national unity, others have developed deep feelings of hatred toward Afghans of other ethnicities. Consequently, the prospects of a united Afghanistan seemed dim to these participants. Most participants, however, were adamant that ethnic tensions were the result of foreign entrepreneurs who had fueled intergroup conflicts to achieve their own goals, rather than an inherent part of Afghan society. According to this view, ethnic divisions were a new phenomenon, standing in stark contrast to a history whose ethnicity was not part of the consciousness of most Afghans.[5]

While the political and socioeconomic discontinuities between post- and preconflict Afghanistan are large, the reconstruction programs are not without some significant links to the country's pre-conflict development. Many of the major donors in the current reconstruction effort provided aid to Afghanistan for years prior to Taliban rule, some extended back to the 1950s. Humanitarian programs continued during the Taliban regime, albeit with great difficulty. Aid financing of intercity highways and modern airports was substantial.

The U.S. aid program, for example, included projects in irrigation, agriculture, rural works, basic health services, primary schools, Kabul University, and locust control. The flagship U.S. project—irrigation of the Helmand Valley—was a well-known disappointment. The current U.S. aid program is working on agriculture in the Helmand Valley once again, but within a more modest scope. American assistance to the education sector, in contrast, was generally successful. If donors' institutional memories can be revived, there is a wealth of experience to draw upon regarding dimensions of development that should be less affected by recent discontinuities.

As donors and a new leadership in Afghanistan resume the quest for modernization and development after a long hiatus, it is encouraging to observe early and complete agreement between the donors and the government on basic concepts for the reconstruction process. The donors enthusiastically endorsed the political and economic agenda the Afghan authorities unveiled at a meeting in Kabul in October 2002. It is not remarkable that the agenda reflected outside lessons from recovery and economic transition experiences, and was guided by professionals; the finance minister, Ashraf Ghani, is a former World Bank official described as "the driving force behind the government's efforts to be taken seriously by the donors and international financial institutions."[6] The government's "vision" was based on orthodox principles of transparency and fiscal accountability. The agenda introduced priorities that should serve to organize reconstruction assistance and programs. Needless to say, common guiding concepts between donors and post-conflict governments is indispensable in establishing the legitimacy and credibility of a new regime and in effectively implementing reconstruction programs. Donor adherence to the government's vision will help to assure Afghan "ownership" of the reconstruction program. A perception held by the government and the population that reconstruction is not being designed and imposed by outsiders, has proven to be important for sustaining redevelopment processes.

Another robust lesson that has been drawn from the 50-year history of development assistance is that aid has had "large" effects (e.g., faster growth and poverty reduction) in countries with "sound policies and institutions." The amount of aid also matters; substantial aid (in sound contexts) produces substantial benefits.[7] Thus, concurrence between the Afghan government and the donors on policies is vital. The institutions clearly remain to be created or strengthened. However, moving beyond a broad agreement on strategy and policy coherence to a coordination of actual programs and projects, is less encouraging.

Planning in the year 2001 for post-conflict rehabilitation in Afghanistan had recent precursors. In 1992 and 1993, the United Nations (UN) agencies (working first in Kabul, then forced to decamp in Islamabad) developed an Afghanistan Rehabilitation Strategy of more than 1,000 pages. At that time Afghanistan ranked 171 out of 173 countries in the United Nations Development Program (UNDP) Human Development Index. By then, 15 years of war had already caused one million deaths, 2.5 million people had been maimed and disabled, and the country suffered from vast physical destruction. Irrigation systems were destroyed and forests denuded for fuel wood. The health and education systems were decimated. The effort to create a centrally planned economy had compounded the country's problems. The conflicts following the introduction of this strategy have merely compounded the toll. As a caution against seeing the present situation through rose-colored glasses, it is worth quoting a judgment from the UNDP in 1993 that humanitarian aid provided in the midst of hostilities that year was efficacious in promoting peace:

> The demonstrable success of these rehabilitation programs, many of which lay the groundwork for longer term, sustainable development, should be a signal to the donor community that, even under the dysfunctional Taliban national government, investment in those broad areas of the country that are peaceful can have a significant effect on stability and the peace process itself.[8]

In a second effort to prepare for post-conflict reconstruction, the UN in 1997 led a process (the so-called Strategic Framework for Afghanistan) to achieve policy coherence among the donors. According to one review, the effort was a failure. Aside from reasons related to the circumstances at the time (e.g., Taliban rule, the focus on humanitarian aid), three of the effort's weaknesses are worth citing to foreshadow problems of coherence that continue to characterize the post-Taliban period: "differing conceptions of politics, assistance, and rights within the international community; the project-level focus of the assistance system; and the failure of donors to agree to the creation of a common fund."[9]

Lessons on Program Content and Process

In chapter two, Dennis Rondinelli has reviewed some lessons from development experience that can be applied to possible development options for Afghanistan. In contrast, the lessons presented in this analysis, focus on the content and process of international post-conflict aid. Because it is impossible to summarize the full range of substantive and procedural lessons in evaluation literature, selected lessons that appear particularly salient for the initial aid effort in contemporary Afghanistan, are as follows:

Center Versus Periphery. Aid generally strengthens the central authorities and the specific ministries and officials responsible for funds and projects by adding to the government's budget funds or resources that increase the organization's ability to extend benefits. However, implementation of the aid flow, alone, may not be sufficiently powerful to enhance political power if the authorities have a weak constitutional or political basis for exercising central governance. Mozambique illustrates the former. Bosnia, with the limited powers assigned to the central government under the Dayton accords, illustrates the latter. Aid in Afghanistan should promote the central authority of the state, as well as assist the development of civil society nongovernmental organizations (NGOs), a decentralized public sector, and local governance capabilities. However, international assistance organizations should try to avoid working against strengthening the center by providing resources to local or regional authorities that are not cooperating in good faith with national institution-building.

In practice, such a guideline will have to be applied flexibly. Aid agencies often face the dilemma that denying aid aimed directly at the needy and powerless (because unacceptable authorities rule the potential beneficiaries), commonly hurts the beneficiaries while leaving the rulers unscathed. At this stage, the central government in Afghanistan has little organization or structure extending into the provinces. Not all of the provincial governors currently support the center. Aid project–implementers in the provinces must work with the local authorities and power-holders that exercise de facto jurisdiction. In the experience of one contractor implementing a project in rural areas, no doors would have opened or local cooperation would have materialized, if personal approval had not been obtained from the provincial warlords. When it is known that the flow of aid depends on approval from these local power-holders, it is probably unavoidable that they will share credit for aid benefits or even claim complete credit.

Many aid projects actually operate below the level of provincial authorities. These projects often place resources in the hands of traditional community leaders or empower new civil society leaders as potential political actors. Then, these direct recipients may reinforce the positions of provincial authorities or may undercut them. Even if undercutting seems likely in an area controlled by a warlord who, in effect, is working against stabilization and recovery, the necessary "scaling-up" of civil society organizations is unlikely to be easily or rapidly accomplished.

Assuming that key players and forces in Afghanistan allow the redrafting of the country's constitution, assistance to that process might be the most important contribution that donors could make. In effect, designing the Afghan constitution will be comparable to designing the peace accords that have set the legal foundation in other countries for post-conflict political and governance structures. The distribution of powers between center and periphery and the structures of political parties and the election system will be critical. There is a long history of constitution and organic law formation, and its subsequent national evolution or failure, in multiethnic countries and in federated states. Scholarly analysis of these experiences is extensive. In recent years, the UN, the World Bank, and governments have provided advice, good offices, and in some cases pressures, to the parties negotiating the terms of a peace settlement. A minimal, but critical, contribution by the donors would be to fund technical assistance in constitution-drafting. Assistance with dispute resolution expertise has also proven useful. The donors already provided essential logistical and other support that made the first assembly in Afghanistan, the Loya Jirga, possible.

Donor experience with preparing for elections is also extensive. The overall lesson from Bosnia is that if an agreement is pressed upon unwilling parties, a return to violence or a collapse of the original design might only be avoided as long as a credible international military presence is maintained. A related lesson, suggested by experience in Bosnia and El Salvador, is that the economic aspects of an accord, such as redrafting of the Afghan constitution, should be given sufficient weight as parties and donors focus on political issues (such as the allocation of revenues as a key determinant of the authority and effectiveness of the center). Regardless of which donors take the coordinating "lead" on the political, legal, or economic dimensions of the constitution process, the most valuable technical assistance might come from multiethnic countries like Malaysia, Mauritius, Belgium, and Switzerland that have devised successful basic solutions.

Aid for Governance. Donor programs to rebuild governance and administrative capacity have been central to post-conflict reconstruction. Post-conflict economies share with developing countries a general need to strengthen the government's macroeconomic management capability, including budgeting, expenditure control, public sector investment management, central bank functions, and revenue collection. They also share the need for rule of law, coherent legislation that enhances the legal framework for economic activity, and an effective and independent judiciary. Although a large body of literature offers lessons from aid experience on these subjects, it will suffice to observe that these basic functions of the state have commonly been in much greater disrepair in post-conflict countries. While the urgency is greater, given the potential for recurrence of conflict in states that fail to establish credibility, so is weak governance capacity. Post-conflict Afghanistan faces serious dangers in this regard.

Likewise, many lessons have been learned on the post-conflict rebuilding of a civil service. As useful as these guides are, they should not be applied mechanically. Some lessons may be dysfunctional or counterindicated in Afghanistan, depending on timing and circumstances. A recent review by Beschel emphasizes the importance of affordability and developing a lean and efficient civil service, focusing on the basics of sound administration, especially an employee database, a simple salary system, and basic establishment controls. Lack of local and donor capacities is critical; donors commonly assign personnel with limited country knowledge and then rotate staff to other locations too frequently. Donors need to develop a pay structure sufficient to lure back skilled émigrés without "breaking" the budget or distorting the local labor market. They must also avoid proliferation of ad hoc project management units that are outside of, and competitive with, the government bureaucracy. To start quickly, many donors will set up Project Implementation Units (PIUs) and attract the best and brightest to work exclusively for them. This contributes to the fragmentation of the nascent civil service and reduces the pool of talent available to the new government.[10]

Creating parallel and overlapping institutions also causes confusion and hinders long-term institutional development. Experience suggests the importance of avoiding excessive "projectization" of aid, a practice that creates distortions in the civil service; providing budgetary support instead; and providing aid in a manner that promotes trust and credibility: Public opinion is often fraught with cleavages and distrust, so it is important that reconstruction efforts place a premium on (enhancing) public participation, voice, and transparency. This will help forge domestic political consensus.

Some disregard of these lessons can be seen in Afghanistan already: Aid in the form of budgetary support has been inadequate. The best and the brightest of skilled Afghans are bid away from government service and from local NGOs work by donors. Competition among international agencies and NGOs for skilled nationals is common in the development assistance business. The competition is especially keen in the initial "gearing-up" period when the aid agencies and their implementing NGOs and contractors are under great pressure to launch programs and move money. The need to bid for nationals, both local residents and diaspora expatriates, is particularly strong in countries where relatively exotic languages are spoken.

The early appearance of this competition in Afghanistan again manifests a seemingly insoluble problem. Returning expatriates have been invaluable in many cases (including current Afghanistan) for providing sorely needed, if short-term, capacity to governments bereft of their former skilled cadres. Nevertheless, as Afghanistan demonstrates, the aid system has never resolved the perennial problems of expatriate hire, such as wage inflation; whether expatriates should be paid on an international salary scale or should accept wages lower than international civil servants; and how to train expatriates to work with their less fortunate compatriots (who remained behind during the years of conflict) without condescension.

NGO proliferation is common in the aftermath of conflicts within developing countries. Afghanistan is no exception. Technically qualified international NGOs provide essential implementation capability where domestic capacity has been severely depleted. NGOs are used widely by donor funding agencies that operate solely through intermediaries, fielding a very small staff for administration and oversight. While Afghanistan is certainly benefiting from the plethora of NGOs, the inflow is also causing familiar governance problems. NGO proliferation adds to the complexities of coordination among donors and between donors and government. Coordination is essential to ensure coherence of policies and programs and consistency and orderliness in the operation of aid programs. On program coherence, for example, donors with different concepts of what is appropriate for health sector assistance have provided costly curative services in some post-conflict cases, inconsistent with the preventive, primary healthcare concept that was serving as the model for initial health services restoration. In a common example of operational inconsistency, international NGOs have often competed with local NGOs for staff and funds. Offering higher salaries than the local NGOs can afford, the international ones often have drawn capable local staff away from the local NGOs. The local-staff competition problem arose early in Afghanistan. Some observers believe that the inrush of some international NGOs that lack prior experience in Afghanistan has hurt the efforts of those NGOs that know the country well from years of prior operations there.

Finally, aid may inadvertently favor one group among the antagonistic or rival communities if the host government authorities stacks the central bureaucracy with appointees selected primarily from one or two ethnic groups over others. Alternatively, aid financing for reconstitution of public administration can contribute significantly to post-conflict stability if the government pursues political inclusion through ethnic representation in the civil service and in policy-formation positions. To accommodate inclusion, civil service recruitment (or retention on the rolls) may have to ignore the otherwise preferable criterion of merit alone, and may have to ignore Beschel's recommendation to keep the civil service "lean."

Decentralization. Decentralization is frequently proposed as an inclusion strategy to help shore up the peace. The strategy assumes that local groups will be more inclined to opt for inclusion in the post-conflict polity if they are granted some meaningful powers that would otherwise be held by a distrusted center. Devolution of such powers would also entail the decentralized distribution of aid resources.

Decentralization has been used by several African countries emerging from conflict, including Uganda, Rwanda, Mozambique, and Eritrea. It is an increasingly attractive policy if it addresses some of the causes of the conflict. To the degree that the war was waged by territorially defined ethnic or religious groups, decentralization could facilitate a war-to-peace transition because it would empower those groups and allow them to settle issues such as land control and land reform, local public spending and employment, and local representation. In Uganda, for example, the policy was expected to assist the emergence of tolerance, development, and consensus, leading to social reconciliation in a country that had suffered high levels of conflict and violence for more than 20 years.[11]

Decentralization has long been a favored policy in the international development community. Under normal circumstances, it is expected to promote the emergence of local and community capabilities, thereby increasing the effectiveness of development programs and services that would otherwise be poorly administered by central authorities with weak implementation capabilities. Mechanical application of this lesson, clearly warranted and useful in other contexts, would be problematic in the case of Afghanistan; the center is struggling to establish its legitimacy, and the commitment of regional warlords to the political reconstruction process remains dubious. The problem is compounded by the financial support that some warlords are allegedly receiving for their cooperation in security operations. Once restoring domestic security is no longer critical, administrative decentralization can strengthen the credibility and reach of the center, while conditional decentralization of development funds and operations can serve as an incentive for orderly political behavior and for adhering to centrally defined policy and performance criteria.

The Private Sector. Aid organizations generally favor promoting the private sector. While this objective is sound, aid administrators have learned to be cautious about expecting significant short-term results. First, domestic investment has typically taken a long time to recover after the cessation of conflict. It would be unrealistic to expect private investment (whether local or foreign) to provide a quick and significant stimulus to Afghanistan's economic recovery. Second, if public sector agencies are likely to perform as efficiently as private entities, privatization should be supported with technical assistance, finance, and monitoring, although the process may not be politically neutral or confidence-building. In other countries, cronyism and corruption have often favored supporters and ethnic compatriots of the groups in authority. Third, aid may promote political favoritism if local governments are administering contract awards and project procurement. This was a problem in Bosnia, for example, where some municipal authorities controlled the local expenditure of aid resources to benefit themselves and their close supporters, including individuals who had been accused of ethnic cleansing crimes. Fourth, in a country lacking any real rule of law, channeling resources only to private entities may induce the excluded "government authorities" to employ or threaten violent means, eliminating the resource competition from the private sector. Bosnia experienced this problem, when aid providers accommodated the "authorities" by giving local public corporations some business.[12]

Promoting the private sector and providing opportunities for individuals to obtain training and advanced schooling that will enable them to command relatively high salaries can create a middle class. If a nascent middle class arises from an ascriptive relationship to the authorities controlling and doling out these opportunities, however, it could simply create a patron–client system that renders the beneficiaries beholden to the political elite.

Inclusion and Bridging. Aid programs normally create opportunities for promoting the inclusion of all groups in a post-conflict society and for punishing spoilers by making them ineligible for assistance. Urban rebuilding projects, for example, may include municipalities located in all ethnogeographic areas so that no group is excluded. Social fund projects can spread assistance widely through small-scale projects administered by NGOs or by district authorities and local communities, as are those funded by the World Bank in Afghanistan.

Along with creating opportunities for inclusion, experience with efforts to bridge ethnic and regional divisions and to reduce the salience of ethnicity may be applicable in Afghanistan. In other post-conflict societies, donors promoted nationwide interethnic professional, business, and cultural organizations; designed development projects in areas that overlap ethno-geographic groupings; included elites from all ethnic groups in the processes of reconstruction planning; and published information about aid programs (especially procurement opportunities) widely and in different local languages.

Gender. Gender-targeted programs have become a regular feature of donor assistance, especially in post-conflict countries. Programs to benefit and empower women—such as extending health services to women, including girls in the school system, raising female adult literacy, and supporting women's organizations—are especially appropriate for Afghanistan. Because of the repression of women under the Taliban, these programs have received more media attention than most other aspects of foreign assistance. Such programs are important for both equity and development. However, as has been pointed out in the case of Bosnia, it was the male gender that made the conflict. The socialization of adult males to accommodation and peaceful habits and pursuits may help prevent the recurrence of conflict and should not be neglected in Afghanistan.

Education. The importance of restoring a decimated education system in Afghanistan is beyond debate. Such an effort would, among others, involve school repair and construction, teacher training, vocational and other skills training for adults, provision of textbooks and school materials, and restoration of higher education facilities. One component—adult skills training—yielded mixed results. It has commonly been assumed that providing marketable skills, especially to demobilized soldiers, would contribute to the peace process by enabling these young males to reenter the civilian economy. The same assumption is being applied to Afghanistan, as indicated in part of USAID's description of its education assistance:

> Education is equally important in combating the war economy. The opportunities gained by education are a critical alternative to this culture for young men who have known nothing but conflict for the past two decades... Skills training and functional literacy will productively engage demobilized soldiers and landless poor so that they might find alternative sources of income.[13]

In several post-conflict situations, the programs for training unemployed and demobilized combatants have succeeded in keeping trainees off the streets and away from any remaining military options. Once these short-term programs have been completed, however, the trainees have generally found few employment opportunities in economies marked by slow recovery and extended unemployment. Many newly trained demobilized soldiers have turned to criminal activity, creating a new source of volatility. Failure to develop lasting wage employment, self-employment in microenterprises, or land settlement programs that reintegrate ex-combatants (especially if explicit promises had been offered as an incentive for peace negotiations), has been destabilizing in some cases.

An essential long-run educational task in many post-conflict countries is to replenish human capital by providing a new generation with advanced skills. This can be a costly and time-consuming process, requiring the rebuilding of secondary and university institutions. Many students who possess the necessary academic preparation and language skills may have to attend advanced degree schooling in donor countries; foreign schooling may be unavoidable when professional education cannot be offered immediately in refurbished local universities. Under the World Bank's emergency education project, university faculties and colleges in Afghanistan will be rehabilitated, a promising indication that long-run human capital reconstitution is recognized as an urgent problem.

Psychosocial Disability. Conflicts characterized by deliberate violence to civilians cause long-lasting psychosocial disabilities. While the existence of post-conflict mental health problems have long been recognized, the surprisingly large-scale persistence of these problems has only recently been demonstrated in contemporary interethnic conflicts. Studies of former Bosnian refugees, for instance, have shown a high incidence and persistence of depression among people who have experienced and witnessed torture, murder of family members, rape, the fears and displacements of ethnic cleansing, and other traumas. Although mental health professionals are still developing effective treatment, adjustment assistance has been introduced in several post-conflict countries with widespread mental health problems. Such programs may restore family self-reliance and economic viability and promote community reconciliation. Although post-conflict mental health programs are still emerging, they are being introduced by donors in Afghanistan.[14]

Demobilization and Reintegration. Donors' experience suggests that the disarming, demobilization, and reintegration of ex-combatants are critical processes for sustaining peace accords and for enhancing prospects for economic recovery. Although the processes have varied depending on country circumstances, a few general lessons applicable to Afghanistan have materialized: First, adequate funding through donors is essential. Lacking sufficient donor support for nonmilitary alternatives, ex-combatants in some cases have slipped back into banditry and lawlessness or into renewed combat.[15] The absorption of some ex-combatants into newly created central government military and police forces is one means of reintegrating them with legitimate jobs. In Afghanistan, however, creating competent and professional central security forces is expected to take a long time. Full funding by donors will be critical to the success of these efforts. The cost of security forces will be charged to the government's general funds, and in the interest of transparent governance, should be included as a category under the government's general budget. If the budget continues to be underfunded, security costs could displace government reconstruction and service programs.

The number of soldiers and militia under the control of "local commanders" in Afghanistan is approximately 175,000.[16] A formal and rapid demobilization may not be politically feasible and may, in fact, be undesirable for the reasons outlined earlier. It is worth reiterating a lesson from past experience. In order for programs to reintegrate former combatants into central police and military forces or into the civilian labor force to work, they should be meshed closely with the development of the new security forces and with the creation of allocated job opportunities and associated training and receive full donor funding.

Aid Delivery. The aid flow to post-conflict countries lags well behind the amounts pledged. Conflict resolution is often based on an expectation that the donor community will provide substantial aid for general recovery and for key components (e.g., demobilization) of peace accords. In the immediate wake of the accords, such expectations are usually validated by financial pledges that the donors have made in previous aid mobilization meetings. Too often, however, the actual amount of donor aid flows falls short of expectations. Donors are usually asked (based on a "needs assessment" likely drawn up by the World Bank or the UNDP) to pledge several years' requirements in advance (three years in Afghanistan). During pledging sessions, the recipient government's representatives typically present favored program and policy packages. The success of the initial pledging sessions raises expectations that reconstruction, employment generation, and polity transformation will be launched enthusiastically.

The actual resource flow and the palpable signs of material benefits of peace are commonly slow to emerge—often resulting in a weak economic recovery, lost opportunities to create and strengthen post-conflict governance, and the squandering of donor leverage.[17] These lags often occur because donors lack confidence in the financial or program management systems of the recipient; because of poor physical security (the staffs of NGOs and contractors are generally more willing to accept some personal risk in the field than are staff or headquarters management of development agencies); because donor legislative or budgeting processes often fail to provide full funding of the amounts their governments have pledged in advance; and because of the "business-as-usual" performance by the more sclerotic of the aid bureaucracies.

Unfortunately, Afghanistan appears to be no exception to this problem. In his first address to the UN General Assembly in 2002 (also the first UN address by an Afghan head of state since 1991), President Hamid Karzai described the aid flow as "insufficient considering the generosity of donors at the Tokyo conference, where over $4.5 billion was pledged to support Afghanistan."[18] The actual numbers appear uncertain, due to disarray in the aid reporting system for Afghanistan. What was clear however, and reiterated in the donor meeting in Kabul the following month, was the disparity in the composition of the aid flows that had materialized. The bulk of the funds had gone to the UN and other agencies for their programs, with relatively little allocated to the Afghan government. In addition, funds directed to the UN and other agencies were allocated largely for emergency relief, not reconstruction. With its budget underfunded, the government was reportedly unable to pay salaries. Some police and soldiers resorted to looting and robbery, as a result of being unpaid for months.[19]

To the extent that the donor explanation for lags and allocation patterns are valid—that is, that Afghanistan must achieve a greater degree of security and stability to improve the chances that higher reconstruction flows will accomplish their purposes—the country faces a dilemma. As President Karzai has argued, the promised aid is essential for achieving necessary stability. In other words, post-conflict situations are inherently high in risk for donors. Aid in substantial amounts must be provided to ensure stability that will then, in turn, enhance the environment for further aid in the long run.

Similarly, the composition of this aid is critical. The allocations of cash for general budget support (as opposed to direct project funding that commonly bypasses the post-conflict government) determine the extent to which the government can demonstrate its value and legitimacy to its population, develop its governance capacities, and finance the inclusion of people from the previously warring factions into central military and civil service. The World Bank stepped into the breach in Afghanistan in mid-2002 to shore up the government's underfunded budget requirements. It remains to be seen if the donor community will repeat this mistake in Afghanistan or will learn from past experience.

Aid Volume. Afghanistan will need sustained and substantial external assistance well into the future. Without large sustained aid inflows, there is little chance that economic activity will improve significantly, that peace will bring about tangible increases in incomes, or that drug crops will not be recultivated. As noted earlier, one reason that aid is likely to play a critical role is because Afghanistan is not likely to attract private foreign investment for some time. Even in the heady days of the mid-1990s, when there was a surge of private capital moving into developing countries, a small number of the beneficiary nations received the bulk of the flow. Thus, in 1996 about 15 percent of the world's developing countries received 95 percent of private transfers.[20] As the experience of Bosnia illustrated, post-conflict countries with highly uncertain political prospects are unlikely to receive a reconstruction push from private external capital.

In perhaps ten years on more, Afghanistan will need substantial assistance beyond the amounts already pledged for the immediate future. The $4.5 billion Tokyo pledge is intended to meet needs in the first three years. The World Bank estimates the five-year need at nine billion. Donors have typically pledged large sums for reconstruction to help warring parties to negotiate a settlement and then cement the peace. The initial per capita aid levels in Afghanistan have been far higher than those provided in most developing countries. The willingness of donors to sustain unusually high aid flows as the post-conflict period stretches over numbers of years has varied from one case to another. When the flows decline, it may be a reflection of declining overall donor interest, including a diminishing involvement in many of the processes that comprise a successful war-to-peace transition. It is hoped that the delivery shortfall problem in Afghanistan thus far is merely another case of the common lagging-performance syndrome, and not a harbinger of "aid fatigue."[21]

Aid Management. With foreign aid providing the bulk of the finances available to the government of Afghanistan, any corrupt diversion of public funds or personal aggrandizement based on public sector expenditures, is likely to be seen as misuse of foreign assistance. The corrosive effects on a fragile peace caused by large-scale, blatant corruption has been described in a recent report on Macedonia by the International Crisis Group (ICG): Corruption in Macedonia, especially at high levels, is endemic. It has evolved from passive exploitation to active coercion and has acquired the capacity not only to retard economic progress but also to foster organized crime and, in turn, political and economic instability. The Framework Agreement in August 2001 stopped a rapidly evolving civil war; however, the agreement depends on the development of democratic institutions and a market economy, for its vitality. "The corruption that eats away at the country is in many ways a cross-community, shared enterprise... [I]t also invites outright collusion between ethnic leaders to heighten tensions and plays a substantial role in making the country ripe for conflict. Left to fester and spread, it will continue to wear down Macedonia's tenuous unity and send dangerous ripple effects throughout the Western Balkans."[22]

The report criticizes the donors for naïveté and negligence. By not "cracking down," by hiding behind the mantra of the need for local "ownership," by claiming to address the problem through "capacity building" (passing laws and training officials), and by arguing that the government would cease cooperating in implementation of the peace accords if pushed on corruption, the donors' "failure [to push] undermines the very agreement on which diplomats have concentrated their energies."[23]

It is striking that the corrupt practices have brought the elites of the different Macedonian ethnicities together in collusion. The fact that here the rival ethnic elites are bedfellows in corruption arises from the coalition governance that Macedonia has enjoyed thus far. The ICG report sees no advantage of biethnic corruption over corruption by a single dominant ethnic elite:

> Endemic corruption is a major contributing factor to the centrifugal forces still at work in Macedonia... The [ethnic] division of "turf" functions as a rehearsal for division of territory as politicians cynically present themselves as defenders of the national interest while in fact conspiring with the other side for personal or party enrichment.[24]

In all post-conflict situations characterized by economic destruction and inactivity, the rush of aid programs and money provides opportunities and temptations for self-aggrandizement. To reduce the incentive for corrupt practices, and simultaneously promote efficiency in the civil service as it is reconstituted, a standard donor recommendation is to keep government small and employees relatively well paid.[25] This lesson appears sensible and helpful for constraining pressures on a government's limited general budget funds. On the other hand, as noted earlier, the exigencies of political inclusion may argue for overriding these financial and technical considerations in order to employ and co-opt elites from ethnic groups that would otherwise view their interests as counter to those of the central government. In other words, the standard International Monetary Fund/World Bank advice to keep a civil service slim in the interests of fiscal discipline might be unwise for Afghanistan, a suboptimal policy when considering the need for political inclusion.

As this chapter suggests, it is important to recognize that there are no facile answers to the problems of aid flow and control. To the extent that donors keep tight policy and financial controls in their own hands, there is little scope for encouraging local "ownership" of government processes like budgeting, planning, and service management responsibility. Tight donor control and program and project management are normally necessary because the government's initial implementation and financial control capacities are weak, but hanging onto such controls may delay local institutional development. Aid officials, who are working under great pressure to "move" money, possess strong incentives to manage projects directly rather than through local ministries that own very limited capability. In Afghanistan, there is an obvious tension between donor control and the donors' desire to strengthen the role and credibility of the country's central government. Tight control, and a reluctance to conduct aid operations in areas that are insecure or controlled by unreliable warlords, reduces the risk of exposing aid to leakage and waste. While slow implementation may be the cost, more creditable aid performance is more likely to enable donors to sustain their own domestic support for longer-term assistance.

The trick, as the World Bank recognized when announcing its first public administration project in Afghanistan, is to manage donor control and implementation in a way that simultaneously contributes to the development of domestic capacity:

> There are large amounts of aid beginning to flow into the country but the domestic capacity to administer this is weak. We need to start building this capacity at once, but at the same time agile and transparent arrangements are needed in the interim. These arrangements also need to be set up in a way that facilitates longer-term capacity building.[26]

The arrangements include assistance to build the finance ministry while contracting with international organizations to handle procurement and auditing. Based on prior experience, the World Bank obviously recognizes in Afghanistan the problems of simultaneously facilitating the flow of resources, building domestic capacity, and maintaining transparent controls. It remains to be seen how well these three purposes are harmonized.

The tension between agility and control lies even deeper, reflecting a fundamental dilemma in post-conflict reconstruction and development assistance. Intervening in post-conflict situations is not "business as usual." There are specific and complex issues, which cannot be dealt with adequately through standard approaches and instruments. Stakes, as well as risks, are high, needs are huge, and capacities are limited. Speed is also key, since "peace dividends" are often essential for conflict-affected groups to regain hope and to work toward consolidating stability.[27]

Speed is essential, as the Afghan case illustrates. The problems of refugee resettlement, poverty reduction, restoration of security, building confidence in a weak polity, and extending basic health and education services, requests immediate attention. The "standard approaches and instruments" of international assistance, designed for nonemergency operations, are replete with requirements for careful thought, technically sound design, and prudent management. The post-conflict environment calls for rapid decision-making; design without benefit of reliable numbers; and flexible management to be able to hire, contract, and spend quickly, and to adjust projects expeditiously in response to unexpected hindrances or opportunities on the ground. Particularly for donors that are very risk-averse, these conditions present difficult challenges.

Intensive monitoring and evaluation offer a partial answer to the greater risks of error inherent in rapid response. Given the uncertainties of knowledge and data, and the volatility of the post-conflict social and political environment, aid activities need to be monitored closely and evaluated recurrently. With regular feedback and the accumulation and sharing of field knowledge, aid managers are better able to adjust programs and projects as they proceed. If projects are designed around a process concept rather than a fixed blueprint, adjustments will be easier to make midstream.[28] In addition, "monitoring needs to be much closer and more frequent than can effectively be managed without a well-staffed resident mission."[29] In late 2002, donors like the World Bank and the USAID were still constrained by the small size of their resident staff in Afghanistan due to a combination of security and logistical conditions, including scarcities of housing, office space, and transportation. As these problems ease, donor management presence is likely to grow, enabling these important lessons of post-conflict management and flexibility to be applied in Kabul.

The extent of aid coordination among donors, and between donors and implementing intermediaries, is a major determinant of the effectiveness of aid management. In virtually every case, evaluations of post-conflict programs have pointed to severe problems of coordination of the agencies involved and demanded rationalizing their programs and projects. Different agencies may offer conflicting policy advice to post-conflict governments. They may have conflicting ideas as to priorities and sector strategies. Some donors, in good faith, may finance facilities and training that are inappropriate for the conditions of a country previously unfamiliar to the provider. These dangers are likely to emerge in Afghanistan simply because of the proliferation of donors and implementing organizations.

Some participants as of late 2002 gauged donor coordination in Afghanistan to be unsatisfactory, worse than par for the course in post-conflict situations. One aid official with experience in several other post-conflict countries, described the coordination situation as cumbersome and dysfunctional. As is sometimes true in aid-receiving countries, post-conflict or not, some ad hoc coordination arrangements were developed on the ground despite the poor coordination at the headquarters levels of the donor agencies. For example, by agreement, different donors have taken "lead" positions for different subjects, such as agriculture and law enforcement. Reconstruction of major roads was divided by agreement among different donors. It remains to be seen if these or other arrangements succeed in sorting out a division of responsibilities or of coordination among donors engaged in similar activities. Much "sorting out" apparently needs to be done. Although the UN mission in Kabul has been designated the lead coordinator, it has been unable (at the time of this writing) to restrain the specialized agencies of the UN system from engaging in endemic turf rivalries and competition for project funds in Afghanistan. In one reported case, an Afghan cabinet minister learned about a project to assist his own ministry—designed and funded by one donor—only when the implementing technicians appeared at his ministry office. Other times, donors have provided expertise duplicating that already being provided by another donor. In another circumstance, two donors independently initiated a provincial project for the same purpose and location; when the technicians from the two countries arrived on-site, mutually surprised, they sorted it out immediately, with one set of experts withdrawing by agreement.

In the face of varying donor objectives (especially competitive commercial objectives) and operating procedures, coordination of aid to developing countries has remained problematic for decades.[30] While it has become commonplace for donors to call for coordination under the host government, such an arrangement is seldom feasible in light of government incapacities in immediate post-conflict circumstances.[31] The lead donors in Afghanistan appear to be concerned with such a coordination problem. Experience in a few exceptional post-conflict cases outside of Afghanistan, such as Bosnia, Mozambique, and East Timor provide varied examples of how coordination can be effective if the donors have the will to harmonize their programs.

Notes

1. World Bank, *The World Bank's Experience With Post-Conflict Reconstruction*, Vol. I Synthesis Report (1998): pp. 35–37.
2. Thomas Carothers, *Aiding Democracy Abroad* (Washington, DC: Carnegie Endowment for International Peace, 2000).
3. Conflict Prevention Initiative (CPI), Harvard Program on Humanitarian Policy and Conflict Research, Securing Communities for Reconstruction in Afghanistan; Final Report of the Conflict Prevention Initiative E-Conference, April 29–May 10, 2002, p. 12.
4. Nicole Ball, *Making Peace Work: Lessons for the International Development Community* (Washington, DC: Overseas Research Council, 1996), pp. 7, 17.
5. Conflict Prevention Initiative (CPI), Harvard Program on Humanitarian Policy and Conflict Research, Securing Communities for Reconstruction in Afghanistan; Final Report of the Conflict Prevention Initiative E-Conference, April, 29–May 10, 2002, p. 14.
6. *New York Times*, October 14, 2002, A8.
7. World Bank, *Assessing Aid; What Works, What Doesn't, and Why* (Washington, DC: Oxford University Press, 1998).
8. UNDP, Development Cooperation Report, 1993–1994, published in 1996.
9. Development Assistance Committee of the OECD, "Aid Responses to Afghanistan: Lessons from Previous Evaluations," draft, March 2001, pp. 2–3.
10. Robert P. Beschel, "Rebuilding the Civil Service in a Post-Conflict Setting: Key Issues and Lessons of Experience," No. 1 (March 2002), at <http://lnweb18.worldbank.org/essd/essd.nsf/CPR/CPR1>.
11. Betty Bigombe, Paul Collier, and Nicholas Sambanis, "Policies for Building Post-Conflict Peace," *Journal of African Economies*, Vol. 9, No. 3 (2000): pp. 344–345.
12. Bosnian examples from Human Rights Watch/Helsinki. "The Unindicted: Reaping the Rewards of 'Ethnic Cleansing,'" Vol. 9, No. 1 (Human Rights Watch, January 1997), at <http://www.hrw.org/reports/1997/bosnia/>.

13. *U.S. Agency for International Development: Afghanistan Recovery and Reconstruction Strategy*, pp. 9, 10, at <http://www.usaid.gov/afghanistan/USAID_Afghanistan_Strategy.pdf>.

14. The Afghan Minister of Health participated in a conference in Sarajevo in September/October 2002 at which representatives from health ministries in several developing countries, the World Health Organization, and other UN agencies, reviewed lessons from, and planned future directions for, mental health recovery programs. The conference was conducted by the Harvard Program in Refugee Trauma. In the case of Mali, e.g., following the peace accords of 1992, "the lack of funding resulted in frustration among ex-combatants, a rise in banditry and eventually, by 1994, a collapse into inter-communal conflict that was more intense than the original conflict." Macartan Humphreys, "Economics and Violent Conflict" (Cambridge, MA: Harvard University, February 2003), p. 19, at <http://www.preventconflict.org/portal/economics/Essay.pdf>.

15. The Economist Global Agenda, June 10, 2002, at <http://www.economist.com>.

16. Ibid.

17. The disconnect between pledges and donor performance is examined in the book by Shepard Forman and Stewart Patrick, eds., *Good Intentions: Pledges of Aid for Post-Conflict Recovery* (Boulder, CO: Rienner Publishers, 2000).

18. *Baltimore Sun*, September 13, 2002, p. 26A.

19. *New York Times*, October 14, 2002, p. A8.

20. World Bank, *Assessing Aid; What Works, What Doesn't, and Why*, p. 11.

21. According to the UN Special Representative to Afghanistan, Lakhdar Brahimi, assistance up to late 2002 was insufficient in restoring peace and stability. *New York Times*, October 14, 2002, p. A8.

22. International Crisis Group, "Macedonia's Public Secret: How Corruption Drags the Country Down" (Skopje/Brussels: August 2002), p. i., at <http://www.intl-crisis-group.org/projects/balkans/macedonia/reports/A400739_14082002.pdf>.

23. Ibid., p. i.

24. Ibid., p. 3.

25. Robert P. Beschel. "Rebuilding the Civil Service in a Post-Conflict Setting: Key Issues and Lessons of Experience," p. 4.

26. World Bank Press Release, "Afghanistan: World Bank Approves $10 Million in Grants to Afghanistan for Public Administration," April 4, 2000. Statement by Linda Van Gelder, project team leader.

27. Serge Michailof, Markus Kostner, and Xavier Devictor, "Post-Conflict Recovery in Africa: A Proposed Agenda for the Africa Region," World Bank Discussion Paper, April 2002, p. 15.

28. World Bank, *The World Bank's Experience with Post-Conflict Reconstruction*, p. 19.

29. Ibid., p. xi.

30. For a recent review of the state of aid coordination, see the World Bank study, "The Drive to Partnership: Aid Coordination and the World Bank," November 1999, at <http://wbln0018.worldbank.org/oed/oeddoclib.nsf/0/d9c32ea0d87f7f6e8525685500 70bfbe?OpenDocument>.

31. Many Afghan government ministries have large but completely untrained staff, lack office equipment or telephones, and lack telecommunication connection between Kabul and the rest of the country.

Part 2

Toward a Stable Civil Society

CHAPTER SEVEN

TOWARD THE RULE OF LAW IN AFGHANISTAN: THE CONSTITUTIVE PROCESS

Charles H. Norchi

A fundamental objective of the international community in attempting to reconstruct a war-torn society is to establish conditions under which people can live in human dignity and contribute to a stable and decent public order of the world community. Experience in many countries has shown the value of establishing a "rule of law" through an inclusive regime of rights under a government that is responsive to citizens' demands and claims. In the case of Afghanistan that was to be done by creating a constitution in which the rule of law would replace the oppressive power of the Taliban.[1] The Taliban regime was an exclusive oligarchy that invoked a narrow interpretation of a divinely inspired legal code offering little prospect for a public order of human dignity or for embodying the people's values in institutions that would generate and protect them.

The tradition of creating and adopting a constitution involves a process of authoritative decision-making in which members of a community clarify and implement their common interest.[2] Nonauthoritative decisions are made and enforced through the exercise of naked power without regard to the preferences of the community, and this has been the experience of much of Afghan history. What the Afghan leadership proposed in 2003, with the participation of the world community, was a new constitutive process broadly grounded in authoritative decision. It would be derived from individuals expected to make basic decisions according to the fundamental preferences of the community, implemented through established procedures, and accepted as "law" because they would be the will of the community.

In all communities there are two types of authoritative decision—those that are "constitutive" and those that manifest and sustain the "public order."[3] Constitutive decisions identify those who are to be the established decision-makers. They allocate bases of power, create the structures of authority and community, and specify procedures that must be followed for a legal or lawful decision. This process includes drafting a constitution that would become part of a community's constitutive process that is established, maintained, and changed by politically relevant elites and sustained by the broad participation of the community. From this process, the ongoing decision processes and formal structure that maintain the public order will flow.

This constitutive process was to be the foundation for Afghanistan's twenty-first-century reconstruction. The process is not about a particular document, such as a constitution, nor is it about a particular moment in time such as a Constitutional Loya Jirga. A true constitution reflects the common interest of a people in constituting their public order.[4] Afghanistan has also had its constitutional texts since the early twentieth century. They have been, in fact, more myths than operational codes. But in 2003, for the first time in their history, the Afghan people were to have a conscious opportunity to construct a constitution.

Constitutive Contexts

The constitutive process in Afghanistan emerged from unique historical events. Features of Afghanistan's constitutive history and context that are collectively distinct are crisis, a lack of centrally combined authority and effective control, widespread customary practices that parallel the state, and Islam as both religion and ideology.

On February 20, 1919 Afghanistan's Amir Habibullah was assassinated and succeeded by his youngest son, Amanullah, who proclaimed Afghanistan an independent state. Soon after, his forces crossed the Khyber Pass into India, and when they were repulsed by British forces he signed the Treaty of Rawalpindi. He then turned his attention from the territorial acquisition of Pushtun tribal territory and initiated an extensive internal modernization program that included improving the judiciary and government administration. In 1923 Amanullah promulgated the first Afghan Constitution and oversaw the establishment of courts and the drafting of secular law codes. Following a visit to Europe in 1927 and 1928, he announced reforms directed at traditional customs, including the wearing of the veil. Like Attaturk of Turkey and Reza Shah of Iran, Amanullah wanted to be a modernizer who would bring secular values and opportunities to his people—an ethnic and tribal patchwork largely dwelling amid deserts, steppes, mountains, and valleys. Many of them resisted the new constitution and legal codes imposed from the center. The 1928 tribal uprisings that began in eastern Afghanistan allowed a fundamentalist Tajik bandit to proclaim himself Habibullah II of Afghanistan, to occupy Kabul, and to force Amanullah to flee first to India and then to Europe.[5]

Thus began a trend in independent Afghanistan's constitutive process: a clash between the urban center's exercise of power increasingly based on narrow secular authority, and the power of religious and customary elites in the rest of the country. This tense ebb and flow of authoritative decision and effective control has shaped the "rule of law" in Afghanistan from the times of Amanullah and Zahir Shah to the Marxists and the Taliban. What the new leaders of the twenty-first century sought, with the support of the international community, was a fundamental change in this constitutive process that had too often slipped into the widespread application of sheer power.

The historical failure of the state to consolidate authoritative decision and effective control paralleled reliance upon customary practices and arrangements as the source of law; no counterpart to the Western state-centric model of law existed in such informal institutions. In its place was social custom, religion, and, in Michael Reisman's terms, "microlaw."[6] The rule of law was exercised outside the formal structure of the state. Ethnic groups overlay tribes and both were animated by religious expectations, whose symbols are often manipulated for political ends. The primary customary code was the ancient *Pushtunwali*,[7] a compendium of micro-norms and mechanisms that imposed social control, enabled dispute settlement, and generally guided behavior. Much of that code turns on the value of respect, especially the preservation of honor and the goal of avoiding dishonor. Pushtunwali values have often served to curtail any unacceptable pursuit of power or status within the community by authoritatively signaling the limits. When violated, dishonor falls upon the violator and even his entire family. If ostracized from the tribe, the individual or the family would become more than *persona non grata*; there would also be loss of a collective security system. In rural areas, anyone ostracized would be forced into the Hobbesian world of Afghanistan beyond the tribe.

One customary feature of Pushtunwali, and the larger Afghan society, has also become a feature of formal government structures: the jirga. When meeting on a grand scale it is called a Loya Jirga. Jirgas regulate many facets of Afghan life, ranging from property issues to the regulation of tribal foreign affairs, to relations with the central government in Kabul. The jirga is an assembly or council that renders decisions on particular issues or cases. The latter are binding on all parties to any conflict. Decisions are based on Pushtunwali and Islamic law. The traditional function of the jirga has been the equitable distribution of power in tribal social organization.

The traditional sanction or "control-intention" exercised by a jirga includes ostracism, fines, and the burning of dwellings. As Reisman notes, "The bite of a sanction is a function of the subjective universe of the target and not of the sanctioner. The critical question is not the magnitude of the sanction, but its effect."[8] Throughout Afghanistan, jirgas and their potential sanctioning effects are endowed with greater expectations of authority than formal governmental structures.

It was an emergency Loya Jirga opened in 2003 by the former King Zahir Shah that picked the transitional government of Hamid Karzai and for most Afghans marked the true beginning of the constitutive process. A jirga, for example, will approve and adopt the constitution.[9] The jirga is a revered, traditional, value-creating institution.

Another pervasive Afghan customary practice is the famous blood feud based on revenge, or Badal, involving whole villages and entire tribes all across Afghanistan. Badal as it has been practiced extends to all the kin of a victim and even his entire tribe. Paradoxically, badal is a limitation on violence because it circumscribes the number of potential participants in a feud based on degrees of separation from the originally invoked dishonoring incident. Badal and other properties of local interaction that over centuries emerged as customary law filled a security need in an environment of personal insecurity. Failure of the implementation of the new formal constitution would only enhance popular reliance on such customary practices and associated microlaw.

The religious dimension is critical to Afghanistan's constitutive context. Eighty percent of the population are Sunni practitioners of the Hanafite rite, most of the remaining 20 percent are Shi'a practitioners of the Jaffarite rite. Islam has been the expression of Afghan's common interest in the context of historically distant and weak central governments, and the peoples' primary loyalties to tribe and community. Olivier Roy has noted,

> Religion ... provides the intellectual horizon, the system of values and the code of behavior, even though this may occasionally involve a clash with other codes of conduct, such as the tribal system; it provides the only source of legitimation based

upon universal values ... the social basis of this religion varies according to whether the context within which it exists is tribal, or non-tribal, rural or urban, and in the same way the link between ideology and religion varies according to whether a group is secularized or fundamentalist, traditionalist or reformist.[10]

Those varying religious perspectives have been key factors in Afghanistan's constitutive contexts. As long as Afghanistan has had constitutions, Islam has been a key component.

The Afghan Constitutive Process and the World Community

Violence and custom imbedded in conflicting Afghan identifications, expectations, and demands existing alongside formal lawmaking, made for a constitutive process that was *sui generis*. Most Afghans have experienced a history of personal insecurity or the expectation of violence. The hope was that history would change with the involvement of the international community marked by the December 2002 United Nations-brokered talks at Bonn, Germany.

The participants in the United Nations (UN) talks on Afghanistan concluded an "Agreement on Provisional Arrangements in Afghanistan Pending the Re-establishment of Permanent Government Institutions," on December 5, 2001. It acknowledged "the right of the people of Afghanistan to freely determine their political future in accordance with the principles of Islam, democracy, pluralism and social justice," and set as a goal, "the establishment of a broad-based, gender-sensitive, multi-ethnic and fully representative government."[11] The Bonn Agreement stipulated that achieving the rule of law would be fundamental to reconstructing Afghanistan. The Agreement committed the new Transitional Government of Afghanistan to international legal obligations to which Afghanistan had been a party, and to an interim legal framework based on the Constitution of 1964 in effect during the time of the last king.

King Mohammad Zahir Shah's 1963 Afghan Interim Government had promulgated a constitution that was quite progressive for the Muslim world at the time. A Constitutional Committee prepared a draft while seeking opinions from Afghans across the country. The Committee also looked to the Universal Declaration of Human Rights and the U.S. Bill of Rights for provisions protecting essential freedoms. The king then appointed a 29-person Advisory Committee, including two women, to review the document. Radio and newspapers were used to convey the details to the general population and a Loya Jirga was convened to review and debate the text article by article, thus beginning what Louis Dupree termed Afghanistan's constitutional period.[12] It is a time many Afghans view as peaceful and prosperous, and by invoking the 1964 Constitution the participants in the UN's meeting at Bonn tapped into that collective memory.[13]

The Islamic Transitional State of Afghanistan, a first stage of reconstruction, was inaugurated on December 22, 2001. The former king, Mohammad Zahir Shah, returned to Kabul after 29 years of exile in Rome, and opened an emergency Loya Jirga on June 9, 2002. An assembly of 1,500 Afghans from all over the world streamed into Kabul to select a government, under the protection of American and allied troops. In the fall of 2004 a subsequent Loya Jirga will serve as the constitutional convention for the new state. With a constitution in place, "free and fair elections" can be held to choose a "fully representative government" as mandated by the Bonn Agreement.

The creation of this important institution has become increasingly common across Asia and was mandated by the Bonn Agreement: "The Interim Administration shall, with the assistance of the United Nations, establish an Independent Human Rights Commission, whose responsibilities will include human rights monitoring, investigation of violations of human rights, and development of domestic human rights institutions." While Afghanistan is formally party to the major international human rights instruments and many of those rights might become enshrined in the new Afghan constitution, those rights will need to be translated into positive human rights policies. To that end, the Afghan Independent Human Rights Commission is potentially an indispensable agent.

Unlike the states that have emerged from post-conflict reconstruction in Europe, Afghanistan is situated in a part of the world that lacks a regional human rights institution. Because there is no pan-Asian human rights regime and because the neighborhood experience has been that constitutive and legislative frameworks have promised more than they could deliver, international organizations, governments, and nongovernmental organizations (NGOs) have pressed for the establishment of national human rights commissions. Experiences across Asia indicate that these commissions have been key value-creating institutions. In many instances they have participated more effectively in the process of claims than have courts, and by translating international human rights into a national rule of law they have acquired broad expectations of authority.[14]

The models of these commissions and the functions they perform vary across Asia.[15] Generally, the commissions increase access to rights, promote a human rights culture, appraise the effectiveness of human rights protection, and invoke substandard human rights behavior. Some commissions also participate in the UN human rights system (notably the UN Commission on Human Rights), maintain formal and informal ties to other national commissions, engage international NGOs, and undertake human rights education. Still others have the powers of investigation, which give them standing to sue their own governments on human rights claims and to serve as a formal arena to which individuals and communities can bring claims. Also, in post-conflict situations they may acquire a critical transitional justice role by bringing past human rights violators to justice and eliminating impunity for previous crimes.

The nascent Afghan Independent Human Rights Commission has received early international support from the wider human rights community, including the UN, governments, and NGOs. Its first chair was Ms. Sima Simar, who had been the Minister of Women's Affairs in the Interim Administration. The inaugural Commission consisted of 11 members, including five women; major ethnic groups were represented. It has begun establishing regional offices and receiving complaints, and has delivered public statements urging an environment free of threat and intimidation in public consultations on the draft constitution.

The role of the Afghan Independent Human Rights Commission in the broader life of the emerging national public order has been evolving slowly,[16] but it has received strong impetus by a Presidential Decree of June 2002.[17] The decree endowed the Commission with important transitional justice powers to address past abuses, and to perform a "Truth Commission" function as in other post-conflict zones. This capacity to document crimes against humanity that have been committed in Afghanistan over the past quarter-century is expected to be an enormous contribution to achieving a rule of law based on human dignity. Under the Presidential Decree, the commission would also have the responsibility to ensure that national laws are consistent with international human rights obligations and to advise on Afghanistan's human rights treaty monitoring obligations. Afghans have expressed great hopes for the Commission, in part because it has achieved early visibility and the attention of the international human rights community and donors.

Yet, even with this support and targeted donor assistance the Commission requires intensive capacity-building. An officer of the Office of the United Nations High Commission for Human Rights was seconded to Kabul to help train commission members, and a former member of New Zealand's Human Rights Commission has been assisting the Afghan Commission in organizing its work including establishing systems to process claims. But staff in Kabul and in the regional offices still requires extensive human rights training. An effective capacity-building program would address all functions typically performed by national human rights commissions. This training would include fact-finding; promoting human rights; conducting investigations; prescribing and applying human rights standards; appraising the developing national and regional human rights contexts; and terminating abusive practices and norms. In the early critical years of the Afghan constitutive process, the Independent Human Rights Commission is an institution that can help insure that the rule of law evolves in the service of human dignity. The UN Special Rapporteur on Afghanistan has declared: "The Afghan National Human Rights Commission should be enabled, through the provision of adequate resources, to develop its capacity at an accelerated pace in order to be able to build a progressively more effective role in investigation and monitoring of human rights violations."[18]

The UN has supported the broader constitutive process through a joint support project of the United Nations Assistance Mission to Afghanistan (UNAMA) and United Nations Development Program (UNDP). This included coordinating international technical and financial support through a Constitutional Support Unit. The Afghan Transitional Administration established three institutions to advance the process: the Constitutional Drafting Commission, the Constitutional Commission, and the Constitutional Loya Jirga. The Italian government assumed the bilateral donor lead in supporting constitutional and judicial activities.

Toward a Constitutive Text

President Karzai appointed a nine-member constitutional Drafting Commission on October 5, 2002 with Vice President Professor Naematullah Shahrani serving as chair. The role of the Drafting Commission was to produce a preliminary draft constitution that would then be taken up by the larger Constitutional Commission, consisting of 35 members also appointed by the president. The Commission's role has been to consult with the people of Afghanistan and produce a final draft for submission to the Constitutional Loya Jirga in late 2004. The Loya Jirga would appraise and presumably adopt the constitution.

Of the early constitutive institutions, the work of the Constitutional Commission may be the most critical. Its tasks were to: (1) prepare and publish the draft constitution; (2) facilitate and promote public information on the constitution-making process during the entire period of its work; (3) conduct public consultations in each province of Afghanistan, among Afghan refugees in Iran and Pakistan, and where possible other countries, to solicit the views of Afghans regarding their national aspirations; (4) receive written submissions from individuals and groups of Afghans within and outside the country wishing to contribute to the constitutional process; (5) conduct or commission studies concerning options for the Draft Constitution; (6) prepare a public report analyzing the views of Afghans gathered during public consultations; (7) educate the public on the Draft Constitution by returning to all the provinces of Afghanistan and to the refugee populations in Iran and Pakistan.[19] Thus the Constitutional Commission was tasked with performing key constitutive process functions of intelligence, promotion, and appraisal.

A preliminary draft constitution was completed in the spring of 2003. It proclaimed, "In Afghanistan national sovereignty belongs to the nation and the nation enforces it directly or through its representatives."[20] It is noteworthy that rather than divinely grounding sovereignty, the draft placed sovereignty in the nation and hence the people of Afghanistan. This is a departure from constitutional practice in surrounding countries. In contrast, the 1979 Iranian Constitution had invoked the "exclusive sovereignty of God," and Pakistan's 1973 Constitution proclaimed, "sovereignty over the entire universe belongs to almighty Allah alone."

Under the draft provisions, a president would be head of state and would appoint a prime minister to form the government. The president would be elected by universal suffrage, and would serve as the supreme commander of the armed forces, have the power to declare war, convene Loya Jirgas, and dissolve the National Assembly. Notably, the draft did not stipulate that the president must be a member of a specific Islamic school such as the Hanafi tradition. A National Assembly would be "... the highest legislative organ ... the express of the will of the people and represent the whole nation." Among its powers would be the ratification of international agreements and treaties, the "dispatch of armed forces outside Afghanistan," and granting "[p]ermission for obtaining loans." Voting power would be based on population, so populous provinces with urban areas would have greater influence on national decisions.

The draft constitution provided for a judiciary. Members of the Supreme Court "[s]hould have higher education in the science of law and Islamic jurisprudence." The draft left open the establishment of religious courts with the provision, "[t]he judiciary power is composed of supreme court and other courts whose number is determined by law."[21] The draft document did not entirely ignore long-standing customary mechanisms, as in previous Afghan constitutions it codified the Loya Jirga. Thus, "the Loya Jirga is the highest expression of the will of the people of Afghanistan."[22] The draft also imposed some limits on the use of the jirga. The Loya Jirga would be convened by the president. It could make decisions relating to "independence, national sovereignty, territorial integrity, and high public interests," to "modify commandments of the constitution," and for "other issues stated in this constitution." Membership of the Loya Jirga would consist of: (1) Members of the national assembly; (2) presidents of provincial councils; (3) representatives of the provinces in population on the basis of general, free, secret, and direct elections in accord with law. Where the National Assembly was termed an expression of the will of the Afghan people, in keeping with traditions, the Loya Jirga was termed the highest expression of that will. Although jirgas are regularly held in communities throughout the country, a Loya Jirga for the nation would only be convened in extraordinary circumstances.

Interim Outcomes

The draft constitution of the Islamic Republic of Afghanistan reflected many lofty goals and common demands of individual Afghans who have suffered years of war and misery. It was but a step in the national constitutive process, and hence the question to be resolved was: Would its core values survive as rights and be implemented as policies? Many of the specified goals tracked important values clarified by the world community in the Universal Declaration of Human Rights (UDHR).[23] In Chapter One, entitled "The State," there was a reference to the UDHR, "[T]he state respects the fundamentals of the Charter of the United Nations Organization, honors the Universal Declaration of Human Rights, ..." While the draft respected and honored important sets of international instruments, it did not incorporate them explicitly. However, a range of human dignity values found expression in the draft. The first clause in Chapter One affirmed the "Islamic Republic of Afghanistan as an independent and indivisible state based on principles of social justice." That is not surprising as respect, a key traditional Afghan value, is considered the foundation of social justice. Furthermore Chapter One stated: "The State of Afghanistan is obligated to adopt necessary measures for the purpose of creation of a prosperous and progressive society based on social justice, protection of human dignity, the realization of democracy, and the maintenance of national unity and equality among all the tribes and clans of the country."[24] The phrase "unity and equality among all the tribes" reflects the historical concern of the central government for maintaining order amidst conflicting demands in the provinces.

Not surprisingly, traditional Afghan concepts of rectitude were reflected throughout the document, beginning with the name of the state, "The Islamic Republic of Afghanistan." Chapter One provided "the religion of Afghanistan is the sacred religion of Islam. The followers of other religions are free within the limits of the law in the exercise of their religious rites. In Afghanistan no law contrary to the fundamentals of the sacred religion of Islam, and other values of this constitution can be promulgated."[25] This provision would allow non-Muslim Afghans to practice their religions. While protection of the Islamic faith was a feature throughout the draft constitution, the document was not heavy-handed and appeared to approach the subject with some caution. Thus, "the state adopts necessary measures for the organization and improvement of conditions of mosques, madrasas and religious centers, and the promotion of moral virtues in society." It is unclear whether the term "organization" includes measures of control, in which case this provision is about power as well as rectitude. Also, in keeping with tradition, the text based the official calendar of the country on the hirjat of the Prophet (PHUH[26]) and made Friday a public holiday.

Chapter Two of the text, "The Fundamental Rights and Duties of Citizens," was a broad expression of respect. It proscribed discrimination toward Afghan citizens. It provided that "[t]he citizens of Afghanistan whether female or male are equal before the law and have equal rights and duties regardless of language, tribal and clan affiliation, religion, place of residence and social position." This explicit gender equality in the draft was especially noteworthy. A further clause affirmatively obligated the state to support human dignity: "The state is responsible for respect and safeguarding of human dignity." Other fundamental rights include the right to life; prohibition of torture; presumption of innocence; limitations on extradition to foreign jurisdictions; right to counsel; personal freedom for debtors; and freedom of movement. The draft stated, "freedom of expression is immune from invasion. With the observance of the values stated in this constitution, every Afghan has the right to express his thought by means of speech, writing, or illustration or other means." The phrase "with the observance of values in this constitution" could open the door to restrictive interpretations.

The freedom of assembly and the right to form associations was preserved in the draft. This affection value, on whose basis associations were formed during periods of war and oppression, has been an important Afghan survival strategy. The draft provided that

> [T]he citizens of Afghanistan have the right to form political parties in accord with provisions of the law provided, *inter alia*, The aims and fundamentals of the party do not contradict the fundamentals of Islam, the scriptures, and the values stated in this constitution .... The setting up and activities of the party based on ethnicity, language, religion and province are not permissible.

Enlightenment was also an important traditional value expressed in the draft constitution. Thus, "Education is the right of all citizens of Afghanistan which the state provides freely."[27] There was a provision aimed at educating women: "[T]he state devises and implements effective programs for the purpose of balanced and further development of female education." Also,

> the state devises and implements a unified educational curriculum within the framework of the sacred religion of Islam, national culture, and in accord with scientific method of international standard. The state compiles the curriculum of religious teaching ... The setting up and the administration of general, higher and professional educational studies is the duty of the state. The state also devises effective programs for the promotion of science, culture, literature and the arts.

In a country of vast illiteracy and a minimally educated population, these educational obligations undertaken by the state will be formidable, expensive, and for many years an aspiration. Perhaps by placing that aspiration prominently in the constitution, the government would be better positioned to attract international donor assistance.

The draft also addressed the well-being of its citizens through health care provisions. Chapter Two provided, "The state is obligated to provide the means of prevention and medical treatment and suitable health facilities freely and suitably to all citizens of Afghanistan." Without extensive assistance from the international community, this major goal could not be achieved for many years. In keeping with Afghan tradition, Chapter Two provided that "family is the fundamental pillar of society, and is under the protection of the state. The state takes necessary measures for the maintenance of bodily and spiritual health of family especially of the child and mother and the training of children." What those "measures" would entail is a matter for clarification. The draft document even included an intellectual property protection component: "The state guarantees the royalties of authors, inventors and discoverers and protects scientific researches in all spheres..." This suggests that domestic legislation and enforcement mechanisms to protect copyrights, patents, and trade secrets would eventually be enacted.

The draft constitution contained many references to "law," but the actual allocation of competence for lawmaking was largely unspecified. At points in the draft text it was unclear who would apply the law, or even which law would be applied. A clause under "The Judiciary" read: "On the issues to be decided the courts apply the provisions of this constitution and the laws of the state." However, where would the laws of the state come from? Who would draft them? It should be noted that legal codes previously existed in Afghanistan. There was the Criminal Procedure Code of 1965, the Commercial Code of 1965, the Civil Code of 1976, and the Penal Code of 1976. However as of this writing, no complete set of any of those laws exists in Afghanistan. International agencies, notably the International Development Law Institute in Rome and the U.S-based Consortium for Response to the Afghan Transition, have embarked on the task of tracking down and reassembling texts. The Afghans would then have to locate the codes in their own constitutive process.

Identifying particular schools of jurisprudence as a unique source of law is a matter of controversy. The draft provided, "When there is no provision in the constitution or laws of the state for an issue among the issues to be decided, the courts decide within the limits of this constitution in accord with the Hanafi jurisprudence in a way to maintain justice in the best possible manner." The Hannafi School of jurisprudence is shared by the majority, but not by all Afghans notably the minority Shi'a. The prominence of the Hannafi school in the draft was less than that of the 1964 Constitution. A preferable solution, serving the broader common interest, would be to invoke both schools, or to invoke neither and instead refer to general principles of Islam.

From the beginning, participants in the Afghan constitutive process wrestled with a dilemma that all Muslim state constitutions have had to resolve—achieving a balance between Islam and Western jurisprudence. There have been conflicting demands about the place and priority of religion in a final document. Faruq Wardak, director of the Constitutional Commission said, "Western minded people say mullahs are making the constitution, the fundamentalist elements say the Americans are making our constitution."[28] Hardliners have pressed for Islam as *the only* source of law, moderate Afghans have preferred invoking Islam as *a* source of law. The outcome of these conflicting demands will determine the nature of judicial review in the life of the new state in a manner acceptable to all Afghans.

The threshold for modifying the constitution was high. The document could be amended on the basis of proposals prepared by a commission "composed of members of the government, the Assembly, the Supreme Court, lawyers, and other qualified persons" under presidential edict. The proposal would be approved by a two-thirds majority of a Loya Jirga meeting convened by the president. There would be an exception, however, as "the principle of adherence to the fundamentals of the sacred religion of Islam, the republican order, and the basic rights of citizens is not modified." In many places, the document was specific about termination arrangements by other procedures such as the National Assembly. The text conveyed fears for the future because it was shaped by personal insecurity expectations based on trends in Afghan history. While its drafters could express lofty aspirations, they were compelled to plan for a less than optimistic alternative future.

Planning the Future, Defying the Past

The planned future might not reproduce the relative tranquility of the 1964 Constitutional period. An alternative future could be more similar to the more recent past, as captured in the 1992 Interim Constitution of the Islamic State of Afghanistan. That past still exists in the values shared in certain regions of the country, especially across the southern border in the northwest frontier province of Pakistan.

The 1992 Interim Constitution of the Islamic State of Afghanistan had expressed the values of those who wielded power at the time, a picture far from that of current planners. The text had bridged the Mujahadin to Taliban period, drawing on symbols of rectitude as a primary base of power. Much of the preamble was a statement of the nature of Islam, and stated a central goal: "The Islamic State of Afghanistan earnestly desires and would take practical steps to relieve its oppressed people of the grips of poverty, deprivation, unjustice, unemployment and idleness by perfect implementation of the holy principles of Islam."[29] It highlighted the family as basic unit of society and asserted "... society should esteem the rights, privileges and the high venerable status of women in light of the tenets of the holy religion of Islam." The Constitution also underscored that the state would be a qualified participant in the international community: "[T]he Islamic State of Afghanistan will support, and abide by, the United Nations Charter and the Universal Declaration on Human Rights provided they do not violate and clash with the basic principles of the holy religion of Islam."

The document left no question as to the strong and narrow religious underpinnings of the text. It proclaimed, "the system of the Islamic Sate of Afghanistan will be based on provisions of the Holy Quran (the Command from none but Allah)."[30] Article Three of the document proclaimed,

> [I]n the Islamic State of Afghanistan, laws governing political, social, cultural and economic aspects will be made in conformity with the tenets and principles of Islam. The procedure of legislation and regulation of the life will be made according to the injunctions of the Quran and Sunnah. ... no law and rule should be made and enforced in contravention of the holy religion of Islam.

Islam was the sole source of law: "In the Islamic State of Afghanistan, invitation to virtue—fostering virtue and suppressing vice—is considered the basic duty of the people."[31] That Constitution invoked a specific school of Islamic jurisprudence, not shared by all Afghans. Thus, "[T]he State will perform religious affairs according to the injunctions of the Hanafite creed. The Shariat Courts will decide cases according to the Hanafite creed." Under Chapter Five, the Judiciary, courts were "... bound to follow the principles of justice and to make concrete and fair judgments under the law which are compatible to the Islamic Shariat. Courts are not entitled to follow the laws, which are not compatible to the Islamic Shariat."[32] Freedom of expression and even thought were limited by applications of Islam as interpreted by the ruling elites.

Although never adopted in any participatory process, the Constitution[33] was a compendium of values many of which remain commonly held in Afghanistan. In practice, it was applied by a narrow elite, which operated effectively as an oligarchy. The regime excluded the participation of much of the population, particularly women. Despite certain textual expressions of the respect value grounded in rectitude, the proof was in the application. Edicts banned women from the workforce and proscribed music, television, video, chess, football, and flying kites. Regular Friday lashings, amputations, and executions were held at the Kabul soccer stadium. Instead of drawing on how Islam could help preserve human dignity, through most of the 1990s, Afghan people lived under a regime that cracked the whip in the name of Allah.

To ensure that Afghanistan's rule of law in the future would not repeat its recent past, the new constitutive process was to be grounded in public and inclusive expectations of authority such that the outcome—a constitution—would be a real Afghan operational code rather than a myth. Such a draft constitution would be a candidate for prescription. Those portions that the Constitutional Loya Jirga would adopt as an authoritative and controlling statement for governing the nation would be prescriptive, and would be effective upon obtaining the signature of the president.

The United Nations Special Rapporteur for Human Rights in Afghanistan declared, "the Transitional Administration and the United Nations must make every effort to ensure the participation of all segments of the Afghan population in the transition process so that Afghan ownership can become a reality."[34] Thus, the Afghan Constitutional Commission stated public participation goals:

> The constitutional commissioners will conduct public consultations to ascertain the aspirations, views and recommendations of the Afghans before finalizing a draft of the constitution for submission to the Constitutional Loya Jirga. The consultations will cover over a two-month period and the commissioners will travel to all 32 provinces and to Iran, Pakistan and, where possible, other countries to consult Afghan refugees. They will meet with the public and key figures in the society. The public will be encouraged to submit written memorandum recommending proposals for the Draft Constitution. The commissioners will strive to place those aspirations within a constitutional framework .... To maximize participation and allow in-depth discussions, the commissioners will have separate meetings with homogeneous groups.[35]

Meeting these goals would be critical for the new state.

Participation in the New State

Because a participatory imperative grounds the new Afghan constitutive process, it breaks with the past. Afghanistan is known as a *chaikana*, or teahouse society. In the *chaikanas* stories are told, poetry is read, and information is exchanged. Though buffeted by the onslaughts of Genghis Khan, Alexander the Great, Tamerlane, the Soviet Army, and the Taliban, ideas and expression animated the *chaikanas*. There, and in other community fora, the constitutive process is expected to take root.

What strategies of participation can allow the constitutive process to reflect the Afghan common interest? One approach is to build on community value–based institutions such as consultative jirgas and shuras, but that are fully inclusive of both men and women. Useful experiences would be drawn from the formerly insecure environment in which customary practices rather than formal institutions have been the operational code.

The Afghan Community Forum introduced by United Nations Habitat as a World Bank–supported activity, is an approach that has worked in rural and urban areas since 1994.[36] The UN Habitat team—initially on a mission to provide rehabilitation in urban areas—noted that despite violence and insecurity, people were surviving and it was crucial to understand what people were doing to survive.

In consulting with local people the team found that values of human dignity (such as respect, well-being, wealth, and the sharing of power) emerged and the challenge was to help people translate these values into project outcomes. People believed that no one recognized their human dignity, in part because no one external to the community listened to their needs or asked them what they wanted. However, people believed they had a right to participate in processes that might affect them.

The UN Habitat team relied initially on authorities to organize local people and thus consultation groups consisted of only men and traditional village elders. The problem was rendering the process inclusive. The team built rapport with the traditional representative councils (shuras) and was thus able to gain access to community women. The women formed their own Community Forum to establish means to consult, associate, and deliberate. A process emerged that became self-sustaining and as awareness of activities spread, the men became interested in the community meetings. Thus, the UN Habitat team was successful in reaching out to excluded groups, and found ways of giving them control—the ability to consult and access information, and to take an active role in decisions regarding their development and fulfillment of their own values as defined by the community. This became the foundation for a community constitutive process.

Throughout the 1990s, the community forum experience was repeated in both urban and rural areas. Grassroots participation in the larger governance and policy process was a key aim. The key tasks were to observe and learn from the community decision-process, for example, what outcomes the community achieved, the aspirations and values they sought to maximize, and the functions and structures they required to achieve aspirations and solve their problems. A central lesson of these experiences is that it is critical to work with the community to enhance their own social processes, and this is a foundation for the constitutive process. These lessons demonstrate that the Community Forum is a workable model to advance public participation in the promotion and appraisal phases of the Afghan constitutive process.

An earlier participatory project also had contributed to the constitutive process of pre-Taliban Afghanistan. In 1990, a Policy Sciences Decision Seminar sponsored by the U.S. government was conducted for Afghans associated with the government-in-exile and civil society groups.[37] Using a set of contextually sensitive tools and procedures, participants generated policies and alternative strategies for addressing governance problems in manners consistent with their clarified goals. Some of those participants have been playing significant roles in the post-Taliban constitutive process. Similar to the Afghan Community Forum, a key lesson of the project was that participants were predisposed to drawing on their own base values to achieve public order outcomes that would fulfill human dignity. However, for years their demands for the opportunity and the means to participate were unfulfilled. With the assistance of the international community, and with a range of methods and techniques that have been used to overcome obstacles through Afghanistan's difficult past, opportunities are available to assist Afghans in securing their future.

Afghanistan's Constitutive Process and Beyond

The Afghan constitutive process will continue beyond the Loya Jirga's affirmation of a text. A constitution is a journey, not a moment. Devising a broadly shared prescriptive text is but one phase in the constitutive process; a bigger challenge could be the implementation phase. Techniques for Afghan participation in the continuing constitutive process will be critical to achieve a longer-term outcome that protects the shaping and sharing of values as demanded by the people. The Afghan experience in both formal and customary law has been that the process must respect the people by providing for their demands and claims, and that the people must be able to express their common interests through participation.

The fundamental characteristic of law is that it "is a process of human beings making choices."[38] Yet at the time of this writing, across most of Afghanistan, the conditions that would enable ordinary people to make choices about a process that will affect the life of their nation and their futures, do not exist. The drafters of the Bonn Agreement included this provision:

> Conscious that some time may be required for the new Afghan security and armed forces to be fully constituted and functioning, the participants in the UN Talks on Afghanistan request the United Nations Security Council to consider authorizing the early deployment to Afghanistan of a United Nations mandated force. This force will assist in the maintenance of security for Kabul and its surrounding areas. Such a force could, as appropriate, be progressively expanded to other urban centers and other areas.

In the early stages of the Afghan constitutive process, the multilateral International Security Assistance Force (ISAF) does not patrol beyond Kabul. Many warlords have resurfaced and they have challenged the assertion of any governmental authority. The prevailing problem has been what Afghans call *"tufangsalari,"* or rule by gunmen. In much of the country, regardless of the Bonn Agreement, real power is in the hands of commanders, many of whom waged a *jihad* against the Soviet government. Some served with the post-Soviet mujahidin government, some were former militia leaders of the communist regime, some changed sides, some worked for the Taliban, and some were used by U.S. forces in military operations.[39]

Rule of law and the entire constitutive process depends on disarming, demobilizing, and reintegrating these former combatants. As Dr. Kamal Hossain, United Nations Special Rapporteur for Human Rights in Afghanistan has declared,

> ... the highest priority in the program for restoration of human rights would be to replace the rule of the gun by the rule of law. The consensus expressed by nearly all Afghans, accords the highest priority to security which necessarily connotes establishing an environment for peace, ending past conflicts, respect for human rights and providing for conflict prevention. The opportunity presented by the 1989 withdrawal of Soviet troops for restoring Afghanistan to all of its people was lost. Instead of the multi-ethnic, representative government promised by the Geneva Accords, the international community allowed the country to become an arena of externally supported conflict between warring factions.[40]

As the Afghan constitutive process unfolds what values will be protected? Will they be transformed into positive policies to protect human rights? The process is part of a larger world constitutive process whose central code is the International Bill of Human Rights (the Universal Declaration of Human Rights and the two Covenants). For most of the planet, the values recognized in the International Bill of Human Rights are protected authoritatively.[41] The world community will measure Afghanistan's unfolding constitutive process against those values and the authoritative protection of related claims. Even those constitutional rights and duties inspired by Afghan microlaw must reflect claims authoritatively protected in the wider world. They will be appraised in terms of the international code of human rights and there will be demands to adjust practices inconsistent with international standards.[42]

Afghanistan's constitutive context is unique because of the crises that have affected every value; of the historical inability of the state to combine authority with effective control; of the entrenched customary practices; and of the pervasive religious perspectives that vary in intensity of demand. However, the context has a hopeful dimension—the participation of the world community. As the process continues, there will be historical trends to buck, conditions to fill, and alternatives to avoid. Dr. Kamal Hossain, UN Special Rapporteur declared to the United Nations Human Rights Commission, "The tragic events of September 11 [2001] in an extraordinary way set in motion events presenting once again an opportunity for change. This opportunity has created the Bonn framework for transition. The international community cannot fail this time to fulfill its responsibility. It cannot once again let down the Afghans."[43]

If the Afghans are once again forgotten, the country will probably revert to a crossroads of nations and armies, a land of everyone's way to someplace else. But there is a bleaker alternative future. A sentiment expressed in the *New York Times* by this writer in 1994 may again become relevant: "Afghans are victims of the games superpowers once played: their war was once our war ... if something is not done ... Afghanistan will only produce radical fundamentalists and terrorists. Then surely, some day, Afghanistan will again be our war."[44] That article was entitled "*Whose War is it Now?*"

Notes

The author would like to thank Dawn Greene Norchi and Andrew R. Willard for their views on drafts of this chapter.

1. Ahmed Rashid, *Taliban: Militant Islam, Oil and Fundamentalism in Central Asia* (New Haven, CT: Yale University Press, 2000).
2. Myres S. McDougal and Associates, *Studies in World Public Order* (New Haven, CT: Yale University Press, 1960).
3. Ibid.
4. Charles Howard McIlwain, *Constitutionalism Ancient & Modern* (Ithaca, NY: Cornell University Press, 1947), p. 14.
5. Vincent A. Smith, *The Oxford History of India* (Oxford: The Clarendon Press, 1958).
6. W. Michael Reisman, *Law in Brief Encounters* (New Haven, CT: Yale University Press, 1999).
7. James W. Spain, *The Way of the Pathans* (London: Oxford University Press, 1962).
8. Reisman, *Law in Brief Encounters.*
9. On jirgas in Afghan politics, see Barnett R. Rubin, *The Fragmentation of Afghanistan: State Formation and Collapse in the International System* (New Haven, CT: Yale University Press, 1995); on jirgas in Afghan customary law generally, see Louis Dupree, *Afghanistan* (Princeton, NJ: Princeton University Press, 1980).
10. Olivier Roy, *Islam and Resistance in Afghanistan* (Cambridge: Cambridge University Press, 1986), p. 30.
11. United Nations Agreement on Provisional Arrangements in Afghanistan Pending the Re-establishment of Permanent Government Institutions, Bonn, Germany (December 5, 2001).
12. Dupree, *Afghanistan.*
13. Rubin, *The Fragmentation of Afghanistan.*
14. See Charles H. Norchi, "The National Human Rights Commission of India as a Value-Creating Institution," in John D. Montgomery, ed., *Human Rights: Positive Policies in Asia and the Pacific Rim* (Hollis, NH: Hollis Publishing Company, 1998).
15. See Sonia Cardenas, "National Human Rights Commissions in Asia," in John D. Montgomery and Nathan Glazer, eds., *Sovereignty Under Challenge: How Governments Respond* (New Brunswick, NJ: Transaction Publishers, 2000).
16. See "Afghanistan: Judicial Reform and Transitional Justice," *Report of the International Crisis Group, Asia Report 45* (Kabul, Afghanistan: ICG, January 28, 2003).
17. "Decree of the Presidency of the Interim Administration of Afghanistan on the Establishment of an Afghan Independent Human Rights Commission" (June 2002).
18. Statement of Dr. Kamal Hossain, Special Rapportuer on the Situation of Human Rights in Afghanistan at the Fifty-Eighth Session of the Commission on Human Rights, March 26, 2002.
19. The Constitution-Making Process in Afghanistan, *Report of the Secretariat of the Constitutional Commission of Afghanistan*, Kabul, Afghanistan, March 10, 2003.
20. Preliminary Draft Constitution of the Republic of Afghanistan (March 2003).
21. Preliminary Draft Constitution of the Islamic Republic of Afghanistan (March 2003), Chapter Seven.
22. Preliminary Draft Constitution of the Islamic Republic of Afghanistan (March 2003), Chapter Six.
23. For an analysis of how values are implicitly recognized in the Universal Declaration of Human Rights, see John D. Montgomery, "Human Rights as Universal Values," in Montgomery, ed., *Human Rights.*
24. Preliminary Draft Constitution of the Islamic Republic of Afghanistan (March 2003), Chapter One.

25. Preliminary Draft Constitution of the Islamic Republic of Afghanistan (March 2003), Chapter One.
26. PBUH: Peace Be Upon Him.
27. Preliminary Draft Constitution of the Islamic Republic of Afghanistan (March 2003), Chapter Two.
28. "Afghanistan: Special Report on the New Constitution," IRIN Report, Kabul, Afghanistan, June 2, 2003.
29. "1992 Interim Constitution of the Islamic State of Afghanistan," *The Constitutions of Afghanistan* (Kabul, Afghanistan: Shah M. Book, 2002).
30. Ibid.
31. Ibid.
32. Ibid.
33. The outlined structure of government was unusual. The constitution provided for a Leadership Council as "the highest authority in the affairs of the country." It was to be chaired by the president, and had powers, *inter alia*, to declare war, appoint the prime minister, and oversee foreign relations. In addition, the Constitution provided for a "Council of Jihad." Its responsibilities were "endorsement of laws," "approval or abrogation" of international agreements, and approval of state budgets. The president was to have the power to approve laws and resolutions of the Jihadi Council, but that organ's relationship to other government entities was unclear.
34. Statement of Dr. Kamal Hossain, March 26, 2002.
35. *The Constitution-Making Process in Afghanistan*, Report of the Secretariat of the Constitutional Commission of Afghanistan (Kabul, Afghanistan, March 10, 2003), p. 7.
36. Samantha Reynolds, "UN Habitat Community Forum Report," *Report on Value-Based Participatory Planning, Monitoring and Evaluation* (World Bank Institute: Washington, DC, June 2003).
37. For an appraisal of the Afghan Decision Seminar project in detail, see: Andrew R. Willard and Charles H. Norchi, "The Decision Seminar as an Instrument of Power and Enlightenment," *Political Psychology*, Vol. 14, No. 4 (1993).
38. W. Michael Reisman and Aaron M. Schreiber, *Jurisprudence: Understanding and Shaping Law* (New Haven, CT: New Haven Press, 1987), p. 595.
39. Marin Strmecki, "America's Afghan Imbroglio, Descending Into the Quagmire?" *Strategic Comments* (London: International Institute for Strategic Studies, August 2002).
40. Statement of Dr. Kamal Hossain, March 26, 2002.
41. Montgomery, "Human Rights as Universal Values."
42. Reisman, *Law in Brief Encounters*.
43. Statement of Dr. Kamal Hossain, March 26, 2002.
44. Charles Norchi, "Whose War is it Now?" *New York Times*, March 3, 1994, PA11.

Chapter Eight

Economic Growth and Development Policy in Afghanistan: Lessons from Experience in Developing Countries

Dennis A. Rondinelli

The reconstruction and development of Afghanistan, following decades of internal conflict and external military intervention, pose challenging dilemmas for international assistance organizations and donor countries that have pledged billions of dollars in aid. Economic growth is essential to generate jobs, income, public revenues, and the capital needed to reconstruct the country's destroyed infrastructure. It is needed to provide some sense of security and to stabilize Afghanistan, politically and socially.

Establishing some degree of social and political stability and military security and at least a minimally effective system of governance, are generally recognized as preconditions for stimulating economic growth. International assistance organizations and donor countries seeking to help Afghanistan through a complex and difficult process of reconstruction, and a longer and equally challenging process of sustainable economic development, must carefully sequence and balance short-term programs and policies for establishing the conditions for growth against longer-term policies and programs for sustaining development.

In a comparative analysis of external assistance to six countries—Cambodia, El Salvador, Mozambique, South Africa, the Palestinian Territories, and Bosnia-Herzegovina—during post-conflict periods, Boyce found that donors confronted crucial tensions in each. These included conflicting pressures to pursue timely implementation of recovery efforts versus long-term capacity-building and development, current expenditure versus investment, and elite pacification versus egalitarian growth.[1] The needs assessments guiding donor assistance for economic growth in Afghanistan reflect these same tensions.

The process of stimulating economic growth in Afghanistan is rendered more complex by the difficult conditions under which it must be initiated and sustained. As noted in previous chapters, much of the basic agricultural and manufacturing infrastructure has been destroyed; economic and political institutions have been weakened; and the domestic and international markets for Afghanistan's food supplies, livestock, and manufactured goods have been disrupted or lost. Ethnic and regional tensions still plague a fragmented society, and human capital has deteriorated from years of interrupted education and training, and from the steady decline in health and social services. Governance systems in Afghanistan are still weak and the state's authority barely extends beyond the capital.

This chapter examines the challenges inherent in assisting poor developing countries, especially those ravaged by wars and internal conflicts, to establish functioning economies and to sustain economic growth. The adverse conditions for economic growth in Afghanistan at the beginning of the twenty-first century were perhaps more extreme in their severity than in many other developing countries; but these conditions are neither entirely unique among developing countries nor unfamiliar to the international assistance and nongovernmental organizations (NGOs) that will be helping Afghanistan's government agencies to implement development programs.[2]

As policies and programs for stimulating Afghanistan's economy emerge over the next decade, the lessons of past experience with economic development should be identified and assessed if donor governments, international aid agencies, and NGOs are not to overlook opportunities, repeat mistakes, ignore threats and complexities, and waste resources. Clearly, while not all of the lessons are universally agreed upon, and some may not be applicable in Afghanistan, a significant body of knowledge about stimulating economic growth has been accumulating over the past 50 years.

This review of those lessons focuses on the initial development strategies outlined in the *Preliminary Needs Assessment* for Afghanistan and in the policies set out in the draft *National Development Framework* of the Interim Authority in Afghanistan in 2002. The *Framework*, especially, offers a reference point for what both the Transitional Authority and donor groups are seeking to accomplish. The *Framework* was formulated by ministries of the Interim Authority in consultation with international assistance organizations and identifies high-priority economic growth policies and development programs. The review of economic development experience in this chapter draws on the findings of comparative studies of developing and transitional countries but also includes specific experiences with development programs in individual countries that may offer insights useful in Afghanistan.

Stimulating Economic Development in Afghanistan: Initial Policies and Conditions

Because of its perceived importance for military and political security among Western industrial countries at the beginning of the twenty-first century, donors drafted a detailed and comprehensive needs assessment for the reconstruction and development of Afghanistan with which to solicit external financial aid and launch international assistance programs in 2002. Informed by the *Preliminary Needs Assessment*, the Board of the Afghan Assistance Coordination Authority drafted the *National Development Framework* in consultation with international assistance organizations and obtained the endorsement of the Interim Administration in Afghanistan. The *Framework* provides one of the few official policy statements on how the Transitional Authority views economic development needs in the country.[3]

Afghanistan's policies and donor strategies explicitly recognize that economic reconstruction and development will have to be driven by the private sector, with the state playing a supporting and facilitating role. The *Framework* emphasizes that "the market and the private sector is a more effective instrument of delivering sustained growth than the state," but that the market cannot function effectively without the state's commitment to creating an enabling environment, developing human capital, establishing a rule of law, and implementing systems of accountability and transparency.[4]

The development policy outlined by the Interim Administration rests on three pillars. First, it seeks to use humanitarian assistance and social policy to provide greater security and to develop human capital. Second, it will use external assistance to build the physical infrastructure for a private sector–led, market-driven growth strategy. Third, it will seek sustainable economic growth and social inclusion through a competitive private sector.[5] The *National Development Framework* emphasizes such immediate reconstruction needs such as establishing an effective system of national governance, resettling refugees and combatants, reestablishing the education and vocational training system, ensuring gender equity, providing food aid, addressing serious health and nutrition problems, creating effective national security and police forces, and clearing mines and unexploded ordnance. But it also identifies the components of a longer-term economic growth plan that includes: (1) revitalization of the agricultural sector; (2) reconstruction and expansion of physical infrastructure; (3) private sector development, especially the expansion of small- and medium-sized enterprises; (4) employment creation; (5) rural development; (6) industrial and mining development; and (7) strengthening the government's capacity for policy-making and implementation in ways that sustain a market economy and increase private sector competitiveness in both domestic and international trade and investment.

The third pillar of the strategy addresses economic growth policies most directly and is therefore the primary focus of this chapter. The goal is "creation of sustainable growth in order for a competitive private sector to become the engine of development and the instrument of social inclusion through creation of opportunity."[6] Policies outlined in the *Framework* look to the private sector as the main force for generating and sustaining economic growth. The government sees the private sector as a creator of productivity growth and employment; a contractor for public investment projects; a source of management and technological expertise; a source of investment capital; and a provider of basic services such as health and education and of infrastructure. In the *Framework*, the state's role is to establish the conditions under which the private sector can become the engine of economic growth. The Interim Authority defined the government's responsibility as providing security and the rule of law, property rights, functioning infrastructure, a sound financial system, and a stable macroeconomic environment.

The plan identifies specific immediate and long-term components of an economic growth strategy for Afghanistan. Immediate goals are to establish an efficient financial sector and a reliable payments system; create a transparent investment regime—including procedures for foreign investment approval, company formation and registration, foreign exchange regulation, land ownership, expatriate work permits, import processing, and business operating licenses; expand small- and medium-sized enterprises and access to credit and microfinance; and prevent corruption. The government took steps to create a new currency and to establish Afghanistan as a free-trade zone in 2002. Over the medium term, the Interim

Authority saw the need to reestablish a legal framework for commerce, attract domestic, Afghan diaspora, and foreign direct investment, and recreate foreign markets for tradable goods including agricultural produce, textiles and carpets, and stone, marble, and leather products.

The Economy of Afghanistan

Any economic growth strategy for Afghanistan must clearly recognize the limiting initial conditions under which growth must be stimulated and sustained. In 2002, per capita gross domestic product was estimated to be less than $200. More than half (53 %) of national production consisted of agriculture and forestry products, 28 percent from mining and light industry, and 8 percent from trade. Construction, transport, communications, and services together accounted for 11 percent. Traditional agricultural production—primarily wheat and livestock—had been devastated by war and by three consecutive years of drought. Agricultural land was believed to be heavily mined and irrigation systems to have been widely destroyed. Exports of fruits and nuts, carpets, wool, and cotton products had dropped to less than $235 million while imports grew to about $900 million in 1999, not including the large illegal trafficking in narcotics. The country accumulated more than five billion dollars in debt or 72 percent of GDP. Because of the government's inability to pay, neighboring Uzbekistan cut off electricity to northern Afghanistan in 2002. The government has not been able to pay civil servants on a regular basis. The national budget for 2002–2003 was expected to be only 83 million (in USD) and expenditures were to exceed 460 million (in USD).[7] In mid-2002, the country was facing a 175,000-ton food shortage. Rapid inflation, widespread counterfeiting of the *Afghani*—the national currency—and the circulation of three or more currencies led the Da Afghanistan Bank to issue a new currency in 2002.

Although the national development framework identified many components of a policy for accelerating economic growth, it did not focus on the structure and characteristics of the Afghan economy. Any discussion of economic growth policies must recognize what Pain and Goodhand have described as the three economic systems that operate in Afghanistan simultaneously: (1) the warlord economy, (2) the black-market economy, and (3) the coping or subsistence economy.[8] The warlord economy is run by what Pain and Goodhand call, "conflict entrepreneurs," that is, by regional and local armed commanders and fighters who engage in hostilities not only to protect ethnic and religious values but also, and perhaps primarily, to make profits and accumulate wealth and power. Their economy is based on smuggling consumer goods, minerals, wheat, and opium, informal taxation of both legal and illicit economic activities, arms trading, economic blockades, asset stripping and looting, and illegal currency trading. The warlord economy is primarily exploitive rather than productive. It has disrupted markets, destroyed economic assets, redistributed resources violently, created illegal entitlements, and further impoverished vulnerable groups. In some regions, warlords have driven out the better-educated population, especially those associated with minority ethnic or religious groups.

The black-market economy may be operated in some places by warlords but consists more widely of noncombatant profiteers, traders in illegal goods, cross-border smugglers, poppy farmers and opium dealers, and truck drivers who constitute the "transport mafia." Black-market economy participants benefit from continuing military conflicts, ethnic and religious tensions, and a weak state. The black-market economy thrives in the absence of other legal means of making profits and creating wealth and is primarily diversionary rather than developmental. Participants derive income from unsustainable extraction of natural resources and minerals; smuggling of antiquities, rare animals, and minerals; the flourishing *hawalla* money-order and currency-exchange systems; and the capture and diversion of international aid resources.

The coping economy in which most of the Afghan population participates is characteristic of a subsistence agricultural sector and a weak system of commercial trade. In the coping economy, poor families and communities often exploit the labor of children in order to survive during periods of widespread asset erosion. Those engaged in the coping economy obtain their livelihoods from diverse low-risk activities such as subsistence agriculture, petty trade, and on- and off-farm low-wage labor. Some participants migrate to Pakistan, Iran, or other countries surrounding Afghanistan and remit part of their earnings to dependents back home. Others survive on income redistribution and support through extended family, local ethnic and religious networks, and humanitarian assistance. The coping economy both results from, and reinforces, the lack of secure and steady employment and long-term investment and the deterioration in health and education standards.

Pain and Goodhand point out that these three economies often overlap but create distinctly different incentives and motivations for participants to continue conflicts or seek a more peaceful society, and for maintaining the status quo or exploring new ways of expanding the productive economy. Creating alternative, stable livelihoods and entrepreneurial opportunities in agriculture, trading, services, mining, natural resource development, and small-scale manufacturing, and the acceleration of macroeconomic growth, may be the only ways to lure participants from the warlord and black-market economies into mainstream economic activities and provide those caught in the coping economy with more fruitful opportunities. Creating those opportunities depends not only on achieving reconstruction objectives quickly, but also on laying the foundation for long-term economic growth.

Faced with this challenge, three critical questions confront Afghan and international development organizations seeking to implement the *National Development Framework*: First, how can economic growth be initiated and sustained over the next decade? Second, how can what is now, for all practical purposes, a subsistence economy—driven in part by the raising of poppies and processing of illegal drugs— be transformed into a productive system? Third, what are the essential conditions for the creation and growth of a market-based, private sector–driven economy? International assistance organizations have addressed all three questions in developing countries and post-conflict societies over the past 50 years.

Initiating Economic Growth and Transforming the Afghan Economy

The questions of how to initiate growth and transform subsistence economies into productive ones have been the subjects of continuing controversy and debate in the international assistance community. Some degree of consensus on essential conditions has emerged from experience, although disagreement continues about optimal sequencing and the most effective drivers of change.

Alternative Growth Strategies

Debates have flourished among and within international development organizations about how best to initiate economic growth in subsistence economies, and international assistance organizations have experimented with a wide range of interventions to help poor countries.[9] Two general strategies emerged—a "big push," or "balanced development" strategy that seeks to promote rapidly a comprehensive set of changes simultaneously in order to create the conditions that launch and sustain economic growth, and a "leading sector" strategy that seeks sequential changes in one or two sectors and relies on the creation of lateral linkages and multiplier effects for spreading growth to other sectors of the economy over time.[10]

The big push strategy relies on observations, primarily in advanced economies, that all sectors are interdependent and that massive investment is needed in both the private sector and the public sector simultaneously, in order to trigger economic growth.[11] The interdependence of all sectors implies that investment in only one sector would not stimulate growth throughout the whole economy. The strategy requires investments, mainly in industry, but also concurrently in agriculture, services, infrastructure, education, technology, and health in order to stimulate macroeconomic growth and to provide mutually reinforcing support in all sectors for continued development.[12] The experience with international development over the past 50 years, however, indicates that in most countries, a big push approach is often difficult to launch and the impacts are not always positive.[13] Such an approach relies on macroeconomic growth from rapid industrialization that primarily benefits, at least initially, capital investors and creates dynamics that, theoretically, allow income and wealth to trickle down to middle- and lower-income groups through opportunities for entrepreneurship and employment.[14]

Often, however, the benefits do not trickle down, or do so very slowly, and economies that have used big push approaches have become polarized between a small wealthy elite and a massive poor population.[15] As the United Nations Food and Agriculture Organization (FAO) pointed out in its 50-year assessment of development experience, "such a strategy, based on industry-led growth and often accomplished through an urban bias in fiscal and social policies largely failed, leaving behind vast rural poverty and food insecurity while accelerating problems linked to rapid urbanization."[16]

The other approach, a leading sector strategy, also sees the interdependence of sectors in the economy but asserts that focused investment in one or two key sectors can drive growth in all others to which they are linked. More importantly, leading sector theorists recognize the limited absorptive capacities, governance and administrative capabilities, entrepreneurial and business skills, and access to capital resources in poor countries that are needed to make a big push or balanced development strategy work.[17] Advocates of leading sector strategy argue that resources should be concentrated in one or two sectors of the economy that will generate multiplier effects by creating demand in other sectors, leading to a more equitable distribution of income and wealth. Often the leading sector chosen for investment is agriculture because the majority of the population in poor countries earns its livelihood from farming, petty trading, and services in rural areas.[18] By focusing on agriculture and rural development, economic growth can be stimulated from the bottom-up rather than from the top-down, benefiting those in farming and rural enterprise more quickly and assuring a more equitable distribution of wealth.

Afghanistan's *National Development Framework* does not outline a specific strategy for initiating growth. It does identify a broad set of economic and social reconstruction projects that might imply a big push approach, but it also recognizes that not all of them are likely to be undertaken together at the same time. Implying a more sequential approach, the *Framework* identifies priorities for immediate reconstruction as well as for longer-term development. The plans of international assistance organizations seem to recognize even more clearly that the existing conditions in Afghanistan and the experience with economic development in other poor and war-torn countries suggest that growth must be initiated in the agricultural and rural sectors. More than 80 percent of the population in Afghanistan derives its livelihood from agriculture, and reestablishing commercial farming and exporting of wheat and grains, fruits, and vegetables, strengthening pastoral and animal husbandry, and developing sustainable forestry are, and will likely remain, the most realistic foundations for initiating equitable economic growth in Afghanistan.

Agricultural and Rural Development as Leading Sectors

Although the *National Development Framework* does not specify a leading sector strategy for stimulating growth, much of the *Framework* and the *Preliminary Needs Assessment* focuses on the reconstruction and development of agriculture and rural areas. Of special importance, especially in drawing Afghans out of the warlord and black-market economies, will be the transformation of agriculture from subsistence to commercial activities, finding farm and nonfarm employment and entrepreneurial activities that offer reliable incomes and livelihoods, and resettling ex-combatants and refugees in communities with viable economic bases.

All the development strategies proposed for Afghanistan recognize that the agricultural sector was devastated during years of conflict and that severe droughts have wiped out crops, livestock, and the resources needed to stimulate food production. Afghanistan's *National Development Framework* sees the objective in the agricultural sector "to enable the farmer to respond to the domestic and international market through better knowledge, tools and linkages with the market."[19] The policy also identifies reconstruction and development of rural and urban infrastructure as preconditions for reestablishing commercial agriculture and meeting the food needs of an undernourished population.

The FAO's assessment of the 50-years experience with economic development led it to conclude, "development strategies that emphasize staple food production have proven to be cost effective in providing the poor with entitlements to food. For most of the undernourished who live in rural areas, extra employment and income derived from staple food production has been—and will continue to be—the key to enhanced food entitlements."[20] FAO's experience with reconstructing and developing the agricultural sector in countries recovering from conflicts—Nicaragua, El Salvador, Guatemala, and Colombia in Latin America; Angola, Burundi, the Congo, Ethiopia, Mozambique, Somalia, and the Sudan in Africa; Sri Lanka and Cambodia in Southeast Asia; and Algeria and Iraq in West Asia, for example— indicates that, in these situations, a focus on agricultural and rural development not only stimulates economic growth and improves food security, but can also reduce the risks of future conflict.

In their extensive review of the process of economic growth in Asian countries, Rosegrant and Hazell document the crucial role that agriculture has played in economic transformation since the 1960s.[21] As a growing sector, agriculture created demand for inputs supplied by nonfarm enterprises, provided materials for processing and distribution, and stimulated demand for tools, equipment, and modern inputs such as improved seeds and fertilizers. As farm household income increased, more people gained access to education, health services, and consumer goods. The Asian Development Bank's (ADB) experience in poor countries of South and Southeast Asia brought it to a similar conclusion, that "agricultural growth is a prerequisite for economic development and rural development in particular" and for reducing poverty and improving the quality of life in rural areas.[22] Recent experience in the Central Asian countries of Kazakhstan, the Kyrgyz Republic, Tajikistan, Turkmenistan, and Uzbekistan indicates that the slow progress in stimulating agricultural development and improving food policy in those countries, and the resulting stagnation in the national economy, places those countries in danger of long-term impoverishment.[23]

The ADB's review of agricultural and rural development experiences both in war-torn countries such as Laos, Cambodia, and Sri Lanka and in poor developing countries such as Pakistan, India, and Indonesia, identifies five conditions for the success of a growth policy initiated through agricultural and rural development that may prove to be useful in Afghanistan. First, the agricultural growth strategy must be equitable so that large numbers of rural residents obtain increased purchasing power from agricultural and related activities. Second, agricultural growth depends on well-developed infrastructure to link farms with nonagricultural sectors. Third, strong rural financial institutions are needed to mobilize resources and allocate them efficiently to promote a wide array of productive activities. Fourth, investment in rural education and human capital is needed to prepare rural workers to participate in nonfarm employment. Fifth, as the agricultural sector grows and food security problems abate, countries must move quickly toward market liberalization, and trade and investment promotion.

Lessons of experience in poor countries in South and Southeast Asia and war-torn countries in Africa may also be applicable in Afghanistan. They indicate that gradually, a package of agricultural and rural development inputs must be provided in order to transform subsistence activities into more productive ones. Drawing on the experience of international assistance organizations, the Interim Administration recognized that in order to stimulate growth in agriculture, development programs would have to focus on provision of seeds, fertilizers, information and techniques of dry-land cropping, affordable credit, more modern agricultural tools, stronger agricultural research and access to land, land registry, and dispute settlement. Rural roads and market facilities would have to be rebuilt and linked to infrastructure systems that would allow easier distribution of inputs and marketing of harvested crops and livestock. The livestock of nomadic groups and settled pastoralists were heavily destroyed by recent prolonged wars and droughts, and reconstruction and development policies call for creating modern methods of livestock raising to stimulate growth in the sector. Afghanistan's development policy will be to reduce the country's vulnerability to drought by expanding the availability and distribution of inputs, repairing rural infrastructure, expanding existing small-scale irrigation facilities, and encouraging water conservation.[24]

Experience in Africa, Latin America, and Asia found that success in developing agriculture and commercializing food production depends particularly on strengthening marketing and distribution institutions.[25] Marketing systems include the organizations, processes, and behaviors for transferring raw materials to producers and products to consumers. Within enterprises, the market system encompasses research and product development, design, and testing in order to meet the needs of consumers. The marketing system involves processes that not only tailor products to consumer demands, but also help enterprises to price products competitively, promote their sale through advertising, distribute products efficiently and effectively through wholesalers and retailers, and service products after they are sold.

Successful international development projects in poor countries of Africa and Asia also have strengthened essential components of the marketing system, including market facilities and supporting infrastructure such as roads, ports, and storage and transfer facilities, as well as adequate communications and transportation services.[26] They have expanded distribution systems—collecting-wholesale, distributing-wholesale—and have expanded retail outlets and organizations that provide marketing information and advertising. Financial and credit institutions and marketing education and training organizations were needed to facilitate the exchange of goods and services; consumer education and protection associations and organizations that develop new technologies and facilitate their transformation into commercial products were essential for improving the efficiency of marketing and distribution. Finally, a system of commercial regulations that provided guidelines and parameters for marketing goods and services have helped prevent fraud and consumer abuse.

Studies of agricultural trade in Benin and Malawi show that projects that help rural traders improve their operations can also contribute to agricultural sector growth. In poor countries, the largest transaction costs of traders are often in search and transport. Policy interventions that help organize brokers and traders into commodity exchanges, improve grading and quality certification, and make it possible for larger quantities of crops to be pooled for transport and storage, increase the efficiency of the system. In Benin and Malawi, benefits to traders and farmers resulted from increasing the traders' asset base, reducing transaction risk, promoting more sophisticated business practices, and reducing the physical aspects of marketing costs.[27]

Based on experience in other poor and war-torn countries, international assistance organizations have found that providing farmers, pastoralists, and nonfarm entrepreneurs with access to credit is vital to stimulate agricultural and rural development. Analyses of successful credit programs that played a crucial role in the economic growth of China, India, Japan, and South Korea from the 1960s through the 1980s reveal some lessons that might be useful in establishing credit for Afghanistan's agricultural and rural nonfarm enterprises.[28] The most successful credit programs were small, focused narrowly, and limited in duration. They were based on clear and objective criteria that were relatively easy to monitor. They gave preference to people with good prospects for reliable repayment. The programs were financed by long-term funds to prevent inflation and macroeconomic instability. The subsidies provided through credit were kept low to minimize distortion of incentives and the tax on financial intermediation, and were aimed at achieving positive externalities, rather than aiding economically declining segments of the agricultural sector. In the nonfarm rural sector, credit was channeled to activities that promoted the manufacturing of export products.

International organizations' experience indicates that revitalizing the agricultural and rural sectors in Afghanistan will require substantial investment in physical infrastructure. In India, Indonesia, and Bangladesh, for example, the extension of rural electrification systems helped subsistence farmers increase production, adopt electrical pumps to irrigate crops, and reduce their dependence on rainfall; it expanded off-farm employment opportunities in village enterprises; and increased handicraft production.[29] Rural irrigation infrastructure in Ecuador decreased household vulnerability, increased food security, and expanded opportunities for women to earn income as irrigators. In Bangladesh, rural irrigation increased poor farmers' access to credit, disseminated knowledge of how to increase productivity, and opened new marketing opportunities.[30]

Rural road projects have helped to stimulate economic growth in the agricultural and rural nonfarm sectors and to expand opportunities for rural residents. In Ghana, rural road rehabilitation allowed farmers to obtain higher prices for their crops by selling directly in local markets, rather than relying on middlemen and enabled shopkeepers to bring goods to rural villages less expensively.[31] In Vietnam, improvements in rural roads and the provision of greater access to rural credit gave farmers the opportunity to reinvest in fertilizer, purchase livestock, and meet basic needs.[32] The task facing development organizations in Afghanistan will be making efficient decisions about the types of infrastructure to provide, where to provide it, how to deliver it, and which level of government should be responsible for providing it if it must be delivered through the public sector. The World Bank notes that it is important to apply commercial principles of operation, broaden competition for suppliers to compete in the market, involve users in infrastructure planning activities, and find the most effective and efficient options for ownership and provision.[33] Those options include public ownership and operation by a public enterprise or government agency; public ownership with operation contracted to the private sector; private ownership and operation with government regulation; or community and user provision. The public and private sectors in Afghanistan will have to develop institutional capacity to work together in planning, designing, building, financing, and operating infrastructure in order to stimulate economic growth.

Finally, international experience with agricultural and rural development in poor and war-torn countries underlines the crucial role that the NGOs and civil society organizations play in stimulating and sustaining growth. Although markets can be efficient mechanisms for allocating resources and delivering goods and services, some groups in society at some periods of time are excluded from or are at a disadvantage in market transactions. Civil institutions can help these groups overcome their market weaknesses. In Burkina Faso, service–asset management groups helped to reduce poverty and inequality by collectively managing community assets such as water and building solidarity within villages and rural towns.[34] In rural Bolivia, community-initiated organizations—agrarian syndicates—were established as collective means of managing local resources. They helped to increase household income, provide economic opportunities for rural women, and improve family welfare and consumption.[35] Through these and more than 60 other types of local organizations and associations, Bolivian farmers and their families share information, reduce the kinds of exploitive or diversionary behaviors seen in warlord and black-market economies, and allow better collective decision-making about economic and social issues.

In Afghanistan's neighbor, Iran, a wide variety of cooperatives and community-based organizations, in which women play an important role, have emerged to address the needs of the rural poor.[36] Production cooperatives for farmers, fruit growers, and livestock raisers help farmers obtain inputs, market products, harvest crops, and process animals for market. Cultivation cooperatives share work related to seeding and to harvesting crops, processing output, and making food products based on the crops grown by members. Trade and credit cooperatives provide interest-free loans based on goodwill and local management of funds. Service delivery cooperatives fulfill philanthropic and charitable work. All the cooperatives contribute in some way that either reduces the impacts of rural poverty or increases the productivity of agricultural and nonfarm enterprises.

Expanding Jobs and Increasing Income Through Small-Enterprise Development

Donors and the government face two other critical tasks in promoting economic growth in Afghanistan. One is expanding job opportunities and sources of income for demobilized combatants and returning migrants, and the other is creating alternative sources of income for those engaged in the warlord, black-market, and coping economies. The International Labor Office's (ILO) experiences in Mozambique, Liberia, the Congo, Sri Lanka, Sierra Leone, and other war-torn countries, led it to conclude that the employment options in the years following the cessation of conflict are limited for ex-combatants and that those who are reintegrated find employment most often in micro- and small-enterprises.[37]

Projects targeted especially to ex-combatants worked well in Mozambique in providing entrepreneurship and job-skill training, but in Central American countries and in Cambodia they were less effective than enrolling former fighters in mainstream retraining programs. Although ex-combatants needed vocational training, skills in basic business practices, and literacy, the ILO concluded that "special courses for ex-combatants exclusively should be avoided" because the programs tended to disappear after external funding ended. Integration of ex-combatants into ongoing government programs for skill development aimed at the general population increased the probability that those programs would be more effective in reaching ex-fighters. Retraining programs provided in mosques, churches, and temples were often more effective for demobilized fighters who could not return to their villages or homes. Relocated or migrant ex-combatants needed assistance with housing, land, medical care, and credit as well as psychological assistance to overcome mental trauma.[38]

The World Bank's successful programs with reintegrating ex-combatants into the economy in postwar Mozambique concentrated on informal sector apprenticeship training and providing grants to master craftsmen and to small- and micro-enterprise employers that included up to a six months' salary equivalent and materials. The grants were provided as an incentive for small business owners to hire and teach ex-combatant apprentices to learn both technical and business skills.[39] The apprenticeship program moved training closest to the point of employment. Sustaining the retraining and employment programs for ex-combatants in Mozambique was closely linked to access to markets, transport, and credit. The program also worked to wean its beneficiaries off of grant dependency quickly so that they developed a self-reliance mentality. One lesson of the World Bank's experience in postwar Mozambique seems especially appropriate for Afghanistan. "During the transition from war to peace," the World Bank's evaluation reported, "given the weak state of local institutions, the use of NGOs, community-based groups, and other private sector intermediaries to assist implementation while simultaneously building counterpart capacity is a critically important strategy."[40]

The experience of the United Nations (UN) with expanding small enterprises and increasing their ability to generate jobs suggests that success depends ultimately on effective national economic growth policies. Assessments of UN programs found that governments in developing countries must implement reforms that allow markets to expand and operate more efficiently, including effective fiscal and monetary policies, legislation that offers investment incentives, efficient market mechanisms and competitive practices, and appropriate pricing policies for basic commodities and services. Success also depends on the ability of government to enact and effectively implement incentive-oriented wage policies and merit reward systems, policies for establishing foreign exchange rates and allocating foreign exchange, and tax and incentive programs to encourage domestic saving and develop financial markets.[41]

Moreover, demand-side policies that increase the purchasing power and income of consumers of informal sector products; expand subcontracting and piece-rate work between formal and informal sector firms; and give small firms equal footing in public procurement, can substantially assist small business development. The World Bank's experience in developing countries suggests that supply-side policies are also crucial.[42] Providing credit for operating small- and micro-enterprises; training informal sector owners and workers in better management practices; creating trade organizations and cooperatives to promote the interests of small enterprises both in procuring supplies and in selling their products; developing technologies used by informal sector firms; and improving working conditions for informal sector participants all enhance the prospects for small-enterprise expansion. Supply-side and demand-oriented policies must complement and reinforce each other. Public investment in urban infrastructure, public services, and human capital (through health and education programs) also creates conditions that allow small enterprises to operate more efficiently.

In Afghanistan, the government will have to maintain a careful balance between policies that create a strong legal environment for small-business expansion and over-regulation of the private sector. The experience in many poor countries is that government policies and regulations become one of the most serious obstacles to small-enterprise expansion.[43] In many developing countries, registering small enterprises can take months or years because of complex bureaucratic procedures or because of nontransparent rules and regulations. During much of the 1980s and 1990s, many of those engaged in informal sector activities in Indonesia, for example, tried to stabilize their customer relationships and offer a sufficient variety of goods to attract new customers, but many could not afford the risks involved in expanding their businesses because of difficulties in obtaining permits or licenses to operate in a fixed location, getting access to cheap credit, and obtaining supplies.[44]

Assistance programs to small enterprises in some poor countries in Africa had mixed results because they were poorly designed and ineffectively implemented.[45] Lessons from more successful programs can, however, provide guidelines for formulating public and private sector policies and managing small-enterprise promotion programs more effectively in Afghanistan. The U.S. Agency for International Development's (USAID) assessments of small-enterprise development projects found that successful programs had a number of common characteristics.[46] Most operated under the strong leadership of a project director who was committed to helping small-scale entrepreneurs raise their incomes. The programs were equipped with concerned and dedicated staff interested in the success of their clients' businesses. Program managers and staff had a developmental philosophy that respected the clients' plans, knowledge, and ideas and that sought to facilitate them. Good programs usually had community-based selection processes that drew on local people's knowledge of the applicants' reliability and character. They reached a reasonable number of clients without creating exhaustive and cumbersome procedures. Managers of these programs avoided paternalism and excessive formality and kept their procedures flexible. For example, they were willing to change to meet clients' needs as they discovered them. Finally, in nearly all of these programs, the managers were concerned about keeping transaction costs low.

Although the capital costs of starting and operating a small-scale enterprise are relatively low in most transitional and developing countries, entrepreneurs have great difficulty obtaining loans from financial institutions. Most rely on personal savings, loans from family or friends, or credit from private moneylenders at high interest rates. Cheap and reliable credit is essential for entrepreneurs to expand. Where governments and the private sector have provided loans to micro-entrepreneurs, they have been used to pay off moneylenders charging high rates of interest, reduce time-consuming trips to purchase small amounts of raw materials or supplies, reach new markets, improve service quality, and start additional businesses. Given the limited success of subsidized credit programs in reaching small-enterprise operators who want to expand, however, those seeking to extend credit in Afghanistan should reassess this form of assistance and explore alternatives. Options include expanding the numbers and quality of banks, financial cooperatives, and other private lending institutions, and helping commercial financial institutions to meet the credit needs of small enterprises. USAID's experience in developing countries suggests that credit programs for small enterprises tend to be more successful when they are responsive to both clients' and lenders' objectives; when beneficiaries are selected on the basis of realistic assessments of the enterprises' viability; and when loan criteria ensure access to credit by women and business operators with little formal collateral. Credit programs are more successful when loans are made at market interest rates, dispersed initially in small amounts for working capital, and increased incrementally based on the borrowers' records of repayment.[47]

The ability of governments to train and educate entrepreneurs has been limited in most poor countries and is likely to be so in Afghanistan. The experience of private organizations in helping to establish training programs for small-enterprise owners and government extension staff involved in assisting entrepreneurs has been more impressive. In Brazil, for example, a private industry organization—the Confedaraçao Nacional da Industría (CNI)—established several programs to assist small- and medium-scale industrial enterprises.[48] These programs provided management development and training for consultants and advisors who worked with small- and medium-sized industries through short courses, seminars, and special meetings. They arranged problem-solving workshops with representatives of larger companies in the industries in which small enterprises had made an important contribution to production. They offered technical advice and information to groups of small enterprises in the same sector and disseminated information on quality control, productivity, technological innovation, and new processes and products. The industry association worked closely with government agencies promoting small-scale enterprise. The paucity of large companies and of private industry organizations in Afghanistan will require recruiting these organizations from other countries surrounding Afghanistan or from Middle Eastern or South Asian countries.

The limited success of government technical assistance programs suggests opportunities for improving performance of small enterprises in Afghanistan by contracting with private institutions or NGOs to provide extension services, run technology and management service centers, and work with cooperatives on improving production and marketing operations. Evaluations of internationally funded assistance programs have found that they were more successful when they provided only a single "missing ingredient"—such as procurement or marketing assistance or common equipment repair and service facilities—to enterprises that could otherwise operate effectively. Successful programs offered assistance that was based on surveys of effective demand and was industry- and task-specific.[49]

Establishing Conditions for Private Sector–Led Economic Growth

The Interim and Transitional Authorities in Afghanistan clearly recognize in the *National Development Framework*, the importance of policy reforms and of creating national and local institutions to support a market-driven, private sector–led economic growth strategy. Experience elsewhere indicates the need for macroeconomic adjustment to encourage the development of market mechanisms. Rosa and Foley point out that strong economic growth in El Salvador in the post-conflict period contributed significantly to the government's ability to implement the Peace Accords during the 1990s.[50] Strong inflows of foreign aid and private capital, along with some international debt forgiveness and exchange rate reforms, helped to stabilize El Salvador's economy and mobilize resources for rapid reconstruction.

Although many cross-country studies in developing countries confirm that promoting a set of policies that establish macroeconomic stability, open the economy to international trade, promote education, and strengthen the rule of law have contributed substantially to fostering economic growth, evidence is inconclusive about how much each of those individual policies affected economic growth and poverty reduction.[51] Studies of 25 transition countries during the 1990s concluded that economic reforms and political liberalization were more powerful forces in stimulating economic growth than changes in economic structures, but that over time the institutional changes resulting from policy reforms had important impacts.[52]

The World Bank's experience in promoting economic growth and transformation in poor countries indicates that policies must focus on four sets of interventions: (1) creating a stable macroeconomy, (2) establishing a competitive microeconomy, (3) strengthening global linkages, and (4) investing in people.[53] These four interrelated and mutually reinforcing sets of policy interventions are likely to be those that the government and international aid organizations in Afghanistan will have to consider. Creating a stable economy permits both small and large enterprises to compete more efficiently and to withstand the external shocks from international trade and investment. Such a system enhances the ability of producers and consumers to respond to market-based price signals. In the World Bank's experience, establishing a competitive microeconomy—a business climate conducive to market transactions—improves financial discipline that contributes to economic stability, produces economic returns that can be used for human resource development, and enhances the ability to attract foreign investment. Strengthening global linkages enhances a nation's capacity for international trade and investment. Global linkages also generate the capital needed to maintain macroeconomic stability and growth. They make possible international transactions and attract new knowledge and technology that contribute to human development. The economic gains from trade increase the competitiveness of the microeconomy. Investments in people contribute to rapid growth in productivity that makes the domestic economy more competitive and creates the capacity to meet international standards. This virtuous cycle of development, the World Bank contends, leads not only to accelerated economic growth and market development but to sustainable economic and social progress.

Macroeconomic Reforms

Since the early 1980s, international assistance organizations and most governments around the world have focused their attention on macroeconomic policy reforms as the key to creating and revitalizing markets for international competition. Over the past 20 years, experience with transforming economies in other developing countries seems to verify the importance of macroeconomic reform in stimulating economic growth. Economic growth policies in Central America focused on comprehensive macroeconomic adjustment and structural reforms that reduced hyperinflation in

Nicaragua in the late 1980s and early 1990s and lowered inflation in other countries in the region, including El Salvador and Guatemala, from an average of 27 percent in 1991 to about 6 percent in 1999.[54] The Central American countries that achieved the most success adopted more disciplined fiscal and monetary policies, consistent exchange rate policies, trade liberalization, and regional integration. Increasing social expenditures substantially improved health and education indicators throughout the region.

Macroeconomic policies in Afghanistan will have to achieve the same results that reform policies sought in other developing countries: to change the economy's structure of production and consumption by increasing the efficiency and flexibility of producers and consumers to respond to market signals. The World Bank's experience with structural adjustment lending, as Toye points out, has focused the attention of governments in developing countries on achieving ten major objectives: (1) strengthening the capacity of government to manage public investment; (2) removing import quotas; (3) improving export incentives; (4) reforming the budget or the tax system; (5) improving the financial performance of public enterprises; (6) revising agricultural pricing; (7) changing public investment priorities; (8) revising industrial incentives; (9) increasing public enterprise efficiency; and (10) improving marketing and other support for agriculture.[55]

Evaluations of World Bank structural adjustment programs in 42 developing countries during the 1980s and early 1990s indicate that, on the whole, these countries accelerated their economic growth rates, improved their internal and external balances, lowered domestic inflation, saw improvements in current account balances, and increased the transparency and reduced the complexity of their trade regimes.[56] Although not all of the countries were successful in all aspects of structural adjustment, more than half of the 42 countries in the sample achieved growth in industrial value added and manufactured exports. In countries in Central Asia and the Balkans—Albania, Azerbaijan, Kyrgyz Republic, and Moldova—where structural adjustment and economic reform have been slow, some of the positive changes in the economy were clearly offset by weak public confidence, political instability, and high levels of corruption.[57]

The World Bank and regional development banks found that institutional development is essential to initiating the virtuous cycle of economic growth and social progress. Doing so, however, depends on strengthening the market system by creating or enhancing effective property rights and economic institutions that improve the capacity of individuals and enterprises to participate in market transactions. Creating this cycle also depends on strong systems of governance and political institutions that support market competition.

Indeed, one of the most important lessons of experience is that economic reforms alone are neither sufficient to create a market economy nor adequate to sustain market growth.[58] In Central and Eastern Europe, it became clear that developing the institutional capacity to produce and distribute goods and services and to engage in international trade was far more important than reformers initially acknowledged.[59] And, reflecting on the ADB's experience, two of its leading economists concluded that "in terms of sequencing reforms, fiscal and monetary policies are less important in the near term and medium term than the standard policy prescriptions would make them appear."[60] They insist that "institutional reforms and price reforms are more important in the early stages."

Without a proper balance of policy reforms and institutional development, poor and war-torn countries may not have the absorptive capacity to use external funding efficiently and effectively for stimulating economic growth. Although external aid was crucial in preventing a weak government from collapsing entirely in Cambodia, donor efforts to generate economic growth during the post-conflict period were undermined by Cambodia's weak absorptive capacity. Especially constraining were the weaknesses in infrastructure, human resources, domestic financial resources, and administrative capability. A failed state pervaded by corruption and an unstable political system ridden with factional tensions made initiating economic growth difficult.[61]

Trade and Investment Policies
Once economic growth begins in agriculture, rural commerce, and manufacturing, sustaining development will depend on increasing international trade and attracting foreign investment. Afghanistan's *National Development Framework* recognizes that "trade is critical to the economic future of Afghanistan. Foreign markets will have to provide the main source of demand for Afghan goods over the short term as poverty will limit the demand for goods within Afghanistan."[62] The *Framework* also notes, "private investment is critical to the recovery and long-term growth of the Afghan economy," and that the government must develop "a supportive and credible strategy for generating foreign investor confidence and trust."[63]

Countries as poor as Afghanistan have benefited from trade liberalization and export promotion policies. Trade liberalization policies were extremely important in overcoming large financial imbalances and recovering agricultural exports in Tanzania during the 1980s.[64] Exports of cash crops such as coffee, cashew nuts, tobacco, tea, and sisal, had declined drastically during the 1970s under the government's socialist economy and when farmers were required to sell products to marketing parastatals. Relaxation of restrictions on exports of nontraditional crops, the replacement of parastatals with cooperatives, dismantling of marketing boards, and liberalization of trade regulations provided incentives for producing and selling cash crops for export. Export expansion also requires policies that reduce barriers to imports, including exchange rate policies that affect the ability of domestic companies to import foreign goods. Import reform policies focus on reducing tariffs and quantitative restrictions through import licensing, quotas, and discriminatory pricing, as well.

The World Bank's experience in China indicates how important trade promotion policies are to providing incentives that encourage both exports and imports.[65] These types of incentives usually include freer access for exporters to foreign exchange and granting them foreign exchange retention rights. Such policies also allow duty-free imports for companies that manufacture export products, tax-free domestic inputs for exporters, and provision of working capital financing for the production of exports. Governments wishing to expand exports must also create legal conditions that reduce discrimination in favor of import-substituting activities and against exporters. Additional incentives may include duty-free imports of capital goods, accelerated depreciation, investment financing, income-tax exemptions for exporting companies, and favorable production and sales financing.

Afghanistan will require external investment and capital transfers for many years to come. Official development assistance is only one source of external funding. For many developing and transitional countries, foreign direct investment (FDI) has helped to develop their domestic and export manufacturing industries. FDI in developing and transitional market economies has helped provide foreign exchange and tax revenues, change regional and personal income generation, modernize social institutions, and change social values.[66] It can bring technical know-how, foreign capital, and imports as well as export marketing capability, and a network of supply and distribution channels.[67] The International Monetary Fund's experience in developing countries indicates that FDI stimulates the transfer of technology and capital inputs in different ways than does trade in goods and services. Many host countries benefit from employee training and human resource development in foreign-owned enterprises.[68] Moreover, FDI can stimulate local investment, and the profits it generates can increase tax revenues in host countries. In a comparative analysis of 58 developing countries in Latin America, Asia and Africa, Bosworth and Collins found that for every $1 of foreign capital inflows during the late 1970s to the mid-1990s, domestic investment in host countries increased by about 50 cents.[69]

The United Nations Conference on Trade and Development (UNCTAD) also found that structural reforms encouraging inbound FDI—especially in sectors requiring external capital, technology, or know-how—are critical to economic growth in poor countries. The UNCTAD emphasizes that creating a favorable investment climate is the single most important change that nations can make to attract and support FDI.[70] Developing countries can generate a favorable investment climate by liberalizing FDI policies, that is, by reducing market distortions and improving standards of treatment and implementing promotion policies. They establish a transparent legal framework for facilitating inbound and outbound FDI and other international economic transactions. Reducing market distortions involves easing restrictions on entry and establishment, ownership and control, operations, and authorization and reporting as well as abolishing unfair trade incentives such as tax advantages, other financial incentives and nonfinancial measures that inhibit or restrict FDI. Improving standards of treatment means providing foreign investors with "national treatment" or "fair and equitable treatment," recourse to international means of settling investment disputes, the ability to transfer funds, and transparency in government-regulated FDI procedures.

The UNCTAD emphasizes that promoting inbound FDI must be part of a liberal trade and investment reform package. Components of such a policy usually include tax concessions for foreign investors in the form of investment write-off provisions, tax holidays, or reduced sales, export or license fees; and reductions of tariffs on imported inputs, and provision of some types of tariff protection.[71] In addition, many governments also provide financial incentives in the form of investment grants, concessional loans, subsidies for exports, training of local workers, research and development assistance, and nonfinancial incentives such as exchange control concessions or more liberal employment requirements.[72]

Human Resource Development

The shortage of human capital, especially of skilled labor and managerial talent, is likely to remain a serious bottleneck to economic growth in Afghanistan for more than a generation to come. The *National Development Framework*'s human and social capital strategy "is to create the conditions for people to live secure lives and lay the foundations for formation of sustainable human capital."[73] The strategy places special emphasis on the need to reestablish educational and health programs and provide social protection during the transition to a growth economy.

The United Nations Development Program (UNDP) experience with promoting economic growth in developing countries indicates that improving human resources is essential to prepare the poor for participating effectively in economic activities.[74] The aspects of human resource development that contribute most to national economic development and social well-being, the UN notes, are health and nutrition, general education, and vocational and managerial training. In Afghanistan, rebuilding the general and vocational education systems will be especially important. The UN experience suggests that literacy, numeracy, and skills developed through primary and secondary education increase labor productivity by increasing people's abilities and capacity to learn. Vocational training focused on agricultural, craft, technical, and trade competencies, and on clerical, accounting, data processing, paralegal, and health service–related skills are essential to build a competent labor force required to provide essential goods and services.

Although Uganda is often cited by international assistance organizations as a model for post-conflict reconstruction, the World Bank acknowledges that structural adjustment and economic growth policies would have been more successful had it and the government given more attention to health sector reforms and found ways of improving the efficiency of educational investment.[75] In its post-conflict macroeconomic reform program for El Salvador, the World Bank more clearly recognized the need to address the requirements of the health and education sectors in order to develop human resources and support economic growth policies.[76] International assistance organizations have found that human resource policies aimed at promoting economic growth in poor countries must not only develop people's capabilities for productive employment, but also provide a safety net for those temporarily disadvantaged by economic transition or unable to participate effectively in a market economy. Ironically, both the success and the failure of economic growth policies can result in increased poverty for some segments of the population in poor countries. The World Bank's evaluation of economic transition experience in Eastern Europe and the former Soviet Union found increasing income inequality in many countries in the region, especially in Lithuania, Croatia, Moldova, Georgia, the Kyrgyz Republic, the Russian Federation, Tajikistan, and Armenia.[77] The success of economic reform policies in many Eastern European countries led to rising returns to education, risk taking, and entrepreneurship, and to decompressing wages, all of which were positive results that benefited some groups more than others. In the former Soviet Union, income inequalities resulted not from differences in educational attainment or wage dispersion, but from the impacts of widespread corruption and rent-seeking, the capture of the state by a narrow group of political interests, and the collapse of formal wages and income opportunities during a period of economic stagnation.

The ADB's experience in developing and conflict-torn countries in Asia suggests that when economies begin to grow, governments must adopt social protection programs to reduce poverty and vulnerability among segments of the population that may not be able to benefit immediately.[78] The ADB's experience leads it to conclude that social protection should focus on labor market policies that stimulate employment expansion and help ensure efficient operation of labor markets as well as on social insurance programs that reduce risks of unemployment, disability, and old age. It recommends that social assistance and welfare service programs for groups such as single mothers and for physically or mentally challenged people, and child protection programs, address the needs of the most vulnerable groups. Micro- and area-based projects that provide micro-insurance, agricultural insurance, and disaster relief help alleviate poverty in areas vulnerable to natural or man-made disasters.

Conclusion

The challenges that Afghanistan faces in stimulating economic growth over the next decade stem not only from adverse initial conditions but also from complex external political, social, and economic forces. Economic growth will be essential to draw Afghans out of the current exploitive and diversionary economic systems in which most participate. Neither the warlord economy nor the black-market economy from which many Afghans derive income and wealth can be made productive. The coping or subsistence economy in which most Afghans survive must be transformed into a commercial surplus economy from which they can earn livelihoods, save, and invest.

The conditions under which external development assistance and Afghanistan's government must operate, and the experience of international agencies in poor and war-torn countries, suggest that a focus on agriculture and rural enterprise may be the most realistic leading sectors through which to stimulate national economic growth. The potential exists—if military and political security can be stabilized and the rural economy begins to grow—to focus later on petroleum, natural gas, and mineral resource development and to reestablish a manufacturing base.

More than 50 years of experience in promoting economic growth in poor countries and postwar societies offers valuable lessons about the components, focus, timing, and pace of economic development that authorities in Afghanistan and international assistance organizations cannot afford to ignore. Many countries in which international assistance organizations have helped to stimulate economic growth share similar conditions and problems with Afghanistan.

Yet, despite all that is known about economic development, stimulating growth in any country remains a great experiment. Policies in one country cannot simply be transferred to another. Strategies that have been successful in the past may offer strong guidelines for future action, but they cannot always be replicated, especially if the conditions that accounted for their success cannot be reproduced.

While donors in Afghanistan cannot ignore the experience of the past and pursue actions in a serendipitous and uncoordinated fashion, neither should they merely replicate programs and policies from other countries blindly. The most important lesson of experience with economic policy reforms is that they must be tailored to the specific needs, conditions, and constraints of individual countries and build on whatever indigenous institutions that can be made more productive. Reviewing the International Monetary Fund and World Bank experience with economic development assistance in poor countries during the 1980s and 1990s, Roumeen Islam concluded, "even after adjusting for systematic differences for example, income, skills, technological sophistication, corruption, existing complementary—institutions—some experimentation and innovation, by countries themselves and by those seeking to help them, may be necessary to accommodate differences in natural endowments and cultural expectations."[79]

The World Bank's evaluation of programs for promoting macroeconomic growth in developing countries during the 1980s and 1990s concluded that they work well only when international assistance organizations recognize the diversity of economic and political structures and the administrative capabilities within the beneficiary countries and avoid supporting overly broad simultaneous reforms in countries with political, economic, and administrative constraints.[80] Experience suggests that international organizations must adjust the level of resource transfers to keep economic adjustment policies on track and to compensate for temporary exogenous shocks. They must also address the backlog of investment in social and economic infrastructure in order to stimulate growth and strengthen the policy framework for private investment that can help develop markets, increase economic flexibility, and improve resource mobilization.

The lessons of past experience can save those seeking to assist Afghanistan from costly and unnecessary errors and can provide valuable guidelines for action in stimulating economic growth. But attempts to impose external prescriptions for economic growth without understanding the social, economic, and political conditions and the modifications and innovations that they demand can result in political backlash and social resistance that seriously undermine the very goals that international assistance organizations and donor governments seek to attain in Afghanistan.[81] By drawing on lessons of past experience—but adapting them to Afghanistan's specific needs—donors can help this war-ravaged country to grow its economy, create jobs, and improve its standards of living, all of which are essential building blocks for constructing a peaceful society.

Notes

1. James K. Boyce, "Beyond Good Intensions: External Assistance and Peace Building," in Shepard Forman and Stewart Patrick, eds., *Good Intentions: Pledges of Aid for Postconflict Recovery* (Boulder, CO: Lynne Reinner Publishers, 2000), pp. 367–382.
2. See, e.g., the profiles of conditions in Mozambique, Sierra Leone, South Lebanon, Kosovo, and Montenegro in Eugenia Date-Bah, "Crisis and Decent Work: A Collection of Essays" (Geneva: International Labour Office, 2001).
3. Interim Administration of Afghanistan, *National Development Framework* (draft for consultation) (Kabul: Islamic Republic of Afghanistan, 2002).
4. Ibid., p. 6.
5. Ibid., p. 6.
6. Interim Authority of Afghanistan, op. cit., p. 37.

7. The Economist Intelligence Unit, *Country Report: Afghanistan* (London: EIU, 2002).
8. Adam Pain and Jonathan Goodhand, "Afghanistan: Current Employment and Socio-Economic Situation and Prospects," Working Paper 8 (Geneva: International Labour Office, 2002).
9. For a summary see Dennis A. Rondinelli, *Development Projects as Policy Experiments: An Adaptive Approach to Development Administration*, 2nd Rev. Ed. (London: Routledge, 1993).
10. World Bank, "The Reform of the Public Sector Management: Lessons From Experience," Policy and Research Series No. 18 (Washington, DC: World Bank, 1991).
11. Walter W. Rostow, *The Process of Economic Growth* (New York: Norton, 1952).
12. R. Nurkse, *Problems of Capital Formation in Underdeveloped Countries* (London: Oxford University Press, 1953).
13. Gunnar Myrdal, *Rich Lands and Poor: The Road to World Prosperity* (New York: Harper and Row, 1957); Paul Streeten, *Frontiers of Development Studies* (New York: Halstead, 1972).
14. Simon Kuznets, *Modern Economic Growth* (New Haven, CT: Yale University Press, 1966).
15. Gunnar Myrdal, *An Approach to the Asian Drama* (New York: Vintage Books, 1970); Irma Adelman and Cynthia Morris, *Economic Growth and Social Equity in Developing Countries* (Stanford, CA: Stanford University Press, 1973).
16. United Nations Food and Agriculture Organization, "What Have We Learned?" *The State of Food and Agriculture 2000* (Rome: FAO, 2000), p. 4, at <http://www.fao.org/docrep/x4400e/x4400e00.htm>.
17. Albert Hirschman, *The Strategy of Economic Development* (New Haven, CT: Yale University Press, 1967).
18. Arthur Lewis, *The Theory of Economic Growth* (London: Allen & Unwin, 1955); T. Schultz, *Transforming Traditional Agriculture* (New Haven, CT: Yale University Press, 1964).
19. Interim Administration of Afghanistan, op. cit., pp. 33–34.
20. United Nations Food and Agriculture Organization, "What Have We Learned?" p. 2.
21. M.W. Rosegrant and P.B.R. Hazell, *Transforming the Rural Asian Economy: The Unfinished Revolution* (Hong Kong: Oxford University Press, 1999).
22. Asian Development Bank, *Rural Asia: Beyond the Green Revolution* (Manila: ADB, 2000), quote at p. 13.
23. Suresh Babu and Alisher Tashmatov, eds., *Food Policy Reforms in Central Asia* (Washington, DC: International Food Policy Research Institute, 2000).
24. Interim Authority of Afghanistan, op. cit., pp. 29–31.
25. Schultz, op. cit.; Uma Lele, *The Design of Rural Development: Lessons from Africa* (Baltimore, MD: Johns Hopkins University Press, 1975).
26. See Dennis A. Rondinelli, *Applied Methods of Regional Analysis: The Spatial Dimensions of Development Policy* (Boulder, CO: Westview Press, 1985).
27. Marcel Fafchamps and Elini Gabre-Madhin, "Agricultural Markets in Benin and Malawi: The Operation and Performance of Traders," Working Paper No. 2734 (Washington, DC: World Bank, 2001).
28. Dimitri Vitas and Yoon Je Cho, "Credit Policies: Lessons from East Asia," Working Paper No. 1458 (Washington, DC: World Bank, 1995).
29. Jocelyn A. Songco, "Do Rural Infrastructure Investments Benefit the Poor?" (Washington, DC: World Bank, 2002).
30. World Bank, "The World Bank and Irrigation," OED Sector Study No. 14908 (Washington, DC: World Bank, 1995).
31. World Bank, *Precis/OED*, No. 199, Winter 1999.
32. Songco, op. cit., p. 22.
33. World Bank, *World Development Report 1994*, pp. 8–10.

34. Paula Donnelly-Roark, Karim Oedgaorgo, and Xiao Ye, "Can Local Institutions Reduce Poverty? Rural Decentralization in Burkina Faso," Working Paper No. 2677 (Washington, DC: World Bank, 2001).

35. Christiaan Grootaert and Deepa Narayan, "Local Institutions, Poverty and Household Welfare in Bolivia," Working Paper No. 2644 (Washington, DC: World Bank, 2001).

36. Nahid Motee and Baquer Namazi, "Traditional Community Based Organizations of Iran: New Partners in Development," paper presented at Mediterranean Development Forum 3, Cairo, Egypt, March 2000.

37. Irma Specht, "Jobs for Demobilized Rebels and Soldiers: Early Preparedness and Sustaining Capacities" (Geneva: International Labour Office, 2000).

38. Ibid., pp. 6–7.

39. World Bank, "War-to-Peace Transition in Mozambique: The Provincial Reintegration Support Program" (Washington, DC: World Bank, 1997).

40. Ibid., p. 4.

41. United Nations, "Creating a Better Climate for Private Enterprise" (New York: United Nations Development Programme, 1987).

42. World Bank, "Developing the Private Sector: A Challenge for the World Bank Group" (Washington, DC: World Bank, 1989).

43. Hernando deSoto, "Constraints on People: The Origins of Underground Economies and the Limits to their Growth," in J. Jenkins, ed., *Beyond the Informal Sector: Including the Excluded* (San Francisco: ICS Press, 1988), pp. 15–47.

44. Demographic Institute, "The Role of Trade in Creating Job Opportunities" (Jakarta, Indonesia: Demographic Institute, University of Indonesia, 1989).

45. Carl Liedholm and Donald Mead, "Small Scale Industries in Developing Countries: Empirical Evidence and Policy Implications" (Washington, DC: U.S. Agency for International Development, 1986).

46. Jeffrey Ashe, *The PICES II Experience, Vol. I* (Washington, DC: U.S. Agency for International Development, 1985).

47. Robert G. Blaney and Maria Otero, "Small and Micro enterprises: Contributions to Development and Fugure Directions for AID Support" (Washington, DC: U.S. Agency for International Development, 1985).

48. Jacob Levitsky, "Brazil—An Alternative to Direct Government-Delivered Support to Small Industries," *Small Enterprise Development*, Vol. 1, No. 3 (1990): pp. 54–56

49. Peter Kilby, "Evaluating Technical Assistance," *World Development*, Vol. 7 (1979): pp. 309–323.

50. Herman Rosa and Michael Foley, "El Salvador," in Shepard Forman and Stewart Patrick, eds., *Good Intentions: Pledges of Aid for Postconflict Recovery* (Boulder, CO: Lynne Reinner Publishers, 2000), pp. 113–157.

51. Paul Cashin, Paolo Mauro, and Ratna Sahay, "Macroeconomic Policies and Poverty Reduction: Some Cross-Country Evidence," *Finance & Development*, Vol. 38, No. 2 (2001): pp. 46–49.

52. Martin Reiser, Maria L. Di Tommaso, and Melvyn Weeks, "The Measurement and Determination of Institutional Change: Evidence from Transition Economies," Working Paper 29 (Cambridge, England: Department of Applied Economics, 2001).

53. World Bank, *World Development Report 1991* (Washington, DC: World Bank, 1991).

54. Leonardo Cardemil, Juan Carlos di Tata, and Florencia Frantischek, "Central America: Adjustment and Reforms in the 1990s," *Finance & Development*, Vol. 37, No. 1 (2000): pp. 34–37.

55. John Toye, *Structural Adjustment and Employment Policy: Issues and Experience* (Geneva: International Labour Office, 1995), pp. 22–23.

56. World Bank, "Adjustment Lending: Lessons of Experience" (Washington, DC: World Bank, 2001).

57. Khaled Sherif, Michael Borish, and George Clark, *Structural Adjustment in the Transition* (Washington, DC: World Bank, 2001).
58. Joseph Prokopenko, "Management Implications of Structural Adjustment," Management Development Program Working Paper (Geneva: International Labour Office, 1991).
59. See Dennis A. Rondinelli, ed., *Privatization and Economic Reform in Central Europe: The Changing Business Climate* (Westport, CT: Quorum Books, 1994).
60. Pradumma B. Rana and J. Malcolm Dowling, Jr., "Big Bang's Bust," *The International Economy*, Vol. VII, No. 5 (1993): pp. 40–43 and 701–702; quote at 702.
61. Sorpong Peau with Kenji Yamada, "Cambodia," in Forman and Patrick, eds., op. cit., pp. 67–111.
62. Interim Authority of Afghanistan, op. cit., p. 42.
63. Ibid., p. 40.
64. Oussama Kanaan, "Tanzania's Experience with Trade Liberalization," *Finance & Development*, Vol. 37, No. 2 (2002): pp. 30–33.
65. See World Bank, *China: External Trade and Capital* (Washington, DC: World Bank, 1992).
66. K. Billerbeck and Y. Yasugi, "Private Direct Foreign Investment in Developing Countries," World Bank Staff Working Paper No. 348 (Washington, DC: World Bank, 1979).
60. See United Nations Industrial Development Organization, *Industry and Development Global Report 1993/94* (Vienna, Austria: UNIDO, 1993).
67. See United Nations Industrial Development Organization, *Industry and Development Global Report 1993/94* (Vienna, Austria: UNIDO, 1993).
68. Prakash Loungani and Assaf Razin, "How Beneficial is Foreign Direct Investment for Developing Countries?" *Finance & Development*, Vol. 38, No. 2 (2001): pp. 6–9.
69. Barry P. Bosworth and Susan M. Collins, "Capital Flows to Developing Economies: Implications for Saving and Investment," *Brookings Papers on Economic Activity*, Vol. 1 (1999), pp. 143–169.
70. United Nations Conference on Trade and Development, *World Investment Report 1994* (New York: United Nations, 1994).
71. United Nations Conference on Trade and Development, *World Investment Report 2002* (New York: United Nations, 2002).
72. K. Billerbeck and Y. Yasugi, "Private Direct Foreign Investment in Developing Countries," World Bank Staff Working Paper No. 348 (Washington, DC: World Bank, 1979).
73. Interim Authority of Afghanistan, op. cit., p. 14.
74. United Nations Department of Economic and Social Development, *World Investment Report 1992* (New York: United Nations, 1992), pp. 164–166.
75. World Bank, "Postconflict Reconstruction: Uganda," Precis No. 171 (Washington, DC: World Bank, 1998).
76. World Bank, "Postconflict Reconstruction: El Salvador," Precis No. 172 (Washington, DC: World Bank, 1998).
77. World Bank, *Transition: The First Ten Years—Analysis and Lessons for Eastern Europe and the Former Soviet Union* (Washington, DC: World Bank, 2002).
78. Asian Development Bank, "Social Protection: Reducing Risks, Increasing Opportunities" (Manila: ADB, 2002).
79. Roumeen Islam, "Institutions to Support Markets," *Finance & Development*, Vol. 39, No. 1 (2002): pp. 48–51; quote at 49.
80. World Bank, "Adjustment Lending: Lessons of Experience" (Washington, DC: World Bank, 2001).
81. See Joan M. Nelson, "The Politics of Stabilization," in R.E. Fineberg and V. Kallab, eds., *Adjustment Crisis in the Third World* (New Brunswick, NJ: Transaction Books, 1984), pp. 99–118; and Paul Streeten, "Structural Adjustment: A Survey of Issues and Options," *World Development*, Vol. 15, No. 12 (1987): pp. 1469–1482.

CHAPTER NINE

ETHNIC DIVERSITY AND THE STRUCTURE OF GOVERNMENT

Milton J. Esman

This chapter argues that the primary objectives of foreign aid donors in post-Taliban Afghanistan should be first, to build the institutions of an effective central government and second, to insure that these institutions provide for equitable participation by members of Afghanistan's major ethnic communities. Rehabilitating the nation's polity and its physical infrastructure and launching programs of sustained economic development will be the task of its indigenous leadership, but they will require major assistance from the donor community for at least the next decade.

Ethnic Pluralism and Warlords

The critical political reality in Afghanistan is its competitive and mobilized ethnic pluralism. In the east and southeast abutting Pakistan are the Pushtun, who comprise an estimated 38 percent of Afghanistan's approximately 25 million people. To the north, adjacent to Tadjikistan, are the Tadjiks, who constitute 25 percent of Afghanistan's people. Uzbeks, living west of the Tadjiks, comprise 10 percent. The center and west are home to Hazara, 20 percent, next to their fellow Shi'a in Iran. The balance consists of Turkmen, Buluchs, and Aimaks. Each of these ethnic communities is under the sway of warlords who, in the turmoil that has wracked the country during the past three decades, have replaced traditional leaders. Each of these warlords has his contingent of fighters and sources of funds and of arms, including revenues from smuggling, import duties, drug traffic, and other criminal activities. There are linguistic and religious differences as well as ethnic ones. While 75 percent of the people are Sunni Muslims, the Persian-speaking Hazara adhere to the Shi'a branch of Islam, as do scattered communities of Ismaeli followers of the Aga Khan.

None of these communities is monolithic. Pushtuns, for example, are divided into eight major tribes, each with its own social structure and its distinctive political interests. The warlords maintain control of their communities by providing protection, by distributing largesse, and by intimidation. All are predatory and aggressively competitive in defense of their turf and in avenging grievances. The *New York Times* reported a story of a Pushtun community in northern Afghanistan that was attacked and devastated by Uzbek fighters, presumably for supporting the Taliban, a movement predominantly of rural Pushtun.[1]

Each warlord is jealous of his autonomy and inclined to resist central authority. At the same time, the warlords demand what they consider a fair share of the offices, jobs, and financial resources available to the central government, including foreign aid. The dominant position of members of the Tadjik and Uzbek Northern Alliance in the interim Karzai government has been noted by personalities from the less-favored ethnic groups.[2] A leading Uzbek warlord, Rashid Dostum, has threatened to withdraw his support because of alleged discrimination and affronts to his dignity. There have been similar threats from other regional warlords, including Padsha Khan Zadran in the southeast and Ismael Khan in the west. Several warlords have been enlisted by the United States military to help hunt down the remaining al-Qaeda and Taliban forces. Warlords have filled the power vacuum created by the elimination of the Taliban and the weakness of the current regime. Defiance of the government and lethal clashes between warlords and their armed followers, suggest the problems certain to confront any future central government.

In quieter times, members of the various ethnic communities coexisted on mostly peaceful terms. There were mutually profitable economic relationships among them, but little social integration. In Afghanistan as elsewhere, during periods of stress, when governments lose their effectiveness, individuals tend to "fall back" on their ethnic communities for security. In failed states, where governments can no longer exercise authority, local strongmen emerge to fill the vacuum; the rule of law, however imperfect, is replaced by the rule of the gun. The strongmen seek to legitimate their power by promising their ethnic followers protection against threatening outsiders, providing security, and organizing rudimentary services. This accounts for the emergence and dominance of regional warlords—men with guns—in such countries as Mexico, after the downfall of the long Diaz dictatorship; in China, after the fall of the last Emperor; in the Congo during the 1980s; and more recently in Somalia. Warlords will continue to hold sway until Afghanistan, with international assistance, succeeds in evolving an effective central government.

Intervention by Outsiders

A further complication is the mischievous influence of outsiders attempting to promote their own interests by manipulating vulnerable fellow ethnics within the country, while insiders look to neighboring states as patrons available to assist them in their struggles. Pakistan's governing elites, for example, have been especially concerned that a movement for a united Pushtunistan, joining Afghanistan's eight million Pushtun with the equal number of fellow ethnics in Pakistan's neighboring northwest territories, could destabilize and threaten the unity of their country, which has already suffered the dismemberment of the former East Pakistan (now Bangladesh). To counteract Pushtun nationalism, Pakistan's government has aggressively cultivated Islamic militancy among its Pushtun neighbors, including ideological and military support for the Taliban movement. They assisted the Saudi regime in spreading the Wahabi version of fundamentalist Islam by financing and providing instructors for schools that trained the Taliban's cadres. Iran, likewise, is committed to protecting Afghanistan's Shi'a minorities (this accounted for Iran's hostility to the Taliban, which promoted Sunni fundamentalism). Russia is intent on containing

Islamic militancy that would threaten its remaining influence in the ex-Soviet Central Asian Republics and promote subversion among Russia's substantial Muslim minorities, as in Chechnya. The vicious effects of external manipulation of ethnic affinities in Bosnia by neighboring Croatia and Serbia, and in Congo by Rwanda, Angola, Zimbabwe, and Uganda, foreshadow the vulnerability of Afghanistan, unless its neighbors can be restrained by international pressure. Any future government in Kabul will have to cope with external interference from many sources, attempting to exploit transnational ethnic affinities.

The Challenge Facing Donors

Landlocked and remote, Afghanistan has barely been touched by the industrial and scientific revolutions of the nineteenth and twentieth centuries. Manufacturing industry is virtually nonexistent, and the nation's meager infrastructure of roads, electric power, telecommunications, health services, and water supply has been devastated by a quarter-century of vicious, uninterrupted warfare. Its educational facilities, limited as they were, were shut down by the Taliban regime, libraries burned, and laboratories destroyed. An estimated five million people, 20 percent of the population, fled the country seeking refuge mainly in neighboring Pakistan and Iran. These refugees must be helped to return to their homes and to rehabilitate their dwellings, farms, and businesses. The damaged infrastructure must be restored so that normal economic life can be revived; the youth—girls as well as boys—may once again enjoy the fruits of education; and young men can visualize a future for themselves in occupations other than as gunmen. Foundations must be laid for agricultural modernization, based on crops other than opium poppies and the development of small industry, so that the growing population may put the damage and despair of the past quarter-century behind them and look forward to a more hopeful future.

Because the Afghan government is bankrupt, financing of the first stages of reconstruction will have to be undertaken by international donors. This includes even salaries and the operating costs of government officials and employees, among them its embryonic security services, until the government gradually gains the capacity to raise its own revenues. Governments and international agencies have pledged to supply at least the first stages of Afghanistan's reconstruction, but these pledges have been slow to materialize and the funds have been used mostly for emergency relief, rather than for reconstruction and development. Should premature donor fatigue deprive Afghanistan of the resources needed to restore its economy and to build sound institutions of government, the country's prospects will be grim. There are accounts, reported almost daily, of violent incidents between rival warlords and of defiance of the central government, because donors, led by the United States, have refused to extend their peacekeeping contingents beyond the capital city. Thus, until its security forces have been trained, equipped, and deployed, the writ of the central government cannot extend beyond Kabul; it will lack the means to enforce its laws and regulations and to face down the warlords.

At present, the national government in Kabul is a government in name only. There is a full panoply of ministers and deputies who are financed and supported by foreign donors, but no structures with the ability to connect the state with society, to extend its authority and services beyond the capital city. Even in Kabul, where a vice president was recently assassinated, the interim president is protected by an American bodyguard. Beyond Kabul, warlords continue to rule. There is a Minister of the Interior, but without an effective police force; a Minister of Finance, but no personnel to collect revenues and manage funds; and a Minister of Public Works, but no staff qualified to build, repair, and maintain highways, airports, water supply, and communications facilities. Until such structures are in place, with sufficient means to provide services to link the central government with local communities and to enable both private enterprise and voluntary associations to operate freely, the national government will be a paper tiger.

Dependent though they are on foreign aid, Afghans are wary of donor promises. They recall how the United States, notwithstanding promises to help restore the economy after the Soviet invasion, lost interest in their country once the Soviet threat had been eliminated. The preoccupation of the United States with Iraq and North Korea tended to confirm these fears. Should the United States and associated donors again abandon Afghanistan, they would be ensuring still another failed state, similar to Somalia, which was abandoned to its warlords a decade ago.

This need not happen. Through sustained and well-directed technical and economic assistance and policy advice over time, donors can provide essential support in building vital military and civil institutions and laying the groundwork for sustained economic development. There are several contemporary examples of efforts by members of the international community, coordinated in most cases by the United Nations (UN), to help countries rebuild political and governmental institutions, restore their physical infrastructure, and renew the process of economic development during the aftermath of devastating internal warfare. These include the cases of Bosnia, Kosovo, Cambodia, Mozambique, and East Timor. Though there are important lessons to be learned from these experiences, they are still too current to allow for reliable judgments. There is, however, one example from recent history that may be instructive, the case of South Korea.

After the Korean War, South Korea was even more devastated than post-Taliban Afghanistan. Its economic infrastructure was in shambles, its government a patchwork of patronage and venality. It was commonly believed that South Korea would be on the international dole for the indefinite future. For example, its exports in 1954 totaled a paltry $24 million, less than 10 percent of the value of essential civilian imports. The U.S. government addressed itself over the next two decades to helping Korea's leadership build the structures of effective government, which in turn, guided and promoted the emergence of a dynamic network of private business enterprises. As a result, Korea's economy grew during the decade from 1962 to 1972 at the compound annual rate of 9.1 percent. This required substantial foreign assistance, but 20 years after the end of the Korean War, South Korea had an effective set of governmental institutions and a dynamic, expanding economy based on an aggressive policy of export promotion. Korea no longer needed foreign aid; it had became an Asian Tiger. U.S. government assistance, supplemented by the World Bank and Japan, filled the gap between Korea's civilian imports and its foreign exchange earnings; financed the rehabilitation and improvement of its physical infra-structure; provided higher education overseas for a generation of professional leader-ship; and engaged in continuing dialogue with government officials on economic policy.[3]

What happened in Korea could happen in Afghanistan. It would require govern-ment leadership committed to strengthening its governmental institutions, to polit-ical reconciliation, and to economic development. Also needed, is a donor presence with sufficient patience and stamina to assist, until the country has gained the capac-ity to manage on its own.

The tendency of donors in the past has been to conceive an aid-recipient country as a single integrated economy and polity, similar to the European countries during the Marshall Plan. The aim has been to maximize macroeconomic growth on the premise that growth "lifts all boats." The neoliberal policies that have been prescribed during the past two decades such as privatization, the elimination of fiscal subsidies, and shrinking of government, or donor-financed projects such as resettle-ment schemes, irrigation works, and waste-management facilities are evaluated mainly in terms of their economic rate of return or benefit–cost ratios. These econ-omistic criteria overlook the distributional consequences of such interventions—who benefits, and who is neglected, disadvantaged, or hurt. In a society such as Afghanistan's, where ethnic sensitivities are at the very heart of domestic politics, fail-ure of donors to consider the interethnic effects of their assistance can contribute to political strife and even undermine the effectiveness of their efforts.

Experiences of donors who have failed to heed this warning have been carefully examined and recorded. A typical example is the Accelerated Mahaveli Project in Sri Lanka, a very large multipurpose irrigation, electric power, and resettlement scheme supported financially by a consortium of donors.[4] Spurred by the enthusiasm of the Sri Lanka government and favorable estimates of the project's economic benefit–cost ratios, donors included Britain, Canada, Germany, Japan, the Netherlands, the UN Development Program, and the World Bank. Though the project was located on land long occupied predominantly by Tamils, a very large proportion of government-selected settlers proved to be Sinhalese. Thus, the project was soon stigmatized by Tamils as a planned colonization of part of their homeland by the Sinhalese-controlled government. When the proposed northern feeder canal that would have served a large area of Tamil farmers was cancelled, ostensibly for financial reasons, Tamil opinion concluded that the scheme, financed by foreign aid, was a deliberate plot to marginalize the Tamil people, a foretelling of what might be expected from any Sinhalese regime. This was typical of many instances of donor failure, despite ample warnings, to consider and act on the likely interethnic consequences of their interventions. The Mahaveli project became one of several triggers of the Tamil rebellion, which has beset Sri Lanka with 17 years of bloody civil war.

Donor myopia, but with less harmful consequences, occurred in Malaysia, where economists associated with donor agencies solemnly warned the Malaysian govern-ment that their New Economic Policy (NEP) designed to eliminate the prevailing identification of "race with economic function" would significantly retard the nation's economic growth. The NEP was initiated following the devastating race riots of May 1969, which were largely believed to have been caused due to Malay resentment at their exclusion from the modern sectors of the economy. The strategy underlying the NEP was to provide preferential assistance to ethnic Malays in gaining educational qualifications, access to capital, government contracts, and ownership shares in modern economic enterprises; thus, Malays would have opportunities to gain experience as entrepreneurs, owners, and managers of medium- and large-scale businesses, without confiscating the property or unduly circumscribing the economic prospects of non-Malay citizens. During the first two decades of the NEP, Malaysia realized annual economic growth rates averaging 7 percent, the size of the economy quadrupled, the official poverty rate declined from 49 to 15 percent, and a significant cadre of Malays began, for the first time, to participate actively in modern industry, finance, and commerce. Though the Chinese complained of government-sponsored discrimination, they shared in the general prosperity; their average per capita income exceeding that of Malays by a substantial margin. The non-Malay share of ownership in a much larger economy actually increased, while the foreign share diminished as the latter sold out primarily to government-backed Malay interests. Here, again donors, blinded by economistic logic, failed to consider what might have happened in Malaysia had the Malay majority continued to be underrepresented in the modern sectors of the economy and in the learned professions.[5]

While these have typified the donors' tendency to overlook ethnic realities in the countries they are assisting, there have been instructive exceptions. Uphoff's report on the Gal Oya project, also in Sri Lanka, describes a program to rehabilitate a large derelict irrigation system, principally by mobilizing the labor and management skills of farmers organized into self-managed irrigation associations.[6] Farmers contributed their labor to rehabilitate and modernize the canals and control structures. Once assured of a steady supply of water throughout the year, the project beneficiaries, Sinhalese and Tamil, would be responsible for operating and maintaining the secondary and tertiary channels. Despite powerful emotions provoked by the vicious ethnic civil war raging about them, the Gal Oya farmers of both ethnic communities continue to cooperate in managing the facilities from which they mutually benefit. A convincing common interest succeeded in sustaining the peace in this unique enclave.

Mary Anderson has identified three formulas that have yielded successful outcomes for donor intervention in ethnically divided countries.[7] The first, the search for *common interests*, as in the Gal Oya project, creates positive-sum outcomes for all parties concerned. The second formula calls for *divisibility*: Instead of a single large project that benefits a single ethnic community, donors should support smaller projects from which all the competing ethnic communities benefit. An example would be several small-scale water management projects instead of a single, large government-managed dam. The third formula produces *interdependence*, where division of labor among ethnic communities creates incentives for, and rewards cooperative versus competitive behavior. As donors develop greater sensitivity to the ethnic dimension of politics, they will discover additional formulas in the design of policies and projects for preventing or mitigating conflict.

In recent years, some donors have expanded the criteria by which they evaluate the activities they support. Donors now consider the environmental impacts of projects; their effects on the welfare and opportunities of women; and their implications for human rights, democratic development, and the rule of law. In Afghanistan, it is important that donors be aware of the realities that motivate so many of the country's political behaviors; they must assess every policy they recommend, and every project they sponsor, according to implications on the ethnic distribution of power and influence. They must be especially wary of possible diversion by elements in the government or by local warlords of donor-provided resources. The Tadjik Minister of Defense, for example, has been accused of loading his ministry and the newly formed national army with members of his own ethnic community. As donors are financing the entire military budget, they can and must prevent this from happening.

The Institutions of Statehood

A prime long-term objective of donors must be to help build the institutions of statehood that donors take for granted in their own countries.[8] Without a viable state apparatus that is capable of protecting life and property and enforcing the law throughout its territory, there can be no security, no law and order, no governmental or private investment, and no economic development. Afghanistan would remain a failed state, a battleground between ruthless warlords, each using its private ethnic-based army for competitive plunder, intimidation, and extortion. The economy would revert to stagnation at subsistence levels; those with portable skills would leave the country. Life for most Afghans would be "solitary, poor, nasty, brutish, and short."[9] Those who advise donors to avoid the futile task of building a central government and instead to work directly with warlords, because the warlords "know how to get things done," condemn Afghanistan to decades of more instability and misery.[10] Donors must instead use their influence collectively, to foster policies and institutions that result at the same time in an *effective* state apparatus and a *legitimate* government.

In the evolution of most modern states, a central authority was forced to confront and overcome opposition from regional potentates in order to build the institutional infrastructure of effective statehood. A key indicator of effective authority is the monopoly of armed forces and the elimination of private armies; this is sometimes achieved by incorporating personnel from private armies into the national militia. In addition to keeping outsiders at bay, effectiveness entails the capacity to protect life and property; to enforce laws and settle conflicts peacefully; and to raise sufficient revenues to sustain the state apparatus and provide basic services, notably public works, education, and the stimulation of agriculture, industry, and commerce. The operations of the state apparatus and the integrating services it provides, develops sentiments of common nationhood that may coexist with, and eventually supersede, ethnic and other parochial attachments. Historically, this process precedes the struggle for democracy, which ultimately succeeds in circumscribing the state apparatus and subjecting it to popular control. This sequence can be observed in recent developments in such successful Asian polities as South Korea, Thailand, and Taiwan, and may also be occurring at its early stages in Russia and China. First, state capacity is established, then controlled to ensure accountability to society and basic human rights.

Resources provided by the central government or by foreign donors for local projects, with the intention perhaps of ensuring interethnic equity, may prove fair game for local warlords until they are displaced by agencies of the national government. As the state demonstrates the capacity and the will to maintain security and enforce its laws throughout the country, the role of warlords will change. This can occur, however, only when the national government has effectively asserted its authority, the rules of the game have changed, and private armies are no longer tolerated. When threatened with irrelevance, these talented men, often with impressive leadership skills, will attempt to adapt to the new set of constraints and opportunities. Some will become national-level politicians, legislators, and cabinet ministers; some will organize provincial or local political machines, serving as power brokers or heading provincial or local governments; others will become businessmen, converting their political influence to economic entrepreneurship. When resistance is no longer feasible, most warlords will not simply fade away; they will apply their skills and contacts to the requirements of the new regime.

In considering the transition of Afghanistan's warlords, the post-Soviet experience of East Europe's communist bosses may be instructive. Once the rules of the game had changed in these countries, many of these former communist commissars adapted their organizational and brokering skills readily to democratic political competition: They organized political parties and competed in elections. Many gained high office in national or regional governments or headed major opposition parties. Some entered the business world, often as executives in newly privatized former state enterprises. What was critical for them, as might be for Afghanistan's warlords, was their recognition that the old political system had changed irrevocably, but that the new rules afforded them fresh opportunities to direct their talents and experience.

Legitimacy: Law and Equity

It is necessary, but not sufficient, for the state to be effective; it must also be seen by those over whom it claims authority as legitimate, and deserving of their respect and obedience. Legitimacy connotes a sense of fairness, of rectitude, and of respect for society's values. It implies that government, in its procedures as well as its outputs, acts not capriciously but according to laws that treat all persons equitably and respect the rights of individual citizens and groups. This requires state bureaucracies that are disciplined by law, an independent judiciary, and access to the courts for citizens.

In the Afghan context, the critical test for legitimacy is the perception that its component ethnic communities are equitably represented in the main organs of the state—the courts and the legislature—but also the civil and military branches of the executive. Rough proportionality to population is the general test of fair and equitable representation, both on symbolic and instrumental grounds. If, for example, the military officer corps should be viewed as dominated by members of a single ethnic community, others will be troubled, not only because they feel entitled to a fair share of these powerful and prestigious jobs, but because they fear that the weight of the armed forces may be employed to the detriment of their underrepresented community. The same applies to the executive agencies, the courts, and indeed, to university admissions. Jobs, contracts, services cannot be treated as ethnic patronage. Exact proportionality may be hard to manage, but the state elites must be seen as striving honestly to insure balanced participation by authentic representatives of its component communities.[11]

Contracts awarded by government and the location of government-financed installations and facilities must take account of ethnic balance. When state enterprises are privatized, ownership should not be allowed to pass exclusively to members of a single ethnic community. Merit criteria for government employment and for university admissions may have to be modified to insure the politically more salient goal of equitable representation. The criterion of formal qualifications must be combined with fair ethnic representation. Even in the absence of rigid proportionality, government elites must be seen as sensitive to the reasonable demands and needs of all ethnic communities and as trying faithfully to keep them in balance. This will counteract attempts by aspiring ethnic politicians to build militant constituencies by claiming that their community has been excluded or victimized by discriminatory treatment.

Political parties or factions are likely to emerge along ethnic lines and to produce governments composed of ethnic coalitions. Early governments are likely to be grand coalitions, with participation from all ethnic groups. Soon, within most ethnic communities, two or more political factions based on extended kinship, economic interests, or ideology may begin to compete for support among their voters. This may, in time, result in competing ethnic coalitions. Each coalition will attempt to maximize its support by including participation from several ethnic communities. As the economy becomes more differentiated and the number of educated men and women expands, political organizations may begin to reflect competing cross-ethnic economic interests and ideological tendencies, but this is a prospect for the next generation. In the short term, however, ethnic identity will be the organizing principle in public affairs; governments will be composed of shifting ethnic coalitions, one of whose principal responsibilities will be to reconcile claims, assuage grievances originating in multiple ethnic communities, and manage conflicts among them. The ability of national-level politicians to fend off violent interethnic conflict will depend on their negotiating skills, the success of moderate leaders in maintaining influence in their own ethnic communities, and the capacity of the national security forces to deter and contain violent disturbances. Encouragement and support of moderate politicians by external donors may be a critical factor in mitigating the ethnic hostility and political vendettas that have plagued Afghanistan's political culture.

Local Authorities and Civil Society

While donors must focus on strengthening the institutions of the central government, many governmental activities should be reserved for regional and local authorities. This policy would capitalize on local initiatives, management skills, and knowledge of local circumstances, and simultaneously prevent overloading the fragile capabilities of the central administration. Among activities that might be devolved are the reconstruction and expansion of local public works and health services, as well as assistance to families in rebuilding their homes and renewing their farms and other means of livelihood. Foreign assistance from governments, international agencies, and nongovernmental organizations (NGOs) should be coordinated through the central government, integrating them with the government's own efforts and promoting equitable distribution among ethnic communities. For the first few years, however, when the emphasis must include relief and rehabilitation as well as development, donors should be encouraged to identify and work on the ground with local author- ities and NGOs that demonstrate the ability to implement projects with reasonable efficiency and probity. In many instances, this may include local warlords and their followers. Many newly independent states in Africa faced the difficult choice of entrusting local government to the traditional chiefs or innovating, as the government elites preferred, more modern systems of elected officials. In some cases, the latter coexisted with the chiefs in unstable divisions of labor, while both shared administra- tive functions with locally posted agents of national departments. In Afghanistan, during the turbulence of the past quarter-century, warlords effectively replaced tradi- tional local authorities and some have become well entrenched in local societies. Once the warlords have been disarmed, the Afghan government must decide which pattern of local government best suits their preferences, so long as the activities reserved for the ex-warlords do not allow them to defy the authority of the central government.

Some donors will be especially inclined to foster and assist domestic private enter- prise, particularly in small-scale manufacturing, agricultural processing, handicrafts, and commerce, and to stimulate initiatives in civil society by working with and through international and indigenous NGOs. Even in supporting grassroots initia- tives of moderate scale, donors would be wise not to overlook the principle of ethnic balance. While beyond the scope of this essay, it is appropriate here to mention that the large number of donors who will be contributing to Afghanistan's reconstruction and development could overwhelm the limited capacities of the government's coordi- nating institutions. Every donor has its own requirements and procedures for project documentation, supplying and accounting for goods and services, financial and progress reporting, and evaluation. They are likely to adopt different terms of employ- ment and set different rates of compensation for local project employees performing similar tasks. To minimize confusion and duplication, prevent operating at cross- purposes, and simplify their procedures, donors should set up machinery in conjunc- tion with the Afghan government to coordinate and facilitate their various efforts.

Conclusion

A major theme of this chapter is that the maintenance of ethnic balance must be a central concern of foreign donors, of Afghan elites, and of scholars and analysts who are committed to the reconstruction and long-term development of Afghanistan and its long-suffering people. Ethnic considerations are certain to dominate Afghan public affairs for the foreseeable future, and voting will occur along ethnic lines. The concern for balanced participation must infuse both the composition of its governing structures and the behavior and outputs of its institutions and agencies.[12] The electoral system, for example, must eschew majoritarian politics, which allows representatives of an electoral majority to control the government, as this would be perceived as enabling the winners to dominate or exclude the losers. Though there will be competition within the various ethnic communities and some electoral deals will be struck across ethnic lines, ethnic communities will not feel secure unless they are assured of representation in the institutions of government in rough proportion to their numbers. In this version of consociational power sharing, there will be inevitable disputes as deputies attempt to convince their constituents that they are diligently promoting and defending their community's interests.[13] The task of statesmanship, then, is to broker compromises and to identify common goals that transcend ethnic interests and grievances.

Outside experience has demonstrated the importance of promoting ethnic balance. In Northern Ireland, the Protestant majority rigorously excluded members of the Catholic minority from executive positions in government, and tilted all the services of government to privilege Protestants and discriminate against Catholics. Though the structures of government were formally democratic—open competition, free elections—the Catholic minority was always outvoted and systematically shut out of any decision-making roles in government. After several decades, this pattern of marginalization and institutionalized discrimination led, predictably, to protests and to an era of interethnic violence that continues and will end only when a power-sharing agreement has been accepted by the militants as well as the moderates on both sides. By contrast, the Swiss system that carefully strives for the proportional participation of members of its ethnic communities in the organs of government and devolves much of governmental activity to its regional cantons, has successfully managed its pluralism and achieved an enviable quality of life for its citizens.

In Afghanistan, the day the nation celebrated the return of its 87-year-old former monarch from a 29-year exile, the Minister of Foreign Affairs, a Tadjik, felt it necessary to issue a statement reassuring the public that though the ex-king is of Pushtun origin, this would not have the effect of distorting the activities of government in favor of Pushtun interests. The predominance of Tadjiks in the interim administration has been noted with alarm by spokespersons for other ethnic communities, fearing that they will use their current advantage to colonize and entrench fellow Tadjiks in government agencies, especially in the embryonic national army and police. The consequent alienation of Pushtuns, the largest ethnic community, from the central government has been identified as the most ominous threat to the future of unity in Afghanistan.[14] This impression will have to be corrected by subsequent governments if they are to enjoy widespread legitimacy.

In the long run, measured in decades, the salience of ethnic identities may diminish as a secure and effective state contributes to the development of sentiments of common nationhood and enables more Afghans to function politically as individuals motivated mainly by economic and ideological concerns, rather than ethnic attachments. Gradual integration of the economy; the influence of urbanization, modern educational experiences, mass media and intermarriage; the effects of the Internet and of cross-cutting memberships in professional and economic interest groups and in recreational associations, may gradually foster the transition to a more individualistic society and a majoritarian democracy. But as the recent histories of the former Soviet Union, Yugoslavia, Spain, and Nigeria demonstrate, this is at best, a long-term project that may never crystallize. Ethnic identities, once mobilized and politicized as they have been in Afghanistan, tend to be long-lasting, especially when they are reinforced and patronized by external, cross-border actors. Peaceful coexistence, rather than integration, is the feasible goal.

For the foreseeable future, the regulation of ethnic tensions, the maintenance and management of consensual and peaceful coexistence will, along with building effective institutions of the central government, remain political prerequisites for the social and economic rehabilitation and development of a stable and prosperous Afghan society. It is imperative that donors not repeat the mistake committed by the United States when it abandoned Afghanistan after the withdrawal of the Soviet Union. The elimination of the Taliban and the al-Qaeda infrastructure is only the first step necessary in the rehabilitation of this stricken country. Helping Afghanistan to build the institutions of effective and legitimate government, and to lay the foundations for sustained economic development, will require substantial financial and technical assistance and donor presence on the ground as trainers and peacekeepers for at least a decade.

Notes

1. *New York Times*, March 2, 2002, p. A1.
2. The Northern Alliance was the last force that resisted and held out against the Taliban. They provided essential assistance to the United States when it launched its campaign against the Taliban after the events of September 11, 2001.
3. Anne O. Krueger and Vernon Ruttan, "Assistance to Korea" (chapter 13) in Anne O. Krueger, Constantine Michalopoulos, and Vernon Ruttan, *Aid and Development* (Baltimore, MD: The Johns Hopkins University Press, 1989).
4. The Mahaveli project has been documented by Ronald J. Herring, "Making Ethnic Conflict: The Civil War in Sri Lanka" (chapter 6) in Milton J. Esman and Ronald J. Herring, eds., *Carrots, Sticks, and Ethnic Conflict: Rethinking Development Assistance* (Ann Arbor, MI: University of Michigan Press, 2001), pp. 140–174.
5. See Milton J. Esman, "Malaysia: Native Sons and Immigrants," in Milton J. Esman, *Ethnic Politics* (Ithaca: Cornell University Press, 1994), pp. 49–74; Just Faaland, J.R. Parkinson, and Rais Saniman, *Growth and Ethnic Inequality: Malaysia's New Economic Policy* (London: Hurst and Company, 1990); and Edmund Terence Gomez and Jomo K.S., *Malaysia's Political Economy: Politics, Patronage, and Profits* (Cambridge, UK: Cambridge University Press, 1997).
6. Norman Uphoff, "Ethnic Cooperation in Sri Lanka: Through the Keyhole of a USAID Project" (chapter 5) in Esman and Herring, op. cit., pp. 113–139.
7. Mary Anderson, "The Experience of NGOs in Conflict Prevention: Problems and Prospects" (Cambridge, MA: The Local Capacities for Peace Project, 1995).
8. This theme has been explored by Andreas Wimmer and Conrad Schetter, "State-Formation First, Recommendations for Reconstruction and Peace-Making in Afghanistan," ZEF (Center for Development Research) Discussion Paper on Development Policy, No. 45, University of Bonn, April 2002.
9. Thomas Hobbes, *Leviathan*, ed. by C.B. MacPherson (Harmondsworth, Baltimore: Penguin, 1968).
10. Marina Ottaway and Anatol Lieven, "Rebuilding Afghanistan: Fantasy versus Reality," Washington, DC: Carnegie Endowment for International Peace Policy Brief #12, January 2002.
11. Like any allocation formula, proportionality is not trouble-free. It may become embroiled in a numbers game, i.e., disputes over the relative numbers of the competing ethnic communities. For example, every census in Nigeria since independence has precipitated violent conflicts over alleged manipulation and falsification of data. See David Kertzer and Dominique Arel, eds., *Census and Identity: The Politics of Race, Ethnicity and Language in National Censuses* (Cambridge, UK: Cambridge University Press, 2001).

12. Milton J. Esman, "Public Administration, Ethnic Conflict, and Economic Development," *Public Administration Review*, Vol. 57, No. 6 (Nov–Dec 1997): pp. 527–533. Also see Esman, "Public Administration and Conflict Management in Plural Societies," *Public Administration and Development*, Vol. 19 (1999): pp. 353–366.
13. On consociational politics, the leading proponent is Arend Lijphart, *Democracy in Plural Societies* (New Haven, CT: Yale University Press, 1977). See also Timothy D. Sisk, *Power-Sharing and International Mediation in Ethnic Conflicts* (Washington, DC: U.S. Institute of Peace, 1996).
14. International Crisis Group, "Afghanistan: The Problem of Pushtun Alienation," Kabul, Afghanistan and Brussels (Belgium: International Crisis Group, 2003).

CHAPTER TEN

WARLORDISM AND DEVELOPMENT IN AFGHANISTAN

Kamoludin N. Abdullaev

On April 17, 2002, Interim Deputy Defense Minister of Afghanistan, Abdul Rashid Dustum, asked a journalist, "What is this warlord thing you journalists keep calling me?" The next day, Dustum, dressed in civilian clothes instead of his habitual fatigues, stood next to the freshly disembarked Afghan ex-king Zahir Shah at a welcoming ceremony at Kabul airport.[1] This was not the query of an odious militia boss, but the demonstration of power of a serious force mobilizing his resources to remain politically influential and to become a key agent in the international reconstruction effort of this poor and ruined country. Indeed, who is an Afghan warlord? How can outsiders deal with the many non-state leaders who possess military strength, the charisma of national liberators, and the ability to capture regional rule in fragmented Afghanistan?

Since the end of the Cold War, donors and national leaders have struggled with the phenomenon of warlordism and warlord politics.[2] "Warlords" are blamed for the disintegration of states and loss of their monopoly over the means of coercion. They are recognized as subnational, militarized leaders who can resist the central authority while participating in illicit activities. Warlordism is considered a destructive sociopolitical phenomenon, from large-scale gangsterism (as in Albania) to quasi-insurgent political movements (as in Chechnya and Kashmir).[3]

"Warlordization," a process involving the creation of "freelance" armed groups and private armies acting beyond the reach of international and national jurisdiction, has escalated from internal to international politics, posing threats to both domestic and world order. In recent decades, the international community has attempted to confront and control "state-based" warlords like Slobodan Milosevic, Franjo Tudjman, and Radovan Karadzic in the former Yugoslavia; Saddam Hussein in Iraq; Pol Pot and Hun Sen in Cambodia; and many others who have established despotic, harsh, and criminal rule where they could. The "warlords of international politics" have been emulated by numerous smaller "drug lords" and "gun lords." Wherever they take root, they create alternative criminal economic systems and warlord organizations, like the National Patriotic Front of Liberia (NPFL) and the Revolutionary United Front (RUF) in Sierra Leone. Western analysts have identified an alarming breakdown of government and society, as a consequence of the rulers of weak states' "mismanagement of, and incapacity to regulate, their physical and biological environments."[4] Rulers in weak and "failed" states of Africa, Asia, and Latin America, allow warlords to strengthen their hand in tax evasion and illegal taxation, arms trading and barter deals, and smuggling, illicit production, narcotics-trafficking, looting, and protection rackets.

Official records all but ignore warlords and warlordism. No precise data exists about their share in "grey," "black," or "bloody" economies and narco-business. There is no way of determining what part of the "Afghan reconstruction pie" has already gone or will go to warlords or how they will attempt to manipulate the donors' recommendations to preserve their social position, political authority, and command over resources. But it is obvious that local warlords have compelled Afghanistan to place security, rather than physical and social reconstruction, at the top of the new agenda. Greater security is needed to encourage donors to invest in reconstruction and to reduce the risk of Afghanistan reverting to war.[5] Likewise, eliminating warlords requires a certain level of economic development in order to transform, gradually, hundreds of thousands of Afghan fighters into peaceful citizens.

Convention describes warlords as an aspect of the "economy of war" that exploits the resources of a failed state.[6] This interpretation suggests the study of external (financial, material, and informational) support from outside sources to their client-warlords. Strategic analysts, military observers, and peace researchers have also considered how their "new wars" are caused by the decline of state power, the breaking apart of professional armies, the lost monopoly of coercion, and violent disintegration between war and peace, military and civil, and of public and private life.[7]

These approaches leave behind many important questions: Who is a warlord? How and when did warlordism emerge in Afghanistan? What distinguishes Afghan warlordism from other varieties? Is there a difference between a legitimate local chief, a *Mujahid*, and a criminal warlord? Are warlords a leading determinant of Afghanistan's *realpolitik*? Drawing lessons from international intervention in countries with similar warlord-related problems, this chapter investigates the complex political, social, and ethnic characteristics of Afghan warlordism. After scrutinizing its main characteristics, this chapter examines Afghanistan's history as a product of its leaders' abandonment of communal self-defense and their preference for operating outside traditional power structures and modern institutional-setting, rather than as a narration of endless and irrational fragmentation and blind pursuit of warfare. A "war on warlords" would raise unwarranted expectations. A better model would provide adequate resources to meet the national aims.

Comparative Perspective

One of the first manifestations of modern warlordism appeared in Chinese politics, from the collapse of Qing dynasty in 1911, until the establishment of a republican regime in 1927.[8] During this period, especially after the death of Yan Shih-k'ai, China's president and strongman, local warlords rose because of the lack of a political force able to unite China and to create a centralized state. Western experts view this period as mostly negative, referring to the regime's weakness and corruption; yet some have also seen the warlords as "performing a constructive role in hastening the destruction of the old imperial civil service."[9] Indeed, Chinese warlords (sometimes referred less negatively as "militarists") often supported efficient local administration within their spheres of influence. Some of the local civil and military rulers, known as *dujuns* (or *tuchuns*) proved to be more than pointless militarists. The governor of the northwestern Xinjiang province, Yang Tseng-hsin (r. 1911–1928), for example, was an effective non-secessionist politician and administrator, at a time when central authority was paralyzed. He conducted his Soviet policy, ignoring the weak Peking government and developing contacts with the adjacent Soviet territories in Central Asia. Yang preferred the policy of imposing strict but rational control over the local non-Hanese population to direct oppression. As a result, he succeeded in keeping this peripheral, multinational, predominantly Muslim region within China's borders, while Russian revolutionary turmoil and the rise of insurgency gripped adjacent Turkestan and Bukhara in 1917–1926.[10] Not surprisingly, the recent demands for democracy in China have evoked interest in this period and animated the debate over warlords, focusing on questions of federalism and devolution of power.[11]

According to Paul Rich, the Chinese form of warlordism has limited relevance for other parts of the world.[12] Unlike warlords in China and elsewhere, those in Afghanistan offered their people not personal prestige or military status or the means for survival, but local support against external threats. Having emerged from popular insurgency, Afghan substate armed force was principally united by the desire to sustain status-groups on the basis of kinship, location, and habitat by establishing political control and a monopoly over illicit economic activities. They coordinated both defense and plunder.

This distinction has important practical implications. Militias based on family, clan, and local loyalties can be destroyed only by force; shared communal loyalties will always remain open to mobilization by future political entrepreneurs. The diffusion and social reshaping of kin-based solidarities cannot be recommended as an immediate development target in post-conflict Afghanistan. These differences notwithstanding, the general effect of warlordization is an unfortunate consequence of state collapse followed by long-lasting violence and migration, which destroy and corrode established hierarchies of kinship, village, and clan. Actual warlordization begins when an insurgent faction fails "to translate military success into any form of social and political responsibility that benefits the population."[13]

Warlords and Afghan State-Building Politics

Is the term "failed state" applicable to Afghanistan? The brief answer is "no" because Afghanistan has never been a "state" defined in the Eurocentric sense. It emerged in 1747 as an association of tribes and ethnic groups ruled by charismatic leaders and cemented through the sharing of loot and state-income extracted from external sources, mostly from India. Pushtun tribal leaders commanded most military forces and provided the emir with an army and cavalry (*lashkar*). To create a force independent from the tribes, the king established non-Pushtun professional units under his direct command.[14] Throughout its history, state-building projects in Afghanistan were doomed to failure. The Afghan state was always too weak to destroy tribal power and to control or disarm the countryside. The periphery, which evaded state control, remained armed to assure the tribes' defense from neighbors, emirs, and the

British, as well as to maintain the rural order of local communities. Riding (looting) as an established institution among central Asian nomads, also required preservation of military order at the local level. Because local leaders were governed only by indirect state rule and needed the armed support of tribes, they were more responsible and less despotic toward the people they ruled. This strong tradition of pastoral non-state survival has been a serious obstacle to the accommodation of centralized power. Townsmen accepted the state, laid their weapons down, and delegated political and military affairs to their rulers. The rural-based leadership, however, did not. Afghan state building relied on a precarious formula of rural communal self-defense with separation of warrior and ruling class from the citizenry in Kabul and other towns. Local military mutual-help associations that fed on the strong pro–self-rule potential along Afghanistan's periphery, survived until the beginning of the twenty-first century.

Relations with external powers have significantly influenced the character of Afghan warlordism. This country is neither a "failed" nor a "new" state nor is it "post-colonial." Far from being a primary goal of conquest, Afghanistan was viewed by the surrounding powers as an empty zone that could serve as a buffer to protect vital interests elsewhere and to secure against expansions by rival empires. For the Russians, Central Asia and Afghanistan defended Siberia and the Caucasus; for the British, they protected India; and for the Chinese, they protected access to Mongolia and northern China. Beginning in the second half of the twentieth century, Pakistan regarded Afghanistan from the position of "strategic depth" in their dispute with India. Because this area was primarily a buffer zone, there was no direct collision between Great Britain, Russia, and China during their two centuries of rivalry in the region. Consequently, none of the empires provided investment or supported durable development in a country belonging to no one. Imperial needs were met in Afghanistan not by civil entrepreneurs, bureaucrats, and capitalists (as in neighboring India, Iran, and Central Asia), but by strongmen able to protect the narrow, often conflicting, interests of the Great Powers. The Afghan state also has no history of self-sustained development; it never depended on revenues generated by its own ownership class. Massive external material and financial support and huge amounts of weapons from mostly Russia, Britain, China, and later the United States, guaranteed the state's questionable sustainability during the second half of the nineteenth and the entire twentieth century. Local leaders, whose power depended on their ability to redistribute resources, were important recipients of external assistance.

Insufficient and irregular external inflows caused continual instability and growing internal fragmentation, which local leaders cultivated to assure their power. Episodically, Afghanistan was shaken by popular revolts targeting the central government's "internal imperialism." These revolts were repeatedly crushed with weapons and money provided by colonial powers—Great Britain and later the Soviet Union. Sometimes this struggle was disguised as a local *jihad*, but it was incapable of mobilizing the masses, transforming communities, or establishing a centralized state. Foreign interference led to paternalism, trading loyalties, the creation of a political economy built on dependency, and clientalism at all levels of Afghan society.[15] The Soviet occupation (1979–1989) revealed both the state and the local powers' inability to lead a popular, unified movement. The anti-Soviet resistance emerged as a spontaneous, disjointed movement of an armed non-state periphery. Supported by the West and regional allies, it was led by traditional elements: local power-holders, informal community leaders, Sufi saints and religious authorities, as well as a new generation of leaders, mutineer officers of the Afghan army, and a variety of teachers, Islamists, and Maoists.

When and how did the Afghan warlord emerge? As a phenomenon of military politics, he surfaced, using Eric Hobsbawm's expression, during "the new era of uncertain or illegitimate government," in the second half of the twentieth century when the superpowers had stabilized frontiers but not reliable regimes.[16] In this situation, armed non-state actors became involved in statewide politics. Emerging as by-products of the superpowers' Cold War rivalry, warlords appeared because of the failure of civilians to control the military. In the USSR, China, North Korea, and Cuba, civilian supremacy was provided through a single political (Communist) party, whereas Algeria, Benin, Burma, Ethiopia, Libya, Syria, and Iraq found themselves ruled by revolutionary militaries. Unlike these countries, Afghanistan had no ideology, political party, or strong army to create and defend viable central power from external and internal threats. Afghan warlords emerged from the remnants of the regular army and tribe-based local militias led by the heads of established local structures, as well as by informal ethnic and regional leaders during and after the Soviet occupation.

Attempts were made in Afghanistan to unite all anti-Soviet resistance groups—composed of *Mujahidin* ("holy warriors") under one Islamic slogan and flag. Yet, despite their shared Islamic ideals, the effort failed. Afghan resistance groups fragmented into regional and ethnic exclusivist groups. One cause for the absence of a unified army lay in the character of guerilla warfare. Afghan society was not homogenous enough to build trust beyond the village, tribe, or ethnic group.[17] In an environment characterized by the absence of reliable central authority, tribesmen were motivated by the goal of strengthening local community and ethnic group structures that could insure immediate security and defend communities against external and internal threats. Thus, warlordism appeared not as a particular kind of politics, as nomadic peoples' innate pursuit for warfare and plunder, but as "a function of the surrounding instability and security." A leftover of military politics, warlordism filled the "void left by the absence of ordinary politics."[18] As the push for independence of external threats increased, this "abnormal" tendency became a "normal" part of Afghan politics.

Meanwhile, conditions on the battlefield called for the separation of powers and tasks within the Mujahidin resistance. Gradually, military leaders known as field commanders crystallized their leadership position, but they were more than mere military leaders. As Naby and Magnus point out,

> They [field commanders] have moderated the political stand of the parties, and, in conditions of civil war, they have created enclaves of peace and reconstruction while Kabul has deteriorated. The appellation of warlord applies to most, and the danger for the future lies in the field commanders unwillingness to surrender political power in favor of a central government or democratic institutions.[19]

During the Soviet occupation, Western donors preferred to deal directly with field commanders, usually pressuring them to form special organs (*shuras*) to implement programs. Being the principal recipients of foreign aid and the immediate physical defenders and service providers to the population, these field commanders gained virtually complete control of the country. By the middle of the 1990s, the resistance was led by five eminent field commanders. In the Herat emerged Ismail Khan (a Tajik), mutinied captain of the Afghan army and an activist of Jamiyat-i Islami-i Afghanistan (currently general, Herat Province governor). Ahmad Shah Masud (a Tajik from Panjsher, assassinated by Arab suicide bombers on September 9, 2001), controlled the west and northeast respectively. Abdul Rashid Dustum (an Uzbek from Juzjan, currently Afghan defense deputy minister and presidential representative in northern Afghanistan) administered Mazari Sharif. Abdul Qadir (an Ahmadzai Pushtun, Afghan vice president assassinated in July 2002) governed Jalalabad and its environs, and finally, Jalaludin Haqqani (a Jadran Pushtun, joined the Taliban in 1995) ruled the Paktia province. There were dozens of less prominent Mujahidin field commanders. Typically, regional militias secured several villages and important strategic points (roads, communications, facilities, etc.) and were generally loyal to mid-level commanders, who controlled parts of the provinces and were usually associated with a regional unit, party, or organization run by a recognized leader. Consistency within the warlord units varied, and shifting loyalties (especially at mid-level) were often responsible for rapid changes and instability.[20]

Though all militias operated within their areas of origin, the war in Afghanistan was not desperately secessionist. Unlike cases in sub-Saharan Africa (Rwanda and Burundi) that did not pursue inclusive nationalism and were drawn into extreme nationalism and genocide, Afghanistan's case allowed the possibility of the eventual establishment of a modern unified sovereign state. Nonetheless, the arms and money provided by U.S., Arab, Iranian, and Pakistani funds, among others, that were distributed unequally to different groups deepened splits, fueling ethnic rivalries and distrust among Afghan factions. On the other hand, Mujahid commanders tried repeatedly to coordinate their activities. Beginning in summer 1987, they met independently within the framework of the All-Commanders Council. In all, from July 1987 to October 1990, the Afghan commanders held three meetings (in Ghor, Quetta, and Badakhshan) to try to establish criteria for cooperation and power sharing. This attempt was not a great success, yet it demonstrated the growing military and political power of field commanders.

Commanders from various parts of the country tried regularly to expand local solidarity networks and integrate into wider—national and Islamic—structures. The most inclusive group was the Jamiyat party, led by Burhanuddin Rabbani, composed of non-Pushtun northerners. Gulbeddin Hekmatyar was the most successful in uniting Pushtun tribesmen without regard to tribal origin. However, forming temporary alliances with Dustum's Uzbek failed, notwithstanding his attempts to manage reliable coalition with Durrani Pushtuns. Due to a widening social base, formation of alliances, and victorious military strategies, the most sophisticated resistance front in Afghanistan, "a veritable protostate" emerged, led by Jamiyat commander Ahmad Shah Masud.[21] In addition to defending his base in northeastern Afghanistan, he succeeded in building social infrastructure and administration and in managing economic activity and local governance.[22] In areas controlled by the Mujahidin, "rudimentary governments" that managed schools, police, and courts were established. Consequently, these local groups evolved into five major regional coalitions, consisting of several provinces each.[23] A non-tribal, Sunni, non-Pushtun, and single-party (Jamiyat)-dominated Mujahid coalition known today as the Northern Alliance, has been less fragmented and more successful in promoting national claims and forming a "state-organized front." On the other hand, commanders from the Pushtun dominated the more politically fragmented south.[24]

A decisive moment for modern Afghanistan came with the signing of the 1988 Geneva Accords and the 1989 Soviet withdrawal. The immediate effects of this seemingly positive political development were the collapse of the Afghan state's ability to collect taxes, a sharp decrease in Soviet aid, and the termination of Afghan natural gas sales to the USSR. President Najibullah's government was soon at the brink of collapse. At the same time, the Mujahidin, which numbered 60,000–70,000 armed militiamen by the end of 1990, was twice the size of the regular army.[25] To keep militias and resistance commanders loyal to the government, Najibullah attempted to buy them off by increasing wages and salaries and subsidizing consumer goods for many sectors of the population.[26] Because he could neither oppose nor co-opt local Mujahidin constituencies, he had to provide them full autonomy, political recognition, money, and titles, and began to rely increasingly on their patronage and brokerage, with USSR financing.[27] These measures further weakened local acceptance of central authority. Najibullah then asked seven major field commanders to participate in national assembly elections rather than treating them as political figures competing for power.[28] All seven rejected the offer and launched an uncoordinated military campaign against the pro-Communist Najibullah regime. Finally, in 1992 they captured Kabul, thus achieving complete victory over the Russians and their internal Communist and atheist clients.

Mujahidin veterans of the Soviet war were held in great esteem among the population.[29] Although successful in waging war against the Soviets, the Mujahidin failed to complete their *jihad*. An armed conflict between commanders destroyed any hope of a communal state-building project almost immediately after Rabbani and Masud entered Kabul in 1992. From then on, the warlordization of Afghan politics increased rapidly, undermining the legitimacy of the Afghan resistance and "privatizing" warfare by Mujahid commanders. The gradual delegitimizing of the Afghan resistance was caused by three main factors: First, the end of the Cold War and the changing global order modified the environment around Afghanistan. After the Soviet withdrawal in 1989, and the fall of Najibullah in 1992, external powers' interest in the Afghan factions' armed leaders, who were their former clients, diminished. Flawed international peace-making efforts and continued U.S. support to some factions undermined the Mujahidin's international and domestic status. Second, the chronic economic deficits of the Afghan state encouraged many gunmen to perform illegal activities as a means of survival. In a virtually stateless and ruined Afghanistan, the postwar revitalization of the economy increased opium production. Regional transport and drug mafias established the basis for a violent and corrupt economy that funded virtually all Mujahid groupings. Many commanders in search of cash, strove for autonomy from ideological and political leadership, further decentralizing the Mujahidin movement. Ideology was a third causal factor in delegitimizing the resistance.

The Afghan case shows how warfare can be an essential, though short-lived, part of *jihad*. The withdrawal of Soviets troops and the fall of their local "infidel" allies completed the military aspect of *jihad*, made the further existence of Mujahidin militarists unnecessary, and contributed to the gradual disintegration and criminalization of the resistance. Many commanders, in need of regular maintenance for their military units, inevitably distanced themselves, both physically and ideologically, from their primary rural social bases as well as from the political leadership and the Mujahidin government in Kabul. This "de-localization" of warfare, lack of cooperation, and rivalry among commanders empowered "war parties" within all constituencies of the resistance. The Mujahidin's inability and unwillingness to lay down weapons, as well as their continuing rivalry and use of terror against the local population, led to the moral degradation of the Mujahidin. This erosion of the previously honored status of "holy warriors" in Afghan society prepared the soil for the emergence of the Taliban, who were considered as having liberated Afghanistan from the Mujahidin disorder and anarchy.

The pressure to continue the war led to a gradual shift of power and authority into the hands of conflict-generating warlords, and away from the local chiefs who had defended the integrity of the community and from Mujahidin liberators. The principal difference between the tribal leaders and old-fashioned Mujahidin was the wish to live within traditional Afghan society and to engage in illegal activities. Some warlords, like Ahmad Shah Masud, Ismail Khan, and Hoja Qadir, used illegal sources like drugs, trafficking, smuggling of emeralds as well as foreign funds to enlarge their military force, build territorially based institutions, develop local self-governance structures, and support local communities. Warlordism usually occurs when a consistent, unified ethnic group with a shared identity, enters into conflict without any positive ideology (such as nationalism or Islamism) under a leader who is a "lord of particular area by virtue of his ability to wage war."[30]

The predatory behavior of warlords is exposed particularly when they try to control the delivery of aid. Claiming to represent local populations, warlords bargain with aid agencies and international donors to maximize the outside resources they can obtain to meet their own military and political interests.[31] Afghan warlordism thus seeks to use and corrupt the traditional social structures and oppose both the state and civil society. The process begins with warlords blocking donor agencies' access to communities and demanding a share of international aid while conducting the unproductive and conflict generating "warlord economy."[32] Subsequently, this leads to drug trafficking, illegal taxation and smuggling, and the financing of ethnic and substate conflicts. In this way, warlords join the "new warrior class" of mercenaries known in many parts of the world.

Warlords and Drugs

From the international perspective, the rise of warlordism and "drugism" in Afghanistan and other parts of the world has coincided with the fall of the Berlin wall and the end of the Cold War, which caused a decline in Russia and the West's capability to monitor international illegal traffic. The Soviet withdrawal and the subsequent relaxed militarization of the countryside, helped relaunch agriculture, trade, and trafficking in the remote Afghan periphery. This improvement reduced opium growing and heroin refining and smuggling, which had been an important source of revenue for internationally supported groups of the Mujahidin.

Opium was one of the most important sources of income for the Taliban. They dealt with narcotics in the same way as the Kuomintang did in China. Chan Kai-shek saw the building of a drug monopoly as part of his campaign to unite China. The Taliban, like Chan, monopolized the drug "industry" with the stated aim of uniting Afghanistan and fighting regional separatists. Though prohibiting the cultivation of opium poppy in July 2000, the Taliban did not forbid the trade in opiates, but rather managed opium cultivation, harvesting, refining, and smuggling, subject to "state" taxes. According to United Nations (UN) data, during the Taliban period, farmers received approximately 1 percent of the harvest profit, dealers 2.5 percent, and regional smugglers 5 percent. The Taliban taxed these amounts variously from 12.5 to 20 percent, or diverted a portion of the raw opium to sell itself. The Taliban taxed drug laboratories at a fixed rate ($70 per kg. for refining and $250 per kg. for transportation in 1999).[33] During 1994–2000, the Taliban drug-based annual revenues totaled approximately $150 million.[34] In exchange for taxing farmers and opium and heroin producers and traffickers, the Taliban assured their protection as well as a stable sale structure and access to transport facilities.

Leaving aside the state-sponsored drug "industry" of the Taliban, the weakness of the state is a key cause of the Afghan nation's involvement in drug trafficking. Here, the Afghan case is similar to what is visible in China, Burma, Somalia, Thailand, Zaire, and South Asia. The experience of these countries indicates a tendency toward warlordism and increased drug trafficking during a decline of centralized authority.[35] During recent decades, Afghanistan has been unable to guarantee adequate border protection, capital flows, custom and traffic regulation, or taxation. The presence of a weak state, transnational criminal organizations, and non-state actors made Afghanistan a haven for drug traffickers.

Afghanistan's geographical location is yet another factor that influenced the rise of drug culture and trafficking. The country is located in the middle of strategically important international trade routes stretching from the Gulf states to the Indian subcontinent, and from Southern Asia to Europe through Central Asia and Russia. Because of their geographical isolation, Afghanistan and Central Asia are loosely integrated into the modern world economy. This makes them, at best, providers of cheap labor for the extraterritorial production and shipment of goods and services to the First World. As much as 80 percent of the heroin seized in Europe and 95 percent of the heroin seized in Great Britain is estimated to originate from poppies in Afghanistan with majority of that transported through Central Asia.[36] International crime syndicates in 2000 received roughly US$100 billion from narcotics trafficked through Afghanistan.[37] Destruction of irrigation systems, drought, and the decline of traditional agriculture also contributed to Afghanistan's involvement in illicit activities.

To date, the Afghan drug trade does not appear to have been significantly affected by the war on terrorism and the U.S. military presence in the region. Having opted for a strategy of nonconfrontation with the warlords, many of whom are deeply involved in drug dealing, the Afghanistan administration risks losing the support it has developed if it initiates a direct, wide-scale attack against drugs production. Harsh measures against poppy cultivation would be ineffective in any case since roughly 50 percent of Afghan peasants are still involved in drug production and trade. With financial support from donor countries, the current Karzai's government tried to ban poppy growing and promised to provide $350 to farmers who agreed not to cultivate poppy on a quarter of a hectare piece of land. The farmers refused the offer, because the income they expected to extract from illegal poppy production was ten times greater. The heroin economy is currently so entrenched that a "war on drugs" and a total ban without the definition of a replacement crop or alternative sources of income could be disastrous for the interim government. Allowing the trade without restraint, however, may also anger the international community, on which Afghanistan depends for reconstruction funds.[38] The counter-narcotics effort undertaken by the government's poppy-eradication campaign in the five provinces in 2003, created tensions simply because alternative livelihood programs did not support this law enforcement endeavor. A study by United Nations International Drug Control Program (UNDCP) estimated that gross income from opium production at the farm level might have been as high as $1.2 billion in 2002. It is unlikely that the international community could afford this sum, which was more than half of the government's expected international aid.[39]

Though some warlords established control over drug production facilities and traffic routes, and some are active in the illicit trade, in general, Afghanistan's warlordism should be regarded as regional, local, and ethnic, rather than being exclusively drugs and arms dealers. Overall lack of security (for individuals and their property), absence of nationwide financial and political structures, the poor transport infrastructure, as well as unstable conditions in neighboring countries in Central Asia, including Pakistan and Iran, prevented uniting of small, competing autonomous commanders and drug dealers into transnational narco-mafia. As a result, in Afghanistan, drugs sustain and promote ethno-regional warlordism—rather than the reverse. The current political situation in Afghanistan allows for warlords to operate in the countryside, and for the expansion of narco-business to continue apace.

The drug problem has a much wider "social dimension" than warlordism. It touches upon the previously neglected cluster of key societal issues, like the violation of human rights associated with gender, family, and ethnicity. Potential donors should be aware that the "war on drugs" is often used as justification by regional governments to reach narrow political ends by suppressing the opposition, targeting particular religious and ethnic groups, limiting civil liberties, and tightening political control.[40]

Both drug business and warlordism are long-term complex problems, conditioned by multiple factors for which there is no simple solution. A weak Afghan central authority, a ruined national economy that is unable to generate enough income for the government or its citizens, and the continual presence and influence of warlords, makes it possible for the drug "industry" to flourish in Afghanistan. The international community's full-fledged commitment is needed to address this issue adequately. Thus far, drug money has been invested heavily in the wars and conflicts in Central Asia. Drugs are a risky mode of survival for Afghan peasantry.

The driving factor in drug business is the enormous profitability of opium trade, heroin manufacturing, and illegal trafficking. It is also clear that in the foreseeable future, reconstruction efforts cannot generate legitimate income that could substitute illegal revenues for Afghan people. Warlords may emerge as principal guardians and keepers of this lucrative business. The case of the anti-drug struggle in Latin America shows that policies which place excessive emphasis on forceful and military solutions are bound to fail. The emphasis should be shifted from pressuring the government to destroy drug crops and wiping out laboratories and intercepting drug transports to helping Afghanistan and its Central Asian neighbors fight drugs trafficking both economically and politically. Narcotics traders and trafficking networks in Iran, Pakistan, and Central Asian states should also be targeted to diminish the demand for opiates within Afghanistan.

Warlords and the Security Situation

The security situation in Afghanistan remains extremely explosive. The Afghan central state became weaker as it faced the armed countryside. By mid-2002, according to the Afghan government, 75,000 armed soldiers worked for warlords, and over 100,000 armed irregular combatants and war veterans were dispersed around the country.[41] Later, President Karzai recognized the crucial importance of security and development by saying, "over a million Afghan combatants cannot be absorbed into the mainstream of society and economy without imaginative development support."[42] In violation of the provisions of the Bonn Agreement, most of the top warlords maintained well-equipped private armies. Moreover, they were officially recognized as regional leaders and the government does not plan to use force to disarm commanders of private armies.[43]

There is little incentive for the warlords to relinquish their military power and control over resources and population. They watch each other closely to take advantage of vulnerability or broken promises. Even those who are in the government have secured an "exit policy" against the possibility of the Karzai's government's failure to defeat them: for example, the second most powerful person in Afghanistan, Marshal Muhammad Fahim (minister of defense and vice president), now keeps 300 tanks and 500 armored cars in his stronghold in the Panjshir valley. In Kabul, he amassed 10,000 troops, which are paid well from government sources.[44] The governor of Herat, Ismail Khan, holds an army of 30,000 troops in the west, using income generated from duties imposed on cross-border trade with Iran. Pacha Khan Zadran of eastern Afghanistan has 6,000 soldiers under his command with 600 being in the direct pay of America.[45] Gul Agha Sherzai (a Qandagari Barakzai Pushtun) in the south and Karim Khalili (a Hazara, Hizb-e Wahdat faction's leader, and Afghan vice president) as well as numerous lesser commanders exist in almost all parts of Afghanistan. Their combined private armies are stronger then those of the state.

Among the main sources of insecurity is continuing rivalry among warlords as well as their challenge to the central authority. Uzbekistan-backed Uzbek Dostum's contest with Fahim-supported Tajik Muhammad Atta in the north, as well as Iran-backed Tajik Ismail Khan's bloody conflict with Pushtun Amanullah Khan in the west, and the stubborn challenge of Karzai by the U.S.-backed Pacha Khan Zadran in the east, in addition to the continuing presence of the al-Qaeda and the Taliban remnants in the south, controlled by countless Pushtun warlords, make the security situation in the country similar to that during 1992–1994.

Placing the international force (ISAF) against non-state military commanders is not possible. By the end of 2002, the U.S. and coalition forces in Afghanistan numbered about 16,000 troops (including 5,000 from the ISAF) equipped mostly with light weapons. To change the military balance in favor of the central government, the international presence would have to be enlarged and extended to all regions of Afghanistan, thus becoming a *de facto* occupying force. The sad example of the Somalia peacekeeping operation suggests that this scenario is doomed to failure, and that the ISAF would be entangled in another long-term conflict with unpredictable consequences. Even if a protracted military conflict could be avoided after the withdrawal of foreign forces from the country, another upsurge of instability would be likely.

Nevertheless, serious programs have been initiated by the international community in the security sector. Its constituencies include the creation of the Afghan National Army (ANA), the formation of a professional police force, and the Disarmament, Demobilization and Reintegration (DDR) program. Under the auspices of the Geneva Conference on security sector reform, major donor countries, including the United States, Germany, and Japan, accepted responsibility for the supervision of each of these programs. This fundamental project was supplemented by Judicial Training (led by the Italian/European Commission) and Counter-Narcotics (U.K.-led) components.[46]

The Afghan government, with the international community, intends to create an 80,000-person army (including 60,000 ground force soldiers, a 12,000-troop border guard, and 8,000-troop airforce).[47] This is the first attempt in Afghan history to create a genuine national army— controlled by the central government and reflecting country's ethnic diversity.

Major warlords, commanders, and regional leaders (Dustum, Ismail Khan, Gul Agha Sherzai, Karim Khalili, Sayyed Hussein Anvari, General Atta Muhammad, General Baryalai, General Muhammad Daud, and General Bismillah Khan) are members of the Afghan Military Commission, formed in June 2002 with the aim of facilitating and monitoring the ANA formation. This is a very promising initiative as it encourages cooperation between the government and warlords.[48] All regional leaders have also agreed to the DDR program and its gradual implementation is underway.

Bringing together recruits from different ethnic and religious communities and avoiding domination by a single group (the Panjshiri Tajik) will not be easy, however. There is a widespread concern that the new army might be used as an instrument to strengthen Tajik control of the government.[49]

Tajikistan's Experience

Generally, the term "warlord" has an extremely negative connotation among Western experts. Such accounts include contrasting "horse people of Gengiz Khan" who "used to live by war alone" to medieval European barons, who "despite their abuse of power also performed important social functions, supporting religion and culture," as John Mackinlay wrote.[50] The demonizing of "horse people" as irrational war-producing barbarians, and equating warlords to nomad riders, depicts the entire region of Central Asia as a weak state zone filled with numerous acting and potential warlords.[51]

This kind of gloomy assessment resonates strongly with "West versus Rest" assumptions that civil society and nationalist movements are in short supply in Central Asia and in much of the Middle East. This philosophy fails, however, to observe important internal dynamics within Central Asian society and provides few clues for freeing this region from warlords. Meanwhile, the experience of neighboring Tajikistan can be helpful in post-conflict security sector reform in Afghanistan.

The 1992–1997 civil war in Tajikistan also resulted in a rapid rise of numerous "people generals" and "field commanders." After the war ended with the signing of a UN-brokered General Peace Agreement in June 1997, the United Tajik Opposition (UTO) was given a 30 percent quota in governmental structures at all levels. The quota did not change much, but it provided a real alternative to war for the most prominent warlords. Almost all the militias (totaling 7,000) were assembled and disarmed under UN supervision. It is important to note that demobilization was a prerequisite giving amnesty to leaders of opposition and legalizing their political parties. Quite surprisingly, the military aspect of the peace-building project was implemented more easily and quickly than the power-sharing agreements. After completing demobilization, the UTO dismissed its military units, granting former combatants the right to join the national army. About 4,500 out of 7,000 UTO fighters joined the army, which, by that time, was composed mostly of pro-government militias. There was a risk that this integration would fail, for initially most of Islamic opposition as well as their pro-governmental opponents remained loyal to field commanders with appalling human rights record and were deeply involved in illegal activities, including narcotics trafficking from Afghanistan. At the same time these hardened detachments (national army by form, ethno-regional military bands by content) were a real, effective, and unique force able to protect the state from uncontrolled bands and insurgents. Indeed, former combatants united in a loose "national army" crushed remnants of non-allied peace spoilers from both the government and UTO, and by 2002, cleared the country of uncontrolled military units deeply involved in drug trafficking and antigovernment activities. In 1999, a quick and effective campaign was undertaken to confiscate arms and introduce a ban on the carrying of weapons by unauthorized persons.

A flexible strategy was applied toward the Tajik field commanders, including: (1) inviting the most influential warlords to enter governmental office in the capital to please their ambitions and make their activities transparent; (2) sending these warlords to military colleges and academies outside the country; (3) providing them with opportunities to enter legal business; and (4) using legal procedures to punish those who committed crimes. The aim was threefold: first, to detach the warlords from ordinary fighters; second, to disengage warlords from the population and destroy their criminal networks; and third, to free the central government from its warlord dependency and restore stable national institutions, by forming a national army, police, and legal system, and by introducing the rule of law.[52] As a result, the warlords were successfully driven out of a risky war-zone into the less dangerous, gray area of open political competition.

During the transition from war to peace, Tajik commanders retained their legitimacy. Many of the former field commanders were integrated into governmental structures, especially in law enforcement bodies, thus solidifying their commitment to the successful implementation of the peace process. In the 1995–1999 parliament (Majlisi Oli) of Tajikistan, among the 181 deputies, there were approximately 20 former field commanders from the pro-governmental "Sitod-i Melli" (Popular Front). The UN-monitored legal reform and elections in 1999 changed the situation. In the current, bi-cameral, professional Majlisi Oli there are virtually no warlords remaining. In conditions of peace and with the restoration of security, local communities did not provide electoral support to "tough guys." Yet, no one regrets that the warlords left the Parliament; some recall their open speeches and fearless challenges to the conformist rhetoric of the post-Communist majority. Most field commanders have exited the country or quit politics to engage in business or sports. Some warlords were sentenced and brought to justice. Many of them, having disengaged from the military, continue to exert influence on communities and to increase their personal wealth. Some maintain control of the drug trade and are thus less likely to willingly squander this power by returning to arms.

Naturally, these activities and the UN intervention did not transform Tajikistan into a modern democracy. Even so, peace building in Tajikistan has largely been considered a success, as it stopped the war and led, at least, to the implementation of a "negative peace."[53] The Tajik government and the former opposition concur on the need to avoid violent conflict and the necessity of protecting the national state-building project. A significant conflict trigger would be the breakdown of this consensus. Vis-à-vis the government, a loosely institutionalized body that struggles to act legally within the international system, the former opposition has a powerful tool, a mechanism of social mobilization (including Ishan-murid groupings, Sufi networks, and the Islamist movement) capable of mustering social masses in a country with few effective political institutions. The situation is fragile, as former warlords might ally with political and regional entrepreneurs to break the status quo. This may lead to a rapid breakdown of civil–military relations—a resurgence of warlords and the hazardous destabilization of the system as had occurred during the first half of the 1990s. Thus far, the government and the Islamic opposition are leading Tajikistan toward the establishment of a relatively stable oligarchy dominated by two rival cliques.

The Tajik case provides ground for both optimism and pessimism. It demonstrates that the disintegration of substate, kin-based political and military alliances is possible through demobilization, subjugation, and repression. The "disintegrators" should be aware, however, that the initial unity of the "disintegrated" may last. Similarly, physical "de-warlordization" is unable to change cardinally the very nature of a country's political culture and to end violence in communities. Meeting human rights standards and transforming the culture of war to a culture of peace are remote aims. A complete freeing of the community from warlord dependency and its actual inclusion into a nation-state framework is possible if a state is created as an alternative haven for communities. But the construction of a unified national army, police, and workable and responsible government that may provide civil services and political participation to communities will take years. In most Third World states, this process is underway with generally depressing results.

Recommendations

Najibullah's experience shows that the politics of buying off warlords is short-lived. The costs increase, as performance lags. International intervention is crucial to prevent a return to total calamity and chaos in the country. A strong and viable state should serve as a central agent for gradual extrication from warlordism.

It is not realistic to expect that the United States, Pakistan, Iran, Uzbekistan, and Russia would stop dealing with their Afghan clients. But it is also irrational not to use their influence in Afghanistan for the benefit of peace. The international community should force regional governments to bear unendurable pressure on warlords, forcing them to reconcile with each other and to recognize the central government. Precedents of this kind have already taken place in Tajikistan in the middle of the 1990s, when Russia and Iran, alarmed by the rise of the Taliban, coerced their clients, the post-Communist secular Dushanbe and Afghanistan and Iran-based UTO, and forced them to make peace. The international community has to relate its development and aid programs in Pakistan, Uzbekistan, Tajikistan, and Russia, as well as other involved countries, with demands to contribute to the peace process in Afghanistan. Governments of neighboring states should be convinced that donor assistance could grow enormously if they help the Afghan government to sustain peace, with all parties benefiting due to stabilization. For those continuing to interfere in Afghan affairs, harsh measures should be applied. Fueling the rivalry between Dostum and Atta, for example, is to a great extent a result of Uzbekistan's intervention.[54] The donor community has an effective instrument to extend its influence to most of Afghanistan's neighbors, as the share of international aid in their budgets is enormous. Current development and aid programs in Central Asia have barely addressed the security issues in Afghanistan. There is a need for an integrated, inclusive, and principled approach to reconstruction, one that is firmly directed toward overall regional security and confidence-building in Central and Southern Asia and the Middle East. This "securitizing" of reconstruction in Afghanistan is crucial for ridding the region of warlords. The United States should stop offering unrestricted support to Afghan warlords with the pretext of the "war on terror." Rather, they should cooperate better with Uzbekistan, aiming for the "de-warlordization" of the north. The United States should also stop empowering Pacha Khan Zadran, who openly challenges Karzai. Remnants of the Taliban can be eliminated with the help of the emerging ANA, as in Tajikistan, when UTO fighters and governmental forces prevented the Uzbekistan-backed warlord Colonel Khudoiberdiev's incursion in 1998.

It is also vital to support the internal "de-warlordization" drive of the Afghans. Afghan communities should express openly their growing antagonism toward criminal warlords. Donors should support human rights nongovernmental organizations (NGOs) that empower local communities and family- and gender-related projects in Afghanistan. Afghan NGOs can play a monitoring role over both government and

UN reconstruction efforts. Local approaches to peace-making should take priority over the international models elaborated in academic peace conferences, at a modest cost compared to direct military engagement with warlords.

Likewise, traditional institutions of power, including *shura*, a mosque-based council, composed of popular representatives, can emerge as key agents in community governance and counterbalance warlords who habitually corrupt communal structures to promote their criminal interests. These traditional institutes and networks have persisted in spite of warlordization, providing grounds for optimism for a future of Afghan politics freed from warlord dependency. Traditionally, Afghan power structures were rooted in a fragile coalition between capital-based elites—who controlled the state apparatus—and local power-holders. The former had subcontracted the latter in a form of state patronage. This personified patron–client connection has provided the illusion that links exist between ethnic communities and the government.

Co-optation is a most promising way to deal with warlords. It implies deliberate convincing of Mujahidin to put down weapons, integrating with central government, and joining legal politics. Creating incentives for this kind of transformation is crucial, as it has important implications for the modeling of an effective power distribution formula for Afghanistan.

The complexity of state building in Afghanistan creates incentives in favor of centralization.[55] The option of restoring a highly centralized Afghanistan, however, contains a danger of confrontation between an externally supported center and peripheral warlords, often backed by regional neighbors and diasporas.

Recently, the debate on institution building in Afghanistan has taken a new turn. Several analysts have begun to advocate federalism and devolution of power given the upsurge of pressures for national self-determination and the need to free the country from "person-centered politics and internal colonialism" associated with the period of Pushtun domination.[56]

The appropriateness for dealing with warlords in peace processes was underlined recently by former Russian prime minister, Eugenie Primakov, who advocated using Tajik peace making as a model for Chechnya. He argues that the core of the talks with Chechen field commanders should be, as in Tajikistan, the definition of conditions under which these commanders would be prepared to disarm, and the benefits they would receive for doing so. This proposal's applicability to the Afghan situation is questionable, because of the differences between these three countries. Afghanistan and Tajikistan were (and remain) independent countries, while Chechnya is (and under any peace proposal acceptable to Moscow, must remain) a constituent part of the Russian federation.[57]

Moreover, in the almost mono-national and generally Sunni Tajikistan, it was not difficult to pacify the two warring Tajik factions under the cover of Tajik nationalism, especially with regard to growing Pushtun nationalism in Taliban-dominated Afghanistan. While in multinational Afghanistan with ardent Shi'a pockets it will not be easy to find an acceptable power-sharing formula. Nevertheless, the primary focus of the Tajik peace process, which is worth taking into account regarding Afghanistan, is the need to settle problems through direct negotiation and bargaining rather than through confrontation with local militarized power- holders.

Power and responsibility sharing is a well-honored principle for situations where protracted conflict has polarized society and politics. The accusing of strongmen as hopelessly illegitimate leaders, as most Western media suggest, by contrasting them with the U.S.-backed "legitimate government," is as counterproductive as is the dichotomization between "traditional versus modern" in Muslim societies.[58] The transition process of the Afghan society from "the abode of war" to the "abode of peace," from militancy to revival, will take years. There is no doubt that Afghan warlords pose serious challenges to the transitional government. But the tactics applied toward them must be based on concession rather than pressure. With crimes committed by all Afghan factions, and the demands to follow international human rights standards being exerted on all, the issue of real national reconciliation must be solved in accordance with Afghan notions of right and wrong.[59]

Focusing donor efforts on local-capacity building requires an effective, representative central government. A cabinet built on a system of quotas (based on region, ethnicity, gender, and sect) will not be as effective as a merit-based professional one. The weak central government should be balanced with a deliberate transfer of power to ethnic and local identities, and the building of their capacities. Armless Mujahidin, supported by a local electorate, legalized and reinstated in due order, may lead their communities. Attempts to create a highly centralized state, even in the interests of dominant ethnic groups, could lead the international community into another long-lasting protracted conflict like Somalia's in the 1990s. A position involving federalism and the decentralization of power among diverse civil society actors is the preferable way to extricate Afghanistan from warlordism and preserve the country's unity. Yet the probability of various warlords supporting federalism as a pretext to exert their control with little interference from Kabul is high. In Afghanistan, the warlords have emerged from a liberation movement. Most of them have the charisma of national heroes. If the international reconstruction effort fails, in the years to come, warlords would attract immediate sympathy among a poor and starving population eager to resist nation and state building and a threatening international force.

Notes

1. Interview conducted by Camelia Enkhetabi-Fard, "More Important Than a Position in the Government is Keeping the Peace: Q&A with Afghan Deputy Minister Abdul Rashid Dustum,"*Eurasia.net*, April 24, 2002, at <http://www.eraianet.org/departments/qanda/articles/eav042402a.shtml>.
2. See, e.g., Edward McCord, *The Power of the Gun: The Emergence of Modern Chinese Warlordism* (Berkley, CA: University of California Press, 1993); Paul B. Rich, ed., *Warlords in International Relations* (London: Macmillan, 1999); and William Reno, *Warlord Politics and African States* (Boulder, CO: Lynne Rienner, 1999).
3. Rich, ed., *Warlords in International Relations*, p. xii.
4. Reno, *Warlord Politics and African States*, p. 217.
5. William B. Durch, "Security and Peace Support in Afghanistan: Analysis and Short- to Medium-Term Options," Rev.5, Henry L. Stimson Center, July 31, 2002, at <http://www.stimson.org/fopo/pubs.cfm?ID=58>.
6. Barnett Rubin, "The Political Economy of War and Peace in Afghanistan," *Eurasia.net*, 1999, at <http://www.eurasianet.org/resource/afghanistan/links/rubin99.shtml>.
7. See, e.g., John Keegan, *A History of Warfare* (London: Hutchison, 1993); Mary Kaldor, *New and Old Wars* (Cambridge, UK: Polity Press, 1999); and John Mackinlay, "Defining Warlords," in *Building Stability in Africa: Challenges for the New Millennium* (2000), at <http://www.iss.co.za/Pubs/Monographs/No46/Defining.html>.

8. See Stephen R. Mackinnon, "The Peiyang Army, Yan Shin-K'ai and the Origins of Modern Chinese Warlordism," *Journal of Asian Studies*, Vol. 32, No. 3 (October 1973).
9. See Paul B. Rich, "The Emergence and Significance of Warlordism in International Politics," in Rich, ed., *Warlords in International Relations*, p. 3.
10. Owen Lattimore, *Pivot of Asia* (Boston, MA: Little, Brown and Company, 1950), p. 53.
11. Rich, *Warlordism in International Relations*, p. 3. See also, Arthur Waldron, "Warlordism versus Federalism: The Revival of Debate?" *China Quarterly*, Vol. 121 (March 1990): pp. 116–128.
12. Paul B. Rich, *Warlords in International Relations*, p. 4.
13. John Mackinlay, *Globalization and Insurgency* (New York: The International Institute for Strategic Studies, 2002), p. 94.
14. Barnett Rubin, *Fragmentation of Afghanistan: State Formation and Collapse in the International System*, 2nd ed. (New Haven, CT: Yale University Press, 2002), p. 46.
15. See M. Nazif Shahrani, "Resisting The Taliban and Talibanism in Afghanistan: Legacies of a Century of Internal Colonialism and Cold War Politics in a Buffer State," *Journal Of International Affairs*, Vol. 5, No. 4 (2001), at <http://www.mfa.gov.tr/grupa/percept/v-4/shahrani.10.htm>.
16. Eric Hobsbawm, *The Age of Extremes: A History of the World, 1914–1991* (New York: Vintage Books, 1996), p. 348.
17. Ralph H. Magnus and Eden Naby, *Afghanistan: Mullah, Marx and Mujahid* (Boulder, CO: Westview Press, 2002), p. 141.
18. Eric Hobsbawm, *The Age of Extremes: A History of the World, 1914–1991*, p. 350.
19. Ralph H. Magnus and Eden Naby, *Afghanistan: Mullah, Marx and Mujahid*, p. 153.
20. International Crisis Group briefing paper, "The Afghan Transitional Administration: Prospects and Perils, Afghanistan," (July 30, 2002), p. 8, at <http://www.crisisweb.org/projects/showreport.cfm?reportid=719>.
21. Rubin, *Fragmentation of Afghanistan*, p. 219.
22. Viktor Spol'nikov, *Afghanistan: Islamskaya Kontrrevolutsia* (Moscow: Nauka, 1987), p. 135.
23. Nazif Shahrani, "Afghanistan Can Learn From Its Past," *New York Times*, October 11, 2001, p. 13.
24. Rubin, *Fragmentation of Afghanistan*, p. 234.
25. Ibid., p. 161.
26. Ibid., p. 161.
27. Ibid., p. 172.
28. Ibid., p. 174.
29. Magnus and Naby, *Afghanistan: Mullah, Marx and Mujahid*, p. 157.
30. Glen Segell, "Warlordism and Drug Trafficking: From Southeast Asia," in Rich, ed., *Warlords in International Relations*, p. 43.
31. Astri Suhrke, Arne Strand, and Kristian Harpviken, *Peace-Building Strategies for Afghanistan. Part 1: Lessons From Past Experiences in Afghanistan*, Commissioned Report (Bergen: Chr. Michelson Institute, January 14, 2002), p. 19, at <http://www.cmi.no/pdf/Peacbuilding%20Afghanistan.pdf>.
32. Adam Pain and Jonathan Goodhand, "Afghanistan: Current Employment and Socio-Economic Situation and Prospects," Working Paper 8 (Geneva: International Labour Office, 2002).
33. Markus Spillmann, "Raw Opium as the Lifeblood of Afghanistan Central Asia Destabilized by Drug Trade," *Neue Zürcher Zeitung* (November 17, 2000).
34. United Nations Office on Drugs and Crime, *The Opium Economy in Afghanistan: An International Problem* (New York: United Nations, 2003), p. 7.
35. Glen Segell, "Warlordism and Drug Trafficking: From Southeast Asia to Sub-Saharan Africa," in Rich, ed., *Warlords in International Relations*, p. 43.
36. Nancy Lubin, Alex Klatis, and Igor Barsegian, *Narcotics Interdiction in Afghanistan and Central Asia: Challenges for International Assistance*, Report to the Open Society Institute (New York, 2002), p. 5.

37. Ibid., p. 5.
38. Thomas Withington, "Afghanistan: Heroin Trade Dilemma," *RCA*, Vol. 99 (January 18, 2002), at <http://www.iwpr.net/index.pl?archive/rca/rca_200201_99_6_eng.txt>.
39. UN Security Council, "Disarming Rival Factions, Creating Strong National Army, Police Crucial for Securing Afghanistan's Fragile Peace" (February 24, 2003), at <http://www.reliefweb.int/w/rwb.nsf/480fa8736b88bbc3c12564f6004c8ad5/bdaceac344753df685256cd700715e58?OpenDocument>.
40. Lubin, Klatis, and Barsegian, *Narcotics Interdiction in Afghanistan and Central Asia*, p. 16.
41. Ahmed Rashid, "United States Faces Fault Lines in Building Afghan Army," *Eurasia Insight* (July 9, 2002), at <http://www.eurasianet.org/departments/insight/articles/eav072602.shtml>.
42. Mark Sedra, "Challenging the Warlord Culture: Security Sector Reform in Post-Taliban Afghanistan," Paper 25 (Bonn: International Center for Conversion, 2002), p. 23.
43. "Kabul Will Not Forcibly Disarm Warlords" (June 8, 2003), at <http://www.eurasianet.org/resource/afghanistan/hypermail/200301/0041.shtml>.
44. Jonathan Steele, "Arms and Warlords," *The Guardian*, July 16, 2002.
45. Sedra, "Challenging the Warlord Culture: Security Sector Reform in Post-Taliban Afghanistan," p. 18.
46. Ibid., p. 28.
47. Ibid., p. 29.
48. Ibid., p. 30.
49. Ibid., p. 30.
50. Mackinlay, "Defining Warlords."
51. Troy S. Thomas and Stephen D. Kiser, "Lords of the Silk Route: Violent Non-State Actors in Central Asia," INSS Occasional Paper 43 (USAF Academy, CO: USAF Institute for Security Studies, May 2002), p. 80.
52. Kamoludin Abdullaev and Catherine Barnes, *Politics of Compromise: The Tajikistan Peace Process* (London: Conciliation Recourses, 2001).
53. In the beginning of 2002, conceivably under the pressure from the United States and/or Russia, the Tajik president dismissed three ministers (custom, border protection, and taxes) who were allegedly and heavily involved in corruption and warlord politics. Besides, two other former militias, commanders of the National Army were suggested, "to change a place of job."
54. Sedra, "Challenging the Warlord Culture: Security Sector Reform in Post-Taliban Afghanistan," p. 15.
55. See Christopher Cramer and Jonathan Goodhand, "Try Again, Fail Again, Fail Better?: War, the State, and the 'Post-Conflict' Challenge in Afghanistan," *Development and Change*, Vol. 33, No. 5 (London: Institute of Social Studies, 2002): pp. 885–909.
56. Nazif Shahrani, "Afghanistan Can Learn From Its Past," *New York Times*, October 11, 2001; see also, James Purcell Smith, "Debate Over Federalism in Afghanistan Continues," *Central Asia-Caucasus Analyst*, October 23, 2002.
57. Radio Free Europe/Radio Liberty Caucasus Report, "Could the Tajik Peace Process Serve as a Model for Chechnya?" Vol. 5, No. 38 (Prague, Czech Republic, November 2002): p. 28.
58. Frederick S. Starr and Marin J. Strmecki, "Afghan Democracy and Its First Missteps," *New York Times*, June 14, 2002.
59. Suhrke, Strand, and Harpviken, *Peace-Building Strategies for Afghanistan*, p. 35.

CHAPTER ELEVEN

HEALTH, HUMAN SECURITY, AND SOCIAL RECONSTRUCTION IN AFGHANISTAN

Paula Gutlove, Gordon Thompson, and Jacob Hale Russell

Introduction

Afghanistan's people suffer from the effects of 23 years of violent conflict driven by internal disputes and foreign interventions. Their health and nutritional status is among the worst in the world, much of their physical and social infrastructure has been destroyed, and their economy barely functions. The outcome of the latest foreign intervention remains to be seen. In some respects, intervention has improved Afghanistan's prospects, but there are signs that the improvement is temporary. Under the eyes of the world, assistance by an array of actors has prevented a full-scale humanitarian crisis, provided an uneven level of internal security, and supported initial steps toward reconstruction. As a result, Afghans have reason to hope for a better future. At the same time, they have reason to fear the loss of interest by foreign donors and the resumption of violence.

Rebuilding Afghanistan's health sector is an essential part of the broader process of national reconstruction. Even greater benefits can be gained by integrating health programs with programs for social reconstruction and the constructive management of conflict. Reconstruction of the social fabric and the development of a culture in which conflict is managed nonviolently will promote stable governance, economic and social development, and, as a result, better health. The potential exists for an upward spiral in the condition of life, in which improvements in different sectors of society are mutually reinforcing. For this reason, there is growing acceptance around the world, endorsed by the World Health Organization (WHO), that prevention of violence is a crucial public health mission.[1] Integration of health programs with programs of social reconstruction will not add a burden on Afghanistan's health sector, but will enhance that sector's productivity. Positive experience in integrating health programs with related programs could provide a model for wider cooperation across sectors and among agencies.

The latest foreign intervention was driven not by concern for the welfare of the Afghan people, but by the desire of the United States and its allies to "root out" the al-Qaeda terrorist organization. As the intervention unfolded, however, the gravity of the humanitarian situation became more evident. Western leaders were compelled to promise support for humanitarian relief and reconstruction, and to some extent, these promises have been kept. Richer nations have implicitly acknowledged their interdependence with Afghanis, recognizing that they will face new or renewed threats if conditions in Afghanistan are allowed to deteriorate. Potential sources of threat include re-emergence of Afghanistan as a haven for terrorists; global spread of diseases such as drug-resistant tuberculosis (TB); increased trade in heroin and opium; and political destabilization in the region, which includes nuclear-armed Pakistan.

Interdependence and mutual vulnerability of the world's peoples are two aspects of a concept known as human security. Other aspects are the imperative of ensuring that all people's conditions of life are above some minimum threshold, and the use of holistic, forward-looking planning to ensure that humanitarian and development initiatives are maximally productive in achieving this outcome. Afghanistan stands out among the world's disadvantaged locations as a place where the principles of human security are especially applicable.

This chapter discusses health, human security, and social reconstruction in Afghanistan. It offers, drawing from experience in other countries, a strategy whereby programs of social reconstruction, community reconciliation, and conflict management can be integrated productively with health programs. Moreover, it argues that human-security principles are appropriate for guiding the process of integration. Social reconstruction is a strand of activity that complements physical reconstruction and political reconstruction. It seeks to gradually rebuild the intangible but crucial fabric of human interactions that allow a society to function, while also meeting the immediate psychosocial needs of a society that has been ravaged by violence. A key component of social reconstruction is community reconciliation, a process involving the restoration of trust and hope within a community, a rise in cooperative behavior, and the development of shared values and expectations. Conflict management is a set of processes that allow conflicts to be managed productively and nonviolently. These processes are necessary for social reconstruction and for all other areas of productive human activity.

A credible strategy for integrating social reconstruction and health in Afghanistan must satisfy five major criteria. First, the strategy must be welcomed by a substantial number of Afghans and be consistent with the policies of the national leadership. Second, it must be rooted in Afghan culture and, to the greatest possible extent, rely on indigenous resources. Third, the strategy must be sufficiently flexible to accommodate large, unpredictable shifts in Afghanistan's political and economic environment. Fourth, it must be adaptable to specific local conditions within Afghanistan. Fifth, it must demonstrate to all parties, including foreign donors, that it adds value and is cost-effective. To satisfy these five demanding criteria, a strategy is proposed in this chapter, which features organic growth and systematic processes for adaptation and coordination.

This chapter begins with a review of the problems facing Afghanistan, with special attention being paid to the health sector. What follows is a discussion of the strategies, both explicit and implicit, that guide the efforts of the various domestic and foreign actors in Afghanistan's reconstruction. Current and planned initiatives that address Afghanistan's problems are then examined, with special attention focused on the health sector and the internal-security sector. Next, human security and its application are described, and experience from other countries in integrating health programs and social-reconstruction programs is reviewed. This leads to a discussion of opportunities for integrating health and social reconstruction in Afghanistan, using a human-security approach. Finally, an organic, adaptive strategy for pursuing these opportunities is articulated.

Information about Afghanistan that is used in this chapter is drawn from current literature as cited, or from interviews of people witih direct field experience. Interviewees are not responsible for any statement in this essay.

Problems Facing Afghanistan

The UN Secretary-General reported in October 2002 that insecurity is "the most serious challenge facing Afghanistan and Afghans today."[2] He further stated, "No region of the country has escaped conflict. These conflicts prevent the delivery of aid, erode Afghans' confidence in the future and continue to cause human, social and infrastructural damage."[3]

While suffering from continuing insecurity, Afghans also face a wide range of grave problems from 23 years of war and disruption. Of all countries worldwide, Afghanistan is the most severely affected by landmines and unexploded ordnance (UXO). There are about 200,000 survivors of mine/UXO accidents, and the death rate prior to 2002 was 150–300 persons per month.[4] Poverty and hunger are widespread. For example, a survey conducted by the UN in September 2002 indicated that in rural areas alone 4.2 million Afghans would require food assistance during 2003.[5]

Table 11.1 provides data that illustrate the humanitarian situation in Afghanistan, with special attention given to health-related indicators. Low levels of access to safe water and sanitation are evident in both urban and rural areas. Immunization rates for children are at somewhat higher levels, reflecting years of effort by agencies including the UN Children's Fund (UNICEF) and the WHO, but many children remain un-immunized. Life expectancy is just over 40 years. One-quarter of babies die in infancy, and about one birth in 60 leads to death of the mother. One child in two is malnourished, which typically leads to stunting of growth. In parts of the country, many children suffer from iodine deficiency, which decreases the average Intelligence Quotient (IQ) by 10–15 points and leads to poor language development.[6] Birth complications and disabling diseases, together with mine/UXO injuries and war injuries, have led to high rates of physical disability. Over 800,000 Afghans, or approximately 3–4 percent of the total population, are physically disabled.[7] Cutaneous leishmaniasis, which produces disfiguring scars that cause social stigma, affects over half-a-million people in Kabul.[8] Mental distress is to be expected in a population that has experienced prolonged war and disruption, and WHO has identified mental health as a concern in Afghanistan.[9] Field investigations by Physicians for Human Rights have found that "a very large percentage of Afghan women suffer from major depression or other mental health problems related to trauma and/or the suffering of multiple losses in their lives."[10] This finding is confirmed by HealthNet International.[11]

The physical and human resources of Afghanistan's health sector were the subject of a detailed survey in mid-2002.[12] This survey identified 904 active facilities,

Table 11.1   The humanitarian situation in Afghanistan

Category	Data	Source
Population status		
Total population	28 million	CIA[1]
Refugees, 2001 est.	3.8 million	UNHCR[2]
Refugees returned, Mar.–Sept. 2002	1.7 million	UNHCR[3]
Internally Displaced Persons (IDPs)	920,000	UNHCR[4]
IDPs returned, 2002	430,000	UNHCR[5]
Health resources and infrastructure		
Access to safe water (total)	13%	UNICEF[6]
Urban	19%	
Rural	11%	
Access to adequate sanitation (total)	12%	UNICEF[7]
Urban	25%	
Rural	8%	
Number of physicians	11 physicians/100,000 persons	WHO[8]
Expenditure of total GDP on health	1%	WHO[9]
Immunization of one-year olds		UNICEF[10]
BCG	48%	
DPT3	35%	
Polio3	35%	
Measles	40%	
Health indicators		
Life expectancy		WHO[11]
Men	41 years	
Women	44 years	
Infant Mortality Rate, to age 5	257 deaths/1,000 live births	UNICEF[12]
Maternal Mortality Rate	1,600 deaths/100,000 live births	UNICEF[13]
Malnutrition of children under 5	49%	World Bank[14]

[1] *CIA World Factbook 2002* (July 2002 estimate of 27.8 million), at <http://www.cia.gov/cia/publications/ factbook/geos/af.html>. Estimates vary; UNICEF approximates the number at 21.8 million.

[2] *UNHCR Statistical Yearbook 2001, Refugees, Asylum-Seekers, and Other Persons of Concern: Trends in Displacement, Protection, and Solutions* (October 2002) at <http://www.unhcr.ch/static/statistical_yearbook_2001/pdfall.zip>.

[3] UNHCR, "Afghanistan Humanitarian Update No. 65" (September 10, 2002), at <http://www.unhcr.ch/cgi-bin/texis/vtx/afghan?page=news&id=3d7f41ff7>.

[4] Ibid. Other reports of the number of IDPs vary from 858,000 (USAID, *Afghanistan: Complex Emergency Situation Report*, October 31, 2002) to 1.2 million (UNHCR, *Refugees by Numbers 2002*).

[5]Ibid.

[6] WHO/UNICEF Joint Monitoring Program for Water Supply and Sanitation, *Access to Improved Sanitation: Afghanistan Coverage Estimates 1998–2000* (September 2001), at <http://www.childinfo.org/eddb/sani/asia/afghanistan_sanitation1.pdf>. Estimates reported are for the year 2000.

[7] Ibid.

[8] "WHO Estimates of Health Personnel," 1997 estimates, at <http://www3.who.int/whosis/health_ personnel/health_personnel.cfm>.

[9] World Health Organization, *World Health Report 2002*, Annex 5 (released October 2002), at <http://www.who.int/entity/whr/2002/whr2002_annex5.pdf>.

[10] WHO/UNICEF, *Review of National Immunization Coverage 1980–1999* (September 2001), at <http://www.who.int/whr/2002/whr2002_annex5.pdf >. Estimates reported for the year 1999.

[11] World Health Organization, *World Health Report 2002*, Annex 1 (released October 2002), at <http://www.who.int/entity/whr/2002/whr2002_annex1.pdf>. WHO cites an uncertainty range of 33.1–48.6 (41.1 mean) for men, and 34.8–52.6 years (43.7 mean) for women.

[12] K. Hill et al., *Trends in Child Mortality in the Developing World: 1960–1996*, unpublished report (UNICEF, January 1998), at <http://www.childinfo.org/cmr/revis/db2.htm>.

[13] Joint study by UNICEF, CDC, and Afghan Ministry of Public Health of four provinces (rural and urban) in Afghanistan, released November 2002, at <http://www.unicef.org/noteworthy/afghanistan/motherhood/index.html>. In one province, Badakshan, the maternal mortality rate was 65,000/100,000—the highest rate ever reported globally.

[14] World Bank Human Development Network, "Health, Nutrition, and Population Statistics," 2000 estimate, at <http://devdata.worldbank.org/hnpstats/HnpAtaGlance.asp?sCtry=AFG,Afghanistan>.
The percentage is based on statistics for underweight children.

consisting of 21 regional or national hospitals, 39 provincial hospitals, 756 facilities that provide basic primary health services (BPHS), and 88 specialized facilities (e.g., malaria centers). About one-third of the active facilities surveyed were severely damaged, mostly (77 percent) by war and the remainder by earthquake. Of the 756 BPHS facilities, about two-thirds had toilets for staff and patients, mostly pit latrines, approximately half had comparatively safe drinking water from hand pumps, and approximately one-fourth had some electricity service. About 45 percent of all active facilities were reportedly owned exclusively by nongovernmental organizations (NGOs), 39 percent were reportedly owned exclusively by an arm of government, primarily the Ministry of Public Health, and about 10 percent were reported as privately owned. Of the government-owned facilities, only about one-quarter are supported solely by government, with much of the remaining support coming from NGOs—the major providers of health care. Indeed, some NGOs have provided health care in Afghanistan for more than 25 years. According to the UN: "For the foreseeable future and until a viable alternative exists, the implementation capacity of NGOs will be required if the Afghan population, particularly in rural areas, is to receive basic health care services."[13]

The survey identified a total of 2,200 general-practice physicians, of whom 604 are women, and 680 specialist physicians, of whom 91 are women. Overall, including not only physicians but also physician's assistants, nurses, midwives, technicians, community health workers, and others, the survey identified a total of 11,785 health providers, of whom 2,936 are women. These personnel are assisted by 6,521 support staff, of whom 1,505 are women. The total number of staff in the 904 active health facilities is, therefore, about 18,000. A gender imbalance in the number of health providers is evident, which is significant in Afghanistan because there are strong taboos against female patients being treated by male health providers. Nationwide, women account for about one-quarter of health providers, and the imbalance is greater in specific parts of the country. Nearly 40 percent of the 756 BPHS facilities lack women health providers.

The UN has remarked that the structure of Afghanistan's health sector dates from the Soviet era and is not well suited to deal with the health problems that the country faces. There is a heavy emphasis on curative care rather than public health, and human and physical resources are concentrated in urban areas.[14] Accordingly, the UN says: "Consultations are taking place to address the severe distortion in health workforce composition, which is presently characterized by a dramatic and increasing oversupply of physicians, and an inadequate number of nurses and allied health personnel, especially female personnel."[15] An independent review of Afghanistan's health sector supports the UN's view that this sector must emphasize public health, correct the gender imbalance in its workforce, and train mid-level health providers rather than doctors.[16]

The picture is not entirely bleak. There are assets that can be built on. The Afghan people have a proven resilience in the face of hardship, and many social connections remain strong at the family and tribal level. Observers report a hunger that is shared widely by Afghans for peace and a normal life. Skills also exist among people within the local population, among returning refugees and in the wider diaspora. The health sector offers special promise in this respect. According to WHO, this sector retained its core capacity to deliver care during the years of crisis, managing "to maintain reasonable coverage in certain parts of the country during the most severe circumstances."[17] Our interviews show that health care is valued highly across Afghanistan and, as a result, has often been sheltered from surrounding conflicts.

Explicit and Implicit Strategies for Afghanistan's Reconstruction

In mid-2002, the Afghanistan Research and Evaluation Unit investigated the status of strategic coordination in the reconstruction of Afghanistan.[18] A key finding was that "there are a multiplicity of strategies being pursued by various foreign governments, donors, NGOs and multilateral agencies in Afghanistan, not necessarily all sharing coherent or even complementary objectives."[19] This situation persists, with exceptions such as the national health strategy. Strategic disarray is evident at the operational level and at the level of broad objectives for the country's reconstruction. Some major actors support one objective explicitly, while their actions imply a different objective. This discrepancy is particularly significant with regard to the building of an Afghan state.

The UN's Transitional Assistance Programme for Afghanistan (TAPA) is committed explicitly to state-building, stating:

> A common thread running through all TAPA activities is support for the enhancement of national capacity to meet humanitarian and reconstruction challenges, through regeneration of public administration at national and sub-national levels, with extensive capacity development and skills-training activities foreseen.[20]

UN programs generally match this commitment. By contrast, foreign governments declare their support for the Afghan Transitional Administration (ATA) led by Hamid Karzai, but their actions often undermine the ATA. They refuse to expand the International Security Assistance Force (ISAF), continue to support warlords who challenge the ATA, are slow to provide financial aid, and direct aid through channels that bypass the ATA.[21]

Among the factors leading to this ambivalent behavior may be an unstated fear that constructing a modern state in Afghanistan is a doomed mission. That view has been articulated by analysts at the Carnegie Endowment for International Peace, who argue, "to begin with a grossly overambitious program of reconstruction risks acute disillusionment, international withdrawal, and a plunge into a new cycle of civil war and religious fanaticism."[22] As an alternative, they favor a compromise approach in which foreign assistance is provided directly to Afghanistan's regions; foreign actors work with warlords and tribal leaders; and the central government has a limited role. Actors in the health sector, however, have shown that the choice is less stark than the Carnegie authors claim. There are opportunities for partnerships among NGOs, tribal leaders, foreign donors, the ATA, and successor governments, whereby the respective strengths of the partners may be complementary.

Donors have pledged about five billion dollars in assistance to Afghanistan for disbursement over a five-year period, or about $42 per person, per year. This is less than has been spent in some other post-conflict situations. Bosnia received aid of

$326 per person, per year, during the years 1996–1999, and Kosovo received $288 per person, per year during the period 1999–2001.[23] The Marshall Plan provided postwar Europe with aid (in 2002 dollars) of $100–200 per person, per year over the course of several years.[24] This comparison illustrates foreign governments' ambivalence about Afghanistan, a problem compounded by the fact that only a fraction of funds consumed in Afghanistan have gone to reconstruction. From October 2001 to October 2002, reconstruction assistance amounted to $370 million, international peacekeeping consumed $540 million, and humanitarian aid was $1.2 billion, while the US and its coalition partners spent $10.2 billion fighting al-Qaeda and the Taliban.[25]

Initiatives to Address Afghanistan's Problems

The major official actors in Afghanistan are government (ATA) agencies, the UN, UN-affiliated agencies such as WHO and UNICEF, foreign governments, development banks, and NGOs. Warlords and tribal leaders are unofficial actors. Reviewing efforts by the various actors in the health sector and the internal-security sector is relevant to social reconstruction in three ways. First, some minimum level of security is a precondition for programs of health and social reconstruction. Second, social reconstruction makes internal security easier to achieve. Third, there are promising opportunities for integrating physical and social reconstruction with initiatives in the internal-security sector.

ISAF now provides an island of security in Kabul, whereas elsewhere the country is plagued by insecurity. As a result, the ATA and many NGOs have called for an expansion of ISAF. The Stimson Center proposes expanding the number of peace-keepers from 5,000 to 18,000 with the primary mission of securing selected cities and road links—still a small force for a country of Afghanistan's size and population.[26] Its successful functioning would depend on other initiatives, including social-reconstruction programs that reduce the potential for violence, and on its ability to call for backup from forces of the U.S.-led coalition.

The ATA intends to build a national army of 60,000 soldiers, a border guard of 12,000 and an air force of 8,000. Training of soldiers has begun, but there are major obstacles to building an effective army.[27] This process could require, at best, a period of ten years. Similar problems will hinder the ATA's plan to build a nationwide police force of about 75,000. Currently, there are about 7,000 policemen, mostly in Kabul.[28] They are said to be poorly equipped and corrupt.[29] Thus, the state will be a limited provider of internal security for the foreseeable future.

Demobilization of former combatants and their reintegration into society pose major challenges. According to one estimate, there are more than 200,000 irregular militia combatants and war veterans dispersed throughout the country.[30] Other estimates indicate that 500,000–800,000 Afghans are currently under arms.[31] Without systematic demobilization and reintegration, many former combatants will turn to banditry. Recognizing this threat, the Japanese government has promoted plans for disarmament, demobilization, and reintegration (DDR). Participants in DDR programs would receive vocational training and be assisted in finding employment in tasks such as demining and repair of physical infrastructure.[32]

In a post-conflict situation, a foreign military force can perform humanitarian and reconstruction tasks, thereby building goodwill. The U.S. military has initiated a program of this kind in Afghanistan, whereby Provincial Reconstruction Teams (PRTs), each composed of 50–100 soldiers and civilians, will be deployed by the United States and other nations. CARE International has expressed concern that this program will be ineffective or harmful.[33] This concern may be justified; with careful training and genuine sensitivity to local needs, however, PRTs could assist Afghanistan's reconstruction. The health sector and related sectors, especially water and sanitation, could provide an appropriate setting.

Many organizations—Afghan, intergovernmental, and nongovernmental—are working in health-related sectors in Afghanistan.[34] Coordination of their varied programs is a difficult challenge. Nevertheless, major actors in the health sector have negotiated a coordinated strategy.

In early 2002, health-policy analysts were concerned that the dominant strategy for reconstruction of Afghanistan's health sector would be to restore the urban-centered, tertiary-care system of the Soviet period—a concern that proved to be baseless. The Afghan Ministry of Public Health, intergovernmental agencies (WHO, UNICEF, UNFPA), development banks, donor governments, and leading NGOs, reached an agreement to adopt a public health approach.[35] The focus will be the provision of a basic package of health services that address the leading causes of morbidity and mortality, and which are targeted to women and children. According to the UN: "Provision of the package will be through a primary health care (PHC) approach, underscored by principles of equity in resource allocation and service provision, good governance, a decentralized and integrated health system, community involvement, and effective inter-sectoral collaboration and cooperation."[36] Components of the basic package are:[37]

- maternal and newborn health (including antenatal care and family planning);
- child health and immunization;
- public nutrition (including micronutrient supplementation);
- communicable diseases (especially tuberculosis and malaria);
- mental health (including community management of mental health problems);
- disability (physiotherapy and orthopedic services); and
- supply of essential drugs.

In light of the major role that NGOs in the health sector, it is inevitable that they will be involved heavily in delivering the basic package of health services. The Afghan Ministry of Public Health will enter into performance-based partnership agreements with selected NGOs, whereby these NGOs will deliver the basic package across the country. NGOs will also collaborate with intergovernmental agencies—especially WHO, UNICEF, and UNFPA—to provide training and capacity building to thousands of health workers. In addition, intergovernmental agencies and donors will help build the capacity of the Ministry of Public Health.[38] Thus, the major actors in the health sector have negotiated a set of partnership arrangements, in which the respective strengths of the partners are complementary. The success of these arrangements will depend upon a number of factors, notably the state of internal security across Afghanistan and the availability of funding from donors.

The UN estimates the health sector's funding needs at $240 million per year, although the sector is, at present, capable of absorbing no more than $170 million per year.[39] The latter amount represents about $7 per person, per year. By comparison, WHO's Commission on Macroeconomics and Health concluded that a set of "essential" health interventions in a low-income country would cost about $34 per person, per year, while current health spending in high-income countries is more than $2,000 per person per year.[40] Still, donors have been slow to provide funding for even the minimal set of health interventions now planned for Afghanistan.[41]

Human Security and Its Application

Human security is an evolving principle for organizing humanitarian endeavors. It places the welfare of people at the core of programs and policies; is community-oriented; seeks to prevent harm; and recognizes the mutual vulnerability of all people and the growing global interdependence that mark the current era. By combining these features in one concept, human security facilitates the organizing of humanitarian initiatives that require cooperation by a variety of actors working in multiple sectors.[42] Human-security principles are especially applicable to the reconstruction of Afghanistan for two reasons. First, the current foreign intervention in Afghanistan is a product of global interdependence, terrorism providing a link between disorder in Afghanistan and the security of prosperous countries. Second, the reconstruction of Afghanistan demands a high level of cooperation across sectors and agencies.

The concept of human security was first defined by the UN Development Program (UNDP) in 1994.[43] Human security entailed the security of persons in seven domains: economic security (assured basic income); food security (physical and economic access to food); health security (relative freedom from disease and infection); environmental security (access to sanitary water supply, clean air, and a nondegraded land system); personal security (security from physical violence and threats); community security (security of cultural identity); and political security (protection of basic human rights and freedoms). A distinction was drawn between human development, which is about widening people's economic choices, and human security, which is about people being able to exercise these choices safely and freely.

The UNDP definition has not been employed universally, as illustrated by the differing interpretations of human security used by the Canadian and Japanese governments.[44] To some extent, such differences reflect differing views on related issues of international policy. For example, the personal- and political-security domains of human security are linked to the controversial issue of "humanitarian intervention" in state affairs.[45] There are also differing perceptions of the utility or "value added" of human security, with the result that a particular government or other actor will emphasize some domains of human security more than others.

Consensus appears to be emerging around an operational definition of human security that combines two ideas. The first idea is that the objective of human security is to provide a "vital core" or minimal set of conditions of life.[46] People whose conditions of life are above this minimal level may live in comparatively undeveloped circumstances, but have a basic level of security that allows them to plan and work for a better future. The second idea is that the minimal set of conditions for a secure life can be specified objectively by setting thresholds for agreed indicators in selected domains of human security. A person is said to be secure if her conditions of life are, in every domain, above the threshold value; conversely, falling below the threshold in any domain places the person in a state of insecurity. With this formulation, there is no need for weights to be assigned to the domains,[47] and, over time, assuming that the state of human security improves, the thresholds can be raised.

The concept of human security adds value when it assists the planning and implementation of practical programs of action. As a general rule these programs will continue a pre-existing strand of activity. Human security can add value in at least four ways. First, it can provide a clear and compelling objective for humanitarian work. Second, it has a preventive aspect, which can stimulate forward-looking contingency planning. Third, it emphasizes global interdependence and can thus mobilize additional resources and new partnerships. Fourth, it addresses interacting threats in multiple domains and can therefore stimulate holistic, comprehensive threat assessment and program planning.

Regarding the fourth point, interacting threats that affect the health domain should be considered. Poor economic conditions, social injustice or bad governance can undermine health care and promote political or criminal violence, which in turn has adverse effects on health—either directly or through collateral effects such as economic dislocation, food shortages, or the degradation of the infrastructure for public health. Adverse effects on health can have adverse implications for the economy, making the potential for a downward spiral in the conditions of life obvious. Such a spiral can be difficult to arrest or reverse.

Experience in Integrating Health and Social Reconstruction

A human-security approach can add value in the health sector by linking health with related objectives such as prevention of violent conflict, improvement of governance, and post-conflict reconstruction. To illustrate, consider the following competing influences. On the one hand, violent conflict and bad governance limit the effectiveness of health interventions.[48] On the other hand, programs for conflict management and social reconstruction have been successfully integrated with health interventions.[49] Thus, the potential exists for an upward, rather than downward, spiral in the conditions of life.

In conflict situations, shared health concerns can create neutral ground for collaboration and establish a basis for addressing fundamental obstacles to peace, such as discrimination, polarization, and manipulation of information. Health care that features cooperation between professionals from different sides of a conflict can be a model for collaborative action and can create the community infrastructure essential for an enduring peace. In post-conflict situations, health programs can be a unifying influence.[50]

Health professionals have a special role to play in healing violence-ravaged communities.[51] They are often well educated, have public stature and access throughout a community, and possess an intimate association with people who have suffered mentally and physically. Health professionals can create a "bridge of peace" between conflicting communities, where the delivery of health care may become a common objective and a binding commitment for continued cooperation. Finally, they can assist reconciliation after the trauma of war, through a healing process that restores relationships at individual and community levels.

In a post-conflict community, the health sector is often aided preferentially by international and NGO assistance, providing options for communication, transport, technology transfer, and public education.[52] During complex emergencies when there is a paralysis of the state, health professionals can fill this void by facilitating the development of institutions that deliver health care, while also contributing to social reconstruction. Furthermore, international medical organizations have experience in building bridges between medical communities in developing and developed countries, north and south, and east and west.

Health care has been the basis for cooperation across conflict boundaries. When the Pan American Health Organization (PAHO) was founded in 1902, for example, one of its basic principles was that health programs can promote cooperation and reconciliation. In the 1980s, PAHO, functioning as WHO's arm for the Americas, applied this principle in war-torn Central America by organizing regional, cooperative public health programs whereby health served as a "bridge for peace, solidarity and understanding." Over time, these efforts grew to support development and democratization as extended aspects of public health. During the period 1991–1997, WHO launched similar programs in Angola, Bosnia-Herzegovina, Croatia, Mozambique, and Haiti, finally consolidating this work by initiating the global program, "Health as a Bridge for Peace," in 1997. A further degree of policy coordination was achieved in October 2002, when WHO published its landmark report on violence and health, establishing violence as a global public health problem.[53]

Other actors have also been involved in combining health care with promotion of cooperation in conflict-ridden areas. UNICEF, for example, has pioneered the promotion of humanitarian cease-fires for pediatric immunizations, and the brokering of "corridors of peace" to allow the transport of medical supplies.[54] The connection between health and peace is now widely accepted within the medical community. Writing in the *Lancet*, pioneers of this connection have argued, "there is a need for a new discipline of 'peace through health' that studies both the downward spiral of war and disease and the positive symbiosis of peace and health."[55]

The Institute for Resource and Security Studies (IRSS), a U.S.-based NGO with which the authors are affiliated, has promoted the integration of health care with social reconstruction and conflict management, working in selected conflict and post-conflict situations. This experience shows that social reconstruction, the healing of intercommunal relationships, and the transformation of violence-habituated systems can be significantly enhanced by training and assistance in conflict management.[56] Several lessons from experience are evident.[57] First, productive management of intergroup conflicts is an essential ingredient of any successful society. Second, conflict-management processes applied by indigenous personnel can provide this ingredient. Third, a strategy that integrates conflict management with selected social activities is the best approach for embedding conflict-management processes in a society. Fourth, indigenous capacity for conflict management can be built with the assistance of external intervenors. Fifth, the health sector represents a particularly promising point of entry for a capacity-building intervention. Sixth, capacity for conflict management can be propagated by building NGO networks.

Drawing upon these lessons, IRSS has worked in the former Yugoslavia and the North Caucasus helping health professionals realize their potential to heal violence-affected individuals and communities. After receiving training in conflict management and community reconciliation, health professionals are assisted in designing and implementing intercommunal activities that integrate community reconciliation and conflict prevention into health care delivery. In the Balkans this work helped to launch the Medical Network for Social Reconstruction in the former Yugoslavia (the Medical Network) in 1997. The Medical Network convenes conferences and workshops, and engages in a range of health care delivery and social-reconstruction activities including war-trauma recovery; special issues in refugee medicine; social reconstruction in cooperation with other professional groups (e.g., police, teachers, social workers); health care for the war-injured physically challenged; and special issues of war-affected children.

Training is recognized within the Medical Network as an effective way to unite professionals from divided communities. Many training programs have involved the training of trainers, and mixed-ethnic teams of trainers have been developed. A training program for psychosocial support—a process to promote psychological and social health of individuals, families, and community groups—was one of the first cooperative projects of the Medical Network.[58] Psychosocial support is especially important in a post-conflict environment, where the stress of violent conflict has impacted individuals and the social network. In this case, the healing process must address the individual's psychological health, his or her ability to function in relationship to others (relational health), and the relational health of the society as a whole. The process of psychosocial support includes training, supervision, facilitation, mentoring, and empowerment, and is pursued in collaboration with the normalization of social sectors (e.g., food, shelter, health, security).[59]

Trauma recovery is a key objective of psychosocial support. For an individual, trauma recovery involves a decrease in loneliness, anger, and bitterness, and the development of a positive outlook. These steps can only occur through relationships with other people. Trauma-recovery training has both content and relational dimensions. Its content changes as the situation evolves, moving from basic trauma treatment to large-scale social reconstruction. The relational dimension also evolves because trainers, caregivers, and clients all need sustainable support structures that can develop as their roles change. This can be achieved by embedding trauma recovery within a program of psychosocial support that is synergistic with related humanitarian and reconstruction efforts.

Building a community-based psychosocial support program creates opportunities for development of NGOs, especially community-based organizations. In the former Yugoslavia, the Medical Network has been successful in mobilizing large numbers of volunteers for these organizations. As in all post-war situations, there is widespread poverty and a dearth of public services. One solution to this problem is for health professionals to promote volunteer action, by training and empowering people to engage in unpaid public service. Volunteers, collaborating with health professionals, can help persons with medical and psychosocial problems. Through voluntary work, the values and practices of solidarity and mutual help, regardless of religious, national or other attributes, are reinforced and promoted. The volunteers become empowered, their self-esteem improves, and they gain new skills.

The Medical Network's experience demonstrates that psychosocial support can contribute to significant social reconstruction in a post-conflict community. With initial training and ongoing support provided by a partnership of indigenous and external actors, psychosocial support develops through a series of steps, in a cycle that begins with training in trauma healing and psychosocial assistance, and ends with the training of additional trainers. Each repetition of the cycle reaches a larger number of people, until a broad and varied community is engaged in social-reconstruction activities. These activities vary depending on the needs of the community and the capacities within it, and can include: planting gardens; repairing public buildings; hospital or school assistance; restoring public spaces; day care assistance; assistance to the elderly; and suicide hotlines. Medical Network psychosocial support programs incorporated an estimated 4,000 volunteers over a three-year period, bringing together Serbian, Muslim, Bosnian, Kosovar, and Croatian participants.

During this process, the community acquires knowledge and capacity, is increasingly able to meet its own social and psychological needs, becomes progressively less reliant on external support, and can eventually contribute to meeting the needs of other, less fortunate communities. There is also a substantial "spillover effect" as the psychosocial support program expands its reach to include, for example, school personnel, police, religious leaders, local businesses, and local politicians in an array of new community programs staffed largely by supervised volunteers. These programs can directly rebuild a violence-ravaged community through assisting in repatriation of refugees, reintegration of former combatants, and the reconciliation of divided communities.[60]

The Medical Network and IRSS have helped to develop the Medical Alliance for Peace through Health in the North Caucasus (Medical Alliance).[61] A key actor in the Medical Alliance is an organization called *Denal* ("dignity"). Based in Ingushetia and with satellite offices in Chechnya, *Denal* provides psychosocial, medical, and educational support to refugees and IDPs in Ingushetia and Chechnya. Members of the Medical Alliance, under the leadership of *Denal*, have collaborated with the Medical Network on training and supervision programs for the North Caucasus region. At the policy level, the WHO and IRSS have brought together representatives of actors involved in health-related humanitarian assistance in the North Caucasus. The objective was to explore how humanitarian assistance programs can provide health benefits to target populations while also facilitating and promoting peace-building, social reconstruction, and in the longer term, the development of a democratic, stable society.[62]

Social reconstruction in Afghanistan poses special challenges due to the large size of the population involved; the degree of damage to social and physical infrastructure; the history of violent conflict; the inadequate security measures currently in place; and the uncertain commitment of foreign governments to the country's future. Nevertheless, programs that have integrated health and social reconstruction in other post-conflict situations provide lessons that can be useful in Afghanistan, are as follows:

- A program should be guided by a broadly representative group of indigenous personnel because only local people can identify accurately the crucial health needs of their communities. Moreover, important resources for understanding and transforming conflict can be found within the culture from which the conflict has emerged.

- International assistance is best offered in the spirit of partnership rather than patronage. Only those international professionals who come to a post-conflict situation with cultural sensitivity and a willingness to learn will be welcome and effective.

- Healing societal trauma can be an essential aspect of social reconstruction, but is often overlooked. Societal trauma does not occur in a vacuum, nor does it heal apart from ongoing social processes. Therefore, societal trauma must not be treated as an individual disorder but one that requires a psychosocial approach. Community-based psychosocial support can be the foundation for social reconstruction, while promoting the growth of the NGO sector and improving the quality of life.[63]

- The greater the ownership local groups exert over any program, the greater is the likelihood that they will find ways to use and sustain it.

- In order for a program to have long-term impact, it must be embedded in a structure that has the potential for long-term sustainability. Thus, the development of local NGOs can be crucial to the success of a program.

- Setting up channels for ongoing communication and information exchange among a range of parties is essential, and may be one of the most important roles of the international community during the social-reconstruction process. Acts of communication and information exchange have symbolic value, acknowledging the gains in trust and human connection that a program achieves, and also have practical value, allowing lessons to be learned and put to use.

- A health and social-reconstruction program is not sustainable or maximally effective unless it establishes links with other actors. To illustrate, the Medical Network was able to grow and gain stability by maintaining communication links with, and developing cooperative projects with, a range of humanitarian and development agencies and NGOs.

- A health and social-reconstruction program is not sustainable or maximally effective unless it actively seeks synergy with other sectors, including water and sanitation, education, and internal security.

- Ongoing program evaluation and a willingness to change goals and methods in response to the findings (i.e., a structured-learning approach) are essential to the efficiency and sustainability of any program. Also, a program must be able to adapt to a changing political landscape.

- It is most efficient and effective to utilize and build upon existing initiatives whenever possible.

- Experience of NGOs and intergovernmental agencies demonstrates that integrated-action programs involving the health sector can function even in difficult times and under unstable conditions. However, some minimum level of stability, security, and external support is required for any program.

Opportunities for Integrating Health and Social Reconstruction in Afghanistan

Factors that hinder the integration of health and social reconstruction in Afghanistan include a lack of internal security; lack of clear commitment to Afghanistan's future by foreign governments; poor coordination of reconstruction efforts; destruction of much of the physical and social infrastructure; and the low status of women. At the same time, there are favorable factors, including a new, global recognition of violence as a public health issue; the presence within Afghanistan of a residual health infrastructure on which to build; agreement on a national plan for the health sector; the resilience of the Afghan people; a history of some successful NGO–government partnerships in health-related programs; and examples of health programs in which community involvement has enhanced local security.

Afghanistan could be a test case for the new recognition of violence as a public health issue. WHO has become a leading advocate of this approach, through its recent report on violence and health and the attendant Global Campaign on Violence and Health.[64] WHO advocates a new paradigm for health in a post-conflict situation, wherein the health sector engages in a wide range of post-conflict activities. Noting that public health needs in the post-conflict period are broad and multi-faceted, WHO calls for an integrated approach across sectors, which is a key principle of human security.[65]

There remains within Afghanistan a residual but functioning health sector that can be rebuilt. The Afghan Ministry of Public Health is moving forward, in partnership with NGOs, to provide decentralized delivery of basic public health services. This arrangement could provide significant opportunities for integration of health with social reconstruction, especially if cross-sector cooperation is encouraged on national and local levels. NGOs will continue to be the major providers of health care, and will be in a good position to pursue social-reconstruction opportunities.

The resilience of the Afghan people has been noted by many observers. Interviews that the authors have conducted indicate that Afghan society has attributes that are under-appreciated by the West. Tribal structures have continued to function in difficult circumstances, and tribal leaders have some accountability to the people they lead. It is important to distinguish between tribal leaders and warlords in this respect, but even warlords are to some degree accountable to local populations. Overall, traditional institutions and long-standing cultural attributes have allowed Afghan society to "bounce back" from repeated disasters. Many observers believe, therefore, that the best way to reconstruct Afghanistan is to focus on supporting and strengthening the traditional tribal structures. This approach would be consistent with the national health strategy that is now in effect.

There are examples of health programs in Afghanistan through which community involvement has enhanced local security. Typically, these are programs in which NGOs play a prominent role, often in partnership with government. Two examples are described here.

HealthNet International has been working in Afghanistan since 1996.[66] This organization seeks to build local capacity for peace-building and reconciliation while improving health care in conflict-prone situations. HealthNet perceives that security can be best addressed by NGOs that work from the bottom up, starting at the rural village level, a progression that is illustrated by HealthNet's "Health Care Support Program" in Nangarhar province. A HealthNet project in a village begins by empowering and enabling local people to provide primary care. People are trained to provide basic health care and health education, to manage a community health clinic, and to train others. In this way local people take ownership of the project and become empowered actors within their community. Often the clinic is the first or only public space that is safe, and it therefore becomes a functional meeting ground for a variety of purposes in addition to health care, including social gatherings, as a market place, and for educational events. The clinic becomes a safe space because the local people are fiercely protective of the health of their children, and will protect this space from violence.

A second example is the "Building Peaceful Societies" project, sponsored by the Centre For Peace Studies, McMaster University, Canada.[67] For this NGO, mental health has been a point of entry. The Centre is engaged in a range of peace-education projects. It trains politicians, intellectuals, and community leaders in conflict-transformation theory and practice, and develops a range of peace-building programs. It has developed, in cooperation with the Afghan Ministry of Education, a peace curriculum for parents and teachers.[68]

These two examples illustrate an existing base of experience in integrating health and social reconstruction in Afghanistan. Opportunities for expanding on this base of experience exist in a number of areas, including infectious disease, mental health, education (including education in public health measures), and demining.

An Organic, Adaptive, and Coordinated Strategy for Integrating Health and Social Reconstruction in Afghanistan

Successfully capturing opportunities for integrating health and social reconstruction in Afghanistan will require a long-term commitment by the international community and at least a minimal level of internal security. It will also require an effective strategy. An appropriate strategy will feature organic growth and systematic processes of adaptation and coordination.

Organic growth implies reliance on existing structures and capacities where possible, building on positive experiences such as those discussed previously. An organic strategy would be adaptive (having multiple, inbuilt feedback loops); would experiment with new approaches and replicate those that are successful, with a phased expansion to increasingly wider audiences; and would be coordinated across sectors, agencies, and communities.

The strategy's first phase would be to set up collaborative "Assessment-to-Action Fora." These fora would gather a range of stakeholders to engage in an ongoing process of assessing needs, assets, opportunities, and achievements. At the local level, these fora might be centered on the country's 756 BPHS facilities, with coordinating networks on regional and national levels. Each local forum would bring together health professionals, community leaders, government and nongovernmental actors to assess the unique needs, assets, and opportunities at that location. Based on this assessment, forum participants would outline pilot programs that address public health concerns (e.g., infectious disease, mental health) while also rebuilding a functional, peaceful society. These programs would be coordinated across sectors (e.g., health, education, DDR, and demining) and among the relevant actors. For example, water- and sanitation-related questions should be an integral part of the public health approach. In the case of infectious diseases like TB and malaria, it is important that the health worker not only provides curative care but also promotes preventive measures. This typically involves working with families, communities, and local authorities.

The adaptive aspect of the strategy would utilize a structured-learning approach that engages all stakeholders in an ongoing process of learning and evaluation. As lessons are learned from pilot programs, goals and methods would be adjusted, and successful programs would be replicated.

Figure 11.1 summarizes the proposed strategy. The inverted-pyramid shape symbolizes a phased expansion of programs over time. At the local level, programs would be developed according to the series of steps shown in the lower part of the figure.

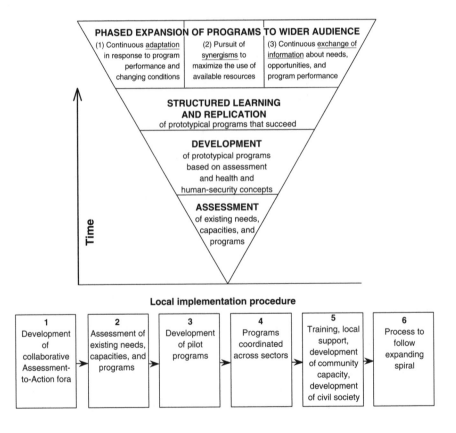

Figure 11.1 Proposed national strategy for integrating health and social reconstruction in Afghanistan

The strategy would need to be coordinated across local, regional, and national levels in order to be sustainable and effective. To that end, the local fora would be connected to each other by coordinating networks, assuring that programs are synergistic. Selected members of local fora in a region would meet with regional government and nongovernmental actors to exchange information and develop a region-wide network. Selected members of regional networks would then meet to form a national network, involving high-level actors as appropriate. The fora and networks would be avenues for interaction among diverse players in the post-conflict milieu. In this strategy, the collaborative "Assessment-to-Action Fora" would provide the foundation of the social-reconstruction process. Each forum would join diverse actors and empower them to develop and engage in programs to build capacity for social reconstruction. Programs would resonate throughout the community, incorporating an ever-expanding number of people in the social-reconstruction process. Interactions among the fora and networks, horizontally and vertically, would contribute to building a national consciousness.

Conclusion

In February 2003, President Karzai visited Washington, DC, to request that the United States fulfill its commitment to rebuilding Afghanistan even as the spotlight shifted to Iraq. Speaking to the Foreign Relations Committee of the U.S. Senate, Karzai warned, "it would be very, very unwise to reduce attention to Afghanistan," given the country's potential to once again, become a haven for terrorists.[69] This statement serves as a reminder that human security is, ultimately, indivisible. Rich and powerful countries would serve their national interests by investing in human security in Afghanistan. One of the key investments they should make is to support the national health strategy and the integration into that strategy of programs for social reconstruction.

Persons Interviewed during the Preparation of this Chapter

- Dr. Lynn Amowitz, MD, MSPH. Senior Medical Researcher, Physicians for Human Rights.
- Dr. Joanna Santa Barbara. Department of Psychiatry and Centre for Peace Studies, McMaster University.
- Willem Van de Put, MA. Director, HealthNet International.
- Dr. Ahmed Abd El Rahman, MD, MPH. Manager, Health Care Support Program in Eastern Afghanistan, HealthNet International.
- Dr. Panna Erasmus, MB, BS, MSc. Manager, Malaria and Leishmaniasis Control Program, Afghanistan, HealthNet International.
- Esmee de Jong, MA. Medical Anthropologist and Liaison Officer, Kabul, HealthNet International.
- Beat Schweizer. Head of Mission to Iran, International Committee of the Red Cross.

Notes

1. World Health Organization, *World Report on Violence and Health* (Geneva: World Health Organization, 2002), at <http://www.who.int/violence_injury_prevention>.
2. UN Secretary-General, *The Situation in Afghanistan and Its Implications for International Peace and Security* (October 2002), p. 4, at <http://daccessods.un.org/access.nsf/Get?OpenAgent&DS=S/2002/1173&Lang=E&Area=UNDOC>.
3. Ibid., p. 8.
4. Asian Development Bank, UNDP, and World Bank, *Afghanistan Preliminary Needs Assessment for Recovery and Reconstruction* (January 2002), p. iii, at <http://lnweb18.worldbank.org/SAR/sa.nsf/Attachments/full/$File/Complete.pdf>.
5. UN Office for the Coordination of Humanitarian Affairs, *Transitional Assistance Program for Afghanistan, January 2003–March 2003* (New York and Geneva: United Nations, December 2002), p. 17, at <http://www.reliefweb.int/appeals/2003/files/tapa03.pdf>.
6. Ibid., p. 26.
7. Asian Development Bank, UNDP, and World Bank, *Afghanistan Preliminary Needs Assessment for Recovery and Reconstruction,* section V.A.
8. HealthNet International Press Release (July 25, 2002), accessed October 1, 2002 at <http://www.healthnetinternational.org/nivo_4.asp?id=154>.
9. World Health Organization, *Reconstruction of the Afghanistan Health Sector: A Preliminary Assessment of Needs and Opportunities* (Cairo, Egypt: World Health Organization, 2002), p. 4, at: <http://www.who.int/disasters/repo/7605.pdf>.
10. Physicians for Human Rights, *Maternal Mortality in Herat Province, Afghanistan: The Need to Protect Women's Rights* (United States: Physicians for Human Rights, 2002), p. 7, at <http://www.phrusa.org/research/pdf/maternal_mortality.pdf>.
11. HealthNet International Press Release (August 1, 2002), accessed October 1, 2002 at <http://www.healthnetinternational.org/nivo_4.asp?id=154>.
12. Management Sciences for Health et al., *Afghanistan National Health Resources Assessment: Preliminary Results* (Kabul: Prepared for the Ministry of Public Health, November 5, 2002).
13. UN Office for the Coordination of Humanitarian Affairs, *Transitional Assistance Program for Afghanistan, January 2003–March 2003,* p. 27.
14. Ibid., p. 26.
15. Ibid., p. 29.
16. Ronald Waldman and Homaira Hanif, *The Public Health System in Afghanistan* (Kabul: Afghanistan Research and Evaluation Unit, May–June 2002), at <http://www.areu.org.pk/publications/waldman_health.pdf>.
17. World Health Organization, *Reconstruction of the Afghanistan Health Sector: A Preliminary Assessment of Needs and Opportunities,* pp. 4–5.
18. Nicholas Stockton, *Strategic Coordination in Afghanistan* (Kabul: Afghanistan Research and Evaluation Unit, 2002), executive summary at <http://www.areu.org.pk/publications/exec_sum_coordination.doc>.
19. Ibid., p. 1.
20. UN Office for the Coordination of Humanitarian Affairs, *Transitional Assistance Program for Afghanistan, January 2003–March 2003,* p. 6.
21. Human Rights Watch, *Afghanistan's Bonn Agreement One Year Later: A Catalog of Missed Opportunities* (New York: Human Rights Watch, December 5, 2002), at <http://www.hrw.org/backgrounder/asia/afghanistan/bonn1yr-bck.pdf>; CARE International Policy Brief, *A New Year's Resolution to Keep: Securing a Lasting Peace in Afghanistan* (CARE International in Afghanistan, January 2003), at <http://www.careinternational.org.uk/news/what_do_care_think/afghanistan/afghanistan_policy_brief_jan_2003.pdf>. See also Sedra, Mark, *Challenging the Warlord Culture: Security Sector Reform in Post-Taliban Afghanistan* (Bonn, Germany: Bonn International Center

for Conversion, October 1, 2002); *Rebuilding Afghanistan: A Little Less Talk, a Lot More Action,* Policy Brief, CARE International in Afghanistan (2002) at <http://www. careusa.org/newsroom/specialreports/afghanistan/09302002_ policybrief.pdf>; International Crisis Group, *The Afghan Transitional Administration: Prospects and Perils,* Afghanistan Briefing (Kabul/Brussels: International Crisis Group, July 30, 2002), at <http://www.crisisweb.org/projects/asia/afghanistan_southasia/reports/A400719_30072002. pdf>.

22. Marina Ottaway and Anatol Lieven, *Rebuilding Afghanistan: Fantasy versus Reality,* Policy Brief 12 (Washington, DC: Carnegie Endowment for International Peace, January 2002).

23. *Rebuilding Iraq: A Little Less Talk, a Lot More Action,* Policy Brief, CARE International in Afghanistan, p. 2.

24. Michael E. O'Hanlon, *The Aid and Reconstruction Agenda for Afghanistan,* Analysis Paper 13 (Washington, DC: Brookings Institution, December 19, 2001), at <http:// www.brook.edu/views/papers/ohanlon/20011219.pdf>.

25. *Rebuilding Iraq: A Little Less Talk, a Lot More Action,* Policy Brief, CARE International in Afghanistan, p. 5.

26. William J. Durch, *Security and Peace Support in Afghanistan: Analysis and Short- to Medium-Term Options,* Presentation (Washington, DC: Henry L. Stimson Center, July 31, 2002), at <http://www.stimson.org/fopo/pdf/afghansecurityoptions310802.pdf>.

27. Sedra, *Challenging the Warlord Culture,* pp. 28–32.

28. Ibid., pp. 32–34.

29. CARE International Policy Brief, *A New Year's Resolution to Keep,* p. 3.

30. Mark Jalali, "Rebuilding Afghanistan's National Army," *Parameters,* Vol. 32, No. 3 (Autumn 2002): pp. 72–86, at: <http://carlisle-www.army.mil/usawc/Parameters/ 02autumn/jalali.pdf>, p. 84.

31. Sedra, *Challenging the Warlord Culture,* p. 39.

32. Ibid., pp. 40–43.

33. CARE International Policy Brief, *A New Year's Resolution to Keep,* pp. 5–6.

34. A list of organizations working in Afghanistan in the areas of health and social welfare and water and sanitation can be found in table 2 and the appendix in Gordon Thompson, Paula Gutlove, and Jacob Hale Russell, *Social Reconstruction in Afghanistan through the Lens of Health and Human Security* (Cambridge, MA: Institute for Resource and Security Studies, May 2003).

35. Waldman and Hanif, *The Public Health System in Afghanistan,* p. 1.

36. UN Office for the Coordination of Humanitarian Affairs, *Transitional Assistance Program for Afghanistan, January 2003–March 2003,* p. 27.

37. Waldman and Hanif, *The Public Health System in Afghanistan,* p. 4.

38. UN Office for the Coordination of Humanitarian Affairs, *Transitional Assistance Program for Afghanistan, January 2003–March 2003,* p. 29.

39. Ibid., p. 27.

40. WHO Commission on Macroeconomics and Health Report, *Macroeconomics and Health: Investing in Health for Economic Development* (Geneva: World Health Organization, December 20, 2001), p. 11 at <http://www3.who.int/whosis/menu.cfm? path= whosis,cmh&language=english>.

41. Thompson, Gutlove, and Russell, *Social Reconstruction in Afghanistan,* table 3.

42. Paula Gutlove and Gordon Thompson, "Human Security: Expanding the Scope of Public Health," *Medicine, Conflict and Survival,* Vol. 19, No. 1 (2003): pp. 17–34.

43. United Nations Development Program, *Human Development Report 1994: New Dimensions of Human Security* (New York: Oxford University Press, 1994).

44. Department of Foreign Affairs and International Trade of Canada, *Freedom from Fear: Canada's Foreign Policy for Human Security* (Ottawa, Ontario: Department of Foreign Affairs and International Trade, 2002); Ministry of Foreign Affairs of Japan, *2000*

Diplomatic Bluebook, chapter II, section 3, at <http://www.mofa.go.jp/policy/other/bluebook/2000>.

45. International Commission on Intervention and State Sovereignty, *The Responsibility to Protect* (Ottawa, Canada: International Development Research Centre, December 2001).

46. Sabina Alkire, *Conceptual Framework for Human Security* (Commission on Human Security, February 16, 2002), at: <http://www.humansecurity-chs.org/doc/frame.html>.

47. Gary King and Christopher J.L. Murray, "Rethinking Human Security," *Political Science Quarterly*, Vol. 116, No. 4 (2002): pp. 585–610.

48. P. Jha, A. Mills, K. Hanson, et al., "Improving the Health of the Global Poor," *Science*, Vol. 295 (March 15, 2002): pp. 2036–2039.

49. Paula Gutlove, "Health as a Bridge to Peace," in WHO Centre for Health Development, *Violence and Health: Proceedings of a WHO Global Symposium, October 12–15, 1999* (Kobe, Japan: World Health Organization, 2000); See also Peter J. Hotez, "Vaccine Diplomacy," *Foreign Policy* (May/June 2001).

50. Gutlove, "Health as a Bridge to Peace."

51. Paula Gutlove, "Health Bridges for Peace," *Medicine, Conflict and Survival*, Vol. 14 (1998): pp. 6–23.

52. War and Health Program of McMaster University, *A Health to Peace Handbook* (Hamilton, Ontario: McMaster University, 1996).

53. World Health Organization, *World Report on Violence and Health*, p. 230; World Health Organization, *Report of the First WHO Consultative meeting on Health as a Bridge to Peace*, (Les Pensieres, Annecy, October 30–31, 1997); World Health Organization, *Health in Social Development: WHO Position Paper, Copenhagen* (Copenhagen, Denmark: World Health Organization); "Local Support for Peace Through Health," in War and Health Program of McMaster University, A Health to Peace Handbook.

54. *Shots of Vaccine Instead of Shots of Artillery*, in War and Health Program of McMaster University, A Health to Peace Handbook.

55. G. MacQueen, J. Santa-Barbara, V. Neufeld, S. Yusuf, R. Horton, et al., "Health and Peace: Time for a New Discipline," *The Lancet*, Vol. 357 (May 12, 2001): pp. 1460–1461.

56. Paula Gutlove, "Health Bridges for Peace: Integrating Health Care with Conflict Prevention and Community Reconciliation," in Smock, David, ed., *Training to Promote Conflict Management: USIP-Assisted Training Projects* (Washington, DC: United States Institute of Peace, July 1999), at <http://www.usip.org/pubs/peaceworks/PDF/ pwks29.pdf>.

57. Paula Gutlove and Gordon Thompson, *A Strategy for Conflict Management: Integrated Action in Theory and Practice* (Cambridge, MA: Institute for Resource and Security Studies, March 1999).

58. Judy Barsalou, *Training to Help Traumatized Populations* (Washington, DC: United States Institute of Peace, December 17, 2001), at <http://www.usip.org/pubs/specialreports/sr79.pdf>.

59. Dean Ajdukovic, "Psychosocial Assistance to Children," in Dean Ajdukovic, ed., *Empowering Children: Psychosocial Assistance Under Difficult Circumstances* (Zagreb, Croatia: Society for Psychological Assistance, 1999).

60. OMEGA Health Centre and Society for Victims of Organized Violence and Human Rights Violation, *European Guidelines on Empowerment and Integration Programs for Refugee Children and Adolescents* (Graz, Austria: Omega Health Centre, 2000).

61. Paula Gutlove, *Health as a Bridge for Peace in the North Caucasus*, Final Report on a Workshop for Health Professionals (Pyatigorsk, Russia, October 29–November 2, 1998; Cambridge, MA: Institute for Resource and Security Studies; and Copenhagen, Denmark: World Health Organization, Regional Office for Europe).

62. Paula Gutlove, *Application of the Peace through Health Approach in the North Caucasus*, Report of an Inter-Agency Consultation (Moscow, April 4–5, 2000, published June 2000;

Cambridge, MA: Institute for Resource and Security Studies; and Copenhagen, Denmark: World Health Organization, Regional Office for Europe).

63. Dean Ajdukovic, "Challenges of Training for Trauma Recovery," in Dean Ajdukovic, ed., *Trauma Recovery Lessons Learned* (Zagreb, Croatia: Society for Psychological Assistance, 1997).

64. WHO, *World Report on Violence and Health; WHO Global Campaign on Violence and Health—January 2003*, Newsletter No. 1 (World Health Organization, 2002), at <http://www5.who.int/violence_injury_prevention/download.cfm?id=0000000655>.

65. WHO (2002), *World Report on Violence and Health*, p. 233.

66. Information obtained from <http://www.healthnetinternational.org> and interviews with HealthNet staff.

67. Graeme MacQueen and Seddiq Weera, *Media and Peace Education in Afghanistan*, Interim Report (Ontario, Canada: Centre for Peace Studies, McMaster University, April 9, 2001); Interview with Joanna Santa Barbara.

68. Seddiq Weera et al., *Breathing a New Breath into the People of Afghanistan: A Peace Curriculum for Teachers and Parents* (Ontario, Canada: Centre for Peace Studies, McMaster University, 2000–2001).

69. *The Boston Globe*, February 27, 2003, p. A18.

PART 3
REGIONAL IMPLICATIONS OF RECONSTRUCTION

Chapter Twelve

The Afghan Neighborhood and Future Stability: A Regional Approach to Reconstruction and Development

Eden Naby and R.N. Frye

Three approaches to reconstruction in Afghanistan distinguish different conceptions of its future development. The first sees Afghanistan as a unique case, with little relevance as a model for other Third World countries or even for other Islamic lands. The second identifies Afghanistan in terms of a model derived from experiences with other Third World countries. The third proposes treating the country as a member of a regional bloc, influenced by, and influencing, its neighbors. This third regional approach shifts the spotlight from one country to the surrounding "neighborhood," because its ethnic groups are separated only by artificial boundaries, living with national neighbors who cannot be ignored in addressing internal problems of reconstruction and development. Since Afghanistan's ethnic-based warlords are beyond the control of neighboring states, international donors must either confront the problems of both or seek cooperation among them.

How is this end to be advanced? There is a limited repertory of possible actions. The creation of a regional tribunal to handle disputes among neighboring countries and ethnic groups is a characteristic endeavor for nongovernmental organizations (NGOs), which can address regional, social, and religious differences, either by regional courts or by institutions created especially to resolve problems between states and among groups that occupy both sides of a national boundary. Although comprehensive regional cooperation is still somewhat of a fantasy, the same can be said of the possibility of isolating Afghanistan and treating it as a single, national identity. Open regional cooperation for common goals is the ultimate desideratum.

Unlike most European states, Afghanistan is a confused mixture of political, economic, and ethnic elements. Several chapters in this book describe Afghanistan's lack of an effective ideology, political party, or army strong enough to consolidate central authority, all of which contribute to warlord domination over all aspects of life. Local tribal and ethnic lords have been a constant feature of Afghanistan's long history, and it seems clear that as "warlords" they will have to be co-opted rather than attacked, and that in the long run the attitudes of the people must change in order to respect, honor, and obey laws and institutions rather than individuals. As institutions, it is the presidency, not the president, and kingship, not the king, that must govern by law.

The suggested regional approach includes three elements. First, it recognizes a recent fundamental change that has dramatically altered the pattern of political relationships in the past two centuries. Competition among colonizing powers since the eighteenth century, when Russia and Britain advanced into Central and South Asia, created a political map that, by 1991, had led to many small sovereign states to perpetuate themselves (known as the "stans": Azerbaijan, Turkmenistan, Uzbekistan, Tajikistan, Kazakhstan, and Kyrgyzstan). As a regional player Afghanistan is not unique, except that 20 years of devastation has diminished it politically, economically, and culturally; helped to remove Cold War's adversarial relations; provided its northern neighbors with sovereignty; and placed Turkey, Iran, and Pakistan in a position to build new relationships with Central Asia and the Caucasus.

Second, this approach finds Afghanistan at the heart of the region. As experienced in the pre-colonial past, the removal of superpower-imposed barriers to transport, trade, and communications, has encouraged the natural impulse in the region to mingle on economic, cultural, and human levels. But formal mechanisms for such activity to occur have not yet fully emerged. Thus without Afghanistan such regional activity can proceed only with difficulty. Even at the height of the Cold War, Afghans traded surreptitiously in illicit goods across the Turkmenistan frontier and elsewhere. Now that Afghanistan has the potential for becoming a stable state, the possibilities for regional cooperation show considerable promise. Donors seeking to assist Afghanistan are entitled to ask to what extent do Afghan leaders see prosperity as lying in the regional network, as opposed to the model of the past 200 years when Afghanistan subsisted on foreign dole.

The third element of the regional approach is Afghanistan's much-discussed multi-ethnicity—a factor leading to internal political instability, cultural institutional weakness, and regional ethnic meddling. A country of 20 to 27 million people, divided by at least three major mutually incomprehensible language sectors—Pushtu, Persian (Dari, Tajik), and Turkic (Uzbek, Turkmen, Kazakh, Kyrgyz)—is handicapped in building educational institutions, running administrative affairs, and creating security organizations. It must be noted that Afghanistan's ethnic diversity was imposed by its borders. The ethnic groups within Afghanistan are extensions of ethnic majorities or minorities across regional borders, raising questions about whether or not there is a viable model for resolving Afghan ethnic woes that exists outside of regional cooperation.

Without examining these three issues in definitive depth, this chapter suggests a regional solution for the next two phases of Afghan history—reconstruction and a hoped-for prosperity succeeding it—in which roads, schools, health care systems, and government ministries will surpass prewar survival standards. Planning must include taking steps to assure that Afghanistan prospers, transcending that dreaded category of "least developed" and ensuring that the country is not, once again, victimized unduly by invasion, religious fanaticism, the opium economy, terrorist networks, and criminal elements.

Afghanistan and Regional Development

Since it began analyzing the broad international relationship of countries with regard to trade and development, the United Nations Commission on Trade and

Development (UNCTAD) has published information about three issues that affect Afghanistan: the list of countries that are landlocked, those countries that are least developed (LDCs), and regional organizations for economic cooperation and trade. Afghanistan heads the first two lists; it is both landlocked and least developed. But because it has become an ardently nonaligned country (due in large part to its problems with Pakistan) Afghanistan did not appear on any regional lists, nor was it recognized in mutual protection alliances such as CENTO (the Central Treaty Organization) or in trade alliances such as ASEAN (the Association of South East Asian Nations).

Prior to World War II, Afghanistan had joined Iran and Turkey in 1937 in the Treaty of Non-Aggression and Friendship signed at Sa'adabad, Iran.[1] After the creation of Pakistan and the onset of the Cold War, Afghanistan was not invited into any regional alliances for defense or trade development except for bilateral arrangements with the Soviet Union and India as the major partners, and some smaller European and East Bloc countries. In 1985, in the midst of the Iraq–Iran War, the Economic Cooperation Organization (ECO) emerged with the main non-Arab countries of west Asia, Turkey, Iran, and Pakistan, to facilitate cooperation in regional trade.

In 1992, the structure of ECO was transformed, with important consequences for Afghanistan. In that year, with the formation of independent states in Central Asia and the Transcaucasus, the end of the Cold War, and the victory of the Afghan Mujahidin, membership in ECO grew to ten, and Afghanistan became an important, if not controversial, part of this group. All of the members were contiguous geographically, and ECO began to envision a grand revival of trade like that of the ancient Silk Road, promoting the development of port facilities on the Mediterranean, the Arabian Sea, and the Indian Ocean. For Iran, Turkey, and Pakistan, transit through Afghanistan to Central Asia acquired great importance, as the potential for contact with that once-cloistered area became possible. By the mid-1990s, serious discussion emerged in ECO about a transport infrastructure that would allow the seven landlocked members to gain access to sea routes, while the littoral states would engage in trade in everything from gas and petroleum to cotton and rice. The new landlocked states were Azerbaijan, Turkmenistan, Uzbekistan, Tajikistan, Kazakhstan, Kyrgyzstan, and Afghanistan.

The promise that ECO would allow for trade-based prosperity to improve the lot of member states; to allow China access to the west through Central Asia; and in the process, help the reconstruction of Afghanistan, faltered because of the instability that ensued following the outbreak of ethnic war in Afghanistan. Moreover, the possible success of ECO alarmed several capitals. Moscow had been scrambling to retain in its sphere the "near abroad," as it referred to its former eponymous Soviet republics. Saudi Arabia, anxious to influence "Muslim" Central Asia and reduce Iran's chances for the same, worked to thwart Iran, in part through its proxy, Pakistan. China feared that Central Asian independence would bring to a boil the irredentism cherished in its northwest region of Xinjiang, a Turkic (Uighur and Kazakh) area almost indistinguishable from ethnic groups on the former Soviet side. And equally important, the United States, unwilling to see Iran play a major regional role, backed Turkey in its bilateral relations with the former Soviet republics, to the extent that it pressed for the construction of an oil pipeline through the difficult terrain of eastern Turkey, rather than allow a far cheaper route to be built through eastern Iran. Similarly, a pipeline through western Afghanistan that might have brought Turkmen gas to Pakistan and its planned port facilities in the underdeveloped Balochistan province wobbled as Afghan warlords clashed. When the Taliban entered the political scene, they brought a level of regional political ineptness matching that of the U.S. abandonment of Afghanistan after the collapse of the Soviet Union in 1991.

Throughout the 1990s, despite frequent episodes of mutual suspicion among the three original ECO members, regular meetings continued in Ashgabad, Islamabad, Baku, Tehran, and other places. The mechanism for regional cooperation stayed in place. Stubbornly, even after the Taliban drove President Burhanuddin Rabbani out of Kabul, ECO continued to seat him rather than the Taliban as the Afghan representative at its meetings. This is the same pattern followed at the United Nations General Assembly where the Rabbani ambassador successfully fought off his replacement until the overthrow of the Taliban.

Despite meetings and discussion, ECO plans faltered because so much of the interconnection of the region depended on stability in Afghanistan. Asphalt roads, railroad extensions, bridges, electrical grids, investment in warehouses, banking systems, air flights, and many other development plans remained on pause. The consequences of the September 11 attack on the United States provided the impetus that ECO needed to emerge from immobility. With the U.S.-led attack on al-Qaeda and its Taliban protégé, the promise of normalcy returned to the region and ECO became active. In the 30 months since November 2001, when Taliban rule ended in Kabul, ECO meetings have been convened at many levels in all the member countries, including Kabul, both as planning committees for specific purposes, such as women, health, and population issues, and as showcase head-of-state gatherings. At all of these meetings Afghanistan's reconstruction appeared prominently on the agenda. It seems clear that for ECO members, the contiguous regional development idea has ignored old rivalries and offered the promise of cultural exchanges and cooperative arrangements with two other neighboring regional groupings, ASEAN and the Black Sea Economic Cooperation Pact (BSECP)—1992. Moreover, Armenia, Georgia, Ukraine, and possibly China may all be seated in observer status at ECO sessions.

Unlike the BSECP, which moved hastily to accept many countries (11) in short order, many of which are now vying to join the European Union (EU), the gestation period for ECO has been long and its antecedents have provided a climate of growing appreciation for regional cooperation. Nonetheless, the question most pertinent to Afghan reconstruction and development is whether Afghanistan might gain greater benefit from working within the cooperative framework of the region, or continuing the twentieth-century pattern of relying on outside donors and its own resources to advance itself.

Land-locked but Developed: Central Asia and Afghanistan

The shift toward regional cooperation in economic and political issues occurred after the end of World War II, when Western Europe began to adopt concepts and built institutions that evolved from the Council of Europe in 1949 to the EU, and also adopted a common currency in 2002. Other regional groups, formed during the past 30 years but active since the decline in Cold War confrontation in the early 1990s, show differing levels of political activism, although all emphasize and act upon principles of economic cooperation.

On an economic level, the landlocked Central Asian states offer a model of regional cooperation that holds implications for Afghanistan and for other members of ECO. Not only do they offer a model of how such cooperative economies can function, but the six Central Asian states offer the experience that ECO members need in the politics of regional cooperative endeavor. For example, under the *aegis*, or strong arm of Moscow, irredentist ethnicity, as between Uzbeks and Tajiks or Uzbeks and Kazakhs, lay dormant in deference to cooperative efforts. Inter-republic economic cooperative arrangements, for example, the supply of hydroelectric power from Tajikistan to Uzbekistan or the shipping of fuel oil to Tajikistan, functioned smoothly for many decades. This cooperative atmosphere began to disintegrate after 1991, with reverberations from the ethnic and Islamic fundamentalist struggle taking place in Afghanistan. Secular versus Islamic tensions and the fear of ethnic redrawing of what had become international borders, led to some attempts at limited inter-republic cooperative arrangements that proved ephemeral. ECO, on the other hand, offers the former Soviet and non-Soviet states a far broader scope for economic cooperation while adding the advantage of combining the mineral and agricultural resources of landlocked and littoral states.

ECO Dependence on Afghan Reconstruction

Geography has outlasted the astounding political changes of the past 15 years. The Soviet Union is no more, and superpower rivalries in the Afghan neighborhood, whether between tsarist Russia and imperial Britain, or the United States and the Soviet Union, have come to a close. Six new sovereign states have emerged to the north of Afghanistan. Despite these facts, plans for development in the country must still consider the geopolitical realities that are unchanging: Afghanistan is landlocked; it is fiercely multiethnic; its core cultural heritage is uncertain; and the political *raison d'être* for the existence of the country as buffer between superpowers has disappeared.

Today, the Afghan neighborhood displays some striking similarities to the period prior to the entry of non-regional players into the politics of the area. About a millennium ago, Afghanistan had prospered as a transit station on the trade routes extending east and west, and north and south. It is possible to argue that reconstruction of the country can lead to a sustainable economy in the future if its historic role is revived, an argument that is driving Afghanistan's Western-trained administrators into active involvement in ECO. The Afghan Minister of Reconstruction stressed this very point in an interview in Mashhad:

> Afghanistan is a country linking the Indian sub-continent to the central Asian countries. It can play a very significant role in trade and the development of the economic sector of this region. However, first it is important to ensure peace and security in Afghanistan and then it will be beneficial for the progress of ECO in the region. We

know that the formation of economic unions are [sic.] basic steps towards ensuring peace and security, order and discipline, cooperation and coordination among all the countries of the region.[2]

Since the formation of Pakistan in 1947 and its entry into the United Nations (UN) in 1948, Afghanistan has depended on this fellow Muslim state for access to the sea and to world trade. Without Soviet agreement to allow cheap transit, the alternative—crossing Asia and Europe to reach the Atlantic by going through the Soviet Union—put Afghan produce (fruits and nuts, carpets, karakul) at a disadvantage. Soviet agreement came at a high price. That price has been costly in political terms since the late 1960s, and especially since 1978. The current political leaders in Kabul understand the price that was paid.

Like Afghanistan, the six Central Asian states that emerged after 1991 are also landlocked. Throughout the 1990s, as before, they continued to depend on the old rail transit routes that bound their cotton and fruits to Russian factories; their new and old gas and petroleum pipelines headed north-northwest to Russia only. Not until China built the railroad and extended pipelines westward toward Kazakhstan was there an alternative available for these landlocked states.[3] The pipeline through Turkey, constructed with U.S. urging and funding, provides another limited alternative for Azerbaijan's mineral wealth. If these former republics are to prosper, however, they will need more alternatives for transport on which trade depends. Into this picture, enters the potential provided by ECO and by Afghanistan.

Humanitarian aid to post-Taliban Afghanistan passed chiefly through Pakistan's main port, Karachi, by truck and sometimes by rail to Peshawar or Quetta, and then by road into Afghanistan. This was the old path for arms to the Mujahidin except for those that came from China across the Khunjarab Pass and into Pakistan. During his last days as president of the Republic of Afghanistan, Muhammad Daoud (1909–1978) had begun to negotiate with the still monarchial Iran, to expand rail traffic from Mashhad toward Herat. Now, 25 years later, among the first subjects discussed at meetings held between President Khatami of Iran and President Karzai of Afghanistan is the extension of the Iranian railroad from Sangam in Khorasan to Herat. Bilaterally, the two countries are also planning for a second border-crossing at Milak, where a bridge will span the Khash River connecting Zaranj (capital of Afghan Sistan) with Zabul (capital of Iranian Sistan).[4] Aside from these bilateral transport projects for resolving the problems associated with being landlocked and dependent on the virtual transit monopolies by Pakistan and the Soviet Union, on a regional basis, ECO discussions call for the construction of north-south roads connecting Tajikistan with Pakistan;[5] a bridge across the Panj River to connect Afghanistan's emerging road system with Tajikistan; the provision of transport vehicles for passengers and freight; and so forth. With the removal of Cold War impediments to contact between Afghanistan and Central Asia, Hairaton, in Uzbekistan, will no longer be the sole trade and transit point.

Stability in Afghanistan and the revitalization of ECO cannot exist separately. In part, geography dictates this central position to Afghanistan in regional planning. On the other hand, it is also true that ECO member states are all pursuing internal development and lack extensive surplus capital to invest in infrastructure development within the region. For this reason, ECO activity is linked to the international reconstruction aid pledged to Afghanistan. Pakistan is among those countries that are counting on Afghan reconstruction aid to fund the extensive plans for laying rail track and supplying equipment for shipping.[6] Pakistan also sees the end of its monopoly on the sea trade of Central Asia, and regards the improvement and competitive efficiency of its transit roads as key to holding its trade advantage.

In recent ECO discussions, other, more realistic plans for financing of regional projects are being laid. For example, a fund for Afghan reconstruction is planned,[7] as is a scheme for reinsurance—one of the weaknesses of any major development project undertaken without U.S. support or that of a major international donor. The problems of funding regional development loom large in ECO discussions, one of which produced consensus in 1995 that Iran, Turkey, and Pakistan, the founding members of ECO, would each donate equally to a fund set at $60 million for the ECO Trade and Development Bank, to be located in Istanbul. Implementation plans reemerged in November 2001 after the security of Afghanistan seemed assured.[8] Iran, which bilaterally pledged $50 million to support Afghan development at the Tokyo donors' meeting in January 2002, illustrates how the temptation to exploit bilateral relations when an outright grant is involved overcomes commitments to the ECO institution. But the need to fund regional projects that require outside financing has driven ECO to seek international donors. The Asian Development Bank, of which Afghanistan was a founding member, has emerged as an important resource.

Advantages of ECO in the Post-Reconstruction Period

In 2006, the target year for Afghan financial independence from current donor efforts, Afghanistan is expected to have created a new polity; put into place basic communications and road infrastructures; established an educational system with gender equity; and developed working relationships with international organizations. Yet many questions remain regarding how Afghanistan will conduct itself in the region after this emergency period is over: For example, will Afghanistan have arrived at a workable transit agreement with Pakistan, the sore point of their relationship since 1948? Will it interact economically with its Uzbek and Turkmen neighbors without fear of disaffection by its Turkic minorities just south of the Amu Darya? And how will its relations with Iran develop as this powerful neighbor monitors the fortunes of Afghanistan's Persianate populations? Most importantly, once Afghanistan is projected to return to normalcy in 2011, will this period of normalcy imply a return to a 1960s state of economic dependency, or does normalcy entail regional integration with a stable, world-linked economy for building the infrastructure needed to maintain a decent standard of life for its diverse citizenry?

All countries in the region share certain distinct anxieties regarding future political threats, encouraging them to seek cooperative solutions. Chief among these threats are the disruption of order by Islamic extremists, narcotics trafficking, and economic stagnation.

Economic regeneration of the ECO region may well be foiled through war or threat of war in the region. The leading source for this stems from U.S.–Iran confrontation, especially since the U.S. president named Iran as a state that "aggressively exports terror" in his January 2002 State of the Union address. This same kind of anti-Iran rhetoric was heard from the head of the National Security Council and others as another round of Palestinian–Israeli talks approached and the U.S.-led coalition prepared for war in Iraq. Barring invasion of Iran, the continued attempts to marginalize its efforts in the region through denial of international funding for infrastructure projects, may in fact have little effect on the creation of trade and transport infrastructure within the ECO region. By pooling resources, as with India in the Chabahar port development, or with the Afghan government in road links to the revitalized "garland" road network, ECO stands a good chance of success in building a viable transit network without help from international funding.

To promote trade, cultural exchange, and to engender other networks such as those of air transport and communications, ECO has created many committees, some of which have ambitious but ill-funded plans that include Afghanistan. Some plans appear fated for failure, however; for example, the Pakistan-supported plan to create a single air service was shelved in 2002. Pakistan had been concerned that its air links with Central Asia suffered due to lack of service. On the other hand, the formation of a body of trade laws intended to reduce tariffs, especially on food stuffs, is well within the capacity of ECO. As far as the Afghan government is concerned, ECO creates the forum for airing and resolving members' political differences, while creating a climate for raising the living standards of all the people in the region.[9] There is also a strong likelihood that by cooperative trade arrangements, the disasters in food supply created by the droughts that periodically hit the geographic plateau running from Iran through Afghanistan and parts of Pakistan may be averted. Isolated Afghanistan had usually suffered the most from droughts, which was one of the reasons behind the dissatisfaction with government (1973) and created incentives for the breakdown of law in the rural regions.

While the advantages to regional economic, cultural, and even political cooperation may be readily seen, Afghanistan faces future dangers in the post-reconstruction period; there may be hegemonic attempts by one or another state. For example, through their offers of reconstruction aid, both Pakistan and Iran are pressing the Afghan government subtly for rights that would give them investment advantages in the Afghan economy: Pakistan has already demanded that its businessmen be allowed to invest in Afghan small industry; and Iran wants a part in the development of the Afghan educational system and proposes to send specialists to revive the minuscule industrial sector. In the cultural sphere, Iran's common language with the chief interethnic language of Afghanistan, Dari (the Afghan form of Persian), gives it an edge over Pakistan, for which the language of communication would have to be English (since Pushtu/Pukhtu is one of the least-developed languages of Pakistan, despite the large and concentrated Pushtun population). If handled bilaterally, these arrangements could endanger Afghan cohesion at a future date. Even if all reconstruction efforts succeed, the danger of ethnic fragmentation could still be alive. If ECO becomes the organizational channel for the importation of regional expertise and investment, however, the dangers from neighbors with hegemonic ambitions might be reduced.

Implications for Donors

How can donors anticipate and prepare for regional networking in order to avoid the pitfalls of prewar development in Afghanistan? Is such an approach unique or should it be considered for other parts of the developing world?

The most detrimental economic factor in the development of Afghanistan has been its lack of access to the outside world. Of the countries that are landlocked, only a handful outside the former Soviet Union—Switzerland, Austria, Paraguay—have avoided falling into the world's poorest, or least-developed, category. The eponymous Soviet republics that have achieved constitutional sovereignty with at least a partial international border, although landlocked, are among the few that have achieved prosperity. From Belarus to Tajikistan, road, rail, air, communications, fuel pipelines, and food distribution networks have allowed for the creation of a single economic zone by which all have gained (sometimes with economic subsidies). But for countries outside such a cooperative network, being landlocked is tantamount to being poor. Even when there are resources to be exploited, such as Afghanistan's natural gas or coal, the costs of both development and export are made prohibitive by the difficulty of access to world markets.

The constraints posed by the Soviet presence no longer exist, however, and indeed the whole region can operate without the checks on its interaction posed by the Cold War. Its members can actively court their neighbors both individually and regionally. The mechanism for regional cooperation is the ECO with its secretariat in Tehran. The controversial position of Iran, a leading force within ECO, presents some obstacles to donors for Afghan reconstruction; countries like the United States would hesitate to fund Afghan projects bilaterally, which would benefit Iran. No doubt, however, some projects can be funded indirectly, following the precedent of United States aid to Afghan refugees in Iran through the Red Cross and the UNHCR.[10] Such indirect funding may take three forms: direct, unrestricted funds to the Afghan government, which can best prioritize its needs; or from the World Bank or other international institutions, which can make financial arrangements with ECO; or through NGOs. In any case, when the United States created obstacles to transporting Central Asian oil and gas through eastern Iran, the action was detrimental to the development of the region.

In preparation for the eventual economic stability of Afghanistan, donors would do well to consider the needs of the broader region represented by ECO. Afghanistan, which has never had a railroad other than the mile of rail laid in a Kabul suburb for King Amanullah in 1925, is in desperate need of rail transport that connects to the existing lines of its neighbors at or near Afghan borders. Like the paved roads that ring the central massive of the Hindu Kush, rail lines can also ring the country, at least in a semicircle in the west, and connect to Pakistan at Chaman, to Iran in Sistan (for Chabahar port traffic) and in Herat (for Iranian and Turkmen traffic), and at Hairaton (for Uzbek and general Central Asian traffic). Railroad planning, like road planning, will help to link the fragmented parts of the country and address the needs for the export–import issues that will help to stimulate the Afghan economy and raise the standard of living.

Replacing poppy cultivation with cash crops is also a part of the regional problem tackled best in cooperation with Afghanistan's potential trading partners. One difficulty in regional economic planning arises from the uniformity in cash crops in the region: cotton cultivation, promoted in Central Asia during the Soviet period, created a crisis in Tajikistan and Uzbekistan after 1991, because these countries needed to find markets for raw cotton when cotton prices were falling. Afghanistan introduced cotton cultivation in the areas adjacent to Soviet cotton-growing areas— the spinzar, Pushtu for "white gold," during the late 1930s. Some of the cotton became fabric at the Gulbahar factory, but mostly met domestic need. Integrating cotton into the manufacturing capacity of Pakistan and Iran would benefit Afghanistan even as Uzbekistan and Tajiksitan reduce their cotton production in favor of diversified food stuffs.

The related issues of shared population, health problems, and the status and condition of women can also be addressed regionally. Initial Soviet propaganda promoted women in the workplace and women as mothers. In Soviet Central Asia during the latter half of the twentieth century, rural women "worked" in village (*kolkhoz*) settings but mainly produced very large families, having on average four to six children per adult woman, especially in Uzbekistan and Tajikistan. Runaway populations have strained post-Soviet health, food, and shelter resources, and created educational and employment problems. A similar approach to the role of women in the early Islamic Revolution period drove Iran's population from 38 million in 1977 to 60 million in ten years. Since then Iran has instituted one of the most advanced population control systems in the Muslim world through the voluntary provision of the Norplant under-skin birth control patch to all women, including those in villages. Afghanistan faces a population crisis complicated by anti–birth control views popularly supposed to be Islamic.

Currently, a German daily birth-control pill, named Yazmin, is being sold in Kabul. Yet such an approach is hardly effective since a sale product that is cumbersome to use will hardly help women who need birth control most, those living in rural areas. Because of the cultural sensitivity of the issue of women and birth control, it is one of those areas best handled regionally. Donors involved in such programs can be most effective by going through the appropriate ECO committee on health, women, and population. Anticipating the ways in which post-reconstruction Afghanistan can function in the region, calls for the exploration of means of cooperation. In many cases, helping Afghanistan today may help to transform the region for the decades ahead.

Other Regional Organizations

Many of the countries considered least-developed appear on the UNCTAD's list because, like Afghanistan, they have experienced the devastation of war within recent decades. Countries like Cambodia, Myanmar, Haiti, Angola, Rwanda, Senegal, or Bangladesh are not resource-poor uniformly, nor do they share Afghanistan's problem of isolation, but most are located in parts of the world where regional organizations are weak or nonexistent. In this respect, Afghanistan is unique because it is a weak country in a relatively strong region where regional political conflicts are declining. Afghanistan also falls within a category of diverse resources and a relatively well-developed infrastructure, including strong educational systems. The cultural affinity prevalent among the ten countries of ECO, based on long centuries of shared culture, including an Islamic one, also makes both this region and Afghanistan's relationships within it unique. For these reasons, Afghanistan stands to benefit from regional cooperation and regional networks if donors pay attention to the integration of Afghanistan into the region.

ECO also has the advantage of having a small and manageable membership with a clear focus and priorities. Since it is undergoing restructuring and possible expansion, it is a coherent entity, more like ASEAN than the African Union, which includes all the 36 member states within the African continent (except Morocco). If Afghanistan succeeds in pulling itself out of the level of poverty in which it has operated for decades, it will be due to its regional networks.

Conclusion

The period beyond reconstruction is currently estimated by the international community to begin in 2006, which gives donors time to consider certain geopolitical realities that condition the manner in which reconstruction is funded and implemented. Chief among these realities are the politics of the region, which are not simply based on the end of the Cold War and the emergence of the United States as the main military and political power in the world, but will be based primarily on the demise of the Soviet Union; the emergence of new sovereign states in the Afghan neighborhood; and the restoration of the pivotal geographic link between Afghanistan and the non-Arab eastern Asian region that shares a Perso-Turkic Muslim culture. The economic structure that currently embodies the cooperative network exemplifying this new configuration is ECO. ECO cannot embark on its ambitious plans for regional cooperation in transit trade, banking, and cultural cooperation however, until Afghanistan is stabilized.

With the promise of Afghan stability nearly assured under the Afghan Interim Administration (AIA), leaders in this Afghan government, tasked with reconstruction of the country, appear to appreciate the benefits of the ECO infrastructure. Nowhere is this better demonstrated than in the opening of the Chabahar port on the Arabian Sea coastline of eastern Iran. Finally, after nearly 50 years since an Afghan government proposed such a project from which it would benefit by having an alternative to the Pakistan transit route, (and supported by Iranian and some Indian funding) this project will facilitate Afghanistan's foreign trade when it is linked by road and rail at Herat and Farah to the Iranian road network.[11] It remains the responsibility of the Afghan government to adopt and implement the kinds of trade laws that will restore the economic position it has not enjoyed since the height of the historic and fabled period of prosperity in Central Asia made possible by the Silk Road. Coordinating all tariff and trade laws within the region would help ensure that the landlocked position of 70 percent of ECO members does not handicap them in dealing with the three littoral states.

The ten countries belonging to ECO share similar threats and possibilities, many of which can be best worked out cooperatively, including Islamic extremism and the narcotics trade trafficking that threatens the economy of Afghanistan and the political stability of the region.

Afghan leaders in the AIA, having observed widespread waste and duplication in aid projects, have put forth a strong plea for directing all reconstruction aid through the current government administration. Donors may have misgivings about placing their funds in the hands of the Afghan government, where central planning from Kabul has historically tripped into the abyss that exists between the capital and the rural provinces, but central planning by Kabul and ECO appear to offer sound alternatives to reversion to the prewar past.

Notes

1. Louis Dupree, *Afghanistan* (Princeton, NJ: Princeton University Press, 1980), p. 479.
2. Mir Mohammad Amin Farhang interview, translated in *BBBC Monitoring International Reports*, February 14, 2003.
3. Ralph H. Magnus and Eden Naby, *Afghanistan: Mullah, Marx, and Mujahid* (New York: Westview, 1998), p. 178.
4. These issues were discussed during a August 14, 2002 meeting between President Karzai and President Khatami.
5. Laila A. Ali, "ECO Renews Interest in Pakistan-Tajikistan Rail Link," *Global News Wire—Business Recorder Financial Times Information*, April 20, 2002.
6. Ibid. Pakistan estimates that the rail project from Chaman to Kushka (through Kandahar and Herat not Kabul) will cost $600 million to build and that another $100 million will be required for upgrading the Karachi–Chaman portion of the rail in Pakistan.
7. "Moving Beyond Cliches," *DAWN*, October 16, 2002, at <http://www.dawn.com/2002/10/16/ed.htm>.
8. "Iran Ratifies ECO Accord to Establish Bank," *Asia Pulse*, November 6, 2001.
9. "ECO to Play Significant Role in Afghan Reconstruction—Afghan Minister," *BBC Monitoring International Reports*, February 14, 2003.
10. Mercy Corps, an American-initiated charity, worked to establish refugee camps for Afghans in southeast Iran in 2001. Its funding includes a grant from the Belinda and Bill Gates Foundation, as well as U.S. Department of State funding for humanitarian assistance to Afghans. For more information see <http://dailytidings.com/2001/news1214/regional/dt-regional-05.php>.
11. *Atlas-E Râh-Hâye Iran-1380* (Road Atlas of Iran), Tehran, 1380/2001. This is the first major atlas of Iran depicting in particular the extensive new road system in the east. The road distance between Mashad and Chabahar is 1647 km. (approximately the distance from New York to Chicago).

Chapter Thirteen

Reconstruction, Development, and Nation-Building: Prospects for Afghanistan

Dennis A. Rondinelli and John D. Montgomery

Although neither foreign aid nor military occupation enjoys high regard in the annals of modern statesmanship, both could claim, modestly, that they deserve a place at the center of foreign policy. International assistance has helped dozens of countries move toward more "modern," "progressive," and "productive" states, and it would be churlish to deny their role in nation-building. The past half-century offers abundant examples of countries that have emerged from colony to state, from authoritarianism to political competition, or from subsistence to productivity, largely because of international assistance. Such foreign interventions have their share of failures, but they have achieved enough to encourage the hope of contributing substantially to a better future in Afghanistan and perhaps in other Islamic countries.

The history of assisted reconstruction and development following war and other devastation suggests both warnings and models for the future. Some of its "lessons" for Afghanistan may appear irrelevant, contradictory, or obvious, but knowing them can protect donors from overlooking essential features of their acts. The recurring problems of failed "institutional memory" in development should serve as warning that even the obvious lessons of experience need retelling; banality is a less serious offense than ignorance.

Three kinds of international assistance have already appeared in Afghanistan: conventional economic and technical assistance for development projects and programs; reconstruction assistance for medium-term rebuilding of the economy and infrastructure; and long-term nation-building efforts to overcome the weaknesses of a failed or collapsed state. All are needed to create a viable society and to support stable governance.

The most ambitious form of donor activity is nation-building, which has become fashionable because some external interventions have had to go beyond merely aiding an existing government's development programs or sector projects. In nation-building programs, external donors seek to create, reestablish, or strengthen the capacity of the state to govern and also to support a policy framework that will enable civil society to achieve political, economic, social, and physical development. Donors are compelled to practice nation-building when war displaces an existing regime or when it can no longer function effectively. This core objective is evident in the donors' and the Interim Authority's plans and policies for Afghanistan, described by Rondinelli in chapter two and implied in the virtual model discussed by Montgomery in chapter three.

Lessons of Experience with Nation-Building and Reconstruction

Although the reconstruction and development plans that were proposed in 2002 for Afghanistan included conventional technical and economic assistance, the major thrust of donor activities—especially those of the United States—was aimed at nation-building. The implications of previous efforts in reconstruction assistance for development and nation-building are especially relevant for Afghanistan.

Nation-Building Interventions
National governments and international organizations have engaged in nation-building since the nation-state first emerged as a dominant political entity more than 300 years ago. In the sixteenth century, foreign governments were already beginning to expand their power by subjecting other states under their influence and by imposing institutions of governance on them.[1] The most recent wave of nation-building occurred after World War II, when the United States began to use foreign assistance and military intervention to rebuild war-torn and conflict-ridden countries that it considered important to its economic or security interests. The U.S. military occupation of Japan and Germany and the Marshall Plan for Western Europe marked the beginning of the modern era of nation-building as a distinct element of foreign policy that sought to secure peace, create democratic governments, and stimulate market economies in war-torn countries.

Both the United States and European countries began to use foreign aid and military intervention for nation-building after World War II. The World Bank, the United Nations (UN), and to a lesser extent, nongovernmental organizations (NGOs), also became important channels for foreign aid and for member countries to pursue their nation-building objectives. More than 40 countries in Africa, Eastern Europe, Asia, Central and South America, and the Middle East that were engaged in or recovering from serious conflict, received peacekeeping forces and donor assistance between 1988 and 1998,[2] and many of them still receive post-conflict reconstruction or nation-building assistance.

Lessons of experience with this intensive form of donor influence emerge not only from attempts to rebuild war-torn countries but also from the rescue of "failed" or "collapsed" states whose capacity to govern had disintegrated because of external and civil wars or from political and administrative weakness, ethnic tensions and conflict, economic or financial crises, totalitarianism, and human and natural devastation.

Although some countries have been able to reconstruct their economies and physical assets and build institutions of democratic governance, many of their nation-building policies had mixed results or were outright failures. As suggested in chapter three, one of the great disappointments of international assistance has been the failure of elections to produce stable, democratic government in countries recovering from war and revolution or emerging from colonial status. Dictators and warlords have sometimes triumphed in cases where constitutional institutions, such as those described in the donors' model, were absent.

Although the performance of less intensive forms of development and reconstruction assistance has also been mixed, because of its complexity, nation-building has been especially problematic. Pei and Kasper's review of 16 major U.S.-led nation-building efforts since 1900 (Panama, 1903–1936 and 1989; Cuba, 1898–1902, 1906–1909, and 1917–1922; Nicaragua, 1909–1933; Haiti, 1915–1934 and 1994–1996; Dominican Republic, 1916–1924 and 1965–1966; West Germany, 1945–1949; Japan, 1945–1952; South Vietnam, 1964–1973; Cambodia, 1970–1973; Grenada, 1983; and Afghanistan, 2001–present) concluded that in only four countries—West Germany, Japan, Grenada, and Panama—did the types of democratic governance systems that the United States sought to build, survive after ten years.[3] In only five cases were democratic regimes sustained for more than three years after the United States had withdrawn. In Cuba, Haiti, Nicaragua, Cambodia, and Vietnam, dictatorships emerged quickly after U.S. military forces had left the country.

Pei and Kaspar concluded that success or failure in these 16 cases depended on four critical variables: the target country's internal characteristics (including the degree of ethnic or religious differences; degree of ethnic homogeneity; sense of national identity, state capacity, and organizational effectiveness; and previous experience with constitutional rule); convergence of geopolitical interests (including sustained commitment by outside powers; alignment of national interests of target country and outside powers; and consensus on shared strategic interests within the society); commitment to economic development (including large amounts of external economic resources from donors; use of external aid to launch self-sustaining economic development processes; and development of indigenous capacity to make productive use of external assistance); and, finally, the international legitimacy of the multilateral interim administration or the temporary surrogate regime of the country. In most of the instances in which the United States took the lead in nation-building, these conditions were weak or absent.

The only significant nation-building successes that the United States can claim since 1900 were post–World War II Japan and Germany. Heffron notes in chapter four of this volume that the conditions that allowed successful nation-building in postwar Japan and Germany are rare. Elsewhere, as Marina Ottoway observed,

> [a]lthough defeated and destroyed, these countries had strong state traditions and competent government personnel. West Germany and Japan were nation-states in the literal sense of the term—they were ethnic and cultural communities as well as political states. And they were occupied by the U.S. military, a situation that precluded choices other than the democratic state.[4]

These features were absent in most of the countries that have been targeted for nation-building since then, and none of them characterize contemporary Afghanistan.

In the absence of a strong state, as Esman argues in chapter nine, and Abdullaev in chapter ten, little can be done about either reconstruction or development in

Afghanistan. Esman insists that donors' highest priorities in Afghanistan should be to build the institutions of an effective central government and to ensure the equitable participation in them by members of Afghanistan's major ethnic communities. Marin Strmecki's studies reaffirmed that state-building is a precondition for securing peace in Afghanistan and the foundation on which to build all other development efforts.[5] The difficulties of state-building are all the more pronounced in Afghanistan, where ethnic and religious tensions continue to fragment the Interim Authority's power and control, and as independent warlords continue to exercise economic and military power and even form alliances with external groups or neighboring countries. These forces strongly inhibit the ability of the Interim Authority to establish its legitimacy, elicit loyalty and support, exercise power, or deliver services far outside of Kabul. Yet, as Strmecki records, Afghanistan had achieved some degree of stability and economic and social progress during the 40-year rule of Zahir Shah before his overthrow in 1973. Then Zahir Shah, unlike the United States and other donors today, was able to see and strengthen the shared sense of Afghan national identity underlying religious and ethnic differences by using "the support of traditional social structures, such as tribal, clan and village leaders to legitimate the state." During that 40-year period, the central government was able to make substantial progress in developing an educated technocratic elite connected to those structures and to begin to modernize them. Strmecki proposes that current efforts at state-building be modeled on Zahir Shah's success in "managing Afghanistan's complex social and political relations, working to ensure that all groups [are] accorded proper status in the system and that all important figures [feel] included in a process of consensual governance."[6]

Strmecki's argument that nation-building must focus on the inherent sense of national identity among Afghans of different religious and ethnic backgrounds is reinforced by Nancy Hatch Dupree, who pointed out,

> in spite of the current emphasis on ethnicity, fueled in large part by outsiders for political purposes, the search for unifying indicators reveals that despite pride of origin, despite episodes of friction, despite plays for power, despite self-serving ethnocentric panegyrics by individuals, a sense of belonging, of being Afghan, is evident among the population at large.

She insists that a "sense of national identity does exist, the elements of divisiveness notwithstanding."[7]

In chapter four of this volume, Heffron surmises, on the basis of his review of U.S. policies on reconstruction and restoration in the American south after the Civil War and in Germany and Japan after World War II, that to ignore local institutions and national pride in Afghanistan would doom state-building efforts to almost certain failure: "Throwing more money at Afghanistan will not have the necessary saving effect without the effort to build the civil institutions and a civil society capable of absorbing such a large development package." Heffron discovers "four simple lessons from the past—the priority of individual and customary rights over political solutions, the need for economic commitments commensurate with moral ones, the comparative advantage of bipartisan, multilateral agreements, and the limitations of pump-priming measures to bolster a weak economy"—that should guide donor policies, a view that is reinforced by Bossin's examination, in chapter five, of earlier failed efforts at nation-building in Afghanistan by Great Britain, Russia, and the United States.

Bossin's description of the history of British, Russian, and American attempts to reshape the Afghan state dims our view of the prospects for donor-led nation-building. Both Esman and Abdullaev also note that previous interventions in Afghanistan attempted to ignore or even suppress ethnic and tribal groups, or to convert them into instruments of indirect rule, which resulted in strengthening the aggressive and divisive warlords. The religious intolerance of the Taliban, with their fanatic ambitions further undermined legitimate expressions of diverse or contrary views.

Thompson, Gutlove, and Russell, in chapter ten, turn to more positive uses of ethnic groups and other elements of civil society to contribute to health, education, and social services and to strengthen human security. This strategy would seek and strengthen common interests, find ways of dividing or matching responsibilities with these groups, and offer inducements to them to perform functions that advance their common purposes. Examples of all three strategies as developed in other countries show how the parallel interests and functions of ethnic groups and other elements of civil society can enhance the reach and effectiveness of international assistance.

In retrospect, internationally led efforts at nation-building offer few examples of comprehensive success, but they yield numerous lessons for assessing potential approaches for strengthening the Afghan state. Even though multilateral efforts to rebuild Kosovo, Bosnia, and the Balkan countries were complex and sophisticated, for example, Carl Bildt, the former prime minister of Sweden, drawing on his service as the first international high representative to Bosnia and the UN envoy to the Balkans, found positive guidance for reconstruction in Afghanistan.[8] He offers far-reaching advice: to secure the environment quickly in order to protect minorities and cease hostilities; to give a higher priority to the choice of an appropriate form of the state than to physical reconstruction; and to address major humanitarian issues without letting them predominate over long-term issues. He proposes creating a strong economic framework (including currency, customs, and taxation systems, debt restructuring, accessing international capital markets, strengthening commercial law and the banking system); and seeking a benevolent regional cooperation from neighboring countries, a point that Frye and Naby develop in detail in chapter twelve. Experience in the Balkans indicates the need to create a strong coalition of international support and to plan for a longer time horizon and more resources than are initially estimated for the complex process of nation-building.

Montgomery points out a disconcerting fact of nation-building that is especially important in thinking about Afghanistan; even the positive elements of the "donors' model" that he describes in chapter three can produce disturbing consequences. Sometimes, in a mistaken perception of the appropriate goals, he argues, donors support procedures they consider to be the heart of "democracy," like elections and partisan competition, without concentrating on more central features of stable governance—such as the rule of law, economic competition, adherence to human rights, open media, and administrative efficiency and effectiveness of government organizations—all of which predominate over the familiar apparatus of popular rule. In the immediate wake of reconstruction, countries such as Afghanistan do not usually benefit much from quick-action elections and sonorous political party platforms; indeed, they do not require the adoption of standard "Western" procedures at all, but take on many different forms as they respond to unique social and cultural needs. Nation-building policies often risk failure when adopted too rigidly: the rule of law can degenerate into the rule of lawyers—litigious, costly, and dilatory; unbridled economic efficiency can become piratical and predatory; freedom of speech can reward superficiality and extremism; the clamor for unfulfilled rights can invite invidious reverse discrimination; and even a checked-and-balanced government can yield gridlock. These extremes may not occur during the reconstruction period itself, but donors should become aware of such possibilities in their continued relations. Experience has shown that these elements interact. If all of them are present in a society, they can provide antidotes to excesses in any of them.

Other lessons of nation-building can be derived from experience with "failed states" and the attempts of international assistance organizations to deal with them. Rotberg provided a profile of failed states, most of whose features are identifiable in Afghanistan, and offers guidelines for rehabilitation or renewal.[9] He agrees with the findings described here, that successful nation-building assistance to Afghanistan will require the creation of a strong state with the ability to provide security, eliminate violent conflict, reconcile conflicting ethnic or religious factions, protect human rights, generate economic opportunities, provide basic services, control corruption, respond effectively to emergencies, and combat poverty and inequality.[10] Because the administration of even modest reconstruction programs requires the participation of existing bureaucracies and contract services in Afghanistan, he suggests that donors provide funding to maintain adequate levels of compensation for displaced managers of public activities. Arranging to do so, without reinforcing their previous ideological commitments, calls for care and sensitivity in aligning their purposes with those of the postwar government. At the same time, the composition of these bureaucracies may have to change to incorporate ethnic, religious, or tribal groups that have been neglected or excluded from public service.

Esman and Abdullaev also conclude that support to a strong but politically neutral army will be important in confronting the extensive military power that is still held by independent local warlords and other figures. Institutional incorporation and training programs can help keep security forces out of the hands of local claimants and other ambitious politicians.

Multilateral Reconstruction and Development Assistance

Internal studies of reconstruction assistance conducted by international organizations themselves affirm many of these principles. By 1996, about half of the UN aid budget and 10 percent of Official Development Assistance was committed to relief and recovery efforts in conflict-torn countries, and postwar reconstruction continues to account for a significant portion of World Bank and other international development organizations' assistance funding.[11] Current interventions in Afghanistan are part of a long series of reconstruction efforts by international organizations in post-conflict situations.

Repeated lessons from previous experience would warn against directly transplanting successful programs and projects from other post-conflict countries to

Afghanistan. Even though it is sometimes expedient to cite other countries' successful reconstruction experience to encourage change, reference to them as "ideal countries" for planning purposes may both give offense and also distort the optimal balance among elements of the suggested model. "Model" countries are usually not ideal in all respects, and little is gained by inadvertently importing their imperfections into Afghanistan. Applying the donors' model requires special attention to the needs and conditions of the recovering country. This is especially true, as Norchi emphasizes in chapter seven, in creating a rule of law in Afghanistan. Few states have been built or survived without a popularly accepted constitution or body of established rules for legitimizing policy making and implementation. In Afghanistan "borrowed constitutions" from other countries are unlikely to be accepted or to create a rule of law by which Afghanistan's regional rulers and commanders will abide. Norchi insists that Afghanistan's constitution, to become legitimate, must evolve from participation of both men and women in the county's diverse ethnic, religious, and tribal communities. Although lessons of development experience in creating a rule of law from other countries may offer guidelines, Afghanistan's unique traditions will require a highly participative process in order to shape a constitution that legitimizes the authority of the central government.

The World Bank's review of its experience with post-conflict reconstruction during the 1980s and 1990s has led it to adopt many lessons that can apply to other donors' plans and policies for Afghanistan.[12] The Bank now treats reconstruction as a specialized activity that has its own dynamics, requirements, and costs when it is to become a foundation for development. Both its short- and long-term activities use a multi-sector approach in the search for comprehensive reconstruction. The Bank incorporates psychological and social as well as physical elements in its reconstruction plans, and it seeks to involve war survivors in rebuilding activities and as active participants in planning and implementing reconstruction projects. It has also begun setting up political and logistical prerequisites before introducing transition activities; it gives priority attention to political issues on the grounds that peace and security must be achieved before funds can be used effectively. Because cultural underpinnings differ among countries and are crucial for the success of reconstruction, the Bank encourages governments to select preferred approaches to rebuilding national institutions. For its reconstruction plans it prefers to take into consideration the dynamics of surrounding countries and the need for cooperation with neighboring governments (the approach Naby and Frye suggest for Afghanistan in chapter twelve). The Bank urges donors to assess the probable impact of ethnic, religious, or other identities on post-conflict relationships. And finally, because of the potential risk that conditionalities will slow the process of reconstruction, it now uses them sparingly in post-conflict situations.

In its reconstruction efforts in Uganda during the late 1980s and early 1990s, the World Bank found that it could improve its economic rebuilding efforts by giving more attention to consensus building and by relaxing its preoccupation with raising tax revenues, "given [a] government's history of predatory taxation."[13] Weak coordination of sector projects and programs among donor organizations and NGOs also initially undermined the effectiveness of reconstruction efforts. Evaluations found that "Bank performance was relatively poor in the social sectors, particularly in strengthening health and education institutions."[14] Many of the reconstruction projects were too short-lived to address the expected duration of the recovery period, which is usually at least two decades of sustained effort.

From its experience in Bosnia and Herzegovina during the 1990s, the World Bank learned of the necessity to respond early and comprehensively to post-conflict reconstruction and recovery needs in order to provide a coherent framework for guiding donors' activities.[15] Factors it found to be important in implementing economic recovery efforts included ensuring a wide dispersion of benefits geographically and among different population groups so that they would involve a wide range of stakeholders in planning and implementation and in building social capital and human resources.

The Private Sector

Although all the contributors to this volume call for strengthening the Afghan state, several also see a strong developmental role for the private sector. The drug trades in Afghanistan, as Abdullaev describes in chapter ten, will call for programs of crop destruction integrated with opportunities for rural development. A major instrument for this purpose, as Rondinelli argues in chapter eight, can be to develop the private sector, a sensitive task that risks exploitation of local resources and opportunities by members of the donor community. Economic assistance programs that encourage local entrepreneurship at all levels are more likely to avoid the charge and the reality of neocolonialism than those that are dominated by public or private organizations of donors.

Both Muscat in chapter six and Rondinelli in chapter eight urge that economic assistance pursue export and other foreign trade opportunities. It is often more important to improve tariffs and other import-export terms than it is to offer other forms of assistance to the private sector. Macroeconomic policies to restrain inflation and revitalize markets are also familiar to the international bankers and other financial organizations whose efforts will support and expand the donors' development programs in Afghanistan.

Rondinelli argues that much of what is to happen in Afghanistan is linked to economic growth, which will require donors and the Afghan government to attend to all three elements of the existing economy (the warlord economy, the black-market economy, and the "coping" or subsistence economy). Economic development in Afghanistan remains severely hampered by the smuggling that dominates the drug industry, with its proclivity for violence, its association with plunder and looting, and its malevolent effect on legitimate markets. Dealing with these dysfunctional economies will be the first requirements of developing and expanding production and creating stable livelihoods and entrepreneurial opportunities.

More than 50 years of development experience also attests to the importance of aid sequencing and growth strategy. Given the huge financial requirements of a "big push" strategy that advances all elements on an economy in order to gain the maximum synergy among them, and the risks that large investments so often involve corruption and distortion of effort, it is likely that an "unbalanced" or "leading sector" approach will be the most appropriate for Afghanistan. Agriculture and rural development will constitute the most promising avenues of investment, concentrating on staple food production that, in the end, will benefit the whole population. All elements of a comprehensive agriculture development program, from the provision of seeds and supplies and physical infrastructure to farmer education and rural credit, will be needed for that purpose.

Civil Society

One recurrent lesson from other countries undergoing reconstruction is the importance of rural organization, especially of farmers. The techniques of organizing and supporting such groups are well known among international development specialists. "Informal-sector" and "non-governmental" organizations are extremely valuable elements in such efforts, and government policies that support them are among the most important elements of agricultural development programs.

Thompson, Gutlove, and Russell emphasize the imperative of integrating health and human security programs in Afghanistan. Among specific reforms that international donors have introduced in transitional countries, those relating to the rights of women are especially significant in the case of Afghanistan. Not only did the Taliban reverse some of the social progress that preceded its rule, but denying opportunities to half the population was especially serious in this case because of the relatively low supply of human and social capital in the country. Gender-based programs of assistance in most countries have helped organize women's groups and provide support to micro-finance services to rural populations, as well as to open educational opportunities for females of all ages. They can also support other "equal opportunity" standards in employment and promotion, including devoting special attention to the needs of veterans and returning refugees, for whom employment opportunities and training have contributed to their reentry into civil society.

Management of Aid

Experience over the past 50 years emphasizes that, as important as the appropriate design of development programs and projects is to their success, the efficacy of foreign assistance also depends on mobilizing, delivering, and managing aid in ways that build the recipient's absorptive capacity. Patrick's study of UN and World Bank aid for reconstruction in more than 40 post-conflict countries since the late 1980s identified several recurring problems of aid management that are also appearing in Afghanistan, including slow disbursement of pledged funds; weak mechanisms for pledging and mobilizing assistance; inadequate devices for tracking aid flows; inappropriate forms of aid and conditionality; poor articulation between relief and development efforts; and weak coordination within the donor community.[16] Muscat accepts the World Bank's conclusion that donor control and implementation must be exercised in a way that contributes simultaneously to strengthening domestic institutions. Even if donors fall short of achieving complete success at nation-building, experience with international development underlines how crucial it is for them to provide consistent and continuing support for institution building in aid delivery. His findings coincide with Bossin's emphasis in chapter five on the wisdom of developing a reliable statistical system in Afghanistan in order to collect data needed for planning and policy analysis and to monitor the performance and results of government and donor reconstruction and development activities.

Montgomery, Bossin, and Muscat all emphasize how donors have been able to expand the influence of their programs as they introduce new institutions by adopting positive administrative practices. The most effective means for delivering aid include sharing responsibility for decisions that affect the host country's future, keeping internal financial records open to scrutiny, and holding public hearings on controversial choices it has to make—all of which illustrate political styles that can contribute to institutional objectives. Even if some of the organizational and institutional innovations do not take root, such procedures may equal in importance other elements introduced in aid programs.

Achieving consistency and coordination in donor programs in Afghanistan will require governments and international organizations to identify and justify their objectives clearly. In his review of the "virtual model" of development assistance, Montgomery concludes that donors are more likely to achieve social and political purposes if they acknowledge their long-term goals than if they bury them in obscure official statements that suggest a hidden agenda. While donors sometimes risk political criticism by appearing to interfere with basic decisions that inhere in an independent sovereign nation, the opposite accusation—that they are doing so secretly—is likely to be damaging to their prestige without having the equal prospect of achieving their desired ends.

Prospects for Afghanistan

Experiences of failure or disappointed hopes expose the problems against which donors have to prepare themselves: the lack of experience in self-government at the national level, leading to inadequate administrative resources for necessary functions; corruption attending secret disposition of resources or unchecked monopoly of opportunities; fierce ethnic or tribal communities that resist incorporation into the national polity; internal insecurity caused by surviving elements of the displaced government or ruling elites; predatory external forces or donor conflict; gross inequities in the distribution of natural wealth and opportunities for selfimprovement; illegal industries such as drug production or weapons smuggling; insufficiency of human or social capital; and inadequate resources for public sector investments. Not all of these conditions can be neutralized if the donor commitment collapses prematurely. Avoiding failure implies both careful attention to such problems and sustained interest in dealing with them. With both direct international aid and knowledge of experience in other countries, Afghanistan had embarked on constitutional reform embodying fundamental concepts of human rights and human dignity by the end of 2003.

Although aid donors tend to concentrate their efforts on central authorities, their potential for local influence can also be decisive in supporting constitutional subnational government at regional or provincial levels. In the case of Afghanistan, where local warlords now exercise governing authority, it will be desirable to channel funds to appropriate local units that offset the exercise of illegitimate power and contribute to security and stability.

As reconstruction, development, and nation-building proceed in Afghanistan, donors will face other complexities. The in-country presence of donor organizations is often a useful means of training civil servants and suggesting organizational improvements, but the negative impact of its temporary nature often contributes to an internal "brain-drain" as higher levels of compensation and responsibility attract qualified personnel away from government posts. The balance between offering opportunities to qualified personnel and drawing down the resources of the public service requires close attention. Using existing administrative machinery rather than creating new organizations is a valuable means toward that balance, once disruptive relics of the past are purged from office.[17] The absorption of demobilized troops into the new national army is a task that will require special attention in Afghanistan, since many of the estimated 175,000 soldiers under "local commanders" are likely to present a security hazard if they are neglected.

Early reports of international aid to Afghanistan warn against premature cessation of support and uncoordinated programs from multiple donors. Experience in other countries provides ample evidence of the long-term costs of inadequate provision of support funds and casual competition among international, bilateral, and nongovernmental organizations on the ground. These problems are likely to be especially severe in Afghanistan in view of the unexpectedly high commitments to postwar operations in Iraq and possibly other countries.

Notes

1. John M. Owen IV, "The Foreign Imposition of Domestic Institutions," *International Organization*, Vol. 56, No. 2 (2002): pp. 375–409.
2. Stewart Patrick, "The Check is in the Mail: Improving the Delivery and Coordination of Post-Conflict Assistance," Working Paper (New York: New York University Center on International Cooperation, 1998).
3. Minxin Pei and Sara Kasper, "Lessons from the Past: The American Record on Nation Building," Policy Brief 24 (Washington, DC: Carnegie Endowment for International Peace, 2003).
4. Marina Ottoway, "Nation Building," *Foreign Policy* (October–November 2002): pp. 16–22; quote at p. 17.
5. Marin Strmecki, "It's the Regime, Stupid: The Imperative of State-Building in Afghanistan," *Georgetown Journal of International Affairs* (Winter–Spring, 2003): pp. 30–47.
6. Ibid., p. 42.
7. Nancy Hatch Dupree, "Cultural Heritage and National Identity in Afghanistan," *Third World Quarterly*, Vol. 23, No. 5 (2002): pp. 977–989; quote at p. 978.
8. Carl Bildt, "Hard Learned Lessons on Nation-Building," *International Herald-Tribune*, May 7, 2003, p. 1.
9. Robert I. Rotberg, "The New Nature of Nation-State Failure," *The Washington Quarterly*, Vol. 25, No. 3 (2002): pp. 85–96.
10. Robert I. Rotberg, "Failed States in a World of Terror," *Foreign Affairs*, Vol. 81, No. 4 (2002): pp. 127–140.
11. Patrick, op. cit., p. 2.
12. World Bank, *The Transition from War to Peace: An Overview* (Washington, DC: World Bank, 1999).
13. World Bank, "Post-Conflict Reconstruction: Uganda," *Precis*, No. 171 (1998), quote at p. 1.

14. Ibid., p. 2.
15. Alcira Kreimer et al., *The World Bank's Experience in Post-Conflict Reconstruction: Bosnia and Herzegovina Case Study*, Report No. 17769 (Washington, DC: World Bank, 1998).
16. Patrick, op. cit., p. 2.
17. John D. Montgomery, "The Purge in Occupied Japan," ORO-T 48 (FEC) (Baltimore, MD: Johns Hopkins University, Operations Research Office, 1953); and *Forced To Be Free, The Artificial Revolution in Germany and Japan*, University of Chicago Press, 1957.

Index